SLUGGY FREELANCE

BOOK 3

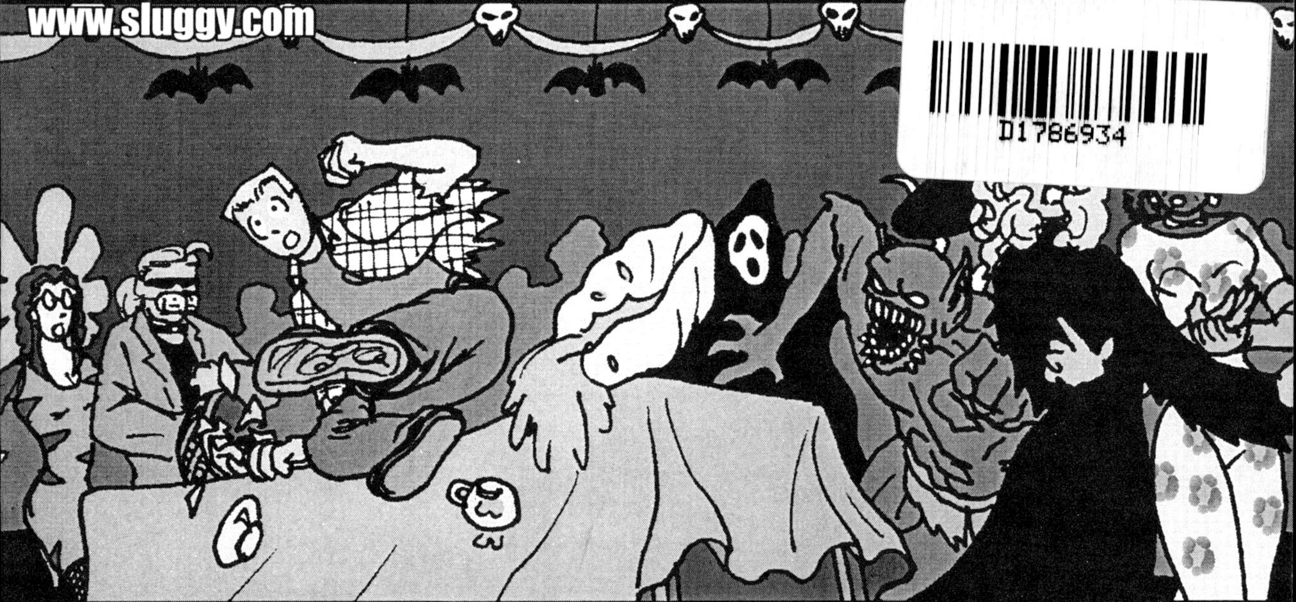

www.sluggy.com

WHEN HOLIDAYS ATTACK!

SLUGGY FREELANCE
www.sluggy.com

Sluggy Freelance: When Holidays Attack is an original publication of Pete Abrams and is published in book form by Plan Nine Publishing.

Contents © 1999 by Pete Abrams
First Printing November 1999.
ISBN 1-929462-00-X

All rights are reserved. No part of this book may be reproduced in any form whatsoever except as provided for by U.S. copyright law. For more information on this book and other *Sluggy Freelance* publications, please contact us via our web site, or write to:

PLAN NINE PUBLISHING

2 Salem St. Suite 314
Thomasville, NC 27360
(336) 472-6463
www.plan9.org

*Bringing you the future tomorrow,
but what's funny today!*

Printed in the U.S.A.

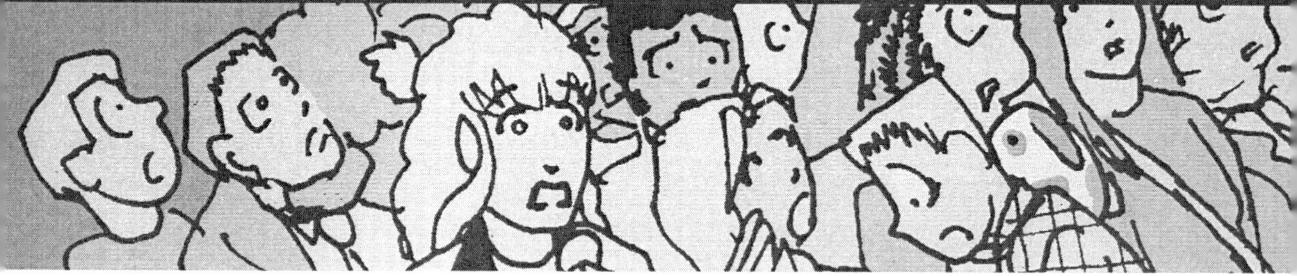

FOR MY PARENTS

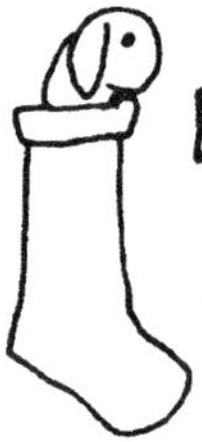

For whom everyday of raising me was a holiday!

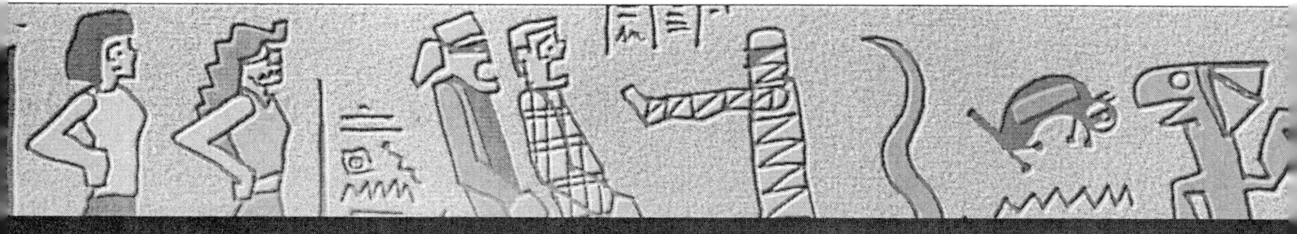

This fine book brought to you by:

PLAN NINE PUBLISHING

2 Salem St. Suite 314
Thomasville, NC 27360
(336) 472-6463
www.plan9.org

Bringing you the future tomorrow, but what's funny today!

WHEN LAST WE LEFT OUR HEROES...

...they were in the fight of their lives and managed victory over a circle of vampires. Sam, their friend-turned-vampire, was able to escape the carnage with the help of his ex-pet, Kiki.

And an ill timed moment of passion between Zoë and Riff leads to complications for both, especially with him currently dating Gwynn.

HEY, I HAD A THOUGHT. IT'S ALMOST HALLOWEEN, AND SAM IS GONE, POSSIBLY FOREVER!

THAT MEANS NO HALLOWEEN PARTY THIS YEAR...

UNLESS WE THROW IT!

Now, Torg and Riff attempt to resurrect the smoke machine from last year's party in preparation for the ultimate Halloween bash.

Meanwhile... in the Dimension of Pain, they plot to reclaim Torg's soul, for he is the one who escaped them so long ago. And they have found a way.

 **Torg:** Guy. Dumb. Dumb Guy.

 **Riff:** Guy. Builds Stuff.

 **Zoë:** Girl. Levelheaded. Doomed. Coed.

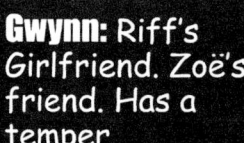 **Gwynn:** Riff's Girlfriend. Zoë's friend. Has a temper.

 **Bun-bun:** Torg's pet rabbit. Has an attitude.

 **Aylee:** Torg's Alien Secretary. Has an appetite.

 **Kiki:** Innocent. Dumb. Curious. Ferret!

 **Sam:** Jerk with fangs.

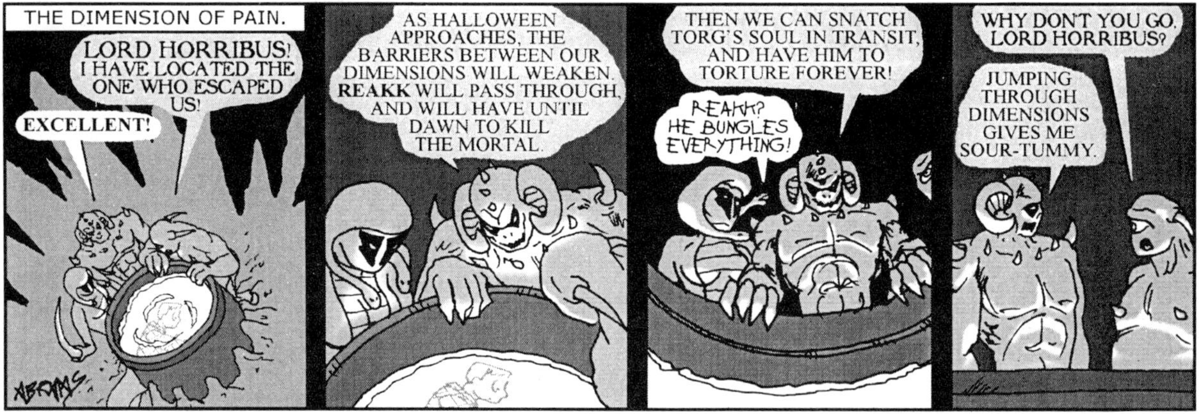
THE DIMENSION OF PAIN.
LORD HORRIBUS! I HAVE LOCATED THE ONE WHO ESCAPED US!
EXCELLENT!
ABRAMS
AS HALLOWEEN APPROACHES, THE BARRIERS BETWEEN OUR DIMENSIONS WILL WEAKEN. REAKK WILL PASS THROUGH, AND WILL HAVE UNTIL DAWN TO KILL THE MORTAL.
THEN WE CAN SNATCH TORG'S SOUL IN TRANSIT, AND HAVE HIM TO TORTURE FOREVER!
REAKK? HE BUNGLES EVERYTHING!
WHY DON'T YOU GO, LORD HORRIBUS?
JUMPING THROUGH DIMENSIONS GIVES ME SOUR-TUMMY.

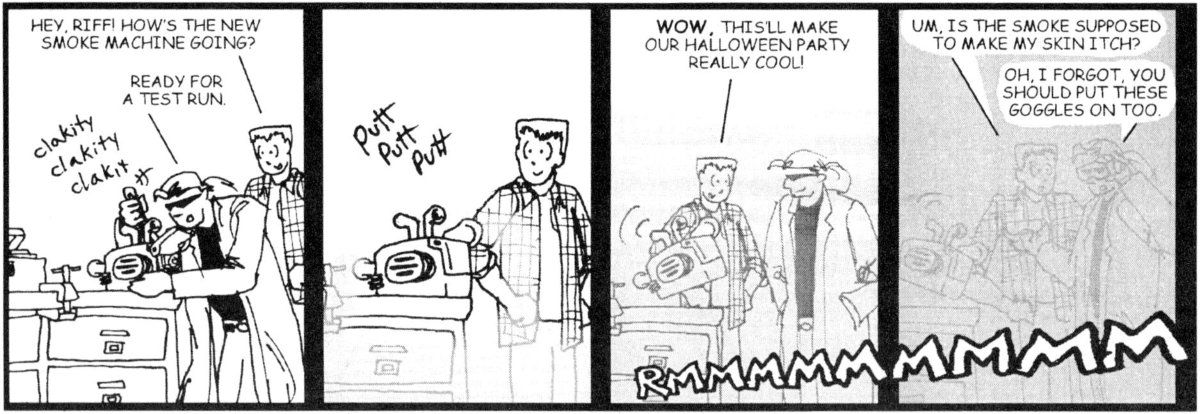
HEY, RIFF! HOW'S THE NEW SMOKE MACHINE GOING?
READY FOR A TEST RUN.
clakity clakity clakit
putt putt putt
WOW, THIS'LL MAKE OUR HALLOWEEN PARTY REALLY COOL!
RMMMMMMMMMMM
UM, IS THE SMOKE SUPPOSED TO MAKE MY SKIN ITCH?
OH, I FORGOT, YOU SHOULD PUT THESE GOGGLES ON TOO.

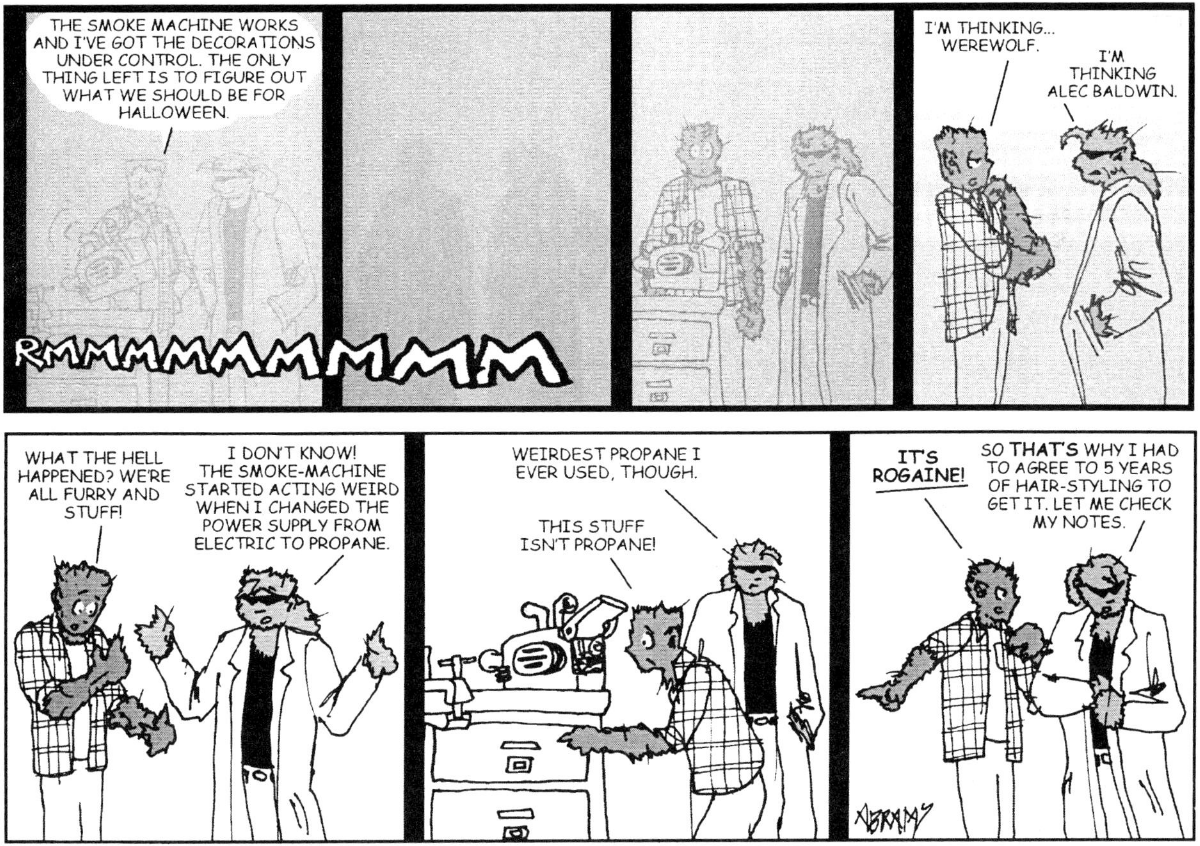
THE SMOKE MACHINE WORKS AND I'VE GOT THE DECORATIONS UNDER CONTROL. THE ONLY THING LEFT IS TO FIGURE OUT WHAT WE SHOULD BE FOR HALLOWEEN.
RMMMMMMMMMMM
I'M THINKING... WEREWOLF.
I'M THINKING ALEC BALDWIN.
WHAT THE HELL HAPPENED? WE'RE ALL FURRY AND STUFF!
I DON'T KNOW! THE SMOKE-MACHINE STARTED ACTING WEIRD WHEN I CHANGED THE POWER SUPPLY FROM ELECTRIC TO PROPANE.
THIS STUFF ISN'T PROPANE!
WEIRDEST PROPANE I EVER USED, THOUGH.
IT'S ROGAINE!
SO THAT'S WHY I HAD TO AGREE TO 5 YEARS OF HAIR-STYLING TO GET IT. LET ME CHECK MY NOTES.
ABRAMS

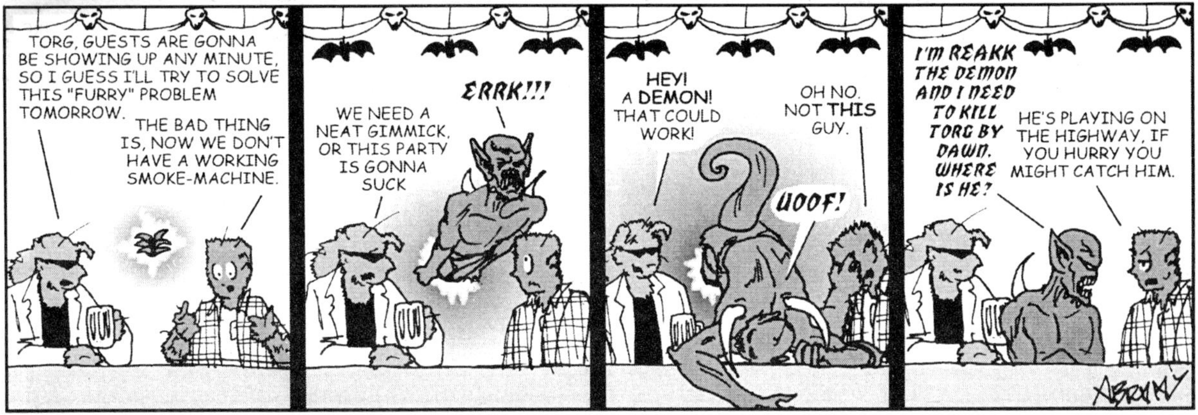
TORG, GUESTS ARE GONNA BE SHOWING UP ANY MINUTE, SO I GUESS I'LL TRY TO SOLVE THIS "FURRY" PROBLEM TOMORROW.
THE BAD THING IS, NOW WE DON'T HAVE A WORKING SMOKE-MACHINE.
WE NEED A NEAT GIMMICK, OR THIS PARTY IS GONNA SUCK
ERRK!!!
HEY! A DEMON! THAT COULD WORK!
OH NO. NOT THIS GUY.
UOOF!
I'M REAKK THE DEMON AND I NEED TO KILL TORG BY DAWN. WHERE IS HE?
HE'S PLAYING ON THE HIGHWAY, IF YOU HURRY YOU MIGHT CATCH HIM.
ABRAMS

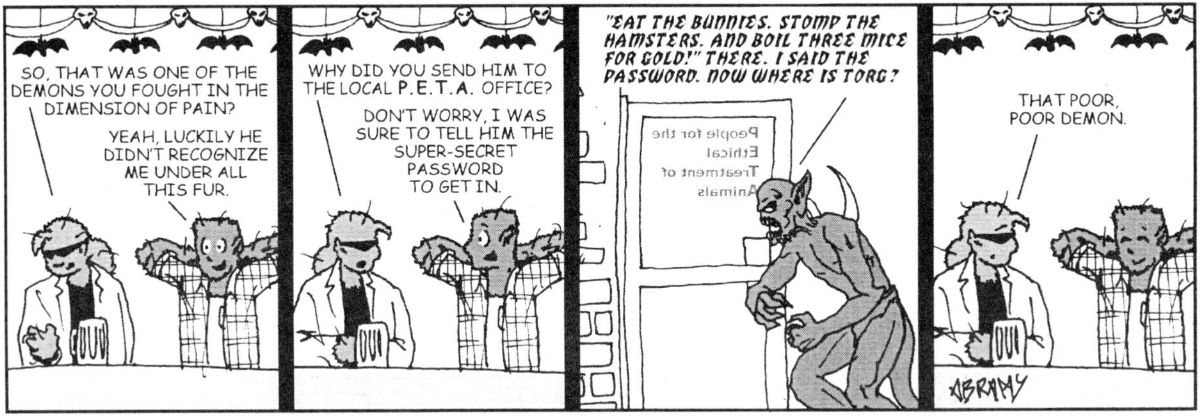
SO, THAT WAS ONE OF THE DEMONS YOU FOUGHT IN THE DIMENSION OF PAIN?
YEAH, LUCKILY HE DIDN'T RECOGNIZE ME UNDER ALL THIS FUR.
WHY DID YOU SEND HIM TO THE LOCAL P.E.T.A. OFFICE?
DON'T WORRY, I WAS SURE TO TELL HIM THE SUPER-SECRET PASSWORD TO GET IN.
"EAT THE BUNNIES. STOMP THE HAMSTERS. AND BOIL THREE MICE FOR GOLD!" THERE. I SAID THE PASSWORD. NOW WHERE IS TORG?
People for the Ethical Treatment of Animals
THAT POOR, POOR DEMON.
ABRAMS

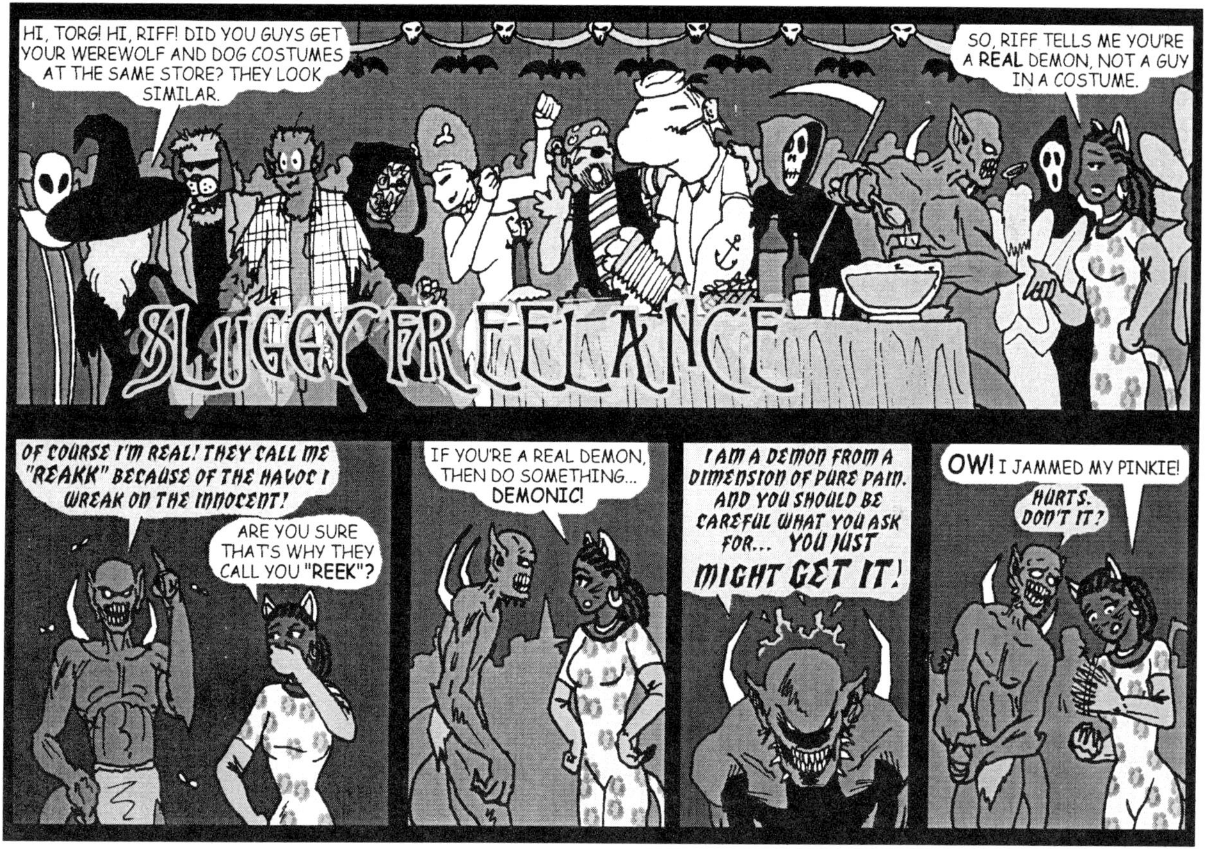

HI, TORG! HI, RIFF! DID YOU GUYS GET YOUR WEREWOLF AND DOG COSTUMES AT THE SAME STORE? THEY LOOK SIMILAR.
SO, RIFF TELLS ME YOU'RE A REAL DEMON, NOT A GUY IN A COSTUME.
SLUGGY FREELANCE
OF COURSE I'M REAL! THEY CALL ME "REAKK" BECAUSE OF THE HAVOC I WREAK ON THE INNOCENT!
ARE YOU SURE THAT'S WHY THEY CALL YOU "REEK"?
IF YOU'RE A REAL DEMON, THEN DO SOMETHING... DEMONIC!
I AM A DEMON FROM A DIMENSION OF PURE PAIN. AND YOU SHOULD BE CAREFUL WHAT YOU ASK FOR... YOU JUST MIGHT GET IT!
OW! I JAMMED MY PINKIE!
HURTS. DON'T IT?

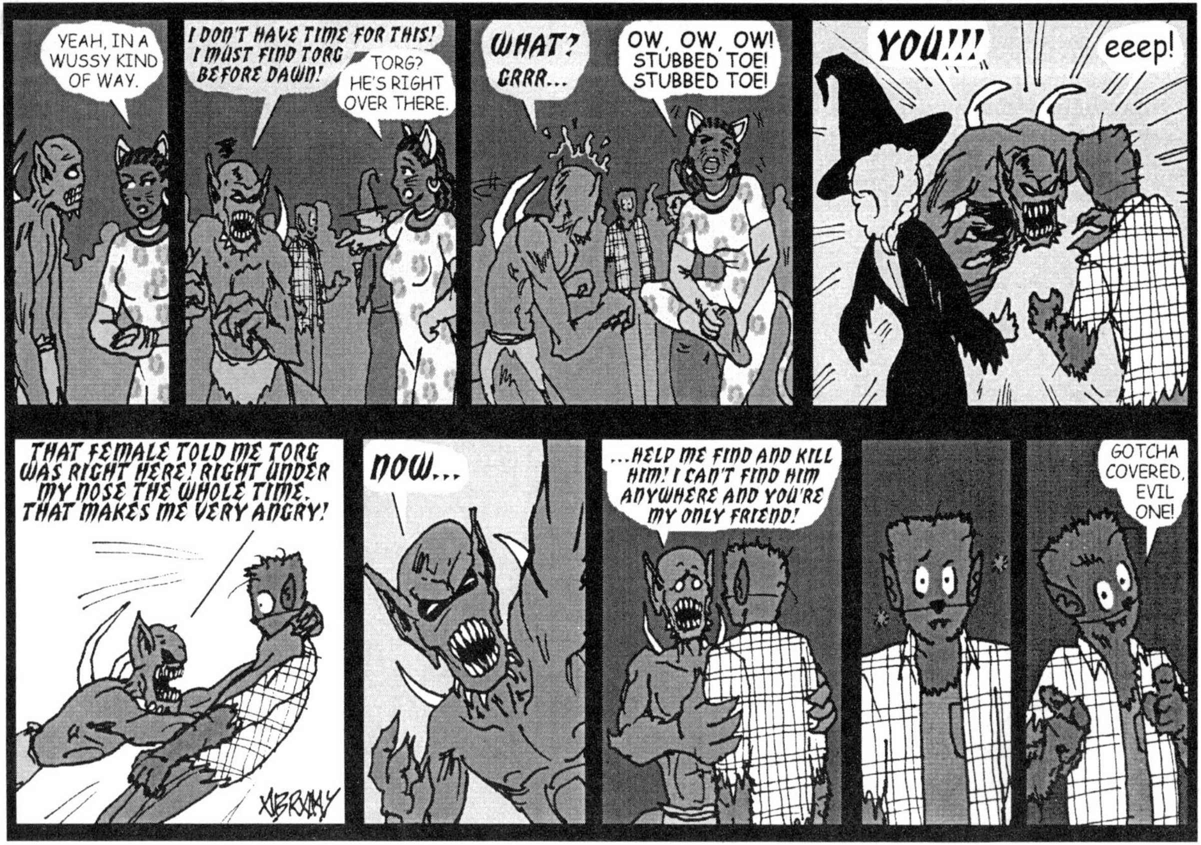
YEAH, IN A WUSSY KIND OF WAY.
I DON'T HAVE TIME FOR THIS! I MUST FIND TORG BEFORE DAWN!
TORG? HE'S RIGHT OVER THERE.
WHAT? GRRR...
OW, OW, OW! STUBBED TOE! STUBBED TOE!
YOU!!!
eeep!
THAT FEMALE TOLD ME TORG WAS RIGHT HERE! RIGHT UNDER MY NOSE THE WHOLE TIME. THAT MAKES ME VERY ANGRY!
NOW...
...HELP ME FIND AND KILL HIM! I CAN'T FIND HIM ANYWHERE AND YOU'RE MY ONLY FRIEND!
GOTCHA COVERED, EVIL ONE!

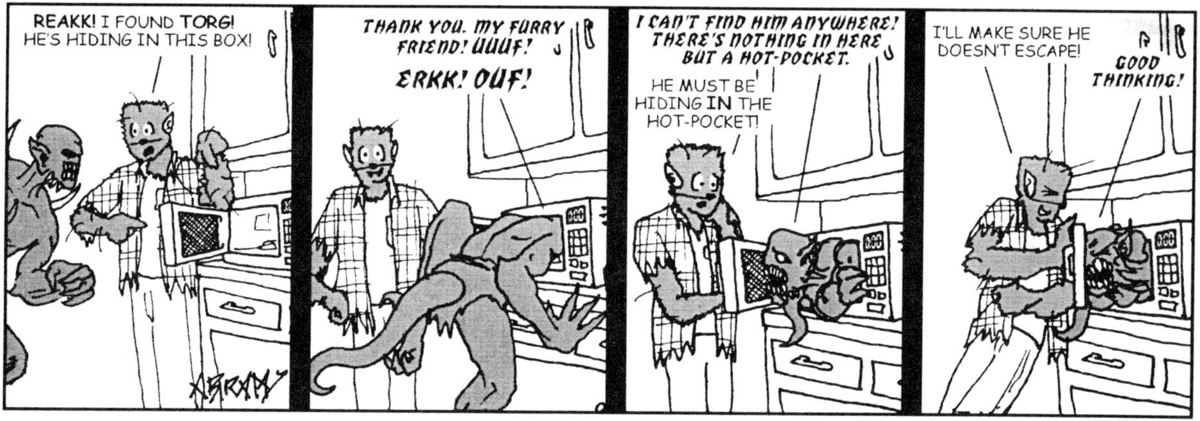
REAKK! I FOUND TORG! HE'S HIDING IN THIS BOX!
THANK YOU. MY FURRY FRIEND! UUUF!
ERKK! OUF!
I CAN'T FIND HIM ANYWHERE! THERE'S NOTHING IN HERE BUT A HOT-POCKET.
HE MUST BE HIDING IN THE HOT-POCKET!
I'LL MAKE SURE HE DOESN'T ESCAPE!
GOOD THINKING!

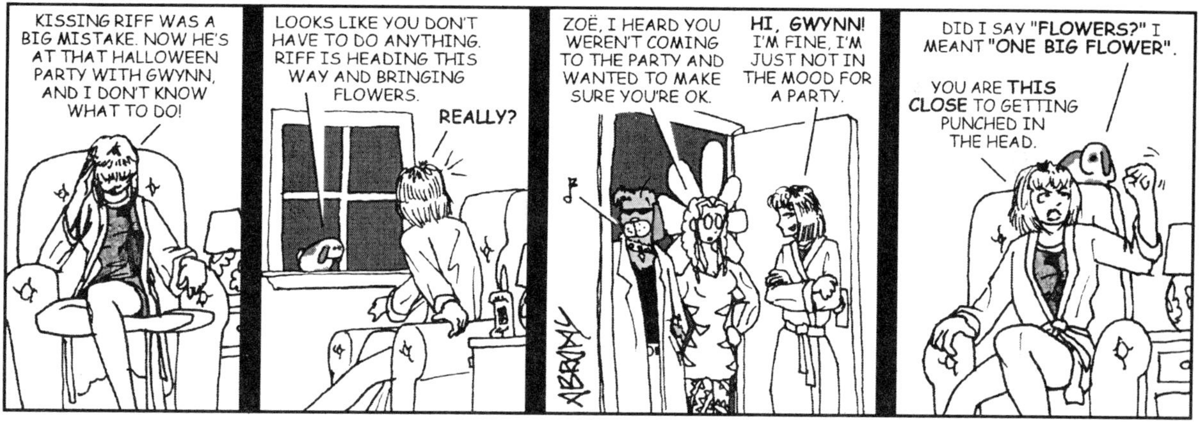
KISSING RIFF WAS A BIG MISTAKE. NOW HE'S AT THAT HALLOWEEN PARTY WITH GWYNN, AND I DON'T KNOW WHAT TO DO!
LOOKS LIKE YOU DON'T HAVE TO DO ANYTHING. RIFF IS HEADING THIS WAY AND BRINGING FLOWERS.
REALLY?
ZOË, I HEARD YOU WEREN'T COMING TO THE PARTY AND WANTED TO MAKE SURE YOU'RE OK.
HI, GWYNN! I'M FINE, I'M JUST NOT IN THE MOOD FOR A PARTY.
DID I SAY "FLOWERS?" I MEANT "ONE BIG FLOWER".
YOU ARE THIS CLOSE TO GETTING PUNCHED IN THE HEAD.

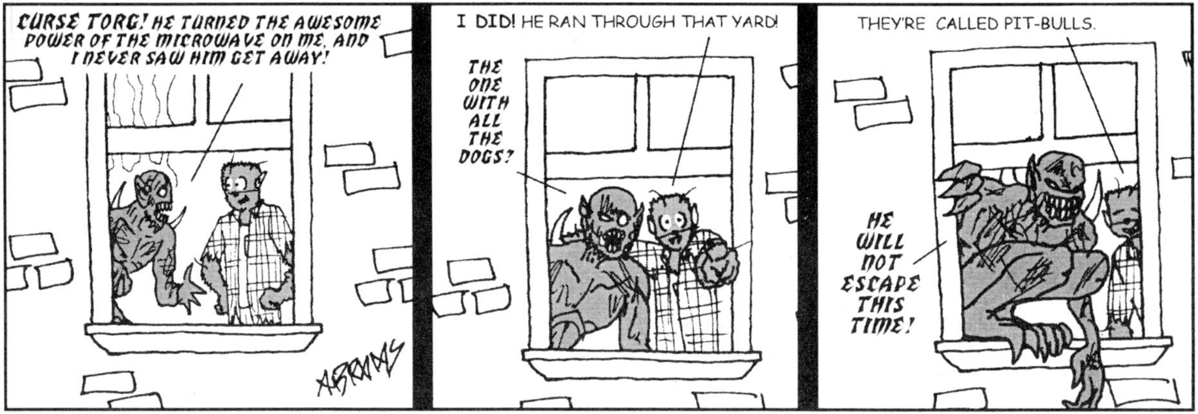
CURSE TORG! HE TURNED THE AWESOME POWER OF THE MICROWAVE ON ME, AND I NEVER SAW HIM GET AWAY!
ABRAMS
I DID! HE RAN THROUGH THAT YARD!
THE ONE WITH ALL THE DOGS?
THEY'RE CALLED PIT-BULLS.
HE WILL NOT ESCAPE THIS TIME!

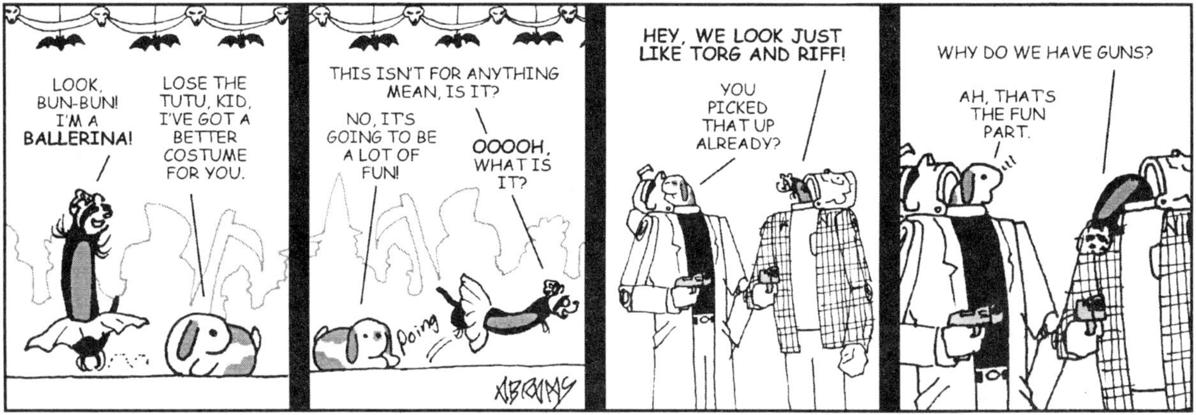
LOOK, BUN-BUN! I'M A BALLERINA!
LOSE THE TUTU, KID, I'VE GOT A BETTER COSTUME FOR YOU.
THIS ISN'T FOR ANYTHING MEAN, IS IT?
NO, IT'S GOING TO BE A LOT OF FUN!
OOOOH, WHAT IS IT?
poing
ABRAMS
HEY, WE LOOK JUST LIKE TORG AND RIFF!
YOU PICKED THAT UP ALREADY?
WHY DO WE HAVE GUNS?
AH, THAT'S THE FUN PART.

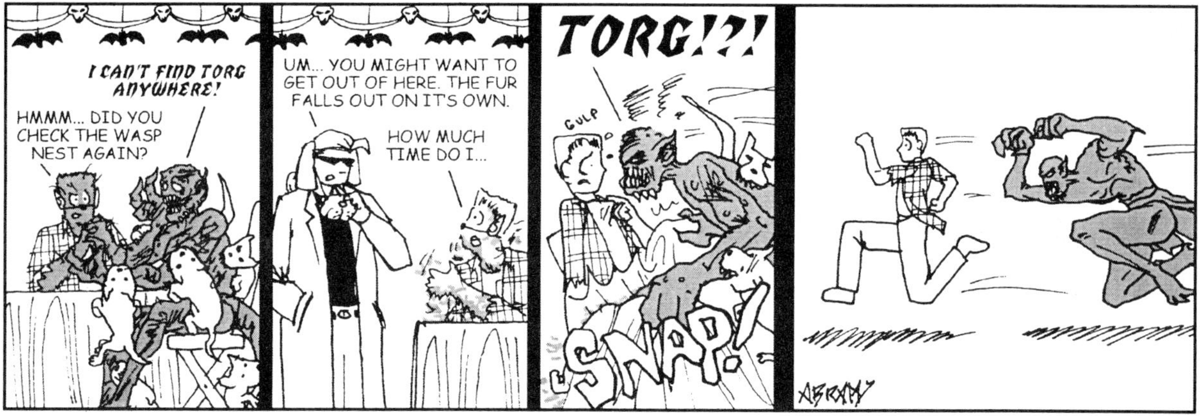
HMMM... DID YOU CHECK THE WASP NEST AGAIN?
I CAN'T FIND TORG ANYWHERE!
UM... YOU MIGHT WANT TO GET OUT OF HERE. THE FUR FALLS OUT ON IT'S OWN.
HOW MUCH TIME DO I...
TORG!?!
GULP
SNAP!

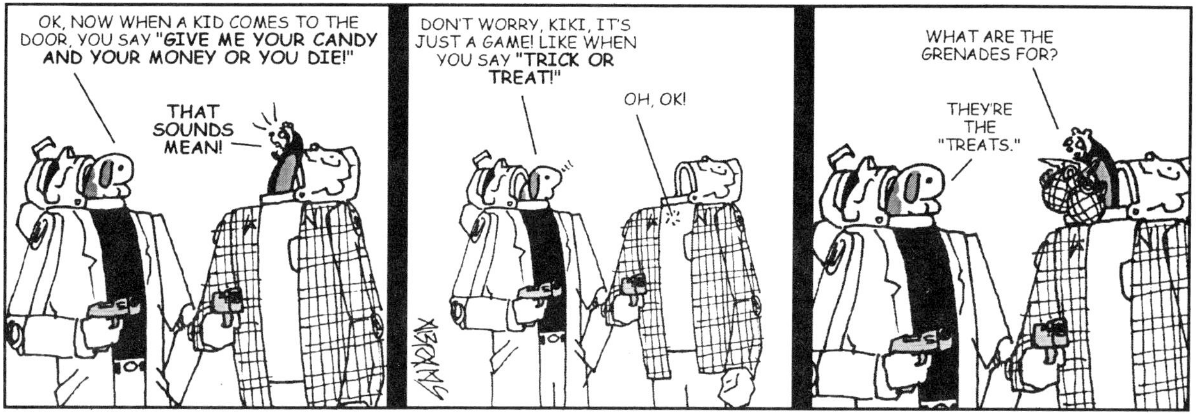
OK, NOW WHEN A KID COMES TO THE DOOR, YOU SAY "GIVE ME YOUR CANDY AND YOUR MONEY OR YOU DIE!"
THAT SOUNDS MEAN!
DON'T WORRY, KIKI, IT'S JUST A GAME! LIKE WHEN YOU SAY "TRICK OR TREAT!"
OH, OK!
WHAT ARE THE GRENADES FOR?
THEY'RE THE "TREATS."

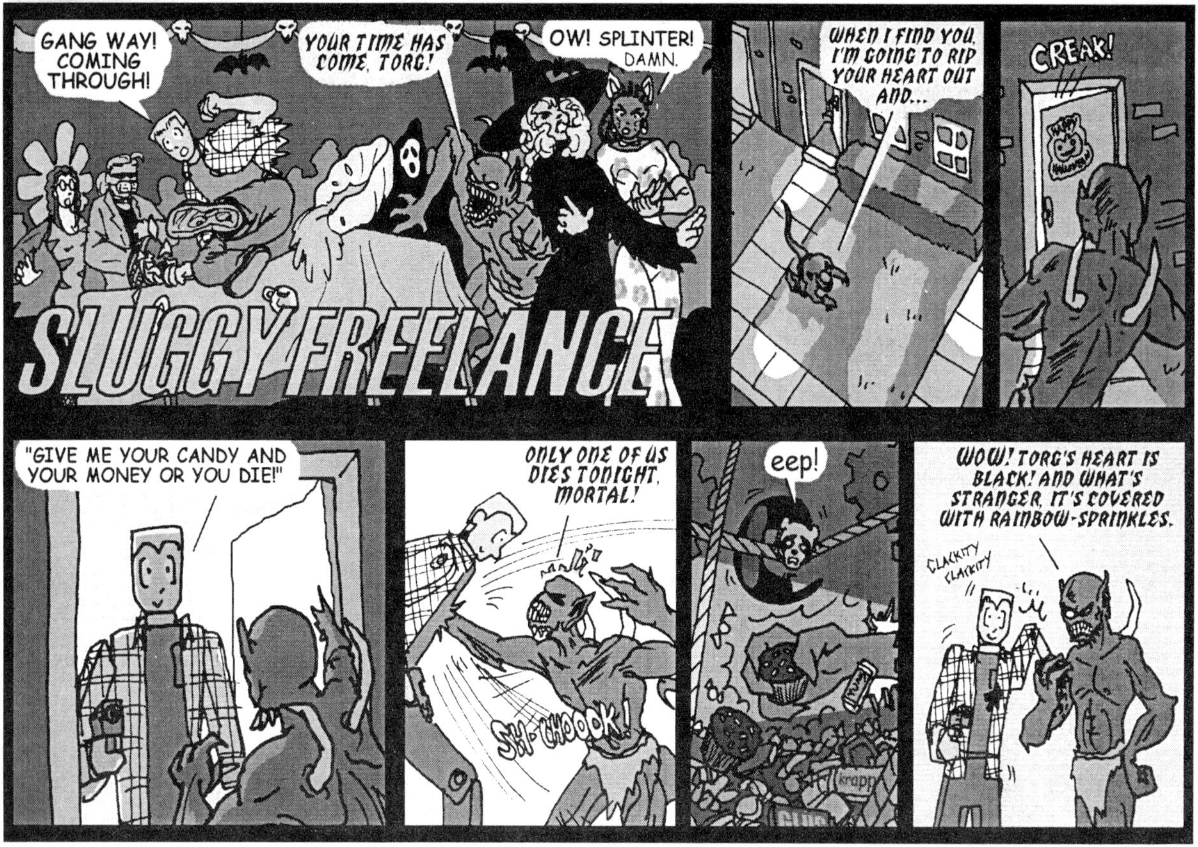
GANG WAY! COMING THROUGH!
YOUR TIME HAS COME, TORG!
OW! SPLINTER!
DAMN.
SLUGGY FREELANCE
WHEN I FIND YOU, I'M GOING TO RIP YOUR HEART OUT AND...
CREAK!
"GIVE ME YOUR CANDY AND YOUR MONEY OR YOU DIE!"
ONLY ONE OF US DIES TONIGHT, MORTAL!
SHP-CHOOOK!
eep!
WOW! TORG'S HEART IS BLACK! AND WHAT'S STRANGER, IT'S COVERED WITH RAINBOW-SPRINKLES.
CLACKITY CLACKITY

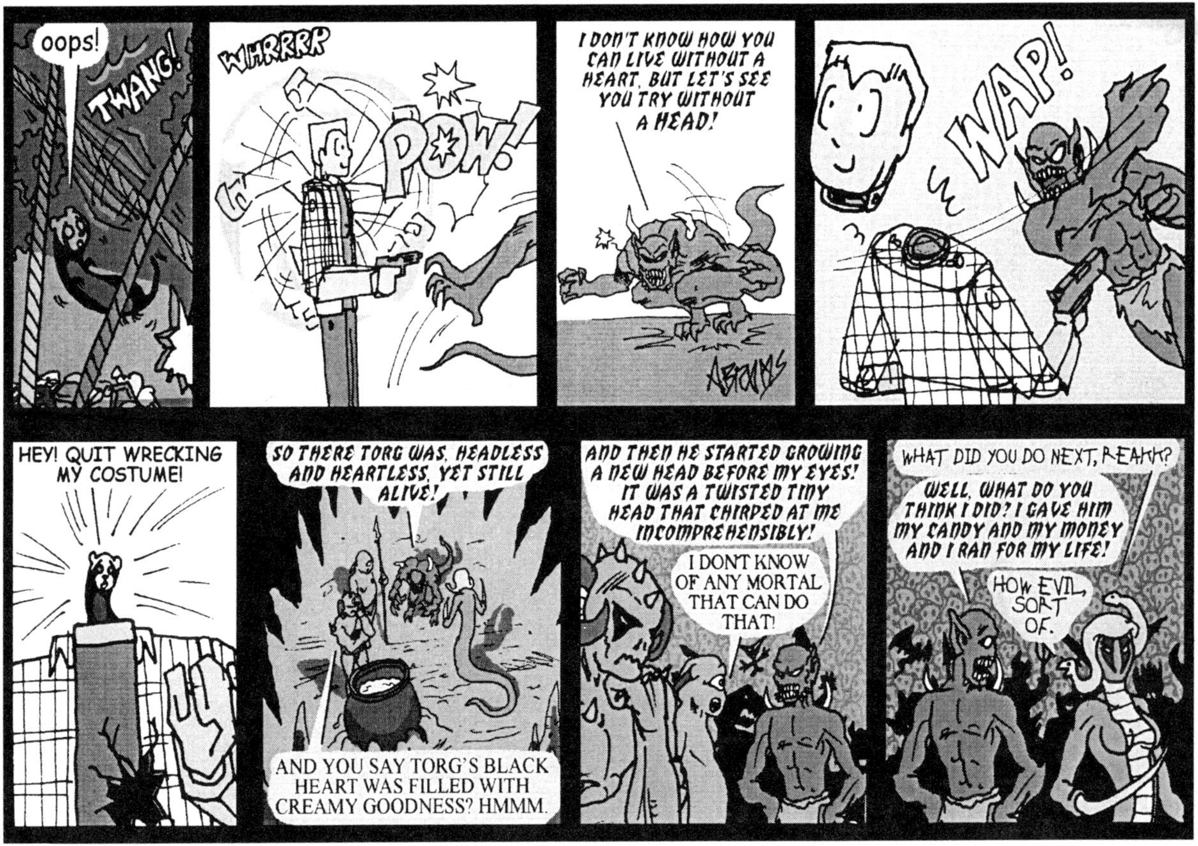
oops!
TWANG!
WHRRRR
POW!
I DON'T KNOW HOW YOU CAN LIVE WITHOUT A HEART, BUT LET'S SEE YOU TRY WITHOUT A HEAD!
WAP!
HEY! QUIT WRECKING MY COSTUME!
SO THERE TORG WAS, HEADLESS AND HEARTLESS, YET STILL ALIVE!
AND YOU SAY TORG'S BLACK HEART WAS FILLED WITH CREAMY GOODNESS? HMMM.
AND THEN HE STARTED GROWING A NEW HEAD BEFORE MY EYES! IT WAS A TWISTED TINY HEAD THAT CHIRPED AT ME INCOMPREHENSIBLY!
I DONT KNOW OF ANY MORTAL THAT CAN DO THAT!
WHAT DID YOU DO NEXT, REAKK?
WELL, WHAT DO YOU THINK I DID? I GAVE HIM MY CANDY AND MY MONEY AND I RAN FOR MY LIFE!
HOW EVIL, SORT OF.

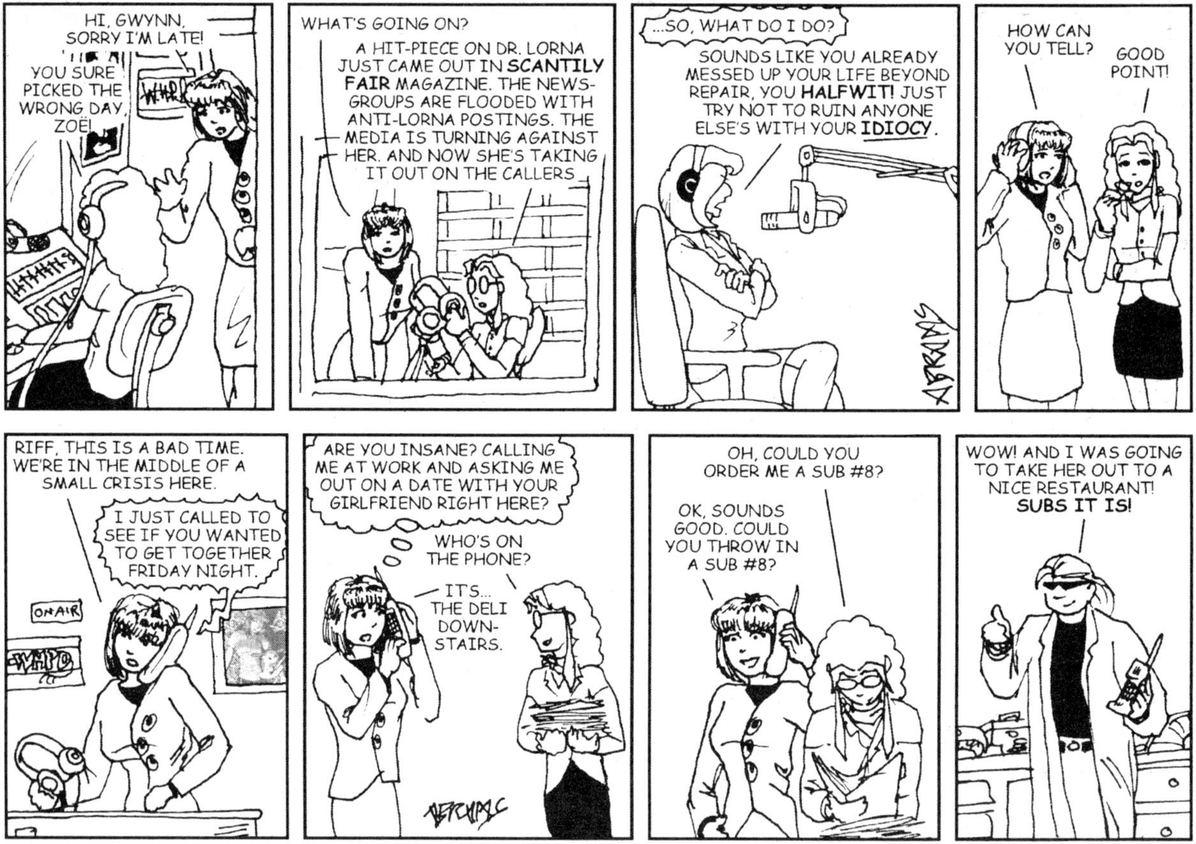
HI, GWYNN, SORRY I'M LATE!
YOU SURE PICKED THE WRONG DAY, ZOË!
WHAT'S GOING ON?
A HIT-PIECE ON DR. LORNA JUST CAME OUT IN SCANTILY FAIR MAGAZINE. THE NEWS-GROUPS ARE FLOODED WITH ANTI-LORNA POSTINGS. THE MEDIA IS TURNING AGAINST HER. AND NOW SHE'S TAKING IT OUT ON THE CALLERS
...SO, WHAT DO I DO?
SOUNDS LIKE YOU ALREADY MESSED UP YOUR LIFE BEYOND REPAIR, YOU HALFWIT! JUST TRY NOT TO RUIN ANYONE ELSE'S WITH YOUR IDIOCY.
HOW CAN YOU TELL?
GOOD POINT!
RIFF, THIS IS A BAD TIME. WE'RE IN THE MIDDLE OF A SMALL CRISIS HERE.
I JUST CALLED TO SEE IF YOU WANTED TO GET TOGETHER FRIDAY NIGHT.
ON AIR
ARE YOU INSANE? CALLING ME AT WORK AND ASKING ME OUT ON A DATE WITH YOUR GIRLFRIEND RIGHT HERE?
WHO'S ON THE PHONE?
IT'S... THE DELI DOWN-STAIRS.
OH, COULD YOU ORDER ME A SUB #8?
OK, SOUNDS GOOD. COULD YOU THROW IN A SUB #8?
WOW! AND I WAS GOING TO TAKE HER OUT TO A NICE RESTAURANT! SUBS IT IS!

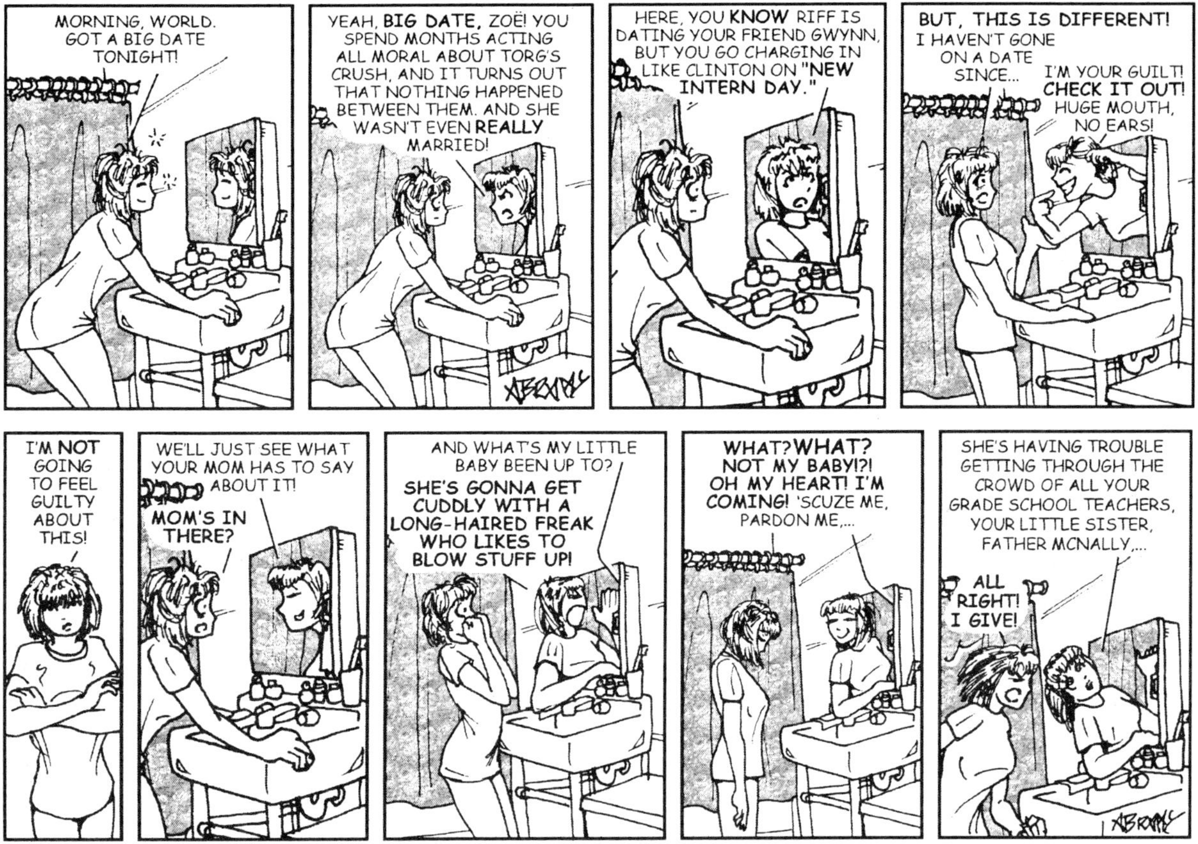

MORNING, WORLD. GOT A BIG DATE TONIGHT!
YEAH, BIG DATE, ZOË! YOU SPEND MONTHS ACTING ALL MORAL ABOUT TORG'S CRUSH, AND IT TURNS OUT THAT NOTHING HAPPENED BETWEEN THEM. AND SHE WASN'T EVEN REALLY MARRIED!
HERE, YOU KNOW RIFF IS DATING YOUR FRIEND GWYNN, BUT YOU GO CHARGING IN LIKE CLINTON ON "NEW INTERN DAY."
BUT, THIS IS DIFFERENT! I HAVEN'T GONE ON A DATE SINCE...
I'M YOUR GUILT! CHECK IT OUT! HUGE MOUTH, NO EARS!
I'M NOT GOING TO FEEL GUILTY ABOUT THIS!
WE'LL JUST SEE WHAT YOUR MOM HAS TO SAY ABOUT IT!
MOM'S IN THERE?
AND WHAT'S MY LITTLE BABY BEEN UP TO?
SHE'S GONNA GET CUDDLY WITH A LONG-HAIRED FREAK WHO LIKES TO BLOW STUFF UP!
WHAT? WHAT? NOT MY BABY!?! OH MY HEART! I'M COMING! 'SCUZE ME, PARDON ME,...
SHE'S HAVING TROUBLE GETTING THROUGH THE CROWD OF ALL YOUR GRADE SCHOOL TEACHERS, YOUR LITTLE SISTER, FATHER MCNALLY,...
ALL RIGHT! I GIVE!

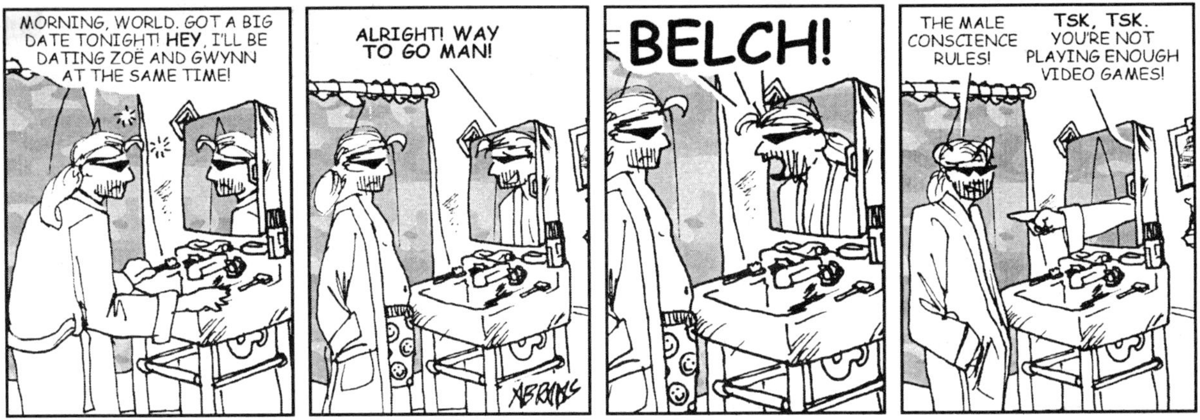
MORNING, WORLD. GOT A BIG DATE TONIGHT! HEY, I'LL BE DATING ZOË AND GWYNN AT THE SAME TIME!
ALRIGHT! WAY TO GO MAN!
BELCH!
THE MALE CONSCIENCE RULES!
TSK, TSK. YOU'RE NOT PLAYING ENOUGH VIDEO GAMES!
ABRAMS

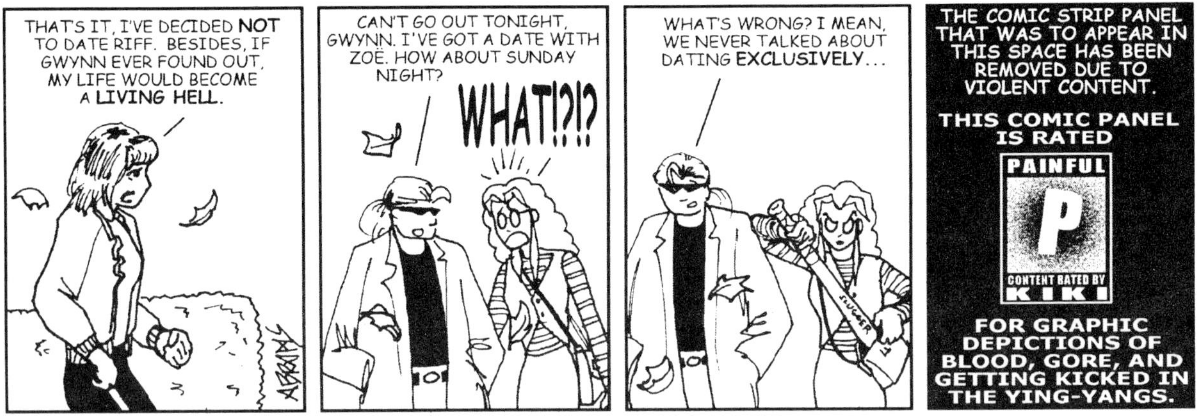
THAT'S IT, I'VE DECIDED NOT TO DATE RIFF. BESIDES, IF GWYNN EVER FOUND OUT, MY LIFE WOULD BECOME A LIVING HELL.
ABRAMS
CAN'T GO OUT TONIGHT, GWYNN. I'VE GOT A DATE WITH ZOË. HOW ABOUT SUNDAY NIGHT?
WHAT!?!?
WHAT'S WRONG? I MEAN, WE NEVER TALKED ABOUT DATING EXCLUSIVELY...
SLUGGER
THE COMIC STRIP PANEL THAT WAS TO APPEAR IN THIS SPACE HAS BEEN REMOVED DUE TO VIOLENT CONTENT.
THIS COMIC PANEL IS RATED
PAINFUL
P
CONTENT RATED BY
KIKI
FOR GRAPHIC DEPICTIONS OF BLOOD, GORE, AND GETTING KICKED IN THE YING-YANGS.

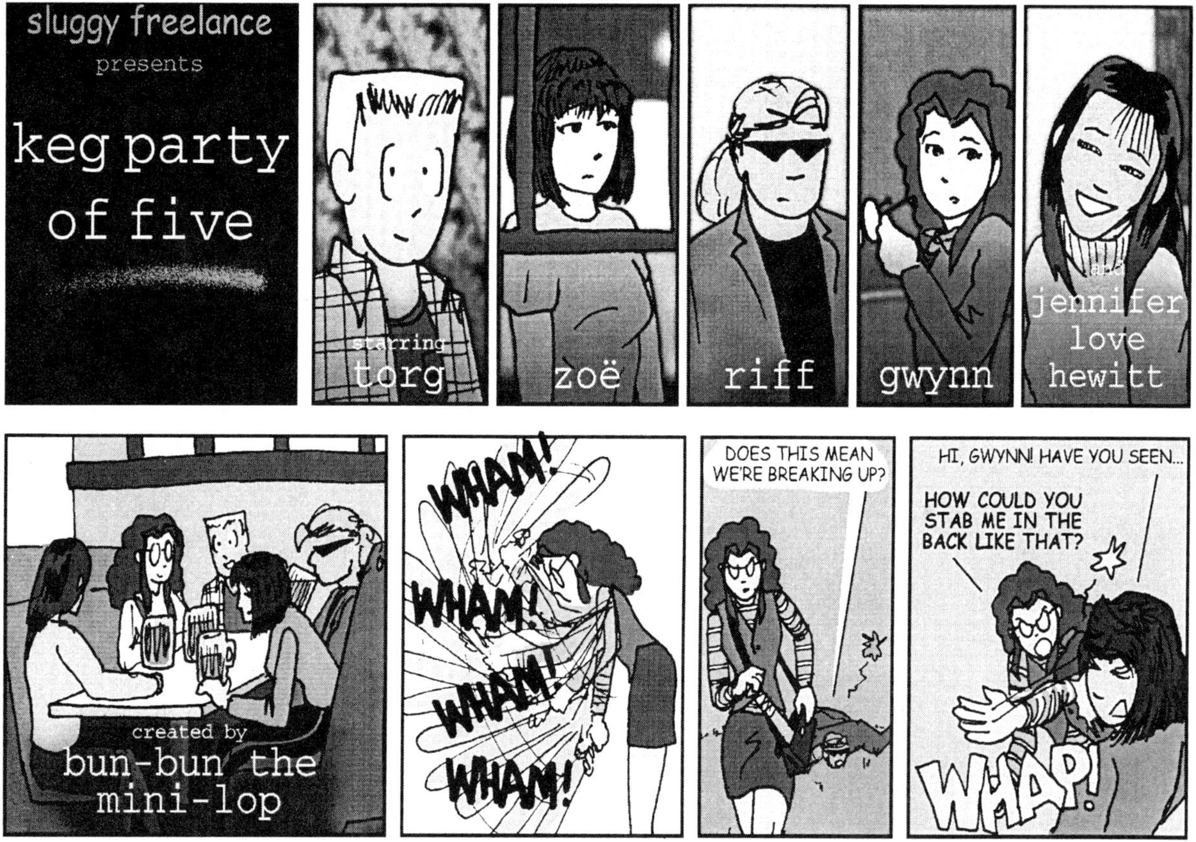
sluggy freelance
presents
keg party
of five
starring
torg
zoë
riff
gwynn
and
jennifer
love
hewitt
created by
bun-bun the
mini-lop
WHAM!
WHAM!
WHAM!
WHAM!
DOES THIS MEAN WE'RE BREAKING UP?
HI, GWYNN! HAVE YOU SEEN...
HOW COULD YOU STAB ME IN THE BACK LIKE THAT?
WHAP!

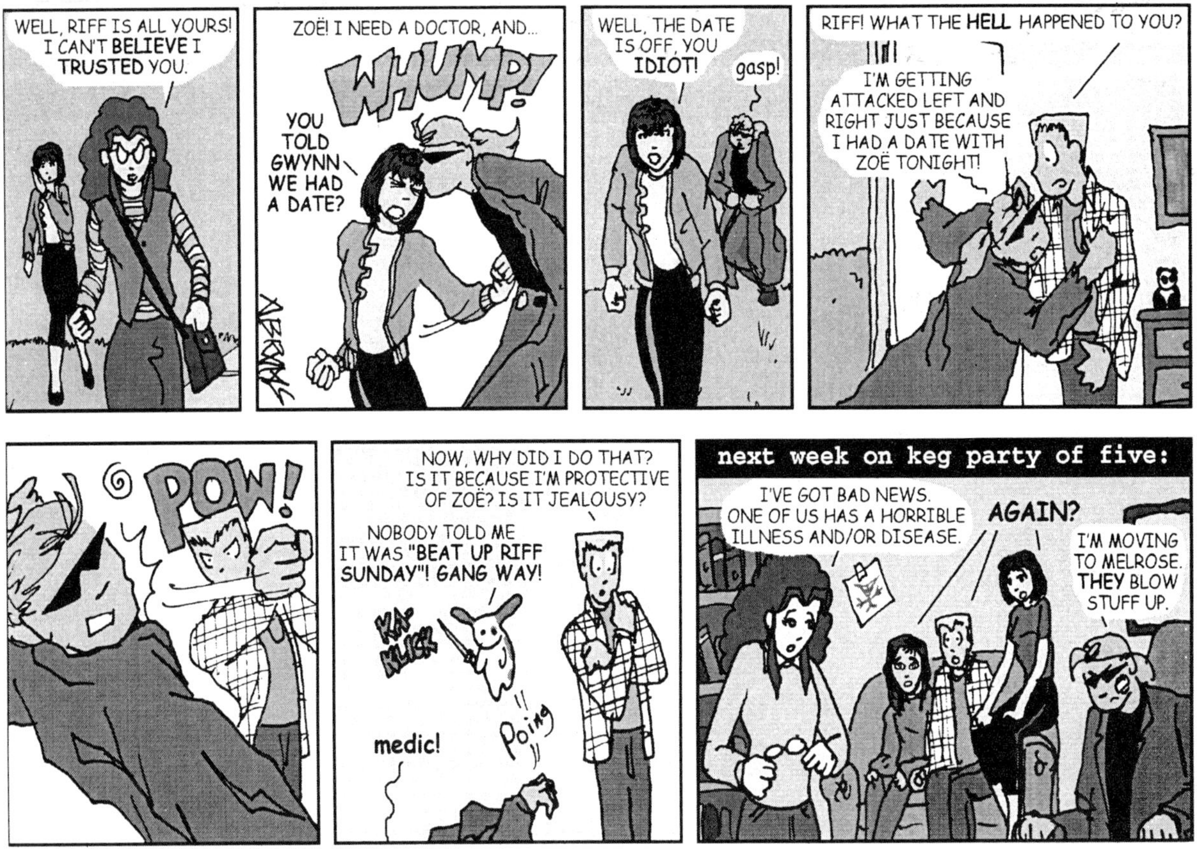
WELL, RIFF IS ALL YOURS! I CAN'T **BELIEVE** I **TRUSTED** YOU.
ZOË! I NEED A DOCTOR, AND...
WHUMP!
YOU TOLD GWYNN WE HAD A DATE?
WELL, THE DATE IS OFF, YOU **IDIOT**!
gasp!
RIFF! WHAT THE **HELL** HAPPENED TO YOU?
I'M GETTING ATTACKED LEFT AND RIGHT JUST BECAUSE I HAD A DATE WITH ZOË TONIGHT!
POW!
NOW, WHY DID I DO THAT? IS IT BECAUSE I'M PROTECTIVE OF ZOË? IS IT JEALOUSY?
NOBODY TOLD ME IT WAS **"BEAT UP RIFF SUNDAY"! GANG WAY!**
medic!
Poing
next week on keg party of five:
I'VE GOT BAD NEWS. ONE OF US HAS A HORRIBLE ILLNESS AND/OR DISEASE.
AGAIN?
I'M MOVING TO MELROSE. **THEY** BLOW STUFF UP.

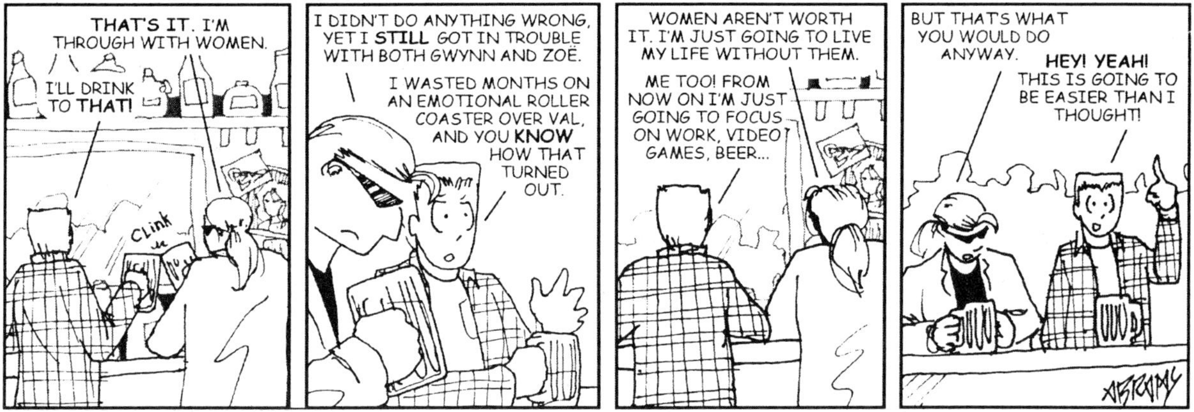
THAT'S IT. I'M THROUGH WITH WOMEN.
I'LL DRINK TO THAT!
CLINK
I DIDN'T DO ANYTHING WRONG, YET I STILL GOT IN TROUBLE WITH BOTH GWYNN AND ZOË.
I WASTED MONTHS ON AN EMOTIONAL ROLLER COASTER OVER VAL, AND YOU KNOW HOW THAT TURNED OUT.
WOMEN AREN'T WORTH IT. I'M JUST GOING TO LIVE MY LIFE WITHOUT THEM.
ME TOO! FROM NOW ON I'M JUST GOING TO FOCUS ON WORK, VIDEO GAMES, BEER...
BUT THAT'S WHAT YOU WOULD DO ANYWAY.
HEY! YEAH! THIS IS GOING TO BE EASIER THAN I THOUGHT!
ABRAMS

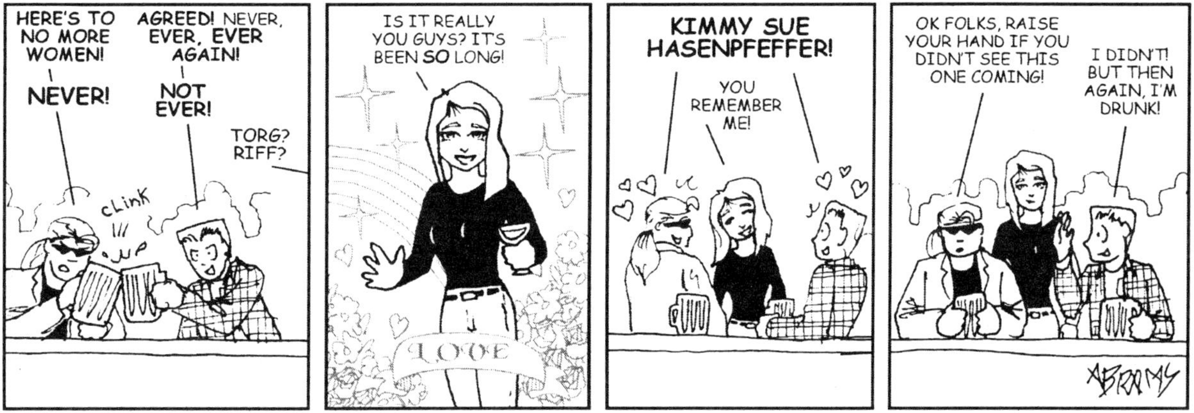
HERE'S TO NO MORE WOMEN!
AGREED! NEVER, EVER, EVER AGAIN!
NEVER!
NOT EVER!
TORG? RIFF?
CLINK
IS IT REALLY YOU GUYS? IT'S BEEN SO LONG!
LOVE
KIMMY SUE HASENPFEFFER!
YOU REMEMBER ME!
OK FOLKS, RAISE YOUR HAND IF YOU DIDN'T SEE THIS ONE COMING!
I DIDN'T! BUT THEN AGAIN, I'M DRUNK!
ABRAMS

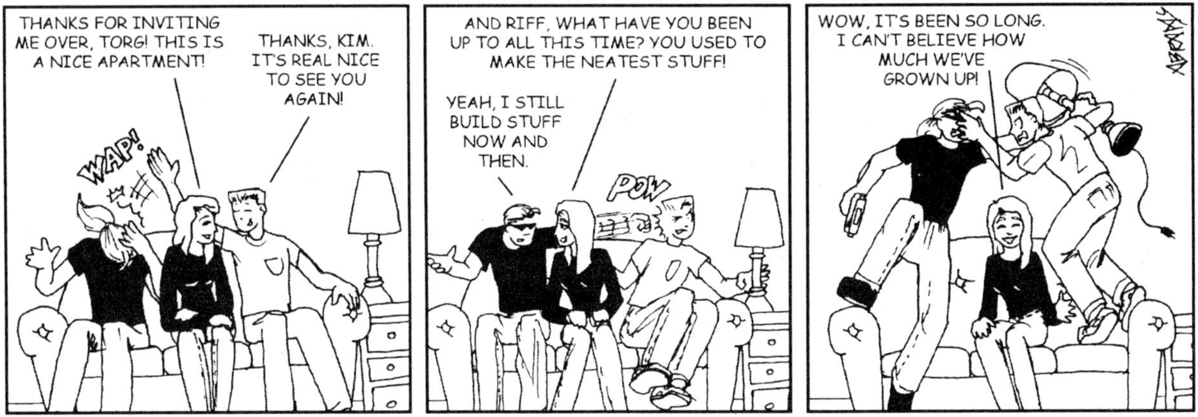
THANKS FOR INVITING ME OVER, TORG! THIS IS A NICE APARTMENT!
THANKS, KIM. IT'S REAL NICE TO SEE YOU AGAIN!
WAP!
AND RIFF, WHAT HAVE YOU BEEN UP TO ALL THIS TIME? YOU USED TO MAKE THE NEATEST STUFF!
YEAH, I STILL BUILD STUFF NOW AND THEN.
POW
WOW, IT'S BEEN SO LONG. I CAN'T BELIEVE HOW MUCH WE'VE GROWN UP!

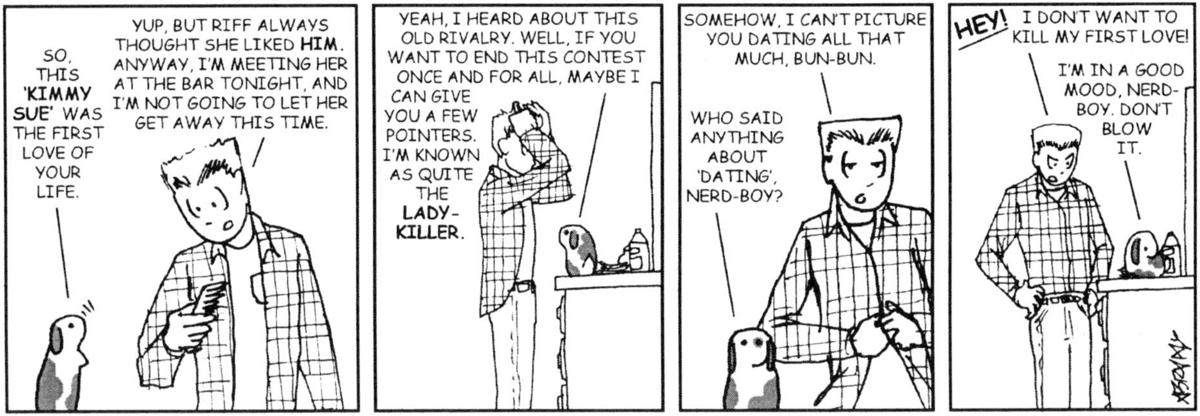
SO, THIS 'KIMMY SUE' WAS THE FIRST LOVE OF YOUR LIFE.
YUP, BUT RIFF ALWAYS THOUGHT SHE LIKED HIM. ANYWAY, I'M MEETING HER AT THE BAR TONIGHT, AND I'M NOT GOING TO LET HER GET AWAY THIS TIME.
YEAH, I HEARD ABOUT THIS OLD RIVALRY. WELL, IF YOU WANT TO END THIS CONTEST ONCE AND FOR ALL, MAYBE I CAN GIVE YOU A FEW POINTERS. I'M KNOWN AS QUITE THE LADY-KILLER.
SOMEHOW, I CAN'T PICTURE YOU DATING ALL THAT MUCH, BUN-BUN.
WHO SAID ANYTHING ABOUT 'DATING', NERD-BOY?
HEY! I DON'T WANT TO KILL MY FIRST LOVE!
I'M IN A GOOD MOOD, NERD-BOY. DON'T BLOW IT.

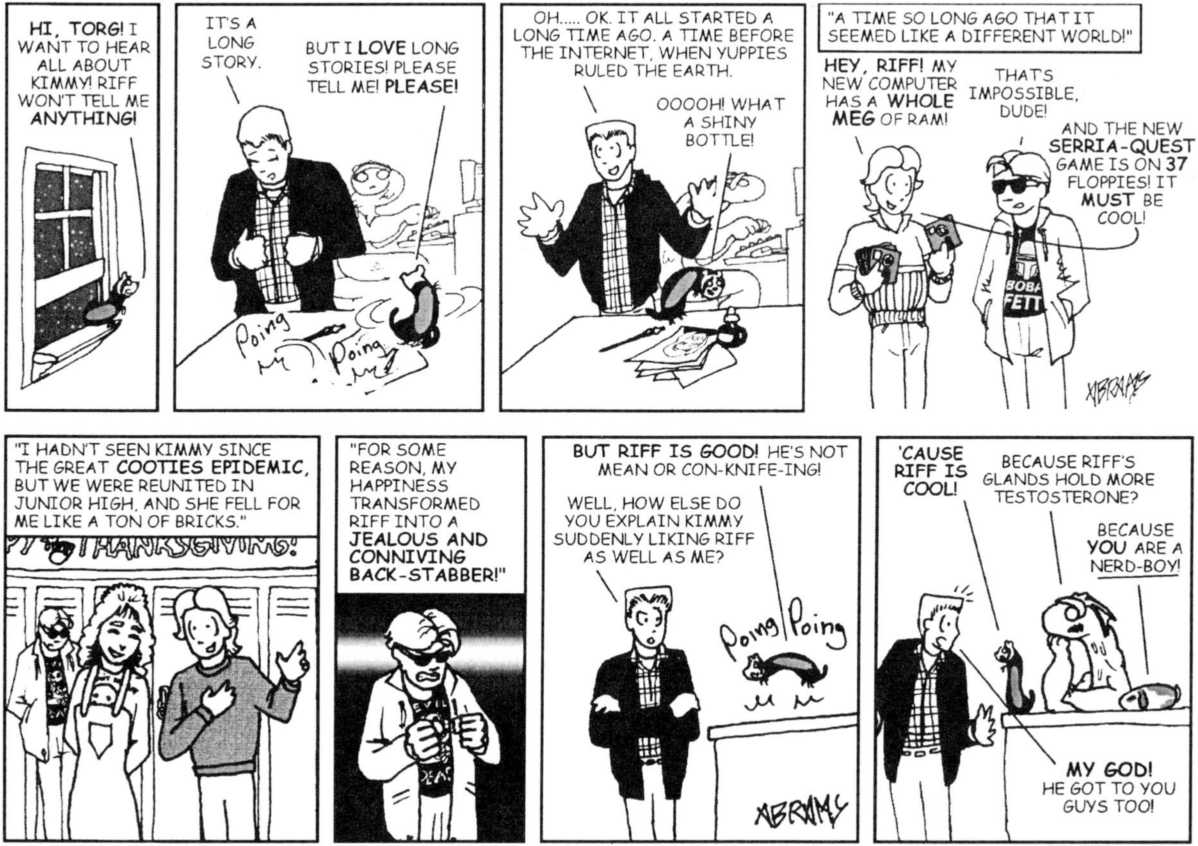
HI, TORG! I WANT TO HEAR ALL ABOUT KIMMY! RIFF WON'T TELL ME ANYTHING!
IT'S A LONG STORY.
BUT I LOVE LONG STORIES! PLEASE TELL ME! PLEASE!
Poing
Poing
OH..... OK. IT ALL STARTED A LONG TIME AGO. A TIME BEFORE THE INTERNET, WHEN YUPPIES RULED THE EARTH.
OOOOH! WHAT A SHINY BOTTLE!
"A TIME SO LONG AGO THAT IT SEEMED LIKE A DIFFERENT WORLD!"
HEY, RIFF! MY NEW COMPUTER HAS A WHOLE MEG OF RAM!
THAT'S IMPOSSIBLE, DUDE!
AND THE NEW SERRIA-QUEST GAME IS ON 37 FLOPPIES! IT MUST BE COOL!
BOBA FETT
ABRAMS
"I HADN'T SEEN KIMMY SINCE THE GREAT COOTIES EPIDEMIC, BUT WE WERE REUNITED IN JUNIOR HIGH, AND SHE FELL FOR ME LIKE A TON OF BRICKS."
THANKSGIVING!
"FOR SOME REASON, MY HAPPINESS TRANSFORMED RIFF INTO A JEALOUS AND CONNIVING BACK-STABBER!"
BUT RIFF IS GOOD! HE'S NOT MEAN OR CON-KNIFE-ING!
WELL, HOW ELSE DO YOU EXPLAIN KIMMY SUDDENLY LIKING RIFF AS WELL AS ME?
Poing Poing
ABRAMS
'CAUSE RIFF IS COOL!
BECAUSE RIFF'S GLANDS HOLD MORE TESTOSTERONE?
BECAUSE YOU ARE A NERD-BOY!
MY GOD! HE GOT TO YOU GUYS TOO!

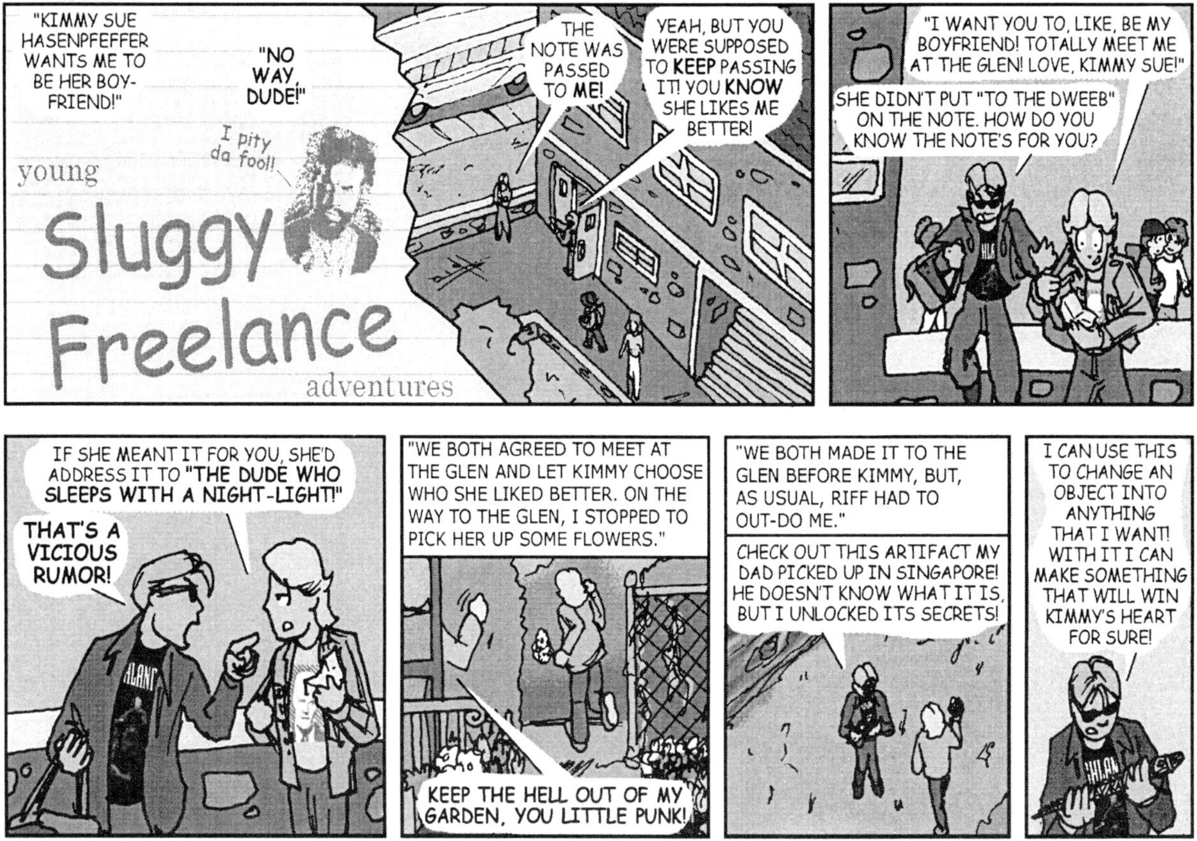
"KIMMY SUE HASENPFEFFER WANTS ME TO BE HER BOY-FRIEND!"
"NO WAY, DUDE!"
I pity da fool!
young
Sluggy Freelance
adventures
THE NOTE WAS PASSED TO ME!
YEAH, BUT YOU WERE SUPPOSED TO KEEP PASSING IT! YOU KNOW SHE LIKES ME BETTER!
"I WANT YOU TO, LIKE, BE MY BOYFRIEND! TOTALLY MEET ME AT THE GLEN! LOVE, KIMMY SUE!"
SHE DIDN'T PUT "TO THE DWEEB" ON THE NOTE. HOW DO YOU KNOW THE NOTE'S FOR YOU?
IF SHE MEANT IT FOR YOU, SHE'D ADDRESS IT TO "THE DUDE WHO SLEEPS WITH A NIGHT-LIGHT!"
THAT'S A VICIOUS RUMOR!
"WE BOTH AGREED TO MEET AT THE GLEN AND LET KIMMY CHOOSE WHO SHE LIKED BETTER. ON THE WAY TO THE GLEN, I STOPPED TO PICK HER UP SOME FLOWERS."
KEEP THE HELL OUT OF MY GARDEN, YOU LITTLE PUNK!
"WE BOTH MADE IT TO THE GLEN BEFORE KIMMY, BUT, AS USUAL, RIFF HAD TO OUT-DO ME."
CHECK OUT THIS ARTIFACT MY DAD PICKED UP IN SINGAPORE! HE DOESN'T KNOW WHAT IT IS, BUT I UNLOCKED ITS SECRETS!
I CAN USE THIS TO CHANGE AN OBJECT INTO ANYTHING THAT I WANT! WITH IT I CAN MAKE SOMETHING THAT WILL WIN KIMMY'S HEART FOR SURE!

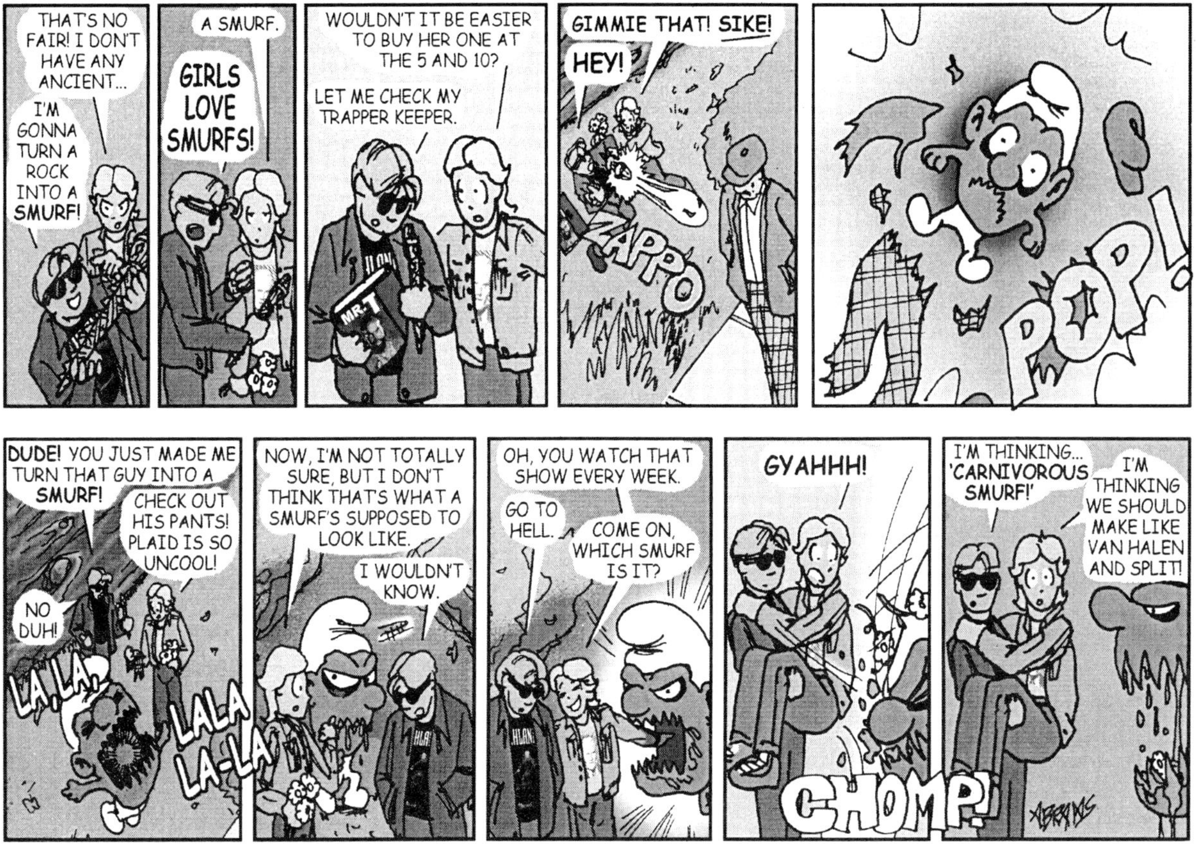
THAT'S NO FAIR! I DON'T HAVE ANY ANCIENT...
I'M GONNA TURN A ROCK INTO A SMURF!
A SMURF.
GIRLS LOVE SMURFS!
WOULDN'T IT BE EASIER TO BUY HER ONE AT THE 5 AND 10?
LET ME CHECK MY TRAPPER KEEPER.
MR. T
GIMMIE THAT! SIKE!
HEY!
ZAPPO
POP!
DUDE! YOU JUST MADE ME TURN THAT GUY INTO A SMURF!
CHECK OUT HIS PANTS! PLAID IS SO UNCOOL!
NO DUH!
LA, LA,
LALA LA-LA
NOW, I'M NOT TOTALLY SURE, BUT I DON'T THINK THAT'S WHAT A SMURF'S SUPPOSED TO LOOK LIKE.
I WOULDN'T KNOW.
OH, YOU WATCH THAT SHOW EVERY WEEK.
GO TO HELL.
COME ON, WHICH SMURF IS IT?
GYAHHH!
CHOMP!
I'M THINKING... 'CARNIVOROUS SMURF!'
I'M THINKING WE SHOULD MAKE LIKE VAN HALEN AND SPLIT!

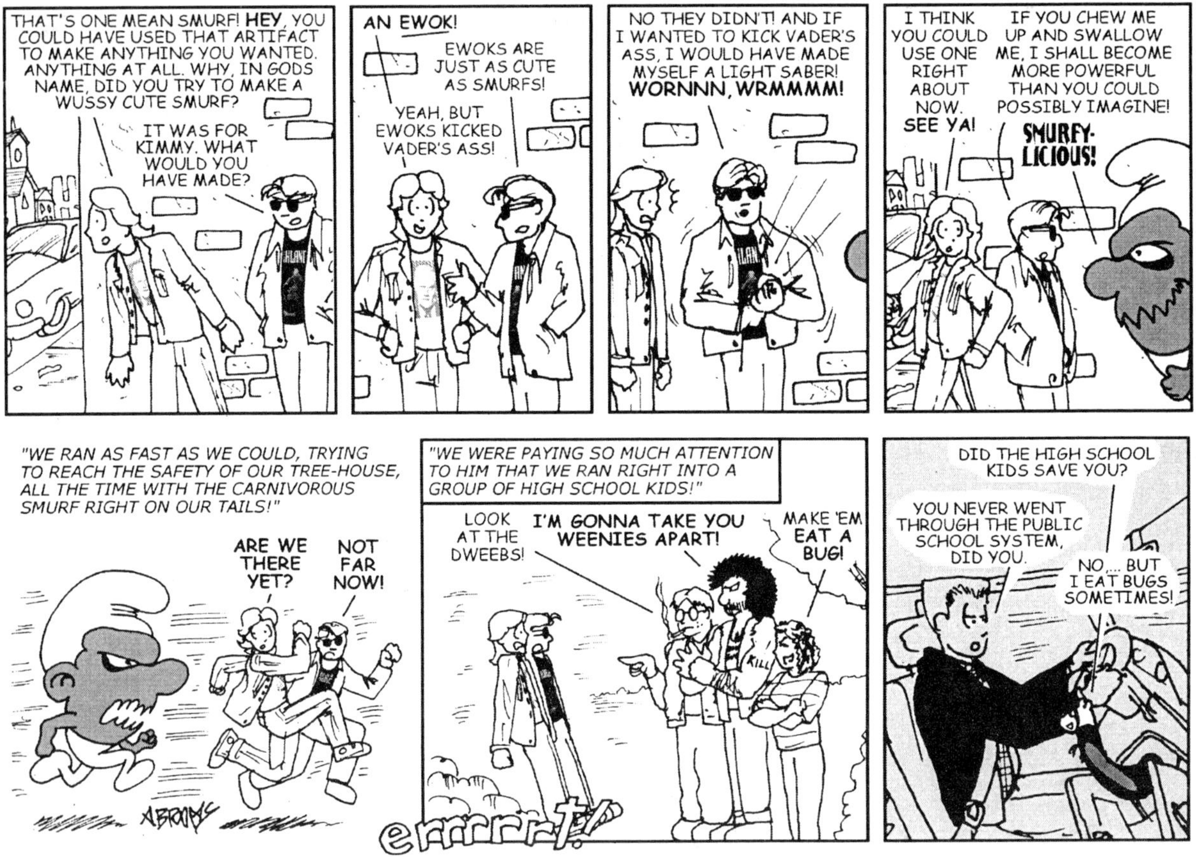
THAT'S ONE MEAN SMURF! HEY, YOU COULD HAVE USED THAT ARTIFACT TO MAKE ANYTHING YOU WANTED. ANYTHING AT ALL. WHY, IN GODS NAME, DID YOU TRY TO MAKE A WUSSY CUTE SMURF?
IT WAS FOR KIMMY. WHAT WOULD YOU HAVE MADE?
AN EWOK!
EWOKS ARE JUST AS CUTE AS SMURFS!
YEAH, BUT EWOKS KICKED VADER'S ASS!
NO THEY DIDN'T! AND IF I WANTED TO KICK VADER'S ASS, I WOULD HAVE MADE MYSELF A LIGHT SABER! WORNNN, WRMMMM!
I THINK YOU COULD USE ONE RIGHT ABOUT NOW. SEE YA!
IF YOU CHEW ME UP AND SWALLOW ME, I SHALL BECOME MORE POWERFUL THAN YOU COULD POSSIBLY IMAGINE!
SMURFY-LICIOUS!
"WE RAN AS FAST AS WE COULD, TRYING TO REACH THE SAFETY OF OUR TREE-HOUSE, ALL THE TIME WITH THE CARNIVOROUS SMURF RIGHT ON OUR TAILS!"
ARE WE THERE YET?
NOT FAR NOW!
"WE WERE PAYING SO MUCH ATTENTION TO HIM THAT WE RAN RIGHT INTO A GROUP OF HIGH SCHOOL KIDS!"
LOOK AT THE DWEEBS!
I'M GONNA TAKE YOU WEENIES APART!
MAKE 'EM EAT A BUG!
errrrrt!
DID THE HIGH SCHOOL KIDS SAVE YOU?
YOU NEVER WENT THROUGH THE PUBLIC SCHOOL SYSTEM, DID YOU.
NO,... BUT I EAT BUGS SOMETIMES!

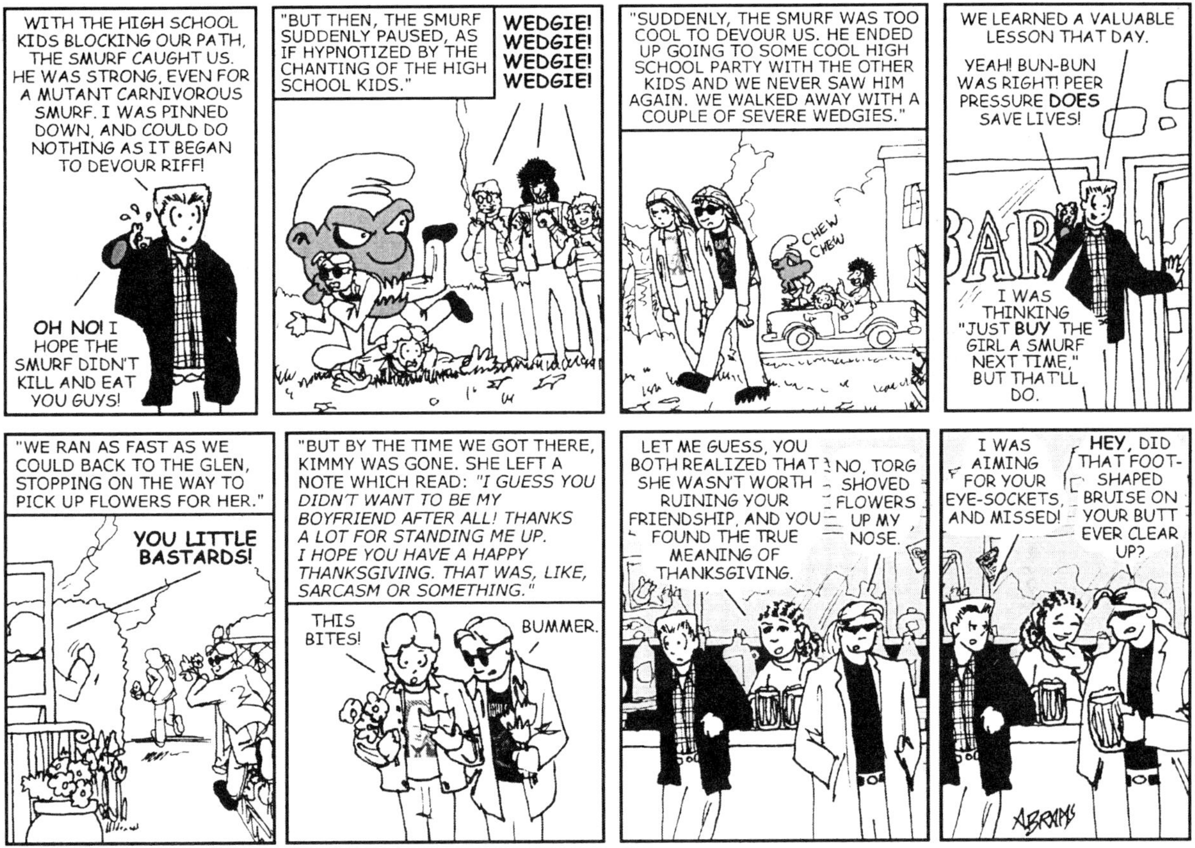
WITH THE HIGH SCHOOL KIDS BLOCKING OUR PATH, THE SMURF CAUGHT US. HE WAS STRONG, EVEN FOR A MUTANT CARNIVOROUS SMURF. I WAS PINNED DOWN, AND COULD DO NOTHING AS IT BEGAN TO DEVOUR RIFF!
OH NO! I HOPE THE SMURF DIDN'T KILL AND EAT YOU GUYS!
"BUT THEN, THE SMURF SUDDENLY PAUSED, AS IF HYPNOTIZED BY THE CHANTING OF THE HIGH SCHOOL KIDS."
WEDGIE! WEDGIE! WEDGIE! WEDGIE!
"SUDDENLY, THE SMURF WAS TOO COOL TO DEVOUR US. HE ENDED UP GOING TO SOME COOL HIGH SCHOOL PARTY WITH THE OTHER KIDS AND WE NEVER SAW HIM AGAIN. WE WALKED AWAY WITH A COUPLE OF SEVERE WEDGIES."
CHEW CHEW
WE LEARNED A VALUABLE LESSON THAT DAY.
YEAH! BUN-BUN WAS RIGHT! PEER PRESSURE DOES SAVE LIVES!
I WAS THINKING "JUST BUY THE GIRL A SMURF NEXT TIME," BUT THAT'LL DO.
"WE RAN AS FAST AS WE COULD BACK TO THE GLEN, STOPPING ON THE WAY TO PICK UP FLOWERS FOR HER."
YOU LITTLE BASTARDS!
"BUT BY THE TIME WE GOT THERE, KIMMY WAS GONE. SHE LEFT A NOTE WHICH READ: *"I GUESS YOU DIDN'T WANT TO BE MY BOYFRIEND AFTER ALL! THANKS A LOT FOR STANDING ME UP. I HOPE YOU HAVE A HAPPY THANKSGIVING. THAT WAS, LIKE, SARCASM OR SOMETHING."*
THIS BITES!
BUMMER.
LET ME GUESS, YOU BOTH REALIZED THAT SHE WASN'T WORTH RUINING YOUR FRIENDSHIP, AND YOU FOUND THE TRUE MEANING OF THANKSGIVING.
NO, TORG SHOVED FLOWERS UP MY NOSE.
I WAS AIMING FOR YOUR EYE-SOCKETS, AND MISSED!
HEY, DID THAT FOOT-SHAPED BRUISE ON YOUR BUTT EVER CLEAR UP?
ABRAMS

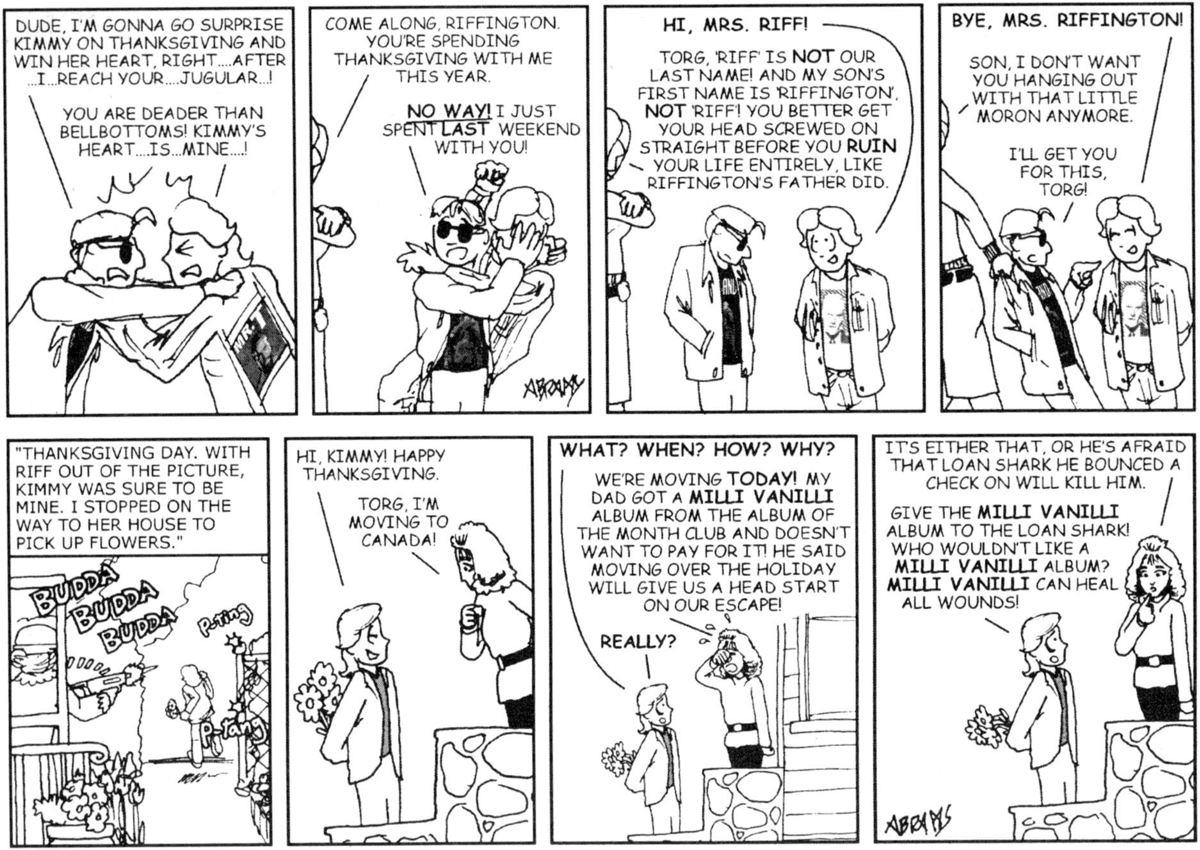
DUDE, I'M GONNA GO SURPRISE KIMMY ON THANKSGIVING AND WIN HER HEART, RIGHT....AFTER ...I...REACH YOUR....JUGULAR...!
YOU ARE DEADER THAN BELLBOTTOMS! KIMMY'S HEART....IS...MINE....!
MR. T
COME ALONG, RIFFINGTON. YOU'RE SPENDING THANKSGIVING WITH ME THIS YEAR.
NO WAY! I JUST SPENT LAST WEEKEND WITH YOU!
ABRAMS
HI, MRS. RIFF!
TORG, 'RIFF' IS NOT OUR LAST NAME! AND MY SON'S FIRST NAME IS 'RIFFINGTON', NOT 'RIFF'! YOU BETTER GET YOUR HEAD SCREWED ON STRAIGHT BEFORE YOU RUIN YOUR LIFE ENTIRELY, LIKE RIFFINGTON'S FATHER DID.
BYE, MRS. RIFFINGTON!
SON, I DON'T WANT YOU HANGING OUT WITH THAT LITTLE MORON ANYMORE.
I'LL GET YOU FOR THIS, TORG!
"THANKSGIVING DAY. WITH RIFF OUT OF THE PICTURE, KIMMY WAS SURE TO BE MINE. I STOPPED ON THE WAY TO HER HOUSE TO PICK UP FLOWERS."
BUDDA BUDDA BUDDA
P-ting
P-tang
HI, KIMMY! HAPPY THANKSGIVING.
TORG, I'M MOVING TO CANADA!
WHAT? WHEN? HOW? WHY?
WE'RE MOVING TODAY! MY DAD GOT A MILLI VANILLI ALBUM FROM THE ALBUM OF THE MONTH CLUB AND DOESN'T WANT TO PAY FOR IT! HE SAID MOVING OVER THE HOLIDAY WILL GIVE US A HEAD START ON OUR ESCAPE!
REALLY?
IT'S EITHER THAT, OR HE'S AFRAID THAT LOAN SHARK HE BOUNCED A CHECK ON WILL KILL HIM.
GIVE THE MILLI VANILLI ALBUM TO THE LOAN SHARK! WHO WOULDN'T LIKE A MILLI VANILLI ALBUM? MILLI VANILLI CAN HEAL ALL WOUNDS!
ABRAMS

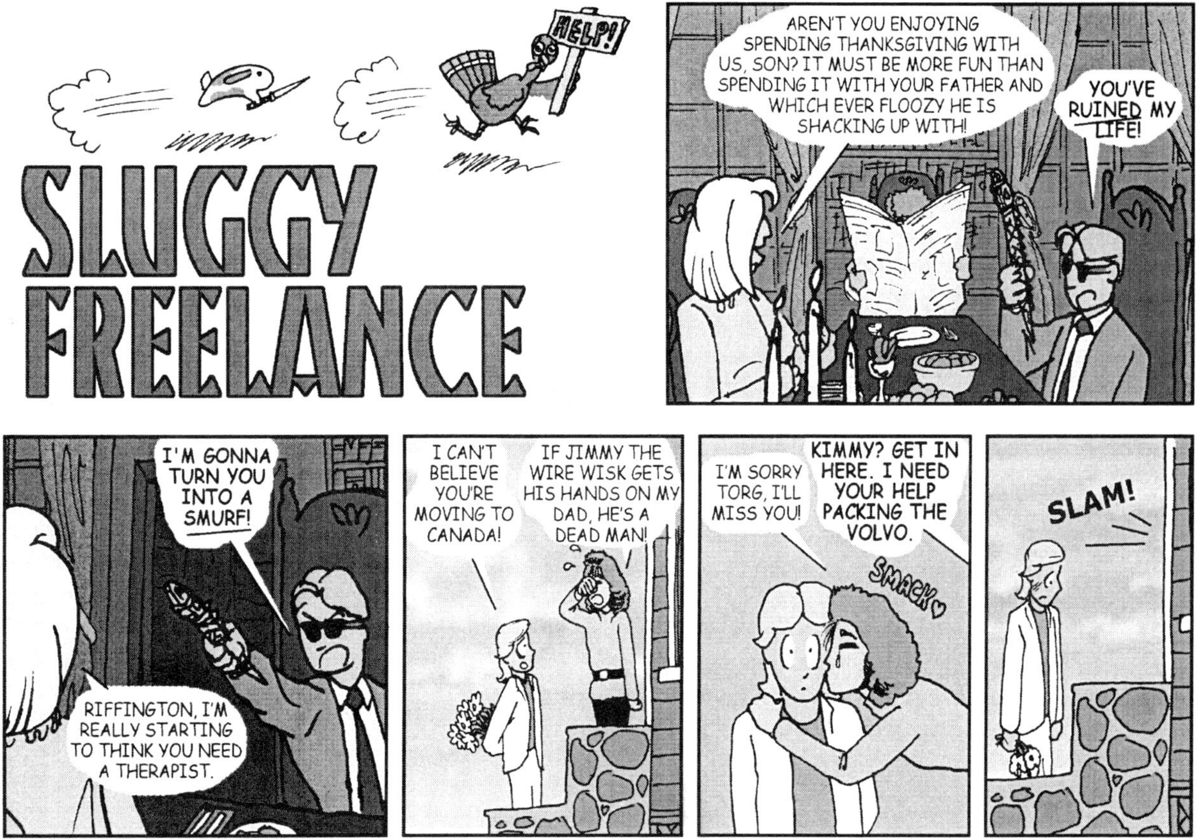
HELP!
SLUGGY FREELANCE
AREN'T YOU ENJOYING SPENDING THANKSGIVING WITH US, SON? IT MUST BE MORE FUN THAN SPENDING IT WITH YOUR FATHER AND WHICH EVER FLOOZY HE IS SHACKING UP WITH!
YOU'VE RUINED MY LIFE!
I'M GONNA TURN YOU INTO A SMURF!
RIFFINGTON, I'M REALLY STARTING TO THINK YOU NEED A THERAPIST.
I CAN'T BELIEVE YOU'RE MOVING TO CANADA!
IF JIMMY THE WIRE WISK GETS HIS HANDS ON MY DAD, HE'S A DEAD MAN!
I'M SORRY TORG, I'LL MISS YOU!
SMACK
KIMMY? GET IN HERE. I NEED YOUR HELP PACKING THE VOLVO.
SLAM!

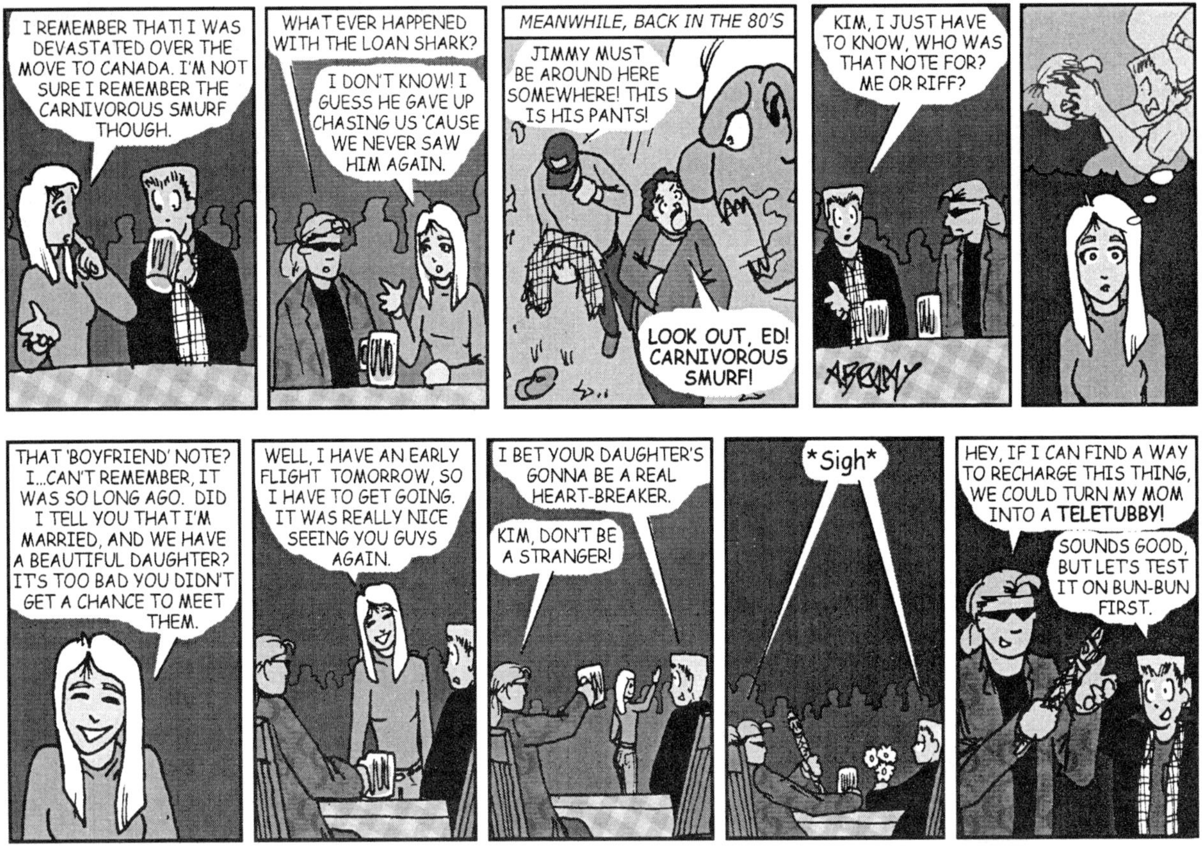
I REMEMBER THAT! I WAS DEVASTATED OVER THE MOVE TO CANADA. I'M NOT SURE I REMEMBER THE CARNIVOROUS SMURF THOUGH.
WHAT EVER HAPPENED WITH THE LOAN SHARK?
I DON'T KNOW! I GUESS HE GAVE UP CHASING US 'CAUSE WE NEVER SAW HIM AGAIN.
MEANWHILE, BACK IN THE 80'S
JIMMY MUST BE AROUND HERE SOMEWHERE! THIS IS HIS PANTS!
LOOK OUT, ED! CARNIVOROUS SMURF!
KIM, I JUST HAVE TO KNOW, WHO WAS THAT NOTE FOR? ME OR RIFF?
THAT 'BOYFRIEND' NOTE? I...CAN'T REMEMBER, IT WAS SO LONG AGO. DID I TELL YOU THAT I'M MARRIED, AND WE HAVE A BEAUTIFUL DAUGHTER? IT'S TOO BAD YOU DIDN'T GET A CHANCE TO MEET THEM.
WELL, I HAVE AN EARLY FLIGHT TOMORROW, SO I HAVE TO GET GOING. IT WAS REALLY NICE SEEING YOU GUYS AGAIN.
I BET YOUR DAUGHTER'S GONNA BE A REAL HEART-BREAKER.
KIM, DON'T BE A STRANGER!
Sigh
HEY, IF I CAN FIND A WAY TO RECHARGE THIS THING, WE COULD TURN MY MOM INTO A TELETUBBY!
SOUNDS GOOD, BUT LET'S TEST IT ON BUN-BUN FIRST.

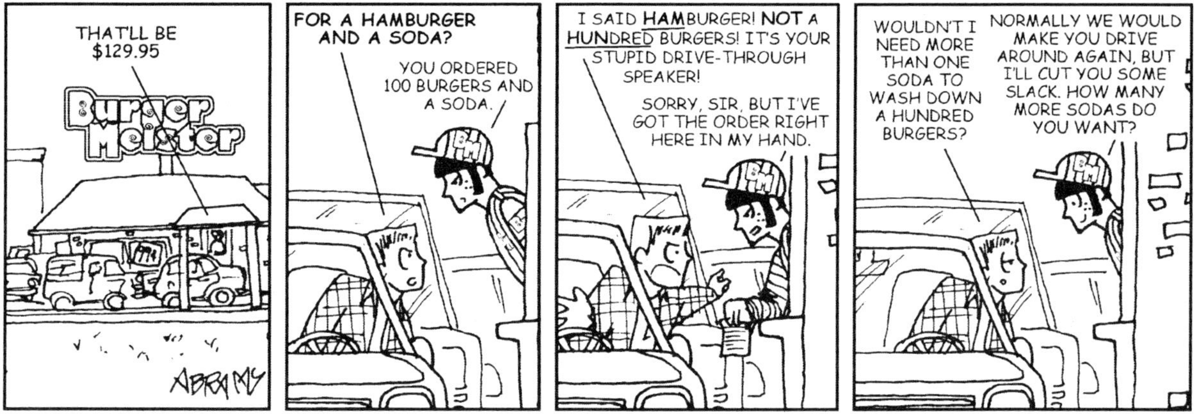
Burger Meister
THAT'LL BE $129.95
FOR A HAMBURGER AND A SODA?
YOU ORDERED 100 BURGERS AND A SODA.
I SAID HAMBURGER! NOT A HUNDRED BURGERS! IT'S YOUR STUPID DRIVE-THROUGH SPEAKER!
SORRY, SIR, BUT I'VE GOT THE ORDER RIGHT HERE IN MY HAND.
WOULDN'T I NEED MORE THAN ONE SODA TO WASH DOWN A HUNDRED BURGERS?
NORMALLY WE WOULD MAKE YOU DRIVE AROUND AGAIN, BUT I'LL CUT YOU SOME SLACK. HOW MANY MORE SODAS DO YOU WANT?

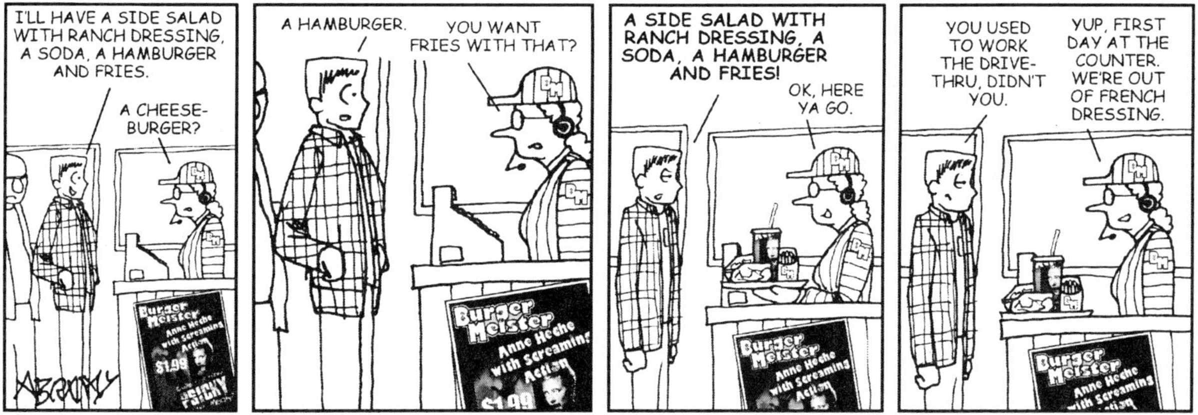
I'LL HAVE A SIDE SALAD WITH RANCH DRESSING, A SODA, A HAMBURGER AND FRIES.
A CHEESE-BURGER?
Burger Meister
Anne Heche with Screaming Action
$1.99
A HAMBURGER.
YOU WANT FRIES WITH THAT?
A SIDE SALAD WITH RANCH DRESSING, A SODA, A HAMBURGER AND FRIES!
OK, HERE YA GO.
YOU USED TO WORK THE DRIVE-THRU, DIDN'T YOU.
YUP, FIRST DAY AT THE COUNTER. WE'RE OUT OF FRENCH DRESSING.

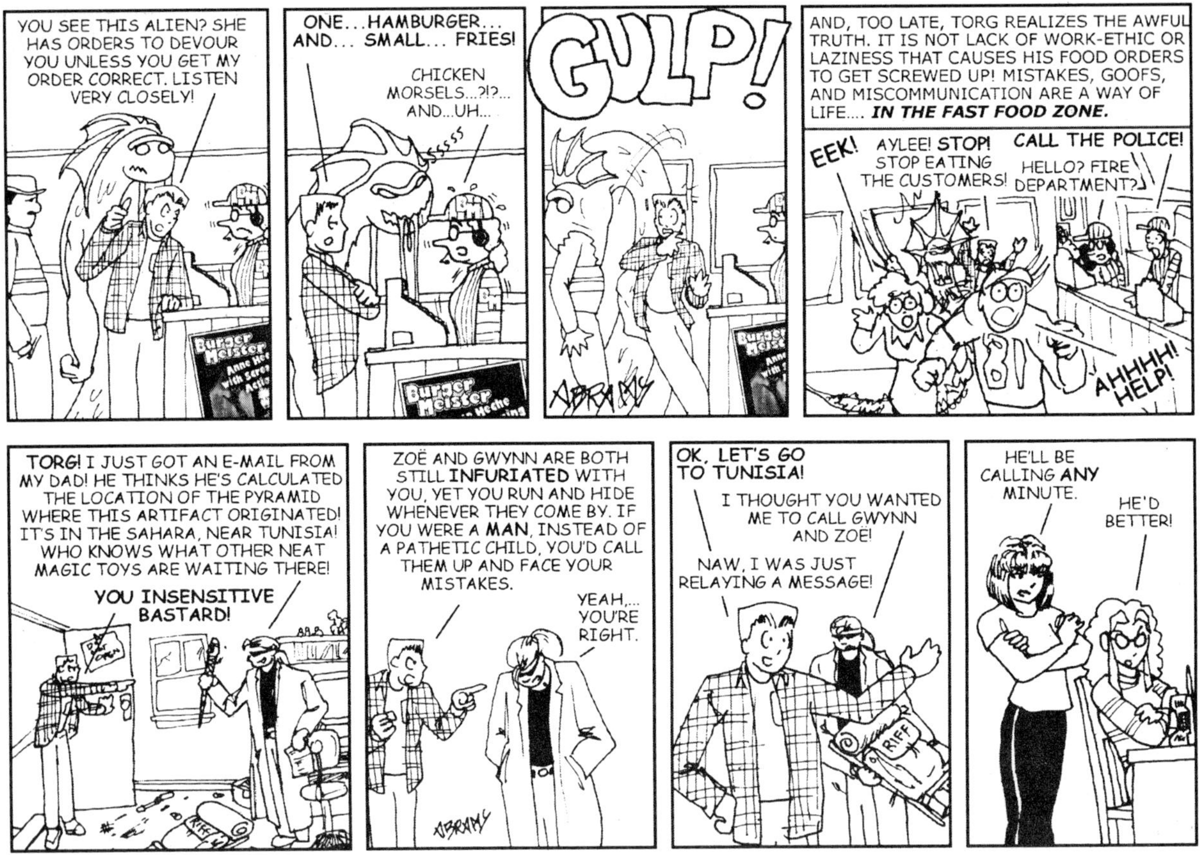
YOU SEE THIS ALIEN? SHE HAS ORDERS TO DEVOUR YOU UNLESS YOU GET MY ORDER CORRECT. LISTEN VERY CLOSELY!
ONE...HAMBURGER... AND... SMALL... FRIES!
CHICKEN MORSELS...?!?... AND...UH...
SSSSS
GULP!
ABRAMS
AND, TOO LATE, TORG REALIZES THE AWFUL TRUTH. IT IS NOT LACK OF WORK-ETHIC OR LAZINESS THAT CAUSES HIS FOOD ORDERS TO GET SCREWED UP! MISTAKES, GOOFS, AND MISCOMMUNICATION ARE A WAY OF LIFE.... IN THE FAST FOOD ZONE.
EEK!
AYLEE! STOP! STOP EATING THE CUSTOMERS!
CALL THE POLICE!
HELLO? FIRE DEPARTMENT?
AHHHH! HELP!
TORG! I JUST GOT AN E-MAIL FROM MY DAD! HE THINKS HE'S CALCULATED THE LOCATION OF THE PYRAMID WHERE THIS ARTIFACT ORIGINATED! IT'S IN THE SAHARA, NEAR TUNISIA! WHO KNOWS WHAT OTHER NEAT MAGIC TOYS ARE WAITING THERE!
YOU INSENSITIVE BASTARD!
RIFF
ZOË AND GWYNN ARE BOTH STILL INFURIATED WITH YOU, YET YOU RUN AND HIDE WHENEVER THEY COME BY. IF YOU WERE A MAN, INSTEAD OF A PATHETIC CHILD, YOU'D CALL THEM UP AND FACE YOUR MISTAKES.
YEAH,... YOU'RE RIGHT.
ABRAMS
OK, LET'S GO TO TUNISIA!
I THOUGHT YOU WANTED ME TO CALL GWYNN AND ZOË!
NAW, I WAS JUST RELAYING A MESSAGE!
RIFF
HE'LL BE CALLING ANY MINUTE.
HE'D BETTER!

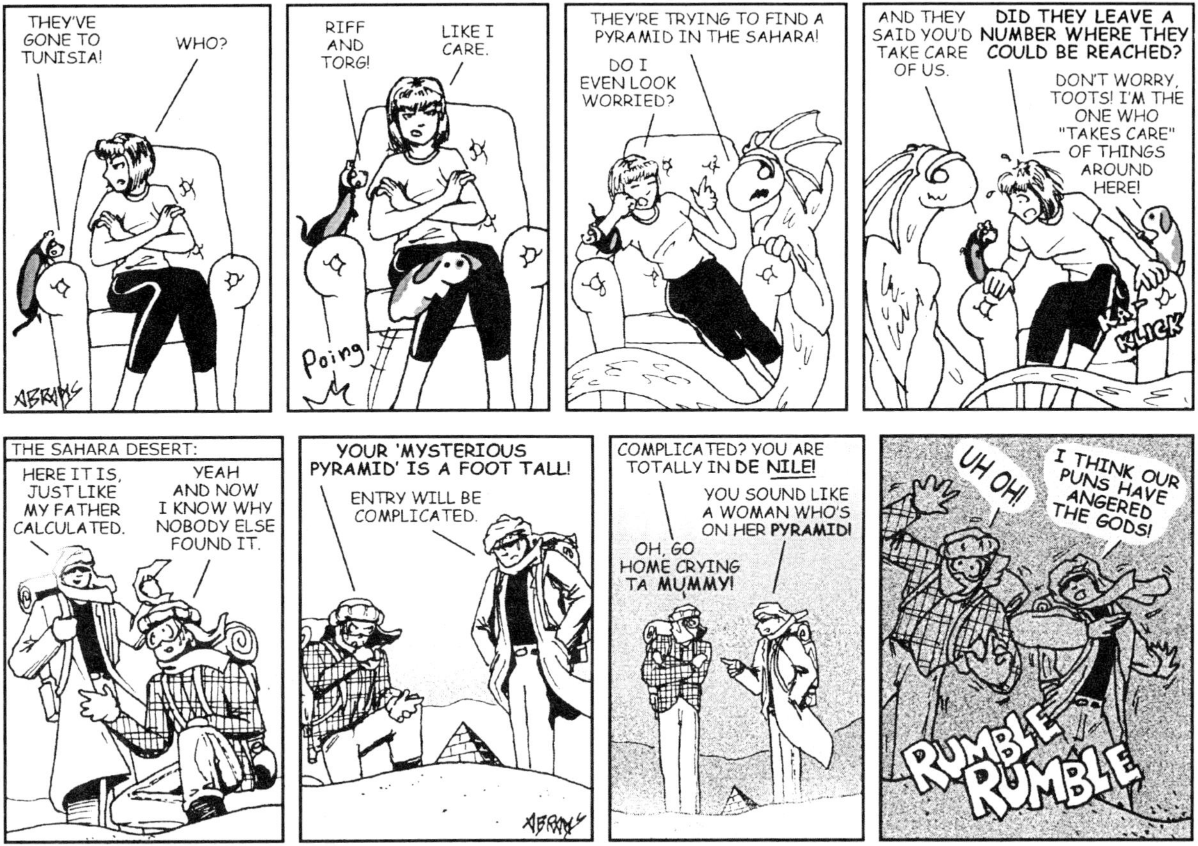
THEY'VE GONE TO TUNISIA!
WHO?
RIFF AND TORG!
LIKE I CARE.
Poing
THEY'RE TRYING TO FIND A PYRAMID IN THE SAHARA!
DO I EVEN LOOK WORRIED?
AND THEY SAID YOU'D TAKE CARE OF US.
DID THEY LEAVE A NUMBER WHERE THEY COULD BE REACHED?
DON'T WORRY, TOOTS! I'M THE ONE WHO "TAKES CARE" OF THINGS AROUND HERE!
KA-KLICK
THE SAHARA DESERT:
HERE IT IS, JUST LIKE MY FATHER CALCULATED.
YEAH AND NOW I KNOW WHY NOBODY ELSE FOUND IT.
YOUR 'MYSTERIOUS PYRAMID' IS A FOOT TALL!
ENTRY WILL BE COMPLICATED.
COMPLICATED? YOU ARE TOTALLY IN DE NILE!
YOU SOUND LIKE A WOMAN WHO'S ON HER PYRAMID!
OH, GO HOME CRYING TA MUMMY!
UH OH!
I THINK OUR PUNS HAVE ANGERED THE GODS!
RUMBLE RUMBLE

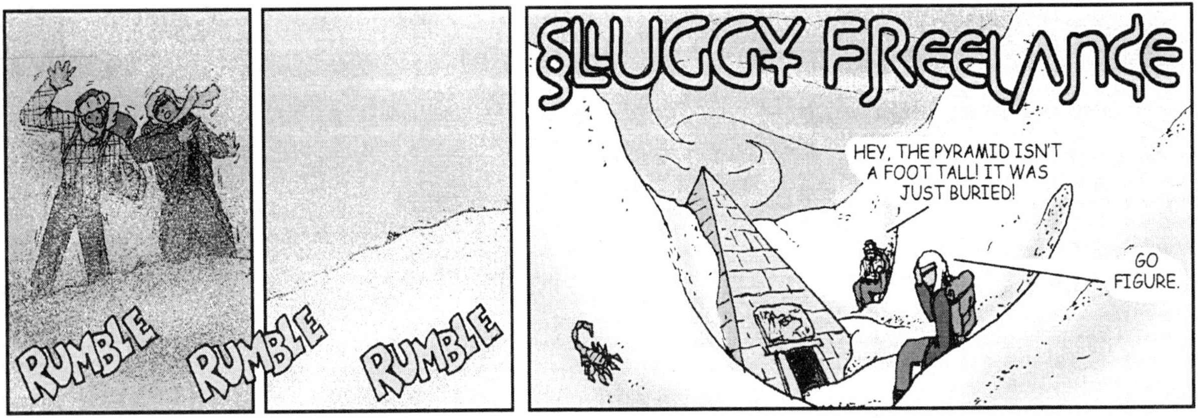
RUMBLE
RUMBLE
RUMBLE
SLUGGY FREELANCE
HEY, THE PYRAMID ISN'T A FOOT TALL! IT WAS JUST BURIED!
GO FIGURE.

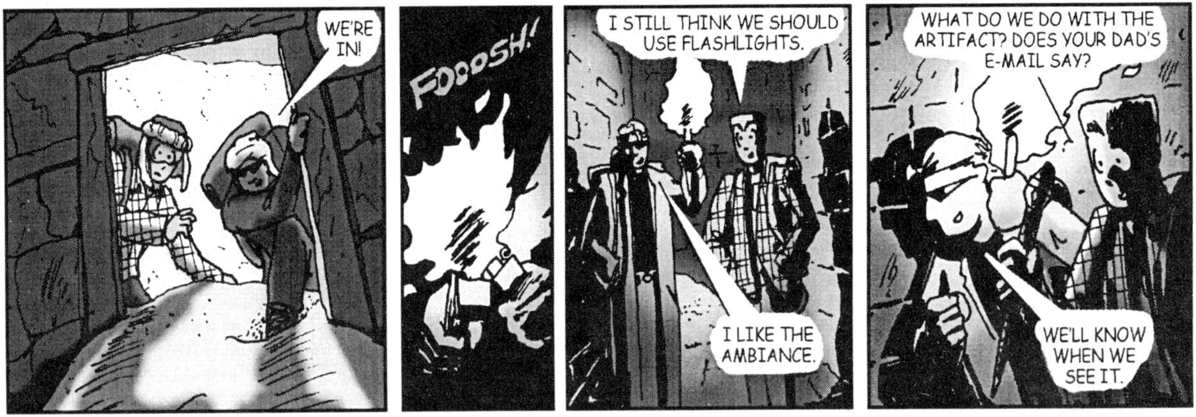
WE'RE IN!
FOOOSH!
I STILL THINK WE SHOULD USE FLASHLIGHTS.
I LIKE THE AMBIANCE.
WHAT DO WE DO WITH THE ARTIFACT? DOES YOUR DAD'S E-MAIL SAY?
WE'LL KNOW WHEN WE SEE IT.

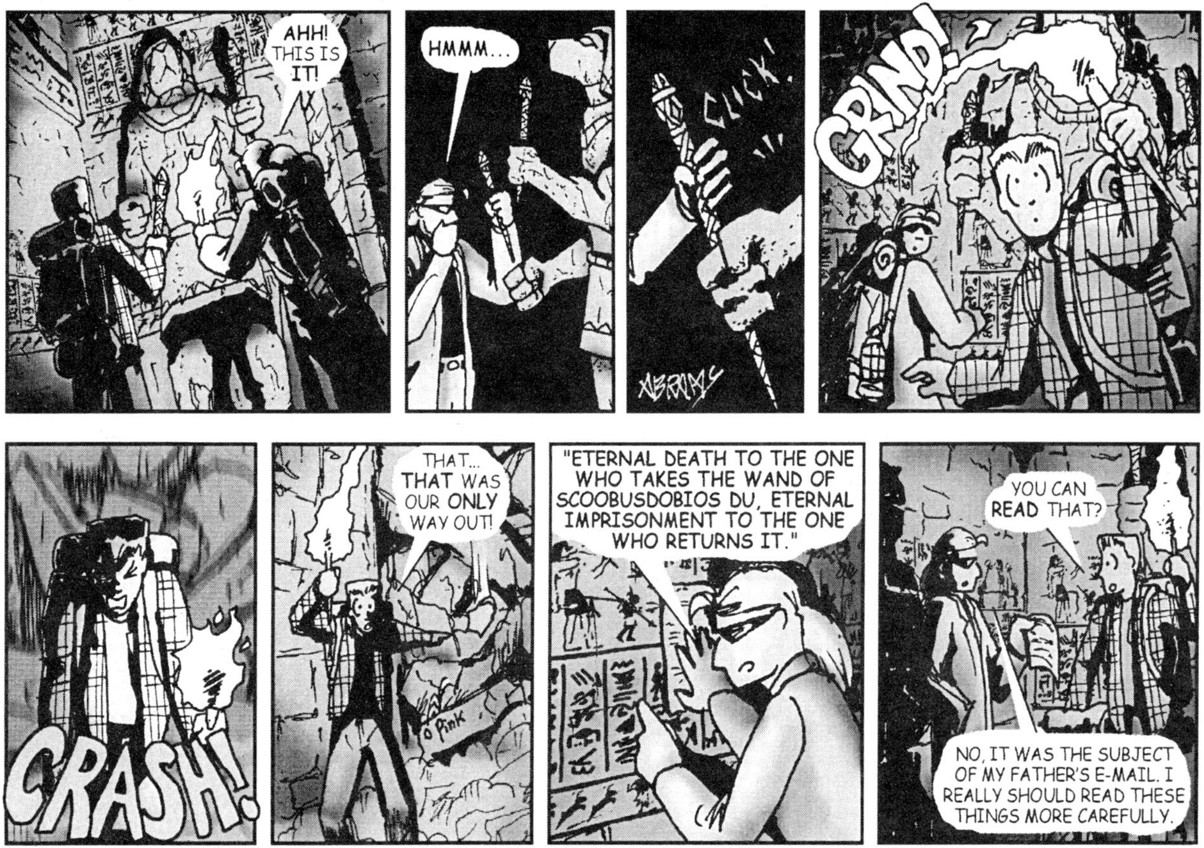
AHH! THIS IS IT!
HMMM...
CLICK!
GRIND!
CRASH!
THAT... THAT WAS OUR ONLY WAY OUT!
"ETERNAL DEATH TO THE ONE WHO TAKES THE WAND OF SCOOBUSDOBIOS DU, ETERNAL IMPRISONMENT TO THE ONE WHO RETURNS IT."
YOU CAN READ THAT?
NO, IT WAS THE SUBJECT OF MY FATHER'S E-MAIL. I REALLY SHOULD READ THESE THINGS MORE CAREFULLY.

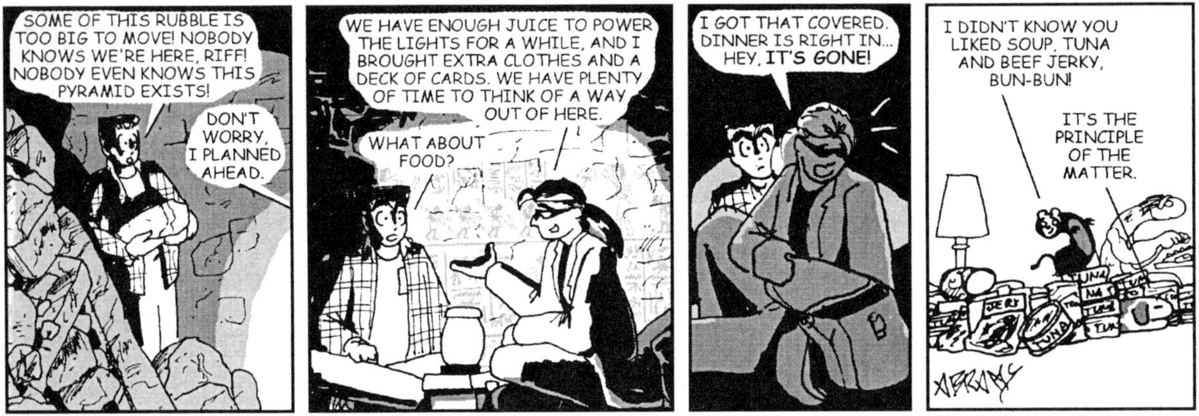
SOME OF THIS RUBBLE IS TOO BIG TO MOVE! NOBODY KNOWS WE'RE HERE, RIFF! NOBODY EVEN KNOWS THIS PYRAMID EXISTS!
DON'T WORRY, I PLANNED AHEAD.
WE HAVE ENOUGH JUICE TO POWER THE LIGHTS FOR A WHILE, AND I BROUGHT EXTRA CLOTHES AND A DECK OF CARDS. WE HAVE PLENTY OF TIME TO THINK OF A WAY OUT OF HERE.
WHAT ABOUT FOOD?
I GOT THAT COVERED. DINNER IS RIGHT IN... HEY, **IT'S GONE!**
I DIDN'T KNOW YOU LIKED SOUP, TUNA AND BEEF JERKY, BUN-BUN!
IT'S THE PRINCIPLE OF THE MATTER.

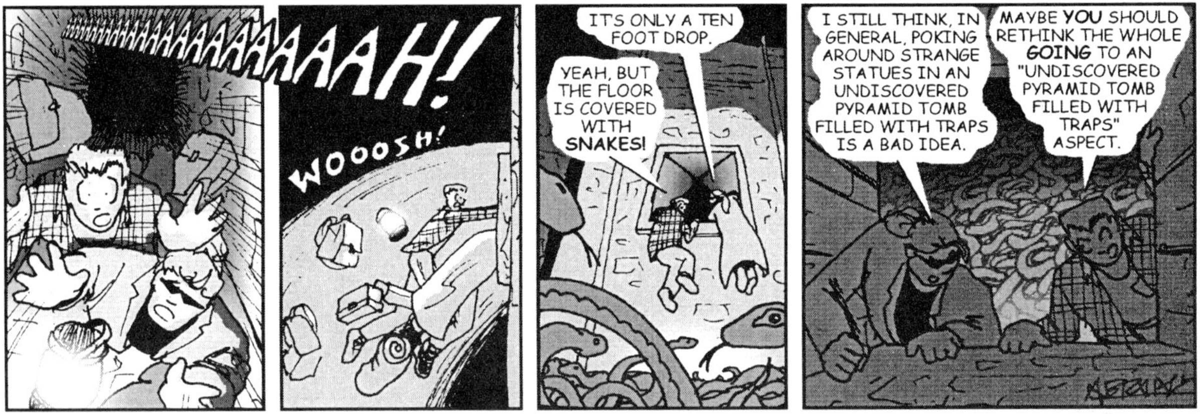
AAAAAAAAAAAAAAAAAAAAAAAAAAAH!
WOOOSH!
IT'S ONLY A TEN FOOT DROP.
YEAH, BUT THE FLOOR IS COVERED WITH **SNAKES!**
I STILL THINK, IN GENERAL, POKING AROUND STRANGE STATUES IN AN UNDISCOVERED PYRAMID TOMB FILLED WITH TRAPS IS A BAD IDEA.
MAYBE **YOU** SHOULD RETHINK THE WHOLE **GOING** TO AN "UNDISCOVERED PYRAMID TOMB FILLED WITH TRAPS" ASPECT.

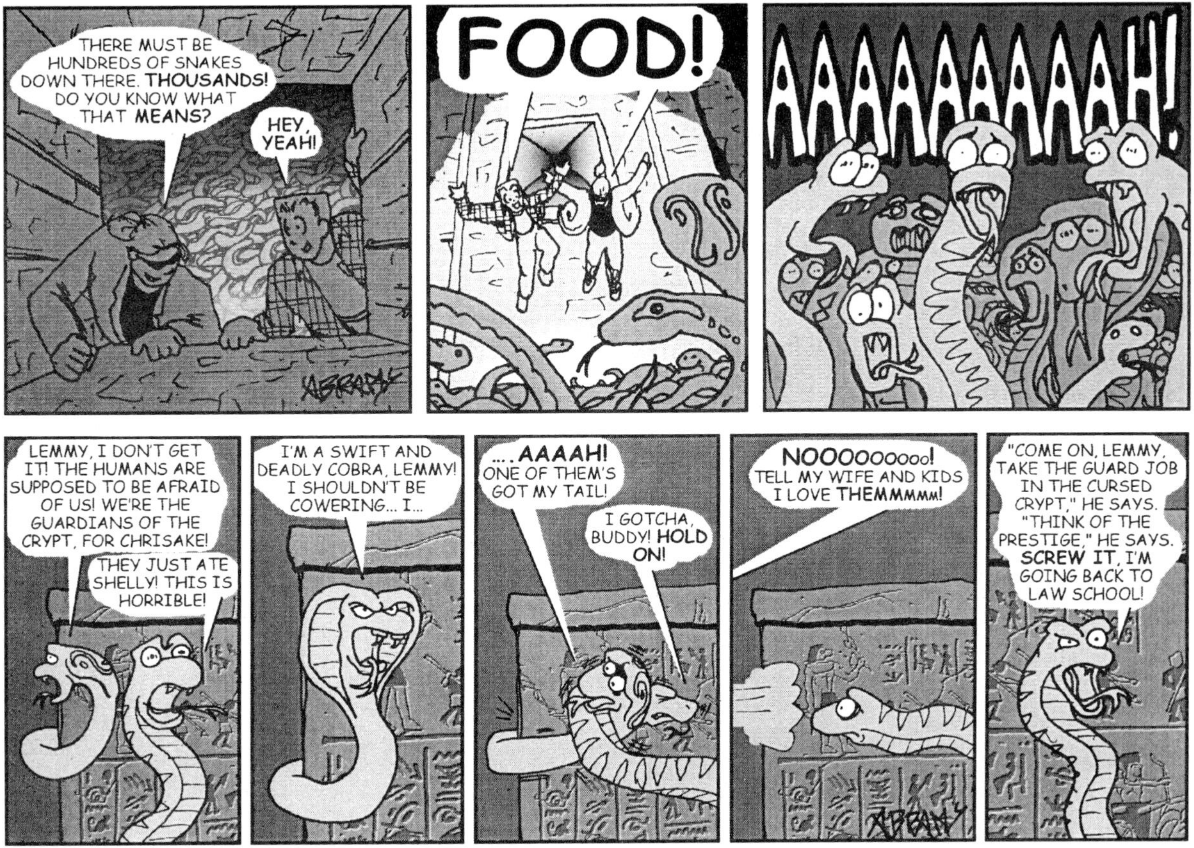
THERE MUST BE HUNDREDS OF SNAKES DOWN THERE. THOUSANDS! DO YOU KNOW WHAT THAT MEANS?
HEY, YEAH!
FOOD!
AAAAAAAAAH!
LEMMY, I DON'T GET IT! THE HUMANS ARE SUPPOSED TO BE AFRAID OF US! WE'RE THE GUARDIANS OF THE CRYPT, FOR CHRISAKE!
THEY JUST ATE SHELLY! THIS IS HORRIBLE!
I'M A SWIFT AND DEADLY COBRA, LEMMY! I SHOULDN'T BE COWERING... I...
....AAAAH! ONE OF THEM'S GOT MY TAIL!
I GOTCHA, BUDDY! HOLD ON!
NOOOOOOooo! TELL MY WIFE AND KIDS I LOVE THEMMMMM!
"COME ON, LEMMY, TAKE THE GUARD JOB IN THE CURSED CRYPT," HE SAYS. "THINK OF THE PRESTIGE," HE SAYS. SCREW IT, I'M GOING BACK TO LAW SCHOOL!

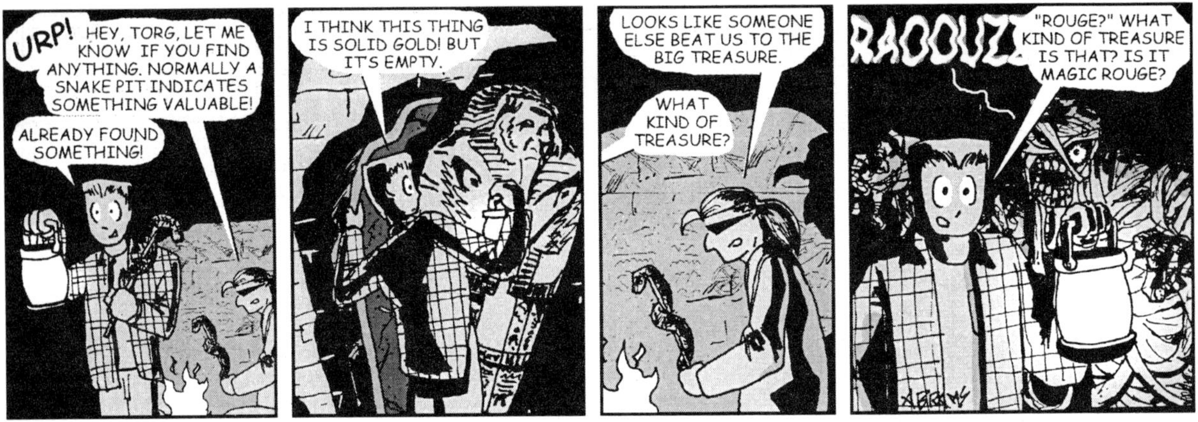
URP!
HEY, TORG, LET ME KNOW IF YOU FIND ANYTHING. NORMALLY A SNAKE PIT INDICATES SOMETHING VALUABLE!
ALREADY FOUND SOMETHING!
I THINK THIS THING IS SOLID GOLD! BUT IT'S EMPTY.
LOOKS LIKE SOMEONE ELSE BEAT US TO THE BIG TREASURE.
WHAT KIND OF TREASURE?
RAOOUZZ
"ROUGE?" WHAT KIND OF TREASURE IS THAT? IS IT MAGIC ROUGE?

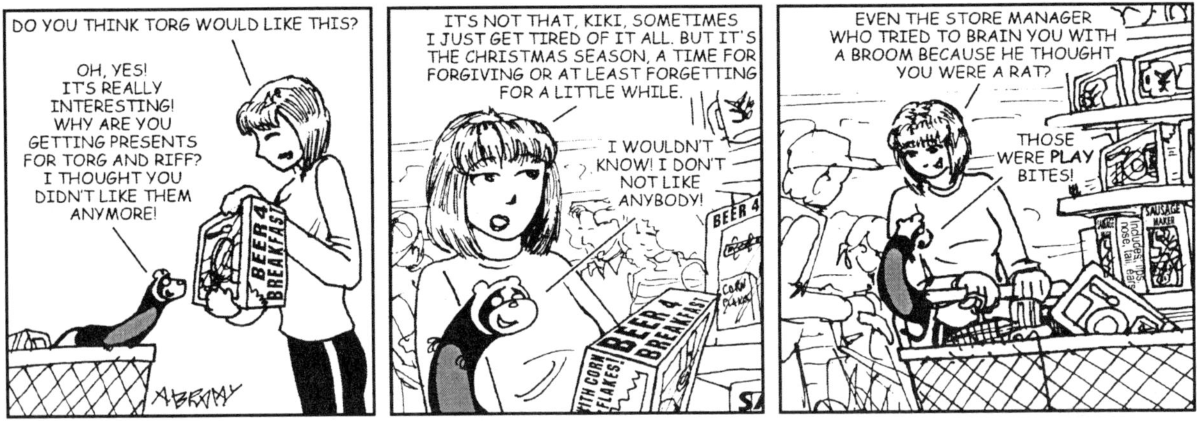
DO YOU THINK TORG WOULD LIKE THIS?
OH, YES! IT'S REALLY INTERESTING! WHY ARE YOU GETTING PRESENTS FOR TORG AND RIFF? I THOUGHT YOU DIDN'T LIKE THEM ANYMORE!
BEER 4 BREAKFAST
IT'S NOT THAT, KIKI, SOMETIMES I JUST GET TIRED OF IT ALL. BUT IT'S THE CHRISTMAS SEASON, A TIME FOR FORGIVING OR AT LEAST FORGETTING FOR A LITTLE WHILE.
I WOULDN'T KNOW! I DON'T NOT LIKE ANYBODY!
BEER 4 BREAKFAST
WITH CORN FLAKES!
EVEN THE STORE MANAGER WHO TRIED TO BRAIN YOU WITH A BROOM BECAUSE HE THOUGHT YOU WERE A RAT?
THOSE WERE **PLAY** BITES!
SAUSAGE MAKER

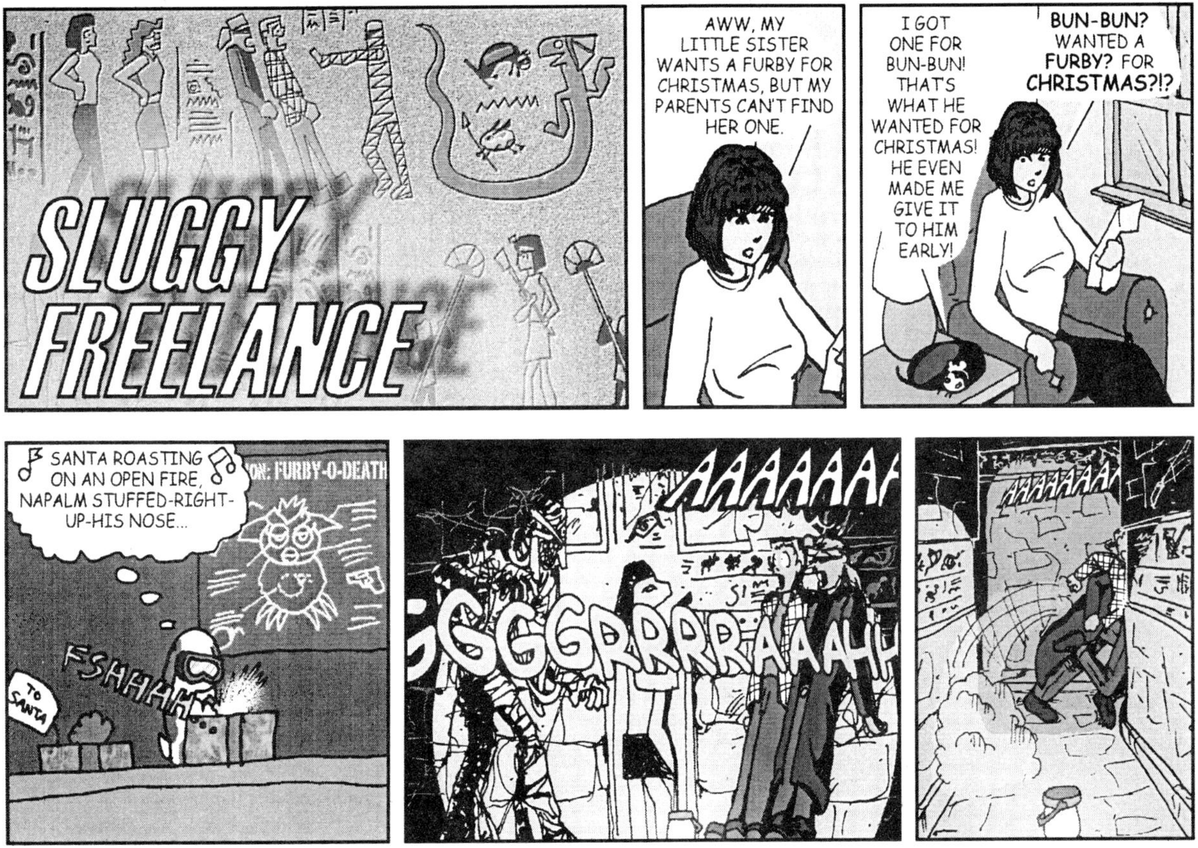
SLUGGY FREELANCE
AWW, MY LITTLE SISTER WANTS A FURBY FOR CHRISTMAS, BUT MY PARENTS CAN'T FIND HER ONE.
I GOT ONE FOR BUN-BUN! THAT'S WHAT HE WANTED FOR CHRISTMAS! HE EVEN MADE ME GIVE IT TO HIM EARLY!
BUN-BUN? WANTED A FURBY? FOR CHRISTMAS?!?
SANTA ROASTING ON AN OPEN FIRE, NAPALM STUFFED-RIGHT-UP-HIS NOSE...
ON: FURBY-O-DEATH
FSHHHH
TO SANTA
AAAAAAA
GGGRRRRAAAHH
AAAAAAA

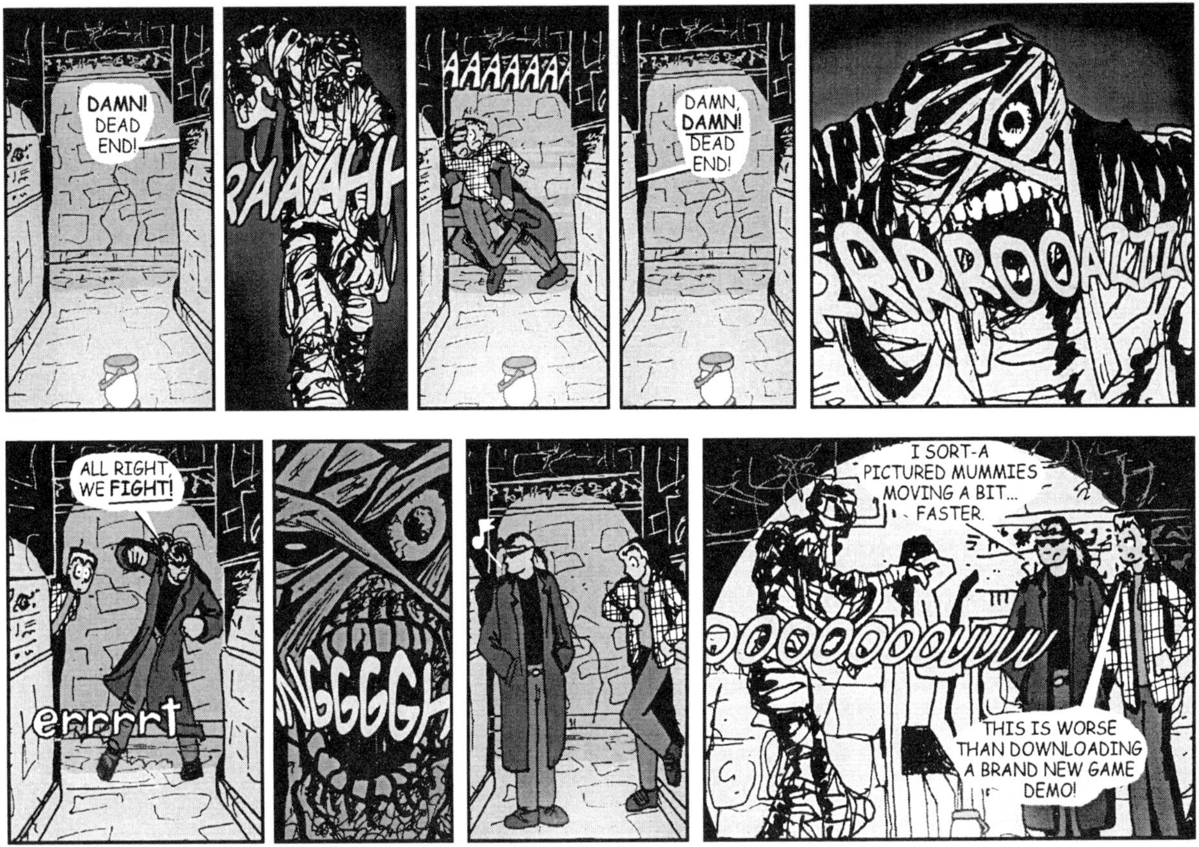
DAMN! DEAD END!
RAAAHH
AAAAAAA
DAMN, DAMN! DEAD END!
RRROOAZZZ
ALL RIGHT, WE FIGHT!
errrrt
NGGGGH
I SORT-A PICTURED MUMMIES MOVING A BIT... FASTER.
OOOOOOOOUUU
THIS IS WORSE THAN DOWNLOADING A BRAND NEW GAME DEMO!

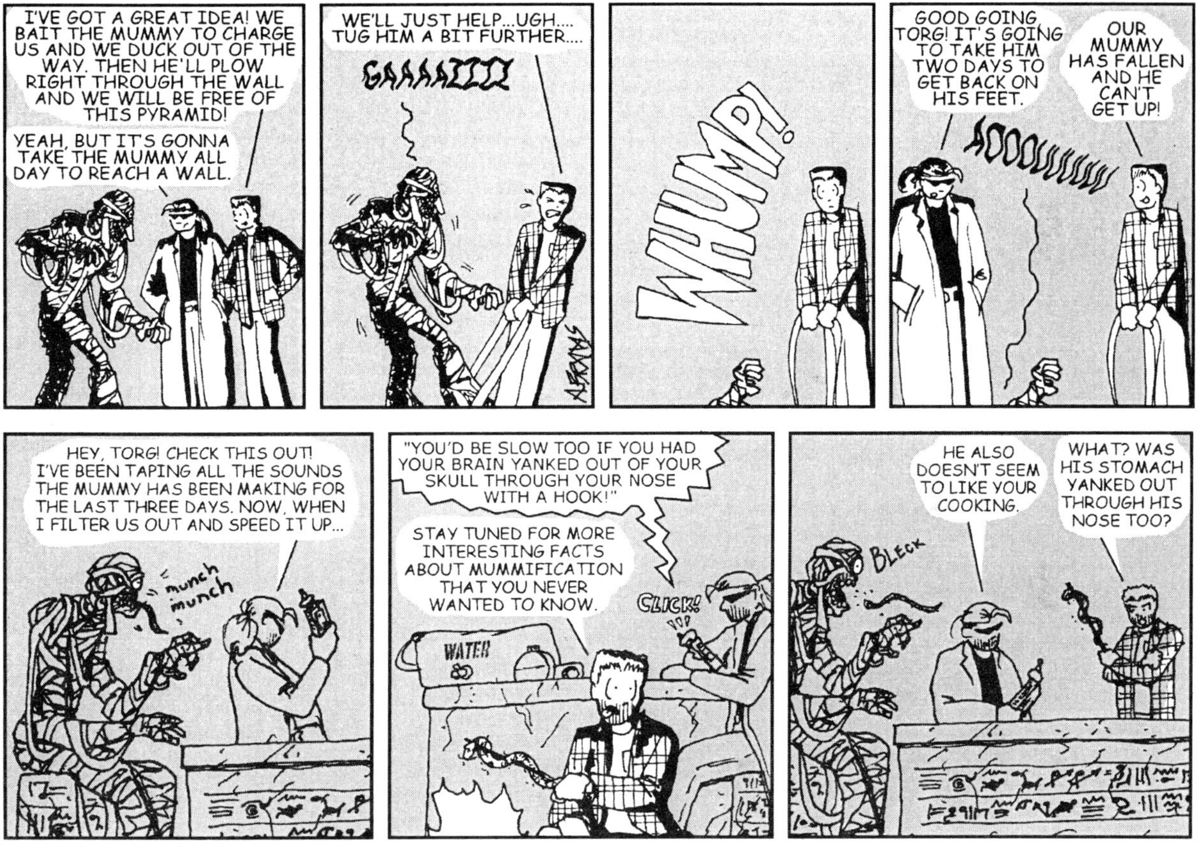
I'VE GOT A GREAT IDEA! WE BAIT THE MUMMY TO CHARGE US AND WE DUCK OUT OF THE WAY. THEN HE'LL PLOW RIGHT THROUGH THE WALL AND WE WILL BE FREE OF THIS PYRAMID!
YEAH, BUT IT'S GONNA TAKE THE MUMMY ALL DAY TO REACH A WALL.
WE'LL JUST HELP...UGH.... TUG HIM A BIT FURTHER....
GAAAAIIII
WHUMP!
GOOD GOING TORG! IT'S GOING TO TAKE HIM TWO DAYS TO GET BACK ON HIS FEET.
AOOOUUUUU
OUR MUMMY HAS FALLEN AND HE CAN'T GET UP!
HEY, TORG! CHECK THIS OUT! I'VE BEEN TAPING ALL THE SOUNDS THE MUMMY HAS BEEN MAKING FOR THE LAST THREE DAYS. NOW, WHEN I FILTER US OUT AND SPEED IT UP...
munch munch
"YOU'D BE SLOW TOO IF YOU HAD YOUR BRAIN YANKED OUT OF YOUR SKULL THROUGH YOUR NOSE WITH A HOOK!"
STAY TUNED FOR MORE INTERESTING FACTS ABOUT MUMMIFICATION THAT YOU NEVER WANTED TO KNOW.
CLICK!
WATER
HE ALSO DOESN'T SEEM TO LIKE YOUR COOKING.
WHAT? WAS HIS STOMACH YANKED OUT THROUGH HIS NOSE TOO?
BLECK

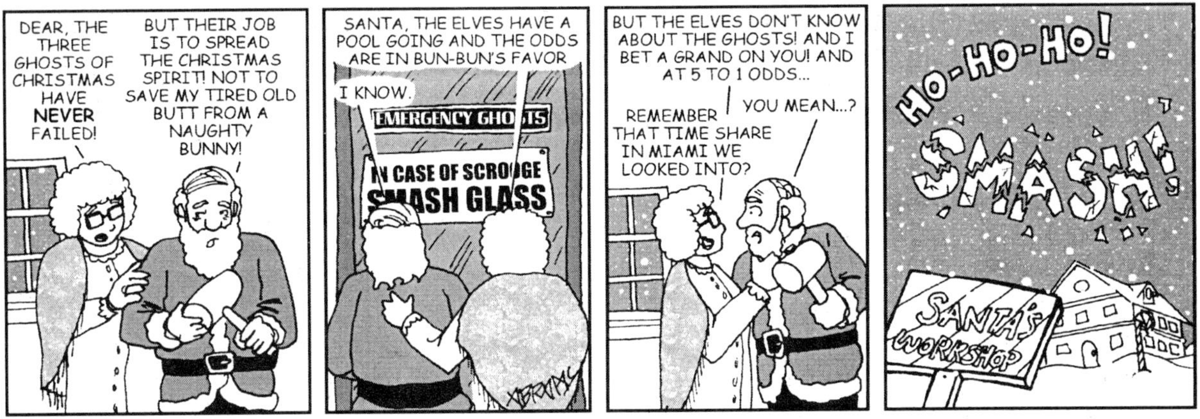
DEAR, THE THREE GHOSTS OF CHRISTMAS HAVE NEVER FAILED!
BUT THEIR JOB IS TO SPREAD THE CHRISTMAS SPIRIT! NOT TO SAVE MY TIRED OLD BUTT FROM A NAUGHTY BUNNY!
SANTA, THE ELVES HAVE A POOL GOING AND THE ODDS ARE IN BUN-BUN'S FAVOR
I KNOW.
EMERGENCY GHOSTS
IN CASE OF SCROOGE SMASH GLASS
BUT THE ELVES DON'T KNOW ABOUT THE GHOSTS! AND I BET A GRAND ON YOU! AND AT 5 TO 1 ODDS...
YOU MEAN...?
REMEMBER THAT TIME SHARE IN MIAMI WE LOOKED INTO?
HO-HO-HO!
SMASH!
SANTA'S WORKSHOP

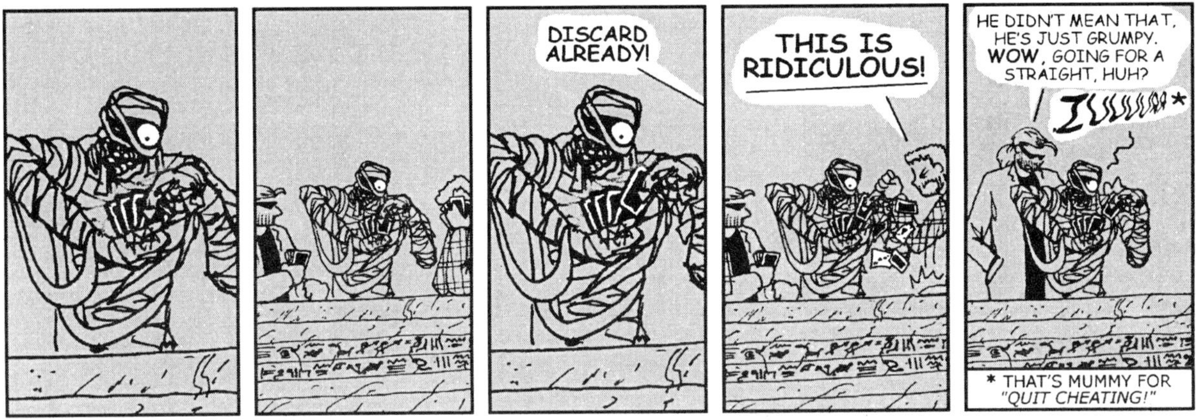
DISCARD ALREADY!
THIS IS RIDICULOUS!
HE DIDN'T MEAN THAT, HE'S JUST GRUMPY. WOW, GOING FOR A STRAIGHT, HUH?
* THAT'S MUMMY FOR "QUIT CHEATING!"

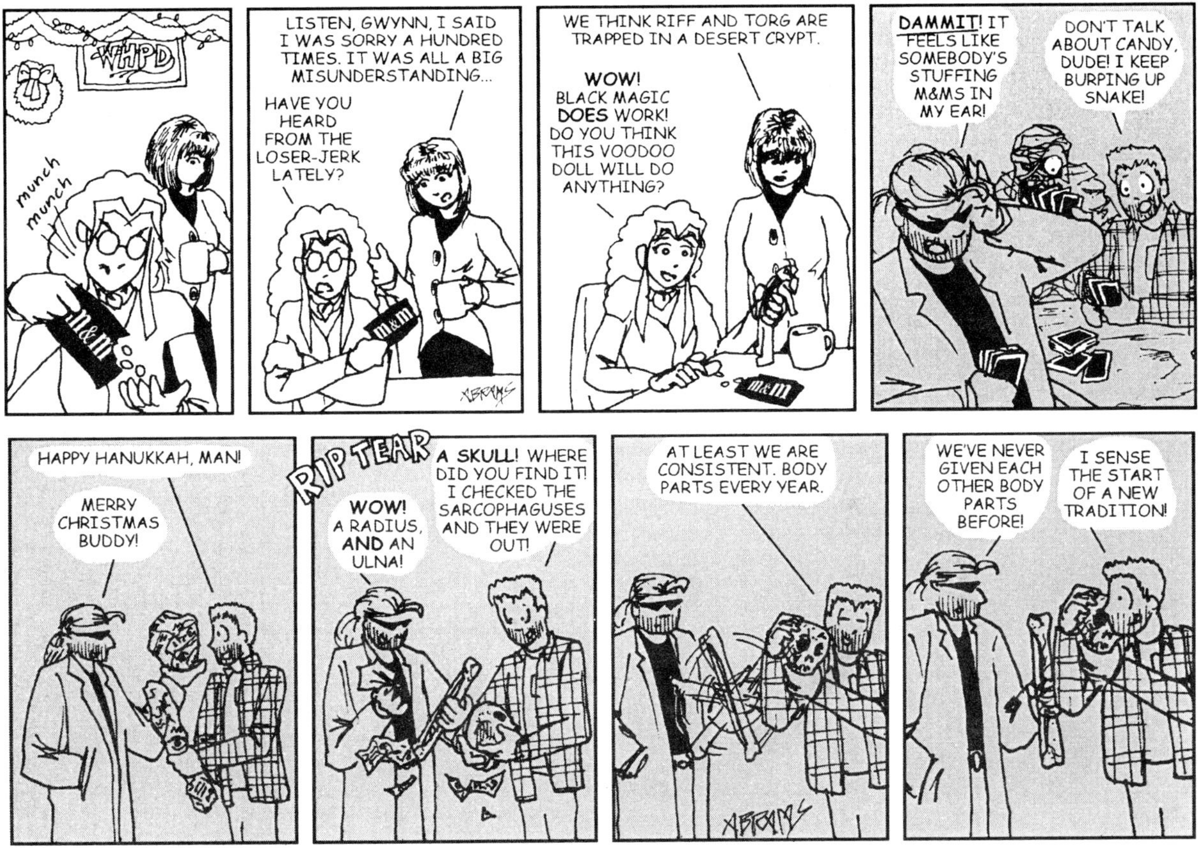

WHPD
munch munch
m&m
LISTEN, GWYNN, I SAID I WAS SORRY A HUNDRED TIMES. IT WAS ALL A BIG MISUNDERSTANDING...
HAVE YOU HEARD FROM THE LOSER-JERK LATELY?
m&m
ABRAMS
WE THINK RIFF AND TORG ARE TRAPPED IN A DESERT CRYPT.
WOW! BLACK MAGIC DOES WORK! DO YOU THINK THIS VOODOO DOLL WILL DO ANYTHING?
m&m
DAMMIT! IT FEELS LIKE SOMEBODY'S STUFFING M&MS IN MY EAR!
DON'T TALK ABOUT CANDY, DUDE! I KEEP BURPING UP SNAKE!
HAPPY HANUKKAH, MAN!
MERRY CHRISTMAS BUDDY!
RIP TEAR
A SKULL! WHERE DID YOU FIND IT! I CHECKED THE SARCOPHAGUSES AND THEY WERE OUT!
WOW! A RADIUS, AND AN ULNA!
AT LEAST WE ARE CONSISTENT. BODY PARTS EVERY YEAR.
ABRAMS
WE'VE NEVER GIVEN EACH OTHER BODY PARTS BEFORE!
I SENSE THE START OF A NEW TRADITION!

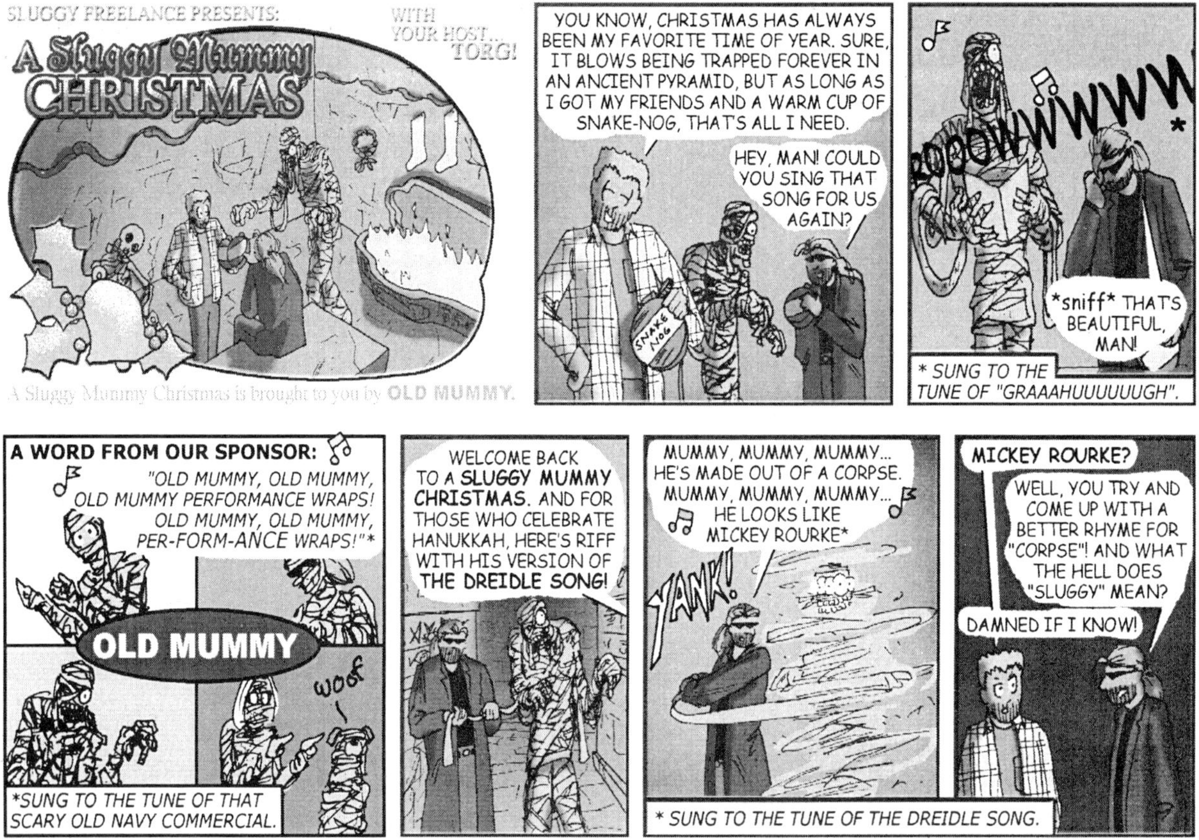
SLUGGY FREELANCE PRESENTS:
A Sluggy Mummy CHRISTMAS
WITH YOUR HOST... TORG!
A Sluggy Mummy Christmas is brought to you by OLD MUMMY.
YOU KNOW, CHRISTMAS HAS ALWAYS BEEN MY FAVORITE TIME OF YEAR. SURE, IT BLOWS BEING TRAPPED FOREVER IN AN ANCIENT PYRAMID, BUT AS LONG AS I GOT MY FRIENDS AND A WARM CUP OF SNAKE-NOG, THAT'S ALL I NEED.
SNAKE NOG
HEY, MAN! COULD YOU SING THAT SONG FOR US AGAIN?
ROOOOWWWWWW*
sniff THAT'S BEAUTIFUL, MAN!
* SUNG TO THE TUNE OF "GRAAAHUUUUUUGH".
A WORD FROM OUR SPONSOR:
"OLD MUMMY, OLD MUMMY, OLD MUMMY PERFORMANCE WRAPS! OLD MUMMY, OLD MUMMY, PER-FORM-ANCE WRAPS!"*
OLD MUMMY
woof
*SUNG TO THE TUNE OF THAT SCARY OLD NAVY COMMERCIAL.
WELCOME BACK TO A SLUGGY MUMMY CHRISTMAS. AND FOR THOSE WHO CELEBRATE HANUKKAH, HERE'S RIFF WITH HIS VERSION OF THE DREIDLE SONG!
MUMMY, MUMMY, MUMMY... HE'S MADE OUT OF A CORPSE. MUMMY, MUMMY, MUMMY... HE LOOKS LIKE MICKEY ROURKE*
YANK!
MICKEY ROURKE?
WELL, YOU TRY AND COME UP WITH A BETTER RHYME FOR "CORPSE"! AND WHAT THE HELL DOES "SLUGGY" MEAN?
DAMNED IF I KNOW!
* SUNG TO THE TUNE OF THE DREIDLE SONG.

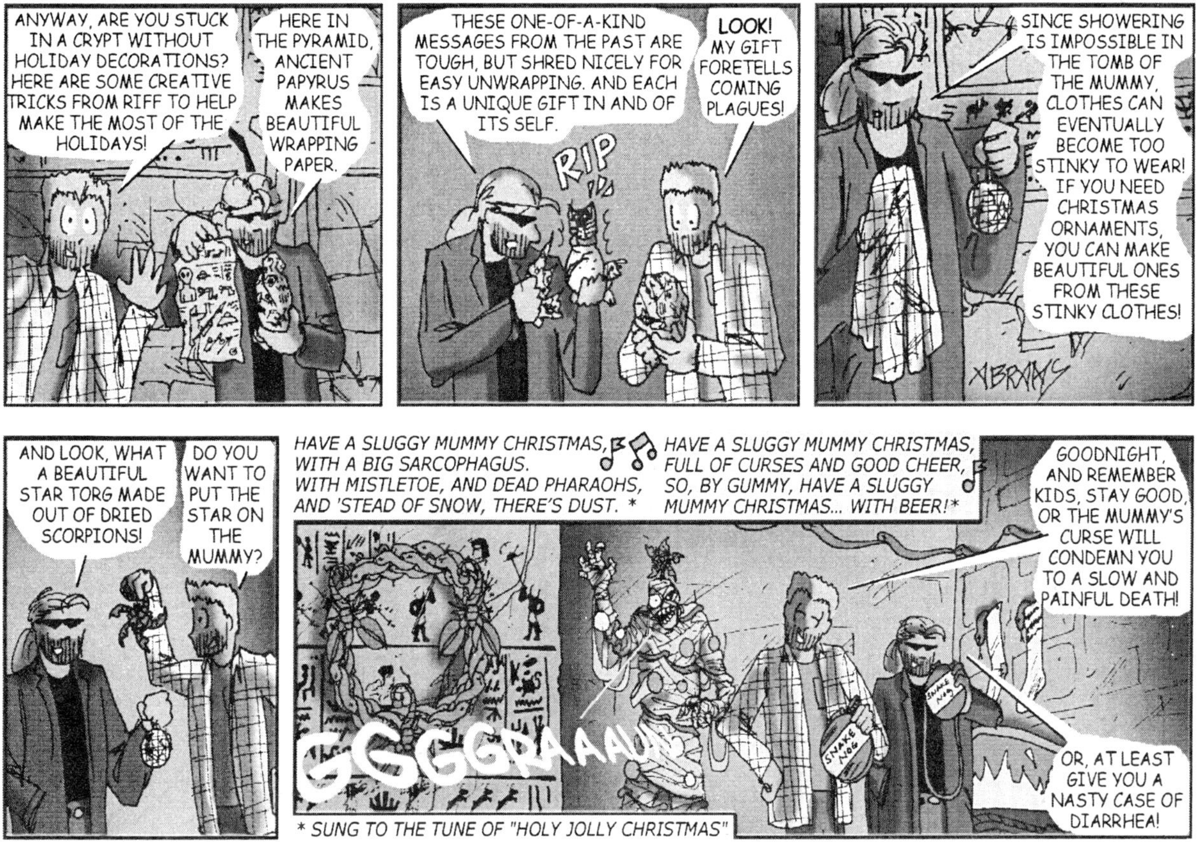

ANYWAY, ARE YOU STUCK IN A CRYPT WITHOUT HOLIDAY DECORATIONS? HERE ARE SOME CREATIVE TRICKS FROM RIFF TO HELP MAKE THE MOST OF THE HOLIDAYS!
HERE IN THE PYRAMID, ANCIENT PAPYRUS MAKES BEAUTIFUL WRAPPING PAPER.
THESE ONE-OF-A-KIND MESSAGES FROM THE PAST ARE TOUGH, BUT SHRED NICELY FOR EASY UNWRAPPING. AND EACH IS A UNIQUE GIFT IN AND OF ITS SELF.
RIP
LOOK! MY GIFT FORETELLS COMING PLAGUES!
SINCE SHOWERING IS IMPOSSIBLE IN THE TOMB OF THE MUMMY, CLOTHES CAN EVENTUALLY BECOME TOO STINKY TO WEAR! IF YOU NEED CHRISTMAS ORNAMENTS, YOU CAN MAKE BEAUTIFUL ONES FROM THESE STINKY CLOTHES!
ABRAMS
AND LOOK, WHAT A BEAUTIFUL STAR TORG MADE OUT OF DRIED SCORPIONS!
DO YOU WANT TO PUT THE STAR ON THE MUMMY?
HAVE A SLUGGY MUMMY CHRISTMAS, WITH A BIG SARCOPHAGUS. WITH MISTLETOE, AND DEAD PHARAOHS, AND 'STEAD OF SNOW, THERE'S DUST. *
HAVE A SLUGGY MUMMY CHRISTMAS, FULL OF CURSES AND GOOD CHEER, SO, BY GUMMY, HAVE A SLUGGY MUMMY CHRISTMAS... WITH BEER!*
GOODNIGHT, AND REMEMBER KIDS, STAY GOOD, OR THE MUMMY'S CURSE WILL CONDEMN YOU TO A SLOW AND PAINFUL DEATH!
GGGGRAAAUH
SNAKE NOG
OR, AT LEAST GIVE YOU A NASTY CASE OF DIARRHEA!
* SUNG TO THE TUNE OF "HOLY JOLLY CHRISTMAS"

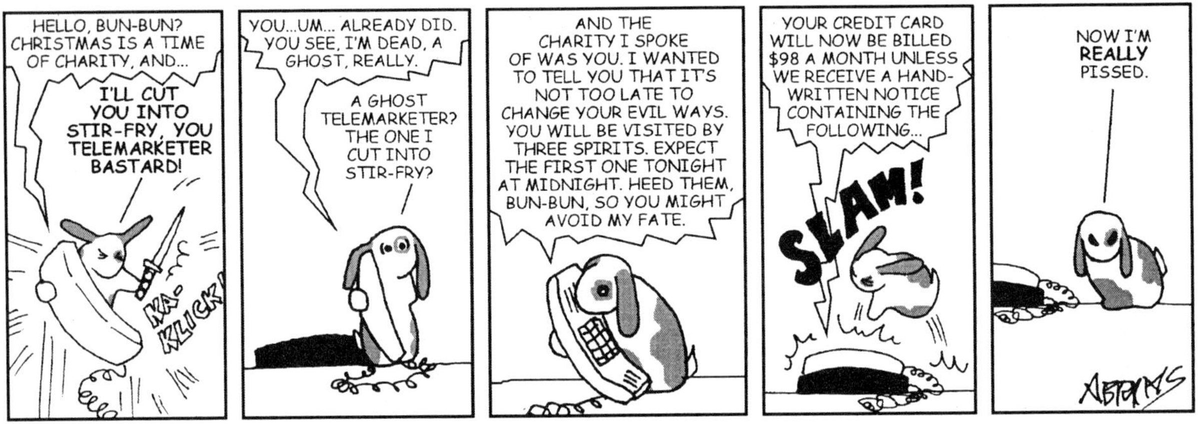
HELLO, BUN-BUN? CHRISTMAS IS A TIME OF CHARITY, AND...
I'LL CUT YOU INTO STIR-FRY, YOU TELEMARKETER BASTARD!
KA-KLICK!
YOU...UM... ALREADY DID. YOU SEE, I'M DEAD, A GHOST, REALLY.
A GHOST TELEMARKETER? THE ONE I CUT INTO STIR-FRY?
AND THE CHARITY I SPOKE OF WAS YOU. I WANTED TO TELL YOU THAT IT'S NOT TOO LATE TO CHANGE YOUR EVIL WAYS. YOU WILL BE VISITED BY THREE SPIRITS. EXPECT THE FIRST ONE TONIGHT AT MIDNIGHT. HEED THEM, BUN-BUN, SO YOU MIGHT AVOID MY FATE.
YOUR CREDIT CARD WILL NOW BE BILLED $98 A MONTH UNLESS WE RECEIVE A HAND-WRITTEN NOTICE CONTAINING THE FOLLOWING...
SLAM!
NOW I'M **REALLY** PISSED.

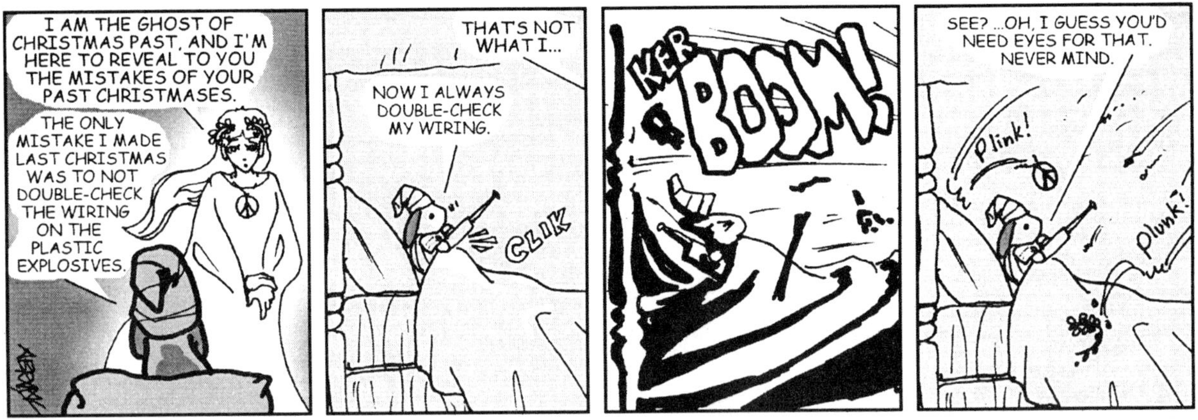
I AM THE GHOST OF CHRISTMAS PAST, AND I'M HERE TO REVEAL TO YOU THE MISTAKES OF YOUR PAST CHRISTMASES.
THE ONLY MISTAKE I MADE LAST CHRISTMAS WAS TO NOT DOUBLE-CHECK THE WIRING ON THE PLASTIC EXPLOSIVES.
THAT'S NOT WHAT I...
NOW I ALWAYS DOUBLE-CHECK MY WIRING.
CLIK
KER BOOM!
SEE? ...OH, I GUESS YOU'D NEED EYES FOR THAT. NEVER MIND.
plink!
plunk!

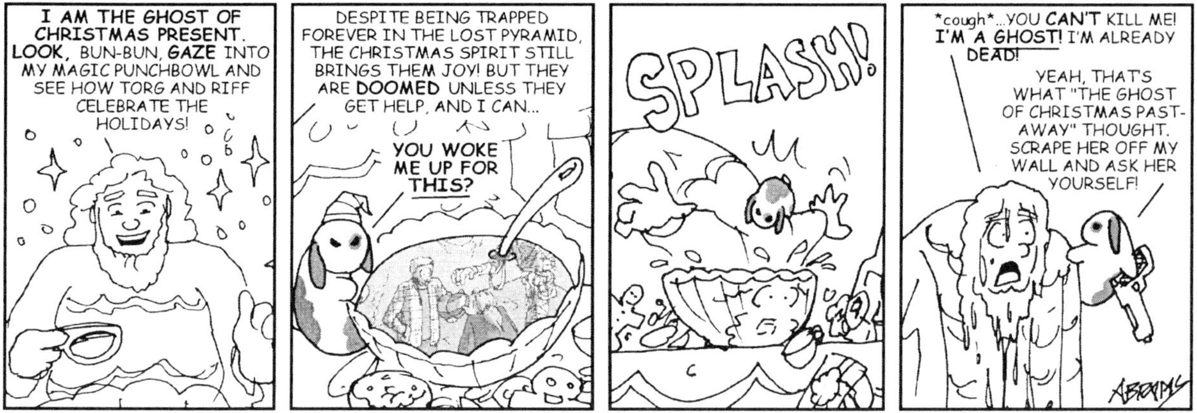
I AM THE GHOST OF CHRISTMAS PRESENT. LOOK, BUN-BUN, GAZE INTO MY MAGIC PUNCHBOWL AND SEE HOW TORG AND RIFF CELEBRATE THE HOLIDAYS!
DESPITE BEING TRAPPED FOREVER IN THE LOST PYRAMID, THE CHRISTMAS SPIRIT STILL BRINGS THEM JOY! BUT THEY ARE DOOMED UNLESS THEY GET HELP, AND I CAN...
YOU WOKE ME UP FOR THIS?
SPLASH!
cough...YOU CAN'T KILL ME! I'M A GHOST! I'M ALREADY DEAD!
YEAH, THAT'S WHAT "THE GHOST OF CHRISTMAS PAST-AWAY" THOUGHT. SCRAPE HER OFF MY WALL AND ASK HER YOURSELF!
ABRAMS

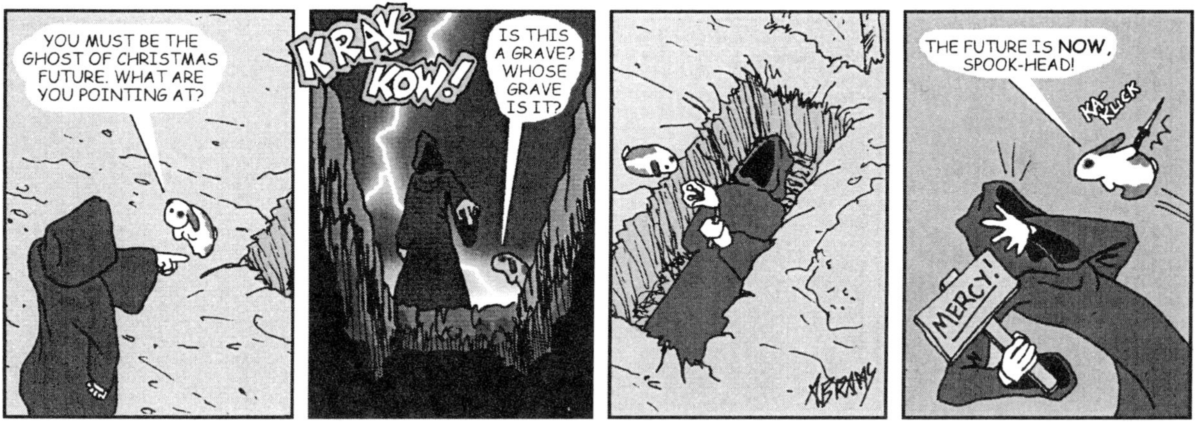
YOU MUST BE THE GHOST OF CHRISTMAS FUTURE. WHAT ARE YOU POINTING AT?
KRAK-KOW!
IS THIS A GRAVE? WHOSE GRAVE IS IT?
ABRAMS
THE FUTURE IS NOW, SPOOK-HEAD!
KA-KLICK
MERCY!

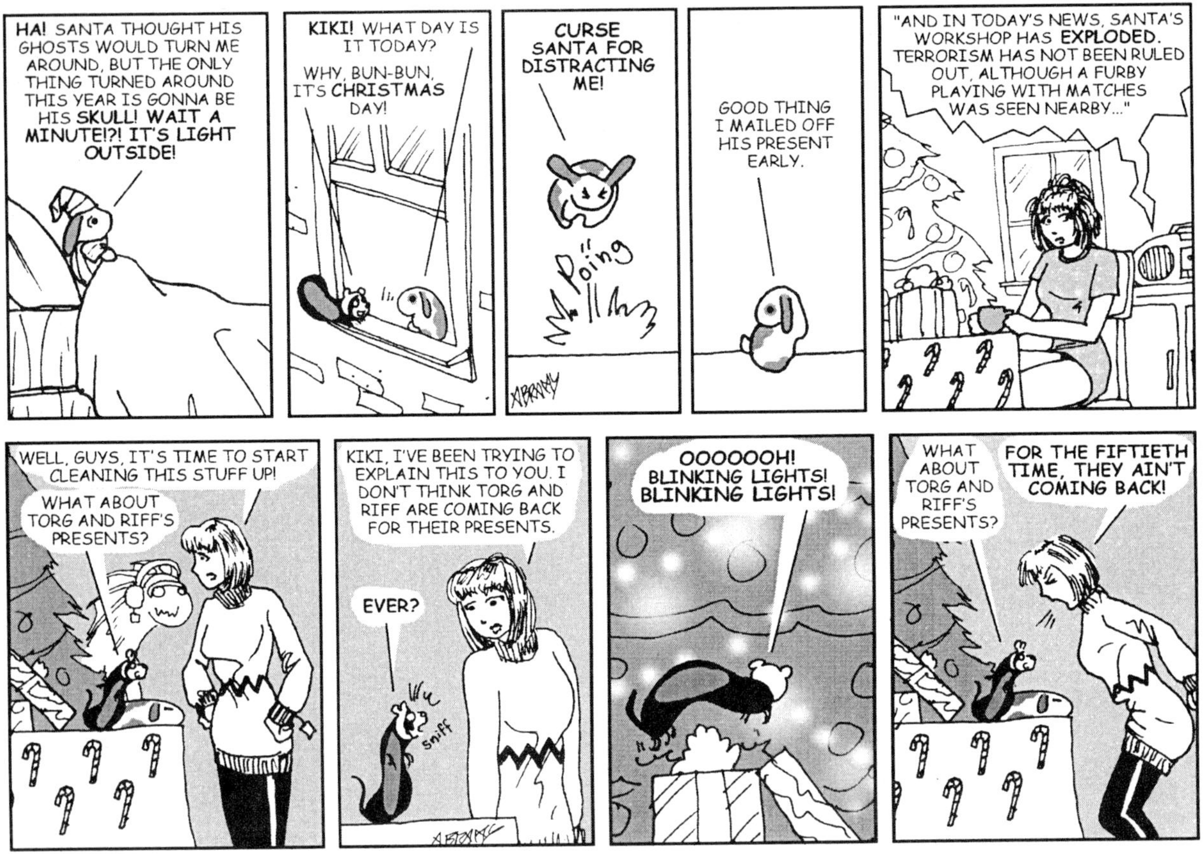

HA! SANTA THOUGHT HIS GHOSTS WOULD TURN ME AROUND, BUT THE ONLY THING TURNED AROUND THIS YEAR IS GONNA BE HIS SKULL! WAIT A MINUTE!?! IT'S LIGHT OUTSIDE!
KIKI! WHAT DAY IS IT TODAY?
WHY, BUN-BUN, IT'S CHRISTMAS DAY!
CURSE SANTA FOR DISTRACTING ME!
POING
GOOD THING I MAILED OFF HIS PRESENT EARLY.
"AND IN TODAY'S NEWS, SANTA'S WORKSHOP HAS EXPLODED. TERRORISM HAS NOT BEEN RULED OUT, ALTHOUGH A FURBY PLAYING WITH MATCHES WAS SEEN NEARBY..."
WELL, GUYS, IT'S TIME TO START CLEANING THIS STUFF UP!
WHAT ABOUT TORG AND RIFF'S PRESENTS?
KIKI, I'VE BEEN TRYING TO EXPLAIN THIS TO YOU. I DON'T THINK TORG AND RIFF ARE COMING BACK FOR THEIR PRESENTS.
EVER?
SNIFF
OOOOOOH! BLINKING LIGHTS! BLINKING LIGHTS!
WHAT ABOUT TORG AND RIFF'S PRESENTS?
FOR THE FIFTIETH TIME, THEY AIN'T COMING BACK!

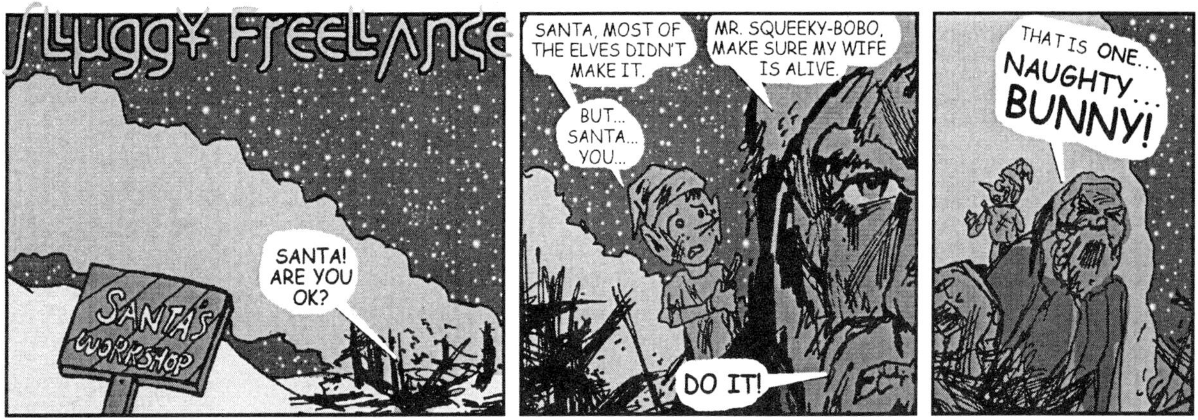
Sluggy Freelance
SANTA'S WORKSHOP
SANTA! ARE YOU OK?
SANTA, MOST OF THE ELVES DIDN'T MAKE IT.
BUT... SANTA... YOU...
MR. SQUEEKY-BOBO, MAKE SURE MY WIFE IS ALIVE.
DO IT!
THAT IS ONE... NAUGHTY... BUNNY!

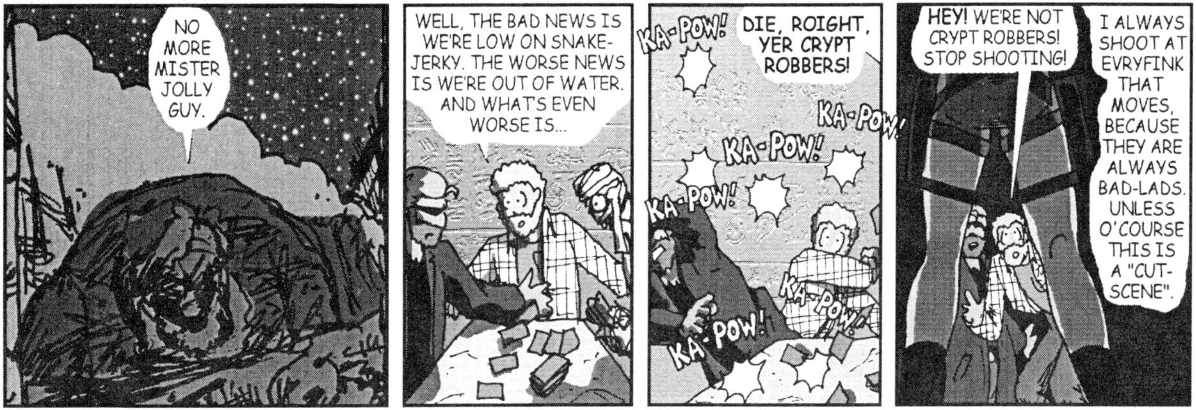
NO MORE MISTER JOLLY GUY.
WELL, THE BAD NEWS IS WE'RE LOW ON SNAKE-JERKY. THE WORSE NEWS IS WE'RE OUT OF WATER. AND WHAT'S EVEN WORSE IS...
KA-POW!
DIE, ROIGHT, YER CRYPT ROBBERS!
KA-POW!
KA-POW!
KA-POW!
KA-POW!
KA-POW!
HEY! WE'RE NOT CRYPT ROBBERS! STOP SHOOTING!
I ALWAYS SHOOT AT EVRYFINK THAT MOVES, BECAUSE THEY ARE ALWAYS BAD-LADS. UNLESS O'COURSE THIS IS A "CUT-SCENE".

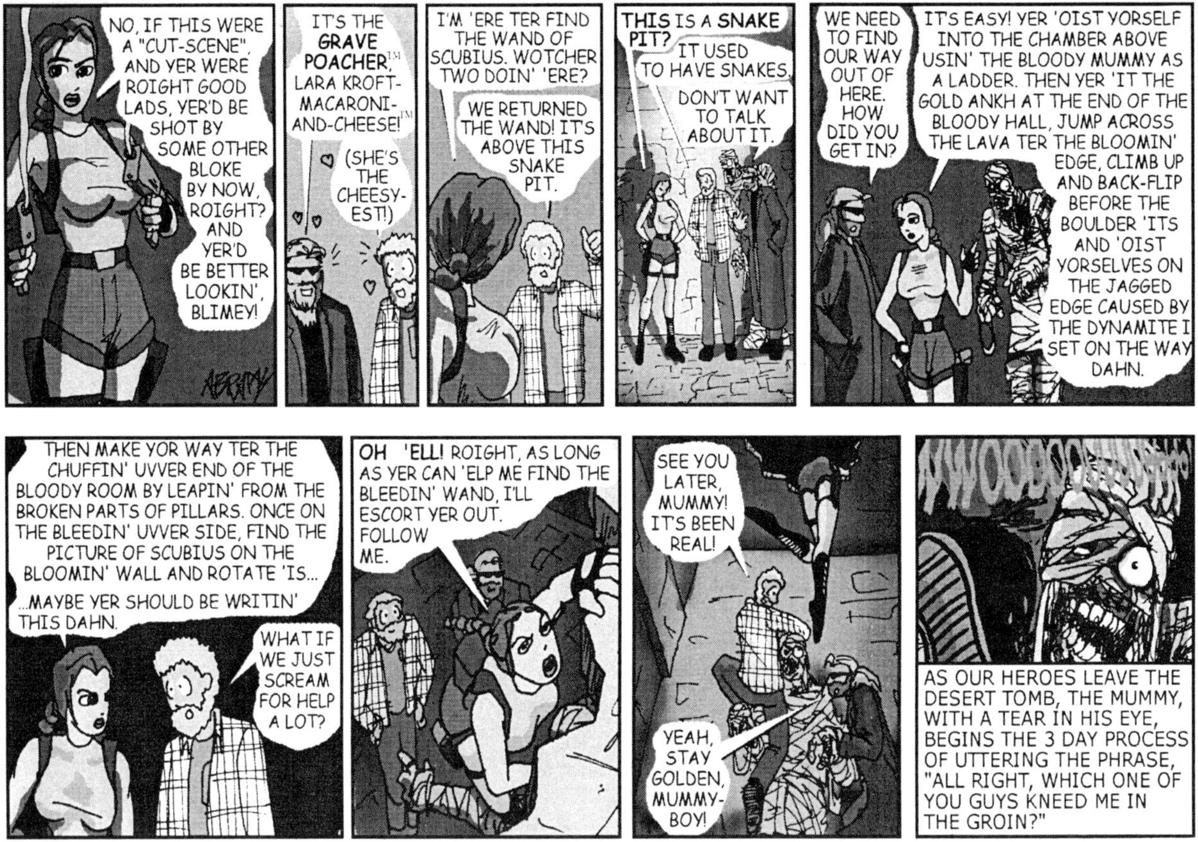

NO, IF THIS WERE A "CUT-SCENE", AND YER WERE ROIGHT GOOD LADS, YER'D BE SHOT BY SOME OTHER BLOKE BY NOW, ROIGHT? AND YER'D BE BETTER LOOKIN', BLIMEY!
IT'S THE GRAVE POACHER™, LARA KROFT-MACARONI-AND-CHEESE!™
(SHE'S THE CHEESY-EST!)
I'M 'ERE TER FIND THE WAND OF SCUBIUS. WOTCHER TWO DOIN' 'ERE?
WE RETURNED THE WAND! IT'S ABOVE THIS SNAKE PIT.
THIS IS A SNAKE PIT?
IT USED TO HAVE SNAKES.
DON'T WANT TO TALK ABOUT IT.
WE NEED TO FIND OUR WAY OUT OF HERE. HOW DID YOU GET IN?
IT'S EASY! YER 'OIST YORSELF INTO THE CHAMBER ABOVE USIN' THE BLOODY MUMMY AS A LADDER. THEN YER 'IT THE GOLD ANKH AT THE END OF THE BLOODY HALL, JUMP ACROSS THE LAVA TER THE BLOOMIN' EDGE, CLIMB UP AND BACK-FLIP BEFORE THE BOULDER 'ITS AND 'OIST YORSELVES ON THE JAGGED EDGE CAUSED BY THE DYNAMITE I SET ON THE WAY DAHN.
THEN MAKE YOR WAY TER THE CHUFFIN' UVVER END OF THE BLOODY ROOM BY LEAPIN' FROM THE BROKEN PARTS OF PILLARS. ONCE ON THE BLEEDIN' UVVER SIDE, FIND THE PICTURE OF SCUBIUS ON THE BLOOMIN' WALL AND ROTATE 'IS...
...MAYBE YER SHOULD BE WRITIN' THIS DAHN.
WHAT IF WE JUST SCREAM FOR HELP A LOT?
OH 'ELL! ROIGHT, AS LONG AS YER CAN 'ELP ME FIND THE BLEEDIN' WAND, I'LL ESCORT YER OUT. FOLLOW ME.
SEE YOU LATER, MUMMY! IT'S BEEN REAL!
YEAH, STAY GOLDEN, MUMMY-BOY!
AS OUR HEROES LEAVE THE DESERT TOMB, THE MUMMY, WITH A TEAR IN HIS EYE, BEGINS THE 3 DAY PROCESS OF UTTERING THE PHRASE, "ALL RIGHT, WHICH ONE OF YOU GUYS KNEED ME IN THE GROIN?"

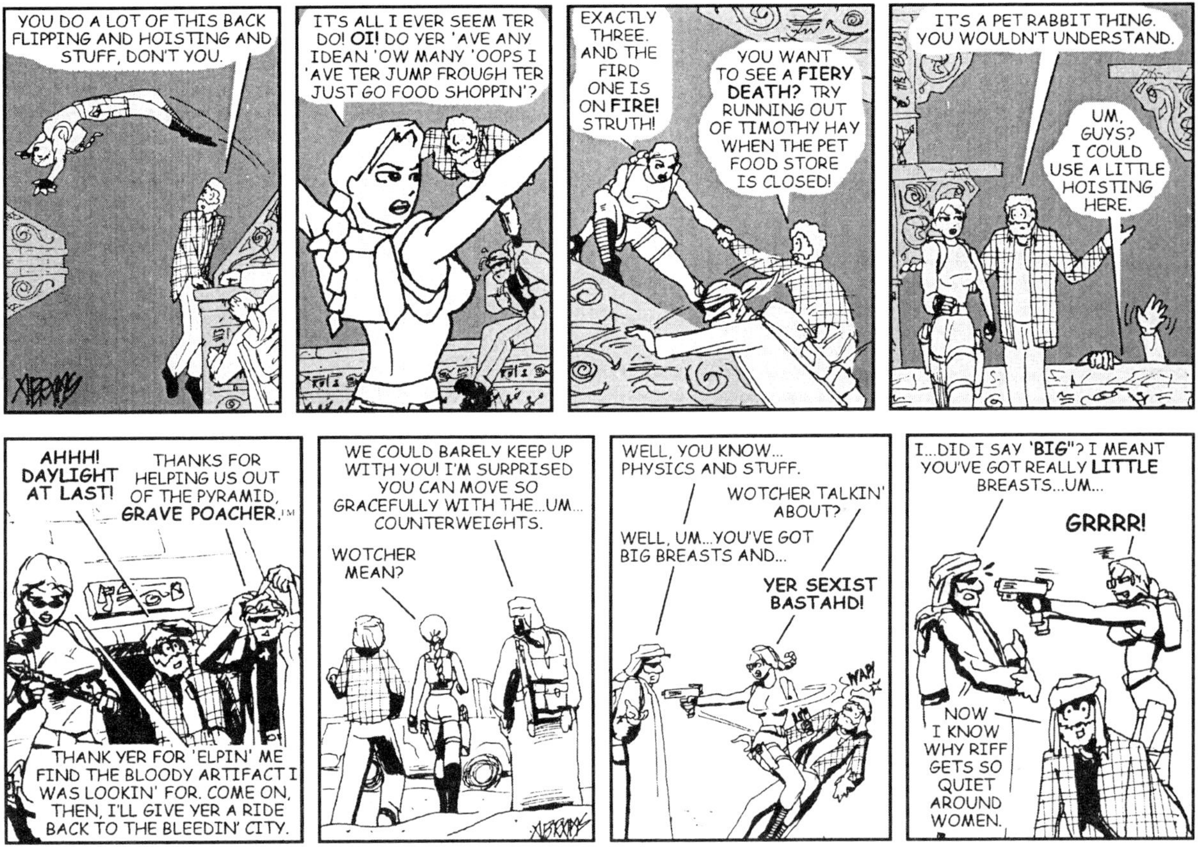

YOU DO A LOT OF THIS BACK FLIPPING AND HOISTING AND STUFF, DON'T YOU.
IT'S ALL I EVER SEEM TER DO! OI! DO YER 'AVE ANY IDEAN 'OW MANY 'OOPS I 'AVE TER JUMP FROUGH TER JUST GO FOOD SHOPPIN'?
EXACTLY THREE. AND THE FIRD ONE IS ON FIRE! STRUTH!
YOU WANT TO SEE A FIERY DEATH? TRY RUNNING OUT OF TIMOTHY HAY WHEN THE PET FOOD STORE IS CLOSED!
IT'S A PET RABBIT THING. YOU WOULDN'T UNDERSTAND.
UM, GUYS? I COULD USE A LITTLE HOISTING HERE.
AHHH! DAYLIGHT AT LAST!
THANKS FOR HELPING US OUT OF THE PYRAMID, GRAVE POACHER.TM
THANK YER FOR 'ELPIN' ME FIND THE BLOODY ARTIFACT I WAS LOOKIN' FOR. COME ON, THEN, I'LL GIVE YER A RIDE BACK TO THE BLEEDIN' CITY.
WE COULD BARELY KEEP UP WITH YOU! I'M SURPRISED YOU CAN MOVE SO GRACEFULLY WITH THE...UM... COUNTERWEIGHTS.
WOTCHER MEAN?
WELL, YOU KNOW... PHYSICS AND STUFF.
WOTCHER TALKIN' ABOUT?
WELL, UM...YOU'VE GOT BIG BREASTS AND...
YER SEXIST BASTAHD!
WAP!
I...DID I SAY 'BIG"? I MEANT YOU'VE GOT REALLY LITTLE BREASTS...UM...
GRRRR!
NOW I KNOW WHY RIFF GETS SO QUIET AROUND WOMEN.

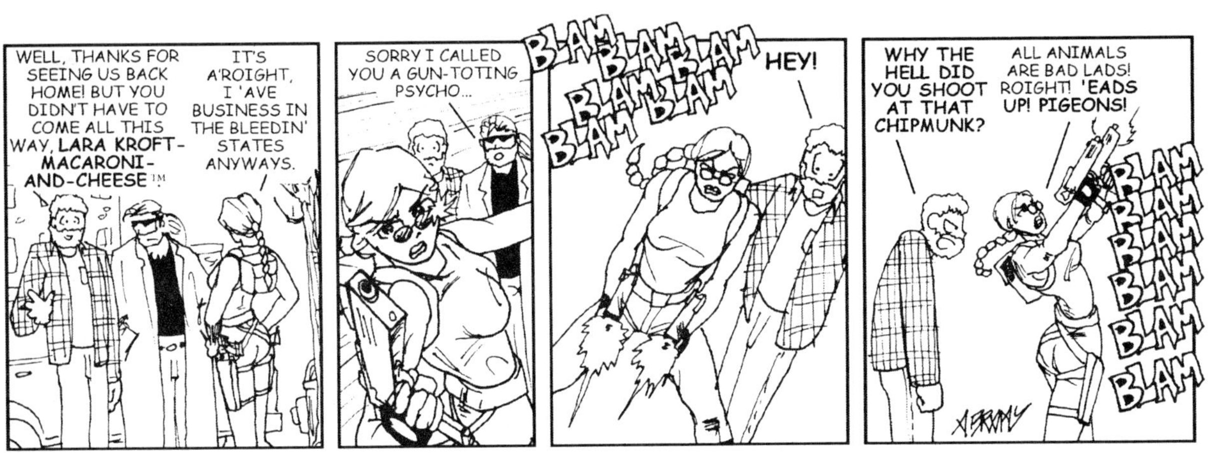
WELL, THANKS FOR SEEING US BACK HOME! BUT YOU DIDN'T HAVE TO COME ALL THIS WAY, LARA KROFT-MACARONI-AND-CHEESE™!
IT'S A'ROIGHT, I 'AVE BUSINESS IN THE BLEEDIN' STATES ANYWAYS.
SORRY I CALLED YOU A GUN-TOTING PSYCHO...
BLAM BLAM BLAM BLAM BLAM BLAM BLAM BLAM BLAM
HEY!
WHY THE HELL DID YOU SHOOT AT THAT CHIPMUNK?
ALL ANIMALS ARE BAD LADS! ROIGHT! 'EADS UP! PIGEONS!
BLAM BLAM BLAM BLAM BLAM BLAM BLAM

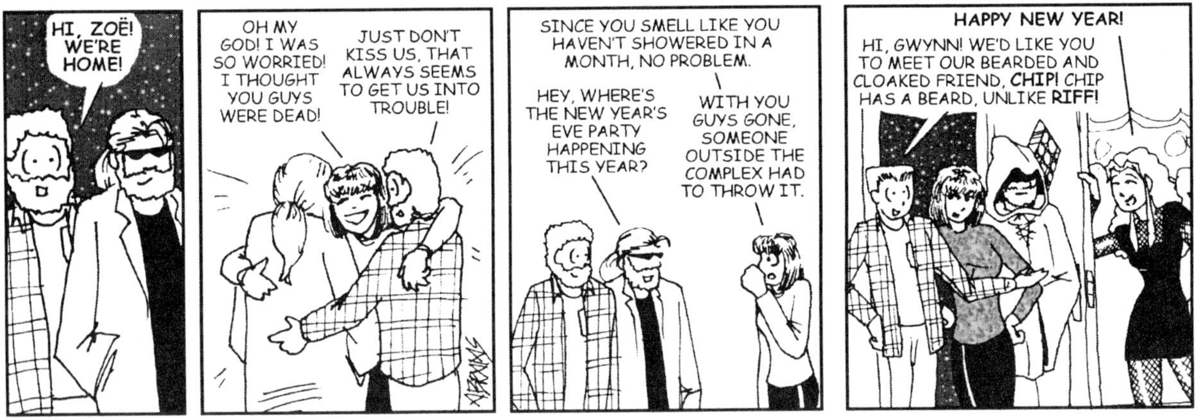
HI, ZOË! WE'RE HOME!
OH MY GOD! I WAS SO WORRIED! I THOUGHT YOU GUYS WERE DEAD!
JUST DON'T KISS US, THAT ALWAYS SEEMS TO GET US INTO TROUBLE!
SINCE YOU SMELL LIKE YOU HAVEN'T SHOWERED IN A MONTH, NO PROBLEM.
HEY, WHERE'S THE NEW YEAR'S EVE PARTY HAPPENING THIS YEAR?
WITH YOU GUYS GONE, SOMEONE OUTSIDE THE COMPLEX HAD TO THROW IT.
HAPPY NEW YEAR!
HI, GWYNN! WE'D LIKE YOU TO MEET OUR BEARDED AND CLOAKED FRIEND, CHIP! CHIP HAS A BEARD, UNLIKE RIFF!

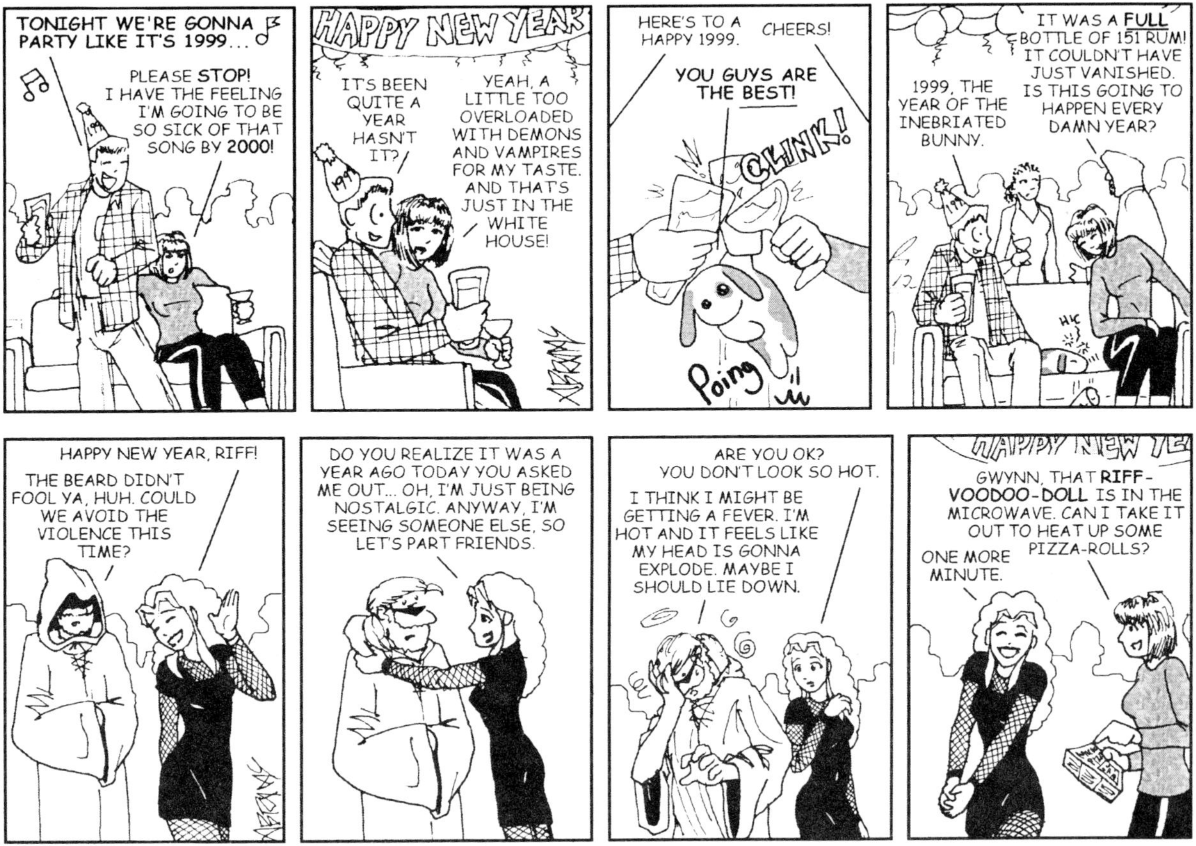
TONIGHT WE'RE GONNA PARTY LIKE IT'S 1999...
PLEASE STOP! I HAVE THE FEELING I'M GOING TO BE SO SICK OF THAT SONG BY 2000!
HAPPY NEW YEAR
IT'S BEEN QUITE A YEAR HASN'T IT?
YEAH, A LITTLE TOO OVERLOADED WITH DEMONS AND VAMPIRES FOR MY TASTE. AND THAT'S JUST IN THE WHITE HOUSE!
HERE'S TO A HAPPY 1999.
CHEERS!
YOU GUYS ARE THE BEST!
CLINK!
Poing
1999, THE YEAR OF THE INEBRIATED BUNNY.
IT WAS A FULL BOTTLE OF 151 RUM! IT COULDN'T HAVE JUST VANISHED. IS THIS GOING TO HAPPEN EVERY DAMN YEAR?
HIC
HAPPY NEW YEAR, RIFF!
THE BEARD DIDN'T FOOL YA, HUH. COULD WE AVOID THE VIOLENCE THIS TIME?
DO YOU REALIZE IT WAS A YEAR AGO TODAY YOU ASKED ME OUT... OH, I'M JUST BEING NOSTALGIC. ANYWAY, I'M SEEING SOMEONE ELSE, SO LET'S PART FRIENDS.
ARE YOU OK? YOU DON'T LOOK SO HOT.
I THINK I MIGHT BE GETTING A FEVER. I'M HOT AND IT FEELS LIKE MY HEAD IS GONNA EXPLODE. MAYBE I SHOULD LIE DOWN.
GWYNN, THAT RIFF-VOODOO-DOLL IS IN THE MICROWAVE. CAN I TAKE IT OUT TO HEAT UP SOME PIZZA-ROLLS?
ONE MORE MINUTE.

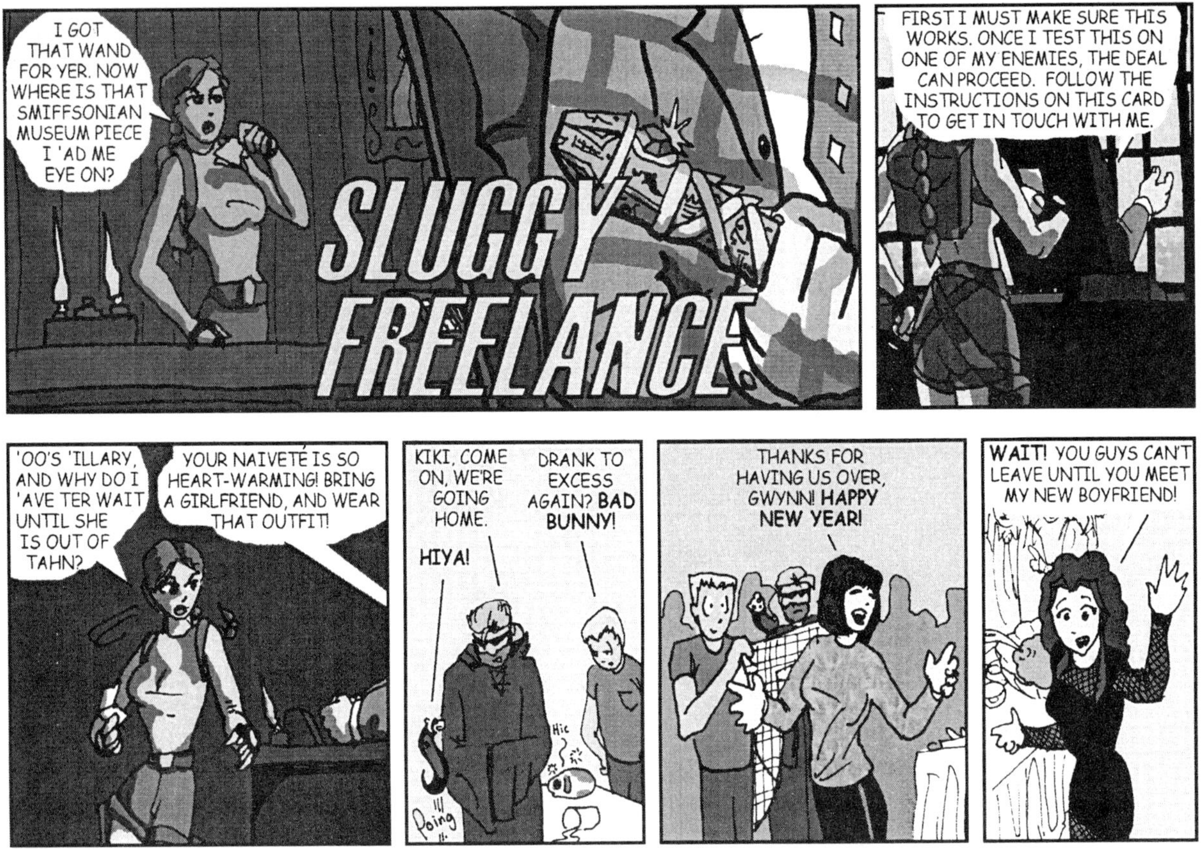
I GOT THAT WAND FOR YER. NOW WHERE IS THAT SMIFFSONIAN MUSEUM PIECE I 'AD ME EYE ON?
SLUGGY FREELANCE
FIRST I MUST MAKE SURE THIS WORKS. ONCE I TEST THIS ON ONE OF MY ENEMIES, THE DEAL CAN PROCEED. FOLLOW THE INSTRUCTIONS ON THIS CARD TO GET IN TOUCH WITH ME.
'OO'S 'ILLARY, AND WHY DO I 'AVE TER WAIT UNTIL SHE IS OUT OF TAHN?
YOUR NAIVETÉ IS SO HEART-WARMING! BRING A GIRLFRIEND, AND WEAR THAT OUTFIT!
KIKI, COME ON, WE'RE GOING HOME.
HIYA!
DRANK TO EXCESS AGAIN? BAD BUNNY!
Hic
Poing
THANKS FOR HAVING US OVER, GWYNN! HAPPY NEW YEAR!
WAIT! YOU GUYS CAN'T LEAVE UNTIL YOU MEET MY NEW BOYFRIEND!

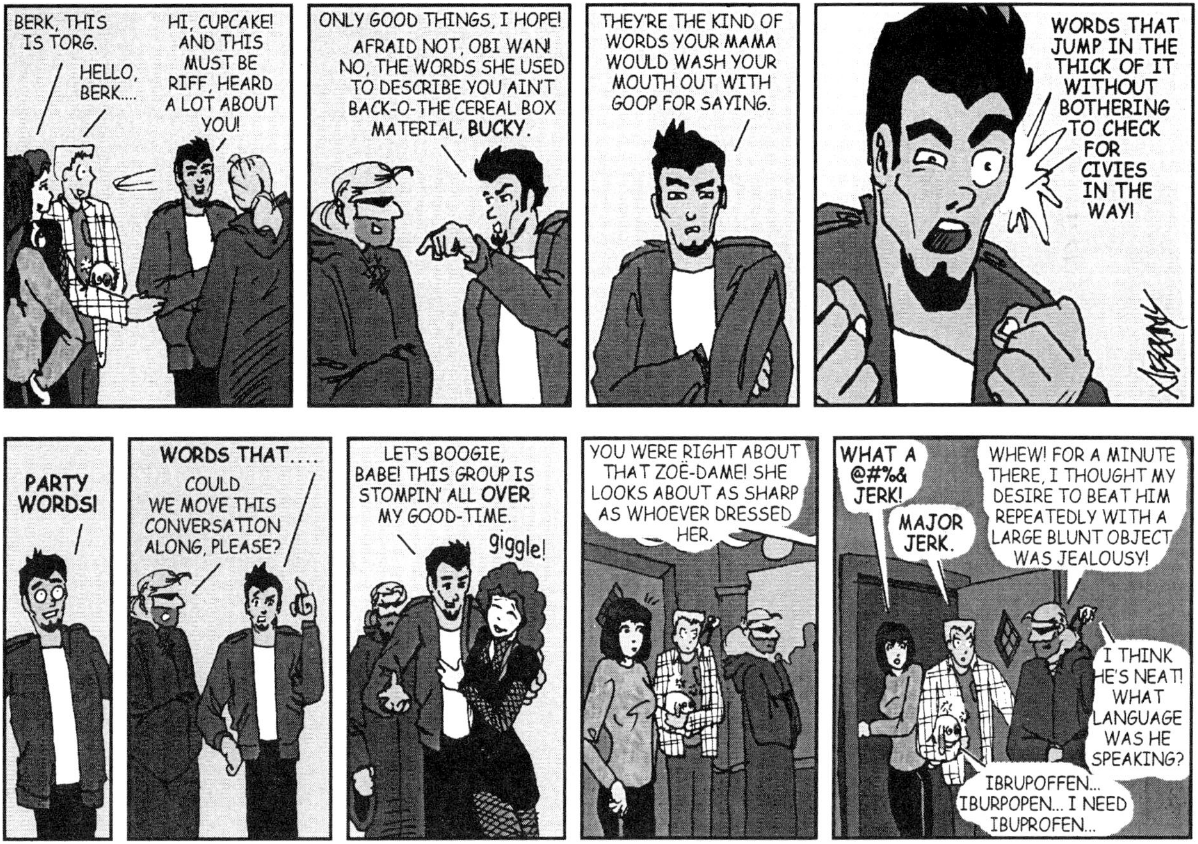
BERK, THIS IS TORG.
HELLO, BERK....
HI, CUPCAKE! AND THIS MUST BE RIFF, HEARD A LOT ABOUT YOU!
ONLY GOOD THINGS, I HOPE!
AFRAID NOT, OBI WAN! NO, THE WORDS SHE USED TO DESCRIBE YOU AIN'T BACK-O-THE CEREAL BOX MATERIAL, BUCKY.
THEY'RE THE KIND OF WORDS YOUR MAMA WOULD WASH YOUR MOUTH OUT WITH GOOP FOR SAYING.
WORDS THAT JUMP IN THE THICK OF IT WITHOUT BOTHERING TO CHECK FOR CIVIES IN THE WAY!
PARTY WORDS!
WORDS THAT.....
COULD WE MOVE THIS CONVERSATION ALONG, PLEASE?
LET'S BOOGIE, BABE! THIS GROUP IS STOMPIN' ALL OVER MY GOOD-TIME.
giggle!
YOU WERE RIGHT ABOUT THAT ZOË-DAME! SHE LOOKS ABOUT AS SHARP AS WHOEVER DRESSED HER.
WHAT A @#%& JERK!
MAJOR JERK.
WHEW! FOR A MINUTE THERE, I THOUGHT MY DESIRE TO BEAT HIM REPEATEDLY WITH A LARGE BLUNT OBJECT WAS JEALOUSY!
I THINK HE'S NEAT! WHAT LANGUAGE WAS HE SPEAKING?
IBRUPOFFEN... IBURPOPEN... I NEED IBUPROFEN...

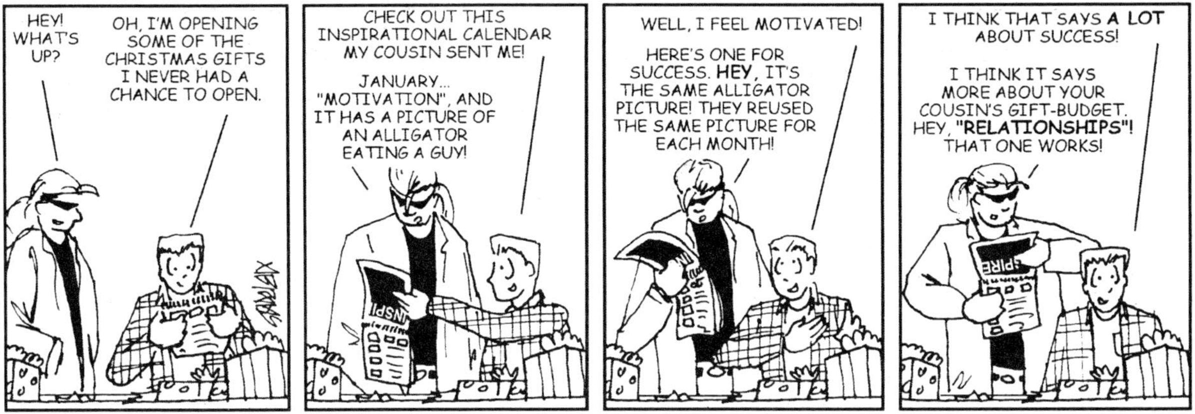
HEY! WHAT'S UP?
OH, I'M OPENING SOME OF THE CHRISTMAS GIFTS I NEVER HAD A CHANCE TO OPEN.
CHECK OUT THIS INSPIRATIONAL CALENDAR MY COUSIN SENT ME!
JANUARY... "MOTIVATION", AND IT HAS A PICTURE OF AN ALLIGATOR EATING A GUY!
WELL, I FEEL MOTIVATED!
HERE'S ONE FOR SUCCESS. **HEY**, IT'S THE SAME ALLIGATOR PICTURE! THEY REUSED THE SAME PICTURE FOR EACH MONTH!
I THINK THAT SAYS **A LOT** ABOUT SUCCESS!
I THINK IT SAYS MORE ABOUT YOUR COUSIN'S GIFT-BUDGET. HEY, **"RELATIONSHIPS"!** THAT ONE WORKS!

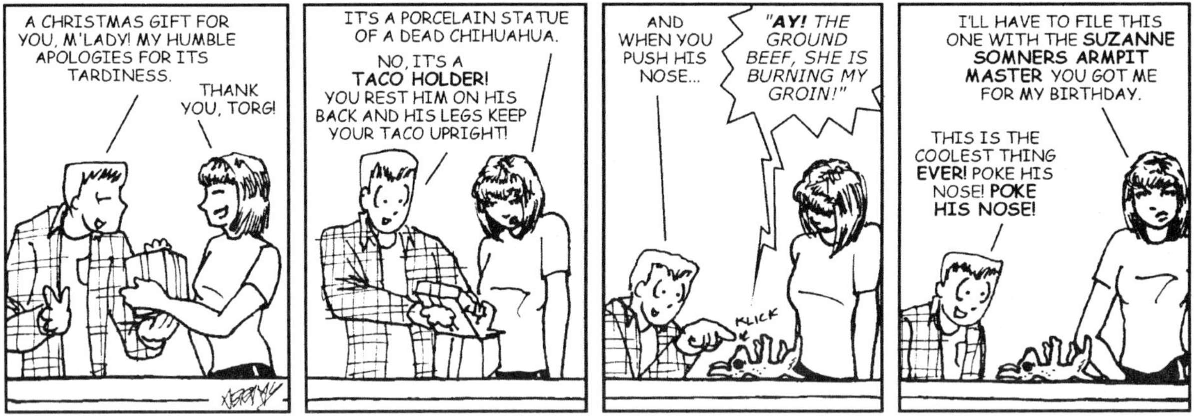
A CHRISTMAS GIFT FOR YOU, M'LADY! MY HUMBLE APOLOGIES FOR ITS TARDINESS.
THANK YOU, TORG!
IT'S A PORCELAIN STATUE OF A DEAD CHIHUAHUA.
NO, IT'S A **TACO HOLDER!** YOU REST HIM ON HIS BACK AND HIS LEGS KEEP YOUR TACO UPRIGHT!
AND WHEN YOU PUSH HIS NOSE...
KLICK
*"**AY!** THE GROUND BEEF, SHE IS BURNING MY GROIN!"*
I'LL HAVE TO FILE THIS ONE WITH THE **SUZANNE SOMNERS ARMPIT MASTER** YOU GOT ME FOR MY BIRTHDAY.
THIS IS THE COOLEST THING **EVER!** POKE HIS NOSE! **POKE HIS NOSE!**

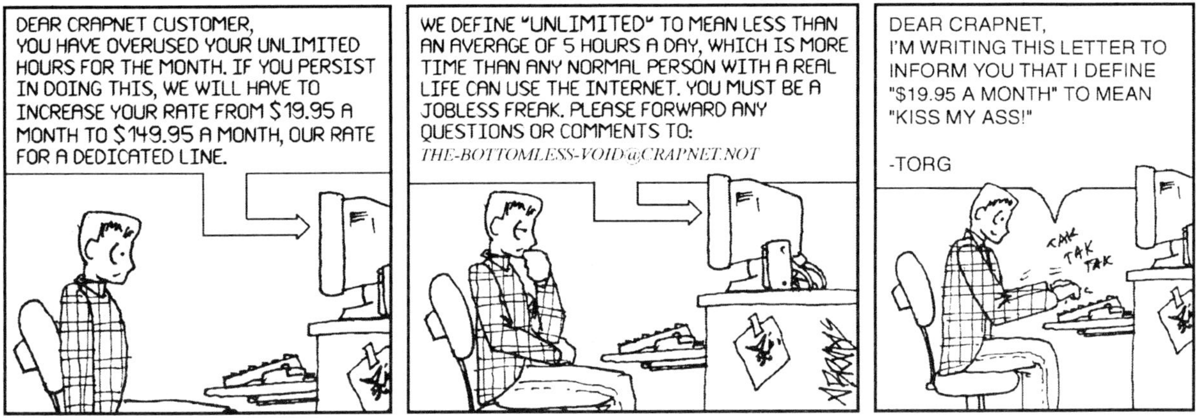
DEAR CRAPNET CUSTOMER,
YOU HAVE OVERUSED YOUR UNLIMITED HOURS FOR THE MONTH. IF YOU PERSIST IN DOING THIS, WE WILL HAVE TO INCREASE YOUR RATE FROM $19.95 A MONTH TO $149.95 A MONTH, OUR RATE FOR A DEDICATED LINE.
WE DEFINE "UNLIMITED" TO MEAN LESS THAN AN AVERAGE OF 5 HOURS A DAY, WHICH IS MORE TIME THAN ANY NORMAL PERSON WITH A REAL LIFE CAN USE THE INTERNET. YOU MUST BE A JOBLESS FREAK. PLEASE FORWARD ANY QUESTIONS OR COMMENTS TO:
THE-BOTTOMLESS-VOID@CRAPNET.NOT
DEAR CRAPNET,
I'M WRITING THIS LETTER TO INFORM YOU THAT I DEFINE "$19.95 A MONTH" TO MEAN "KISS MY ASS!"
-TORG
TAK TAK TAK

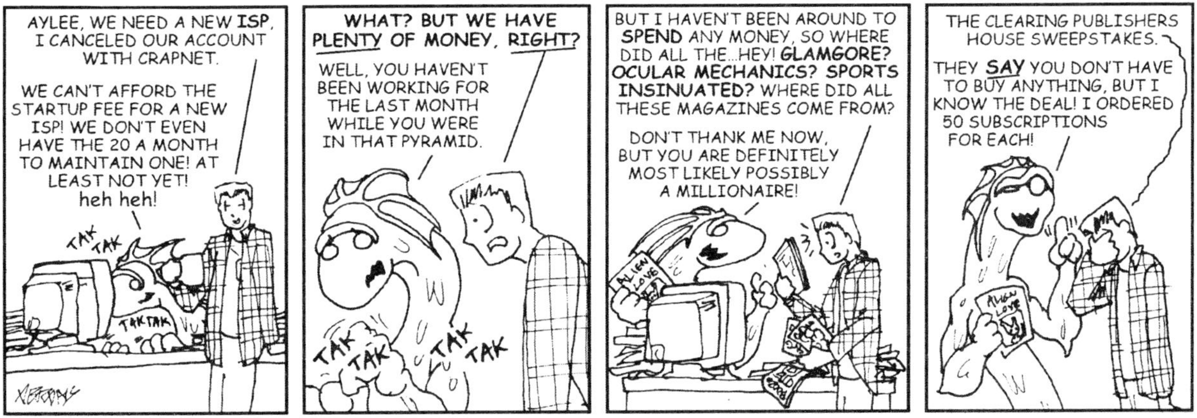
AYLEE, WE NEED A NEW ISP, I CANCELED OUR ACCOUNT WITH CRAPNET.
WE CAN'T AFFORD THE STARTUP FEE FOR A NEW ISP! WE DON'T EVEN HAVE THE 20 A MONTH TO MAINTAIN ONE! AT LEAST NOT YET!
heh heh!
TAK TAK
TAKTAK
WHAT? BUT WE HAVE PLENTY OF MONEY, RIGHT?
WELL, YOU HAVEN'T BEEN WORKING FOR THE LAST MONTH WHILE YOU WERE IN THAT PYRAMID.
TAK TAK TAK TAK
BUT I HAVEN'T BEEN AROUND TO SPEND ANY MONEY, SO WHERE DID ALL THE...HEY! GLAMGORE? OCULAR MECHANICS? SPORTS INSINUATED? WHERE DID ALL THESE MAGAZINES COME FROM?
DON'T THANK ME NOW, BUT YOU ARE DEFINITELY MOST LIKELY POSSIBLY A MILLIONAIRE!
ALIEN LOVE
THE CLEARING PUBLISHERS HOUSE SWEEPSTAKES.
THEY SAY YOU DON'T HAVE TO BUY ANYTHING, BUT I KNOW THE DEAL! I ORDERED 50 SUBSCRIPTIONS FOR EACH!
ALIEN LOVE

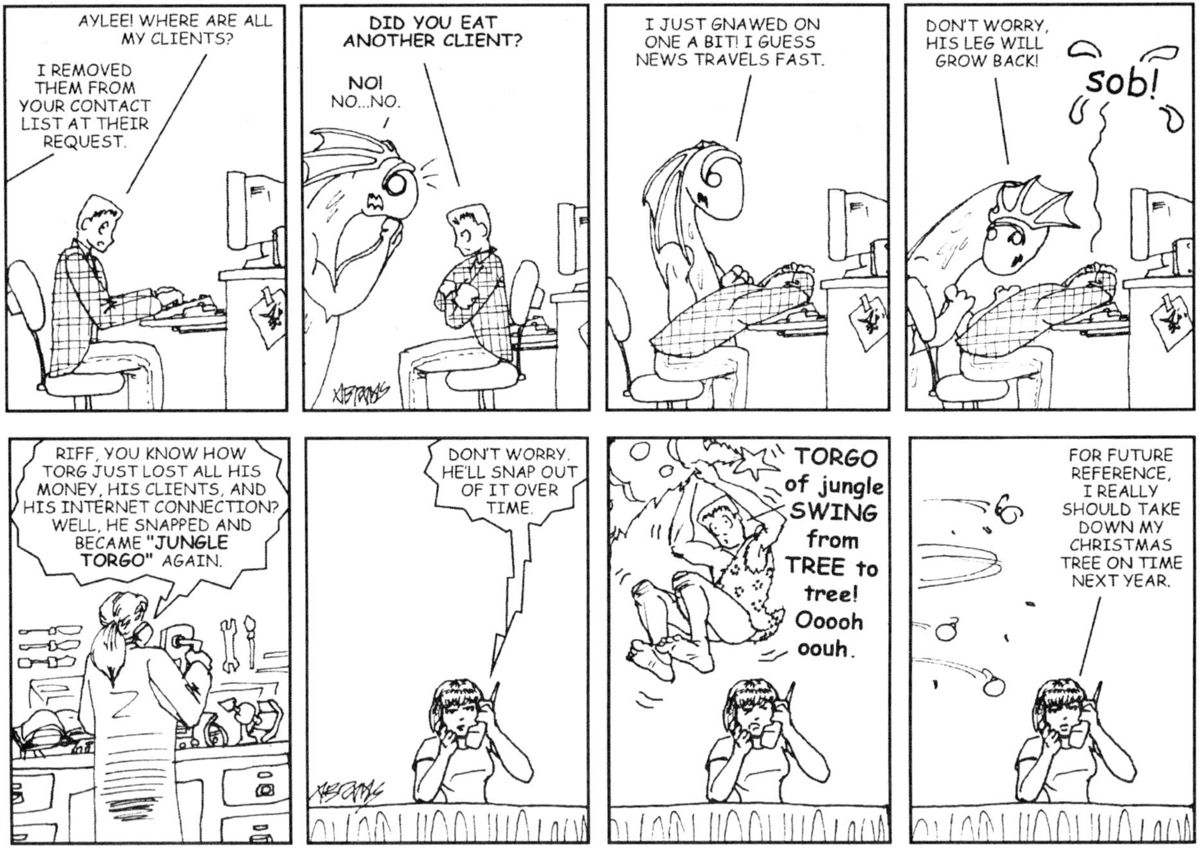
AYLEE! WHERE ARE ALL MY CLIENTS?
I REMOVED THEM FROM YOUR CONTACT LIST AT THEIR REQUEST.
DID YOU EAT ANOTHER CLIENT?
NO! NO...NO.
I JUST GNAWED ON ONE A BIT! I GUESS NEWS TRAVELS FAST.
DON'T WORRY, HIS LEG WILL GROW BACK!
sob!
RIFF, YOU KNOW HOW TORG JUST LOST ALL HIS MONEY, HIS CLIENTS, AND HIS INTERNET CONNECTION? WELL, HE SNAPPED AND BECAME "JUNGLE TORGO" AGAIN.
DON'T WORRY. HE'LL SNAP OUT OF IT OVER TIME.
TORGO of jungle SWING from TREE to tree! Ooooh oouh.
FOR FUTURE REFERENCE, I REALLY SHOULD TAKE DOWN MY CHRISTMAS TREE ON TIME NEXT YEAR.

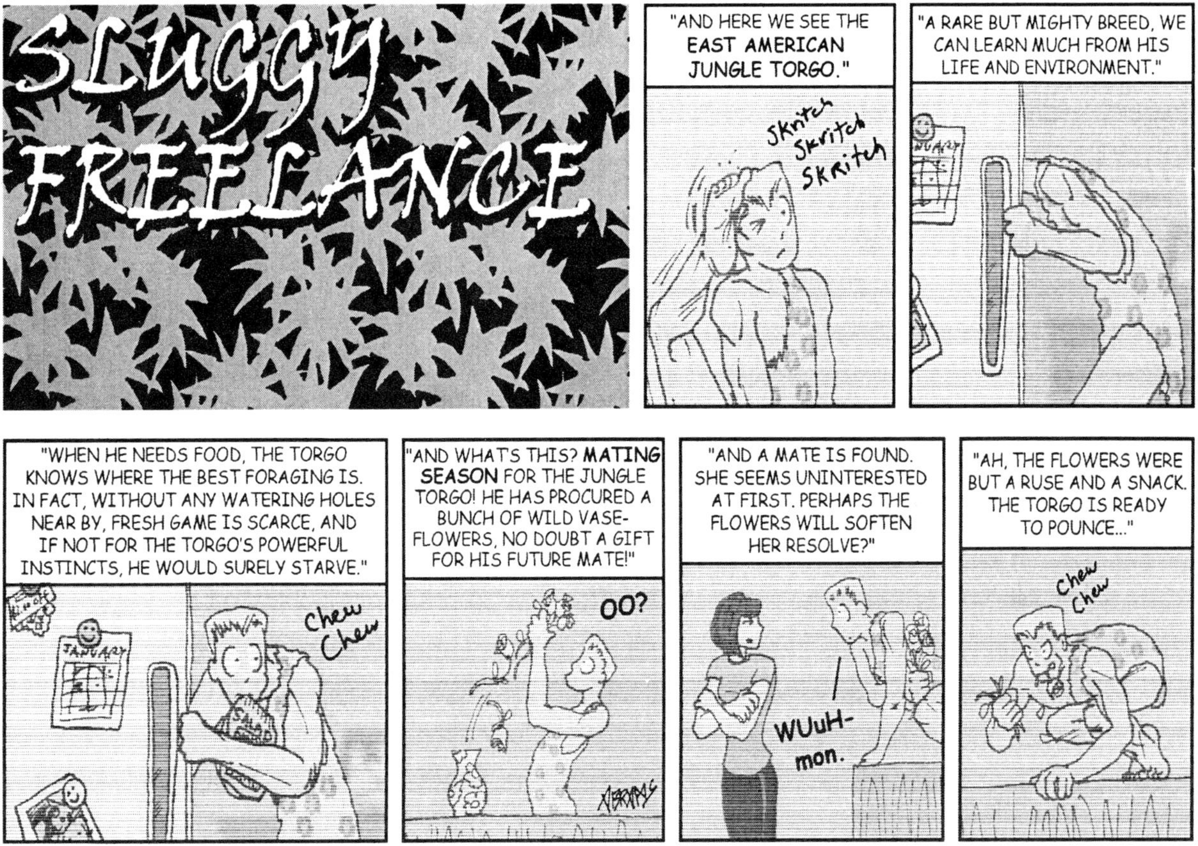
SLUGGY FREELANCE
"AND HERE WE SEE THE **EAST AMERICAN JUNGLE TORGO.**"
SKRITCH SKRITCH SKRITCH
"A RARE BUT MIGHTY BREED, WE CAN LEARN MUCH FROM HIS LIFE AND ENVIRONMENT."
"WHEN HE NEEDS FOOD, THE TORGO KNOWS WHERE THE BEST FORAGING IS. IN FACT, WITHOUT ANY WATERING HOLES NEAR BY, FRESH GAME IS SCARCE, AND IF NOT FOR THE TORGO'S POWERFUL INSTINCTS, HE WOULD SURELY STARVE."
JANUARY
Chew Chew
"AND WHAT'S THIS? **MATING SEASON** FOR THE JUNGLE TORGO! HE HAS PROCURED A BUNCH OF WILD VASE-FLOWERS, NO DOUBT A GIFT FOR HIS FUTURE MATE!"
OO?
"AND A MATE IS FOUND. SHE SEEMS UNINTERESTED AT FIRST. PERHAPS THE FLOWERS WILL SOFTEN HER RESOLVE?"
WUuH-mon.
"AH, THE FLOWERS WERE BUT A RUSE AND A SNACK. THE TORGO IS READY TO POUNCE..."
Chew Chew

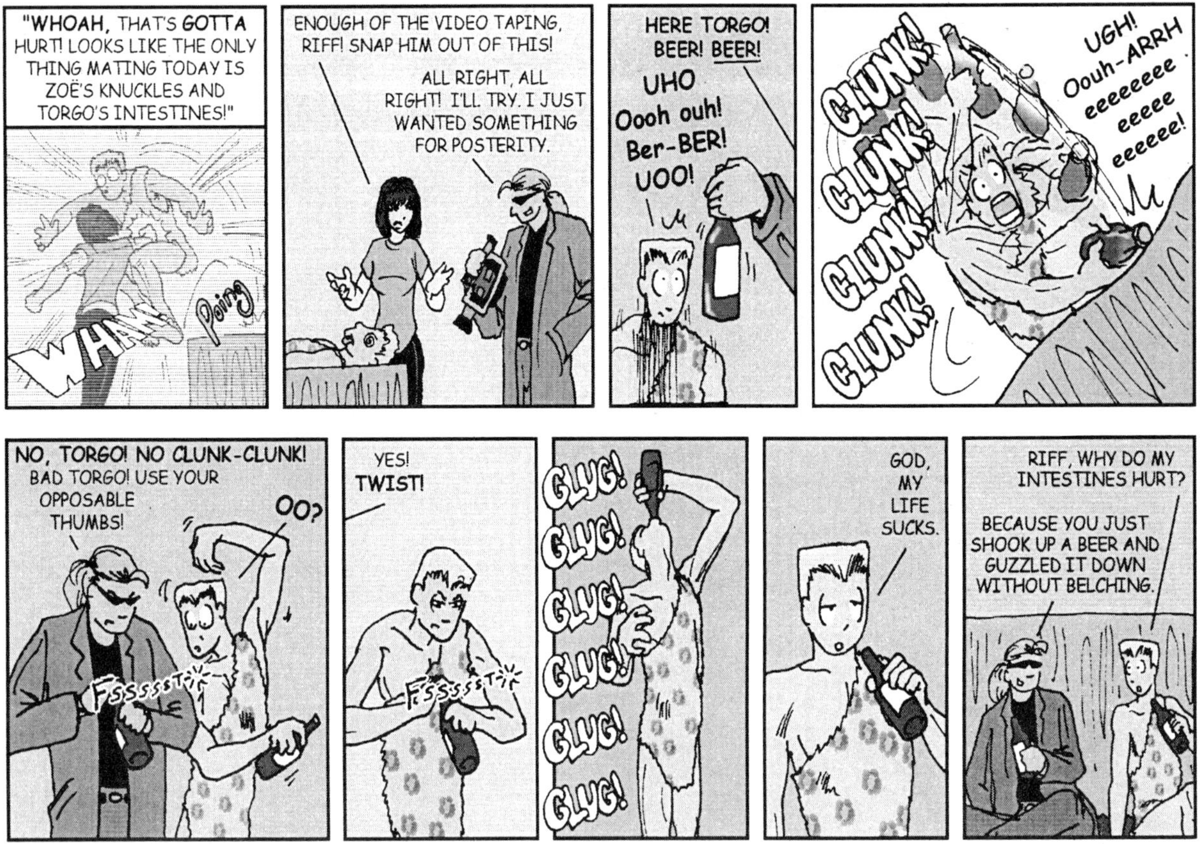
"WHOAH, THAT'S GOTTA HURT! LOOKS LIKE THE ONLY THING MATING TODAY IS ZOË'S KNUCKLES AND TORGO'S INTESTINES!"
WHAM
Poing
ENOUGH OF THE VIDEO TAPING, RIFF! SNAP HIM OUT OF THIS!
ALL RIGHT, ALL RIGHT! I'LL TRY. I JUST WANTED SOMETHING FOR POSTERITY.
HERE TORGO! BEER! BEER!
UHO Oooh ouh! Ber-BER! UOO!
CLUNK! CLUNK! CLUNK! CLUNK!
UGH! Oouh-ARRH eeeeeee eeeee eeeee eeeeee!
NO, TORGO! NO CLUNK-CLUNK!
BAD TORGO! USE YOUR OPPOSABLE THUMBS!
OO?
FSSSSST
YES! TWIST!
FSSSSST
GLUG! GLUG! GLUG! GLUG! GLUG! GLUG!
GOD, MY LIFE SUCKS.
RIFF, WHY DO MY INTESTINES HURT?
BECAUSE YOU JUST SHOOK UP A BEER AND GUZZLED IT DOWN WITHOUT BELCHING.

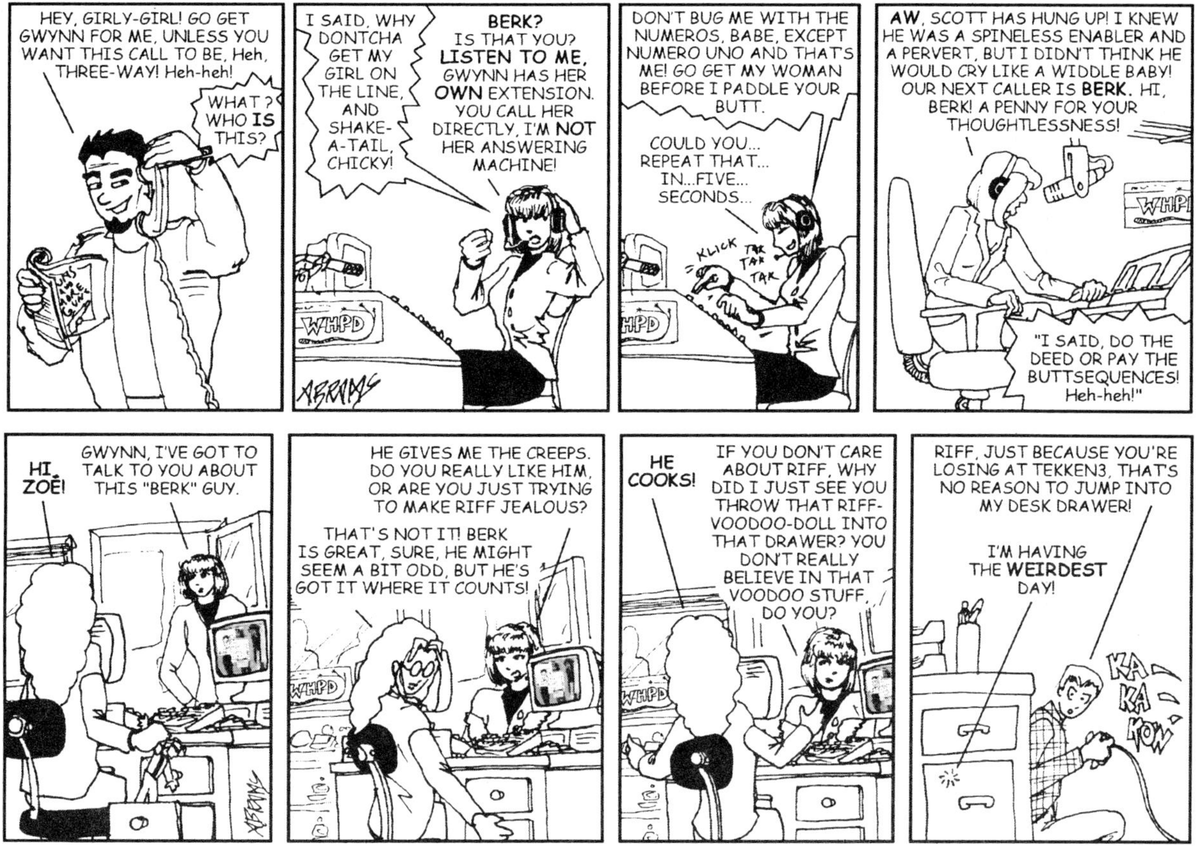
HEY, GIRLY-GIRL! GO GET GWYNN FOR ME, UNLESS YOU WANT THIS CALL TO BE, Heh, THREE-WAY! Heh-heh!
WHAT? WHO IS THIS?
I SAID, WHY DONTCHA GET MY GIRL ON THE LINE, AND SHAKE-A-TAIL, CHICKY!
BERK? IS THAT YOU? LISTEN TO ME, GWYNN HAS HER OWN EXTENSION. YOU CALL HER DIRECTLY, I'M NOT HER ANSWERING MACHINE!
WHPD
ABRAMS
DON'T BUG ME WITH THE NUMEROS, BABE, EXCEPT NUMERO UNO AND THAT'S ME! GO GET MY WOMAN BEFORE I PADDLE YOUR BUTT.
COULD YOU... REPEAT THAT... IN...FIVE... SECONDS...
KLICK
TAK TAK TAK
AW, SCOTT HAS HUNG UP! I KNEW HE WAS A SPINELESS ENABLER AND A PERVERT, BUT I DIDN'T THINK HE WOULD CRY LIKE A WIDDLE BABY! OUR NEXT CALLER IS BERK. HI, BERK! A PENNY FOR YOUR THOUGHTLESSNESS!
"I SAID, DO THE DEED OR PAY THE BUTTSEQUENCES! Heh-heh!"
HI, ZOË!
GWYNN, I'VE GOT TO TALK TO YOU ABOUT THIS "BERK" GUY.
ABRAMS
HE GIVES ME THE CREEPS. DO YOU REALLY LIKE HIM, OR ARE YOU JUST TRYING TO MAKE RIFF JEALOUS?
THAT'S NOT IT! BERK IS GREAT, SURE, HE MIGHT SEEM A BIT ODD, BUT HE'S GOT IT WHERE IT COUNTS!
HE COOKS!
IF YOU DON'T CARE ABOUT RIFF, WHY DID I JUST SEE YOU THROW THAT RIFF-VOODOO-DOLL INTO THAT DRAWER? YOU DON'T REALLY BELIEVE IN THAT VOODOO STUFF, DO YOU?
RIFF, JUST BECAUSE YOU'RE LOSING AT TEKKEN3, THAT'S NO REASON TO JUMP INTO MY DESK DRAWER!
I'M HAVING THE WEIRDEST DAY!
KA KA KOW

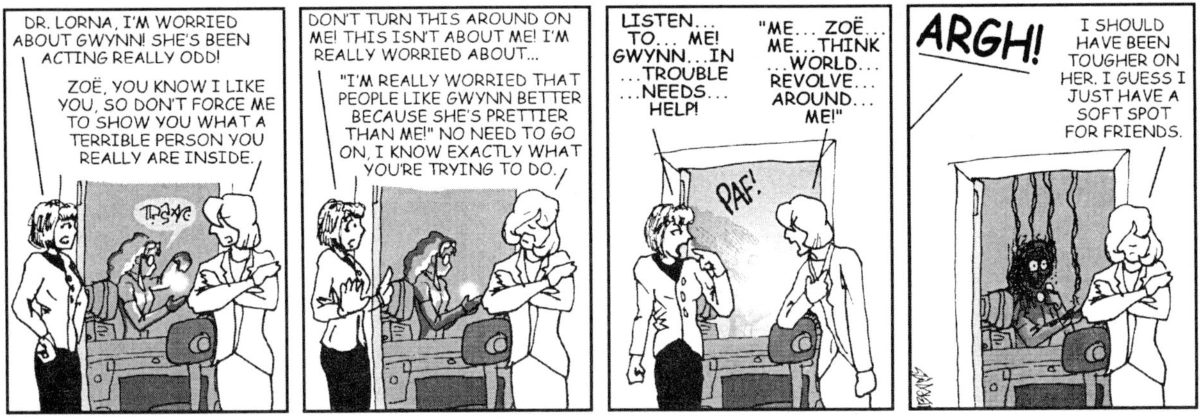
DR. LORNA, I'M WORRIED ABOUT GWYNN! SHE'S BEEN ACTING REALLY ODD!
ZOË, YOU KNOW I LIKE YOU, SO DON'T FORCE ME TO SHOW YOU WHAT A TERRIBLE PERSON YOU REALLY ARE INSIDE.
DON'T TURN THIS AROUND ON ME! THIS ISN'T ABOUT ME! I'M REALLY WORRIED ABOUT...
"I'M REALLY WORRIED THAT PEOPLE LIKE GWYNN BETTER BECAUSE SHE'S PRETTIER THAN ME!" NO NEED TO GO ON, I KNOW EXACTLY WHAT YOU'RE TRYING TO DO.
LISTEN... TO... ME! GWYNN...IN ...TROUBLE ...NEEDS... HELP!
"ME... ZOË... ME...THINK ...WORLD... REVOLVE... AROUND... ME!"
PAF!
ARGH!
I SHOULD HAVE BEEN TOUGHER ON HER. I GUESS I JUST HAVE A SOFT SPOT FOR FRIENDS.

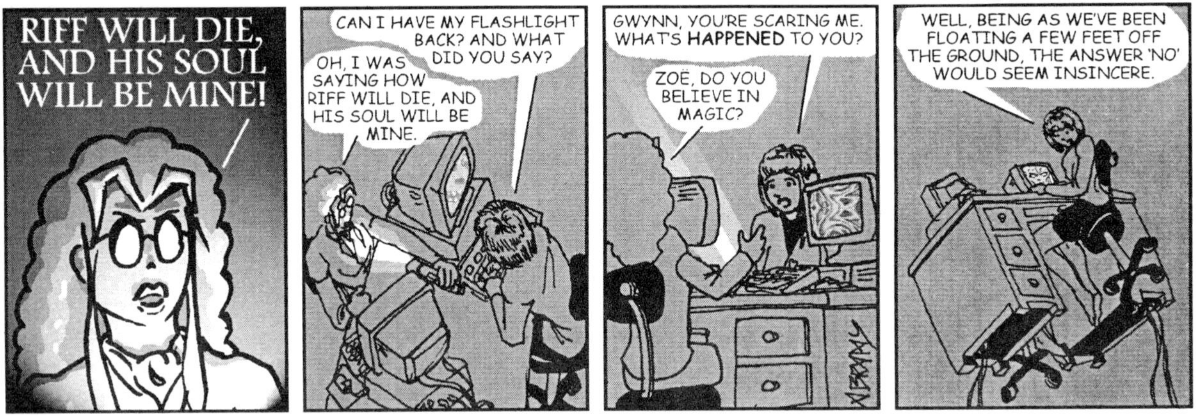
RIFF WILL DIE, AND HIS SOUL WILL BE MINE!
CAN I HAVE MY FLASHLIGHT BACK? AND WHAT DID YOU SAY?
OH, I WAS SAYING HOW RIFF WILL DIE, AND HIS SOUL WILL BE MINE.
GWYNN, YOU'RE SCARING ME. WHAT'S **HAPPENED** TO YOU?
ZOË, DO YOU BELIEVE IN MAGIC?
WELL, BEING AS WE'VE BEEN FLOATING A FEW FEET OFF THE GROUND, THE ANSWER 'NO' WOULD SEEM INSINCERE.

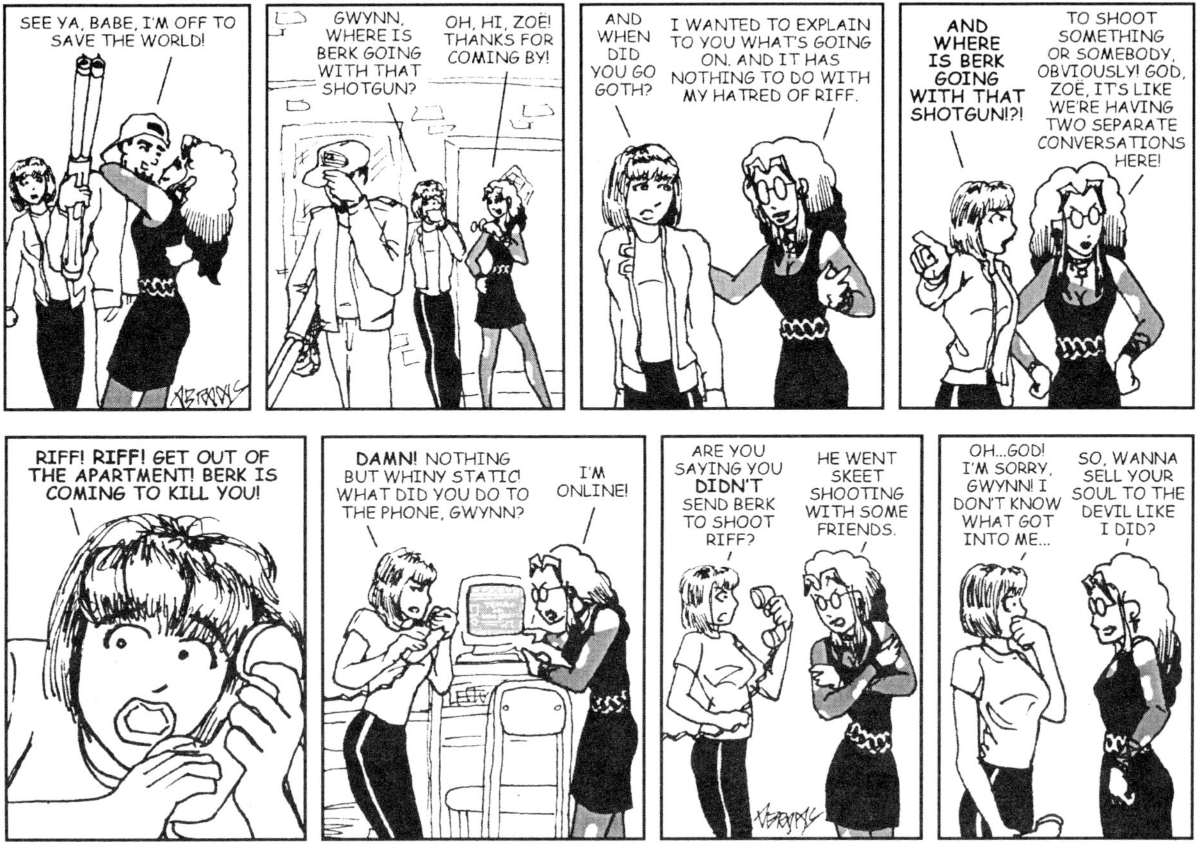

SEE YA, BABE, I'M OFF TO SAVE THE WORLD!
GWYNN, WHERE IS BERK GOING WITH THAT SHOTGUN?
OH, HI, ZOË! THANKS FOR COMING BY!
AND WHEN DID YOU GO GOTH?
I WANTED TO EXPLAIN TO YOU WHAT'S GOING ON. AND IT HAS NOTHING TO DO WITH MY HATRED OF RIFF.
AND WHERE IS BERK GOING WITH THAT SHOTGUN!?!
TO SHOOT SOMETHING OR SOMEBODY, OBVIOUSLY! GOD, ZOË, IT'S LIKE WE'RE HAVING TWO SEPARATE CONVERSATIONS HERE!
RIFF! RIFF! GET OUT OF THE APARTMENT! BERK IS COMING TO KILL YOU!
DAMN! NOTHING BUT WHINY STATIC! WHAT DID YOU DO TO THE PHONE, GWYNN?
I'M ONLINE!
ARE YOU SAYING YOU DIDN'T SEND BERK TO SHOOT RIFF?
HE WENT SKEET SHOOTING WITH SOME FRIENDS.
OH...GOD! I'M SORRY, GWYNN! I DON'T KNOW WHAT GOT INTO ME...
SO, WANNA SELL YOUR SOUL TO THE DEVIL LIKE I DID?

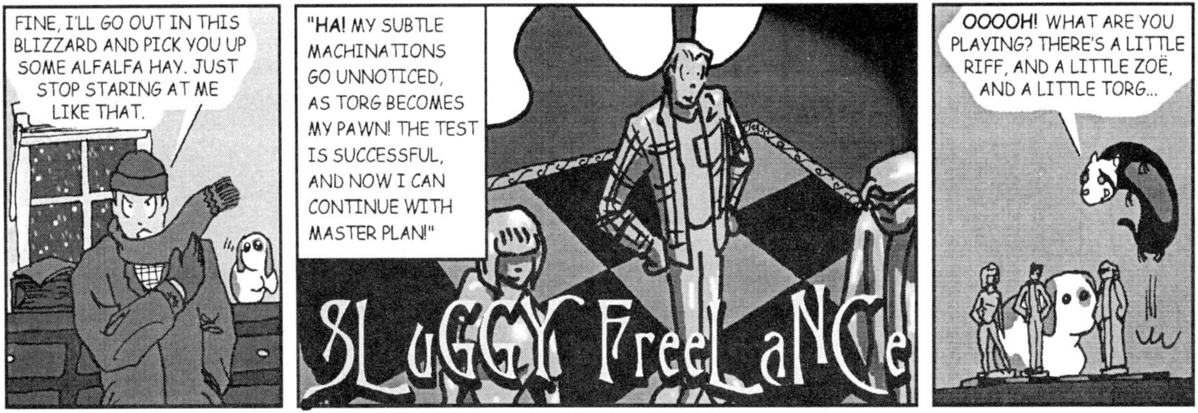

FINE, I'LL GO OUT IN THIS BLIZZARD AND PICK YOU UP SOME ALFALFA HAY. JUST STOP STARING AT ME LIKE THAT.
"HA! MY SUBTLE MACHINATIONS GO UNNOTICED, AS TORG BECOMES MY PAWN! THE TEST IS SUCCESSFUL, AND NOW I CAN CONTINUE WITH MASTER PLAN!"
SLUGGY FreeLaNCe
OOOOH! WHAT ARE YOU PLAYING? THERE'S A LITTLE RIFF, AND A LITTLE ZOË, AND A LITTLE TORG...

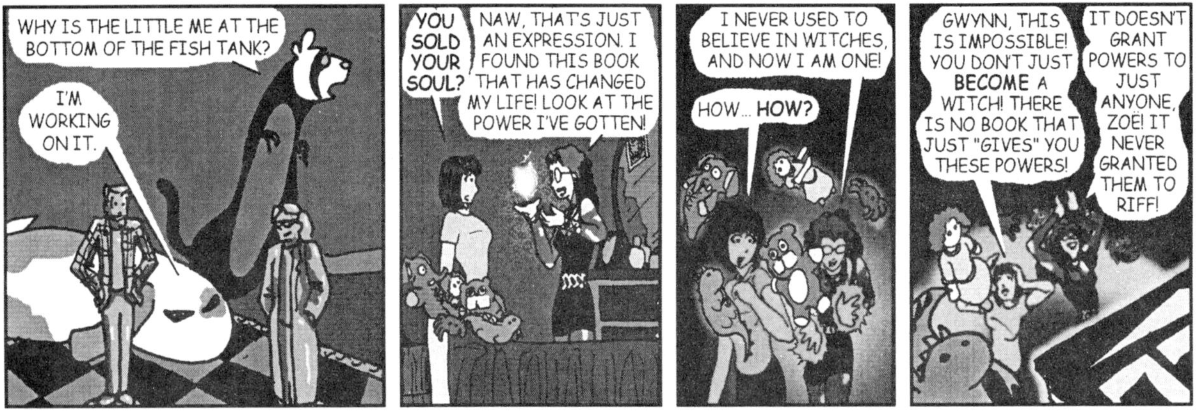

WHY IS THE LITTLE ME AT THE BOTTOM OF THE FISH TANK?
I'M WORKING ON IT.
YOU SOLD YOUR SOUL?
NAW, THAT'S JUST AN EXPRESSION. I FOUND THIS BOOK THAT HAS CHANGED MY LIFE! LOOK AT THE POWER I'VE GOTTEN!
I NEVER USED TO BELIEVE IN WITCHES, AND NOW I AM ONE!
HOW... HOW?
GWYNN, THIS IS IMPOSSIBLE! YOU DON'T JUST BECOME A WITCH! THERE IS NO BOOK THAT JUST "GIVES" YOU THESE POWERS!
IT DOESN'T GRANT POWERS TO JUST ANYONE, ZOË! IT NEVER GRANTED THEM TO RIFF!

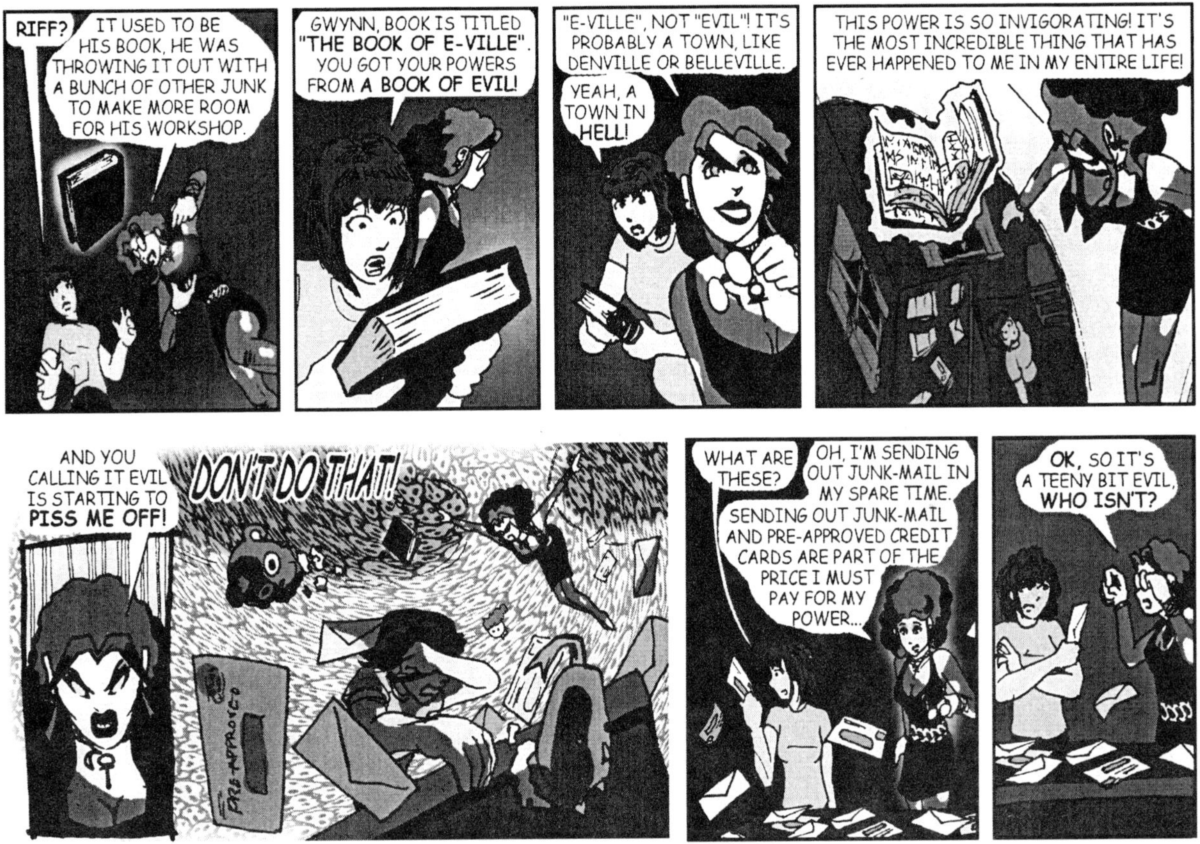
RIFF?
IT USED TO BE HIS BOOK, HE WAS THROWING IT OUT WITH A BUNCH OF OTHER JUNK TO MAKE MORE ROOM FOR HIS WORKSHOP.
GWYNN, BOOK IS TITLED "THE BOOK OF E-VILLE". YOU GOT YOUR POWERS FROM A BOOK OF EVIL!
"E-VILLE", NOT "EVIL"! IT'S PROBABLY A TOWN, LIKE DENVILLE OR BELLEVILLE.
YEAH, A TOWN IN HELL!
THIS POWER IS SO INVIGORATING! IT'S THE MOST INCREDIBLE THING THAT HAS EVER HAPPENED TO ME IN MY ENTIRE LIFE!
AND YOU CALLING IT EVIL IS STARTING TO PISS ME OFF!
DON'T DO THAT!
WHAT ARE THESE?
OH, I'M SENDING OUT JUNK-MAIL IN MY SPARE TIME.
SENDING OUT JUNK-MAIL AND PRE-APPROVED CREDIT CARDS ARE PART OF THE PRICE I MUST PAY FOR MY POWER...
OK, SO IT'S A TEENY BIT EVIL, WHO ISN'T?

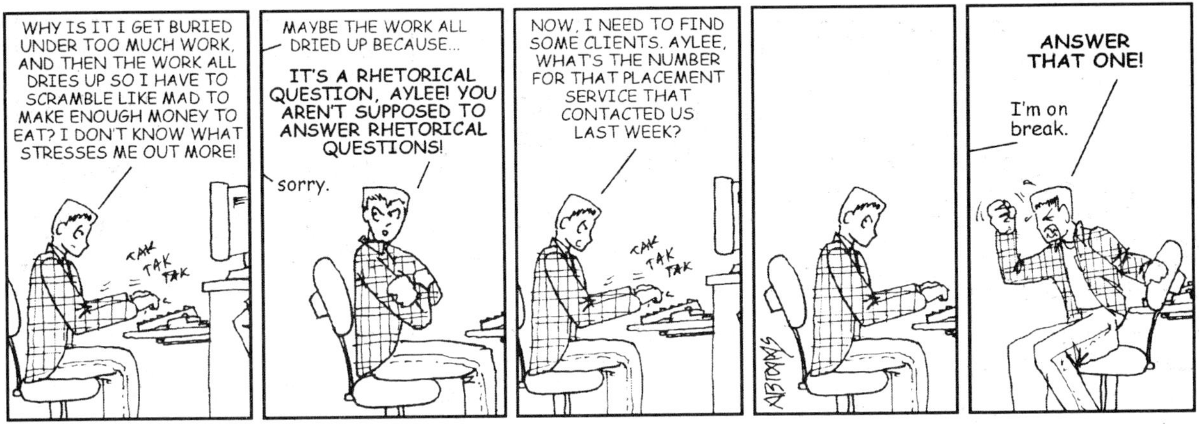
WHY IS IT I GET BURIED UNDER TOO MUCH WORK, AND THEN THE WORK ALL DRIES UP SO I HAVE TO SCRAMBLE LIKE MAD TO MAKE ENOUGH MONEY TO EAT? I DON'T KNOW WHAT STRESSES ME OUT MORE!
TAK TAK TAK
MAYBE THE WORK ALL DRIED UP BECAUSE...
IT'S A RHETORICAL QUESTION, AYLEE! YOU AREN'T SUPPOSED TO ANSWER RHETORICAL QUESTIONS!
sorry.
NOW, I NEED TO FIND SOME CLIENTS. AYLEE, WHAT'S THE NUMBER FOR THAT PLACEMENT SERVICE THAT CONTACTED US LAST WEEK?
TAK TAK TAK
ANSWER THAT ONE!
I'm on break.

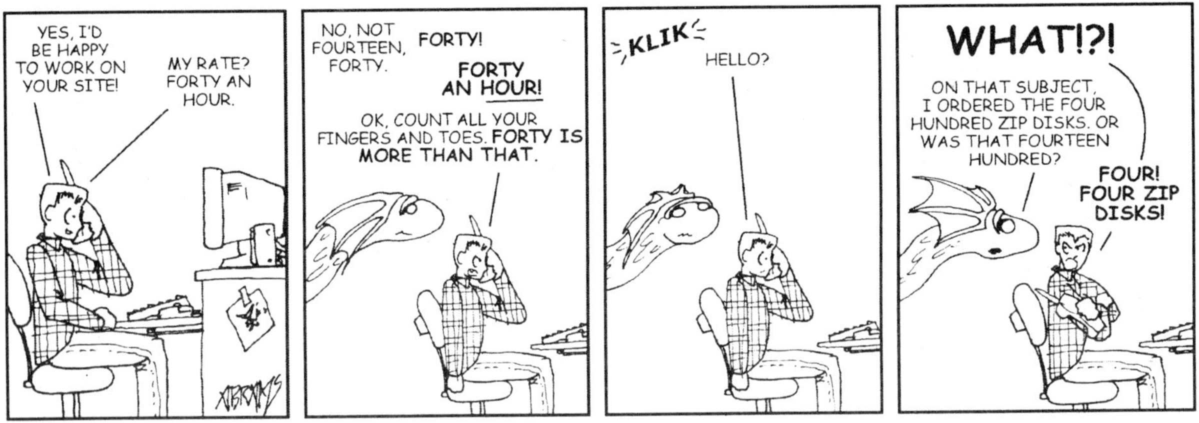
YES, I'D BE HAPPY TO WORK ON YOUR SITE!
MY RATE? FORTY AN HOUR.
NO, NOT FOURTEEN, FORTY.
FORTY!
FORTY AN HOUR!
OK, COUNT ALL YOUR FINGERS AND TOES. FORTY IS MORE THAN THAT.
KLIK
HELLO?
WHAT!?!
ON THAT SUBJECT, I ORDERED THE FOUR HUNDRED ZIP DISKS. OR WAS THAT FOURTEEN HUNDRED?
FOUR! FOUR ZIP DISKS!

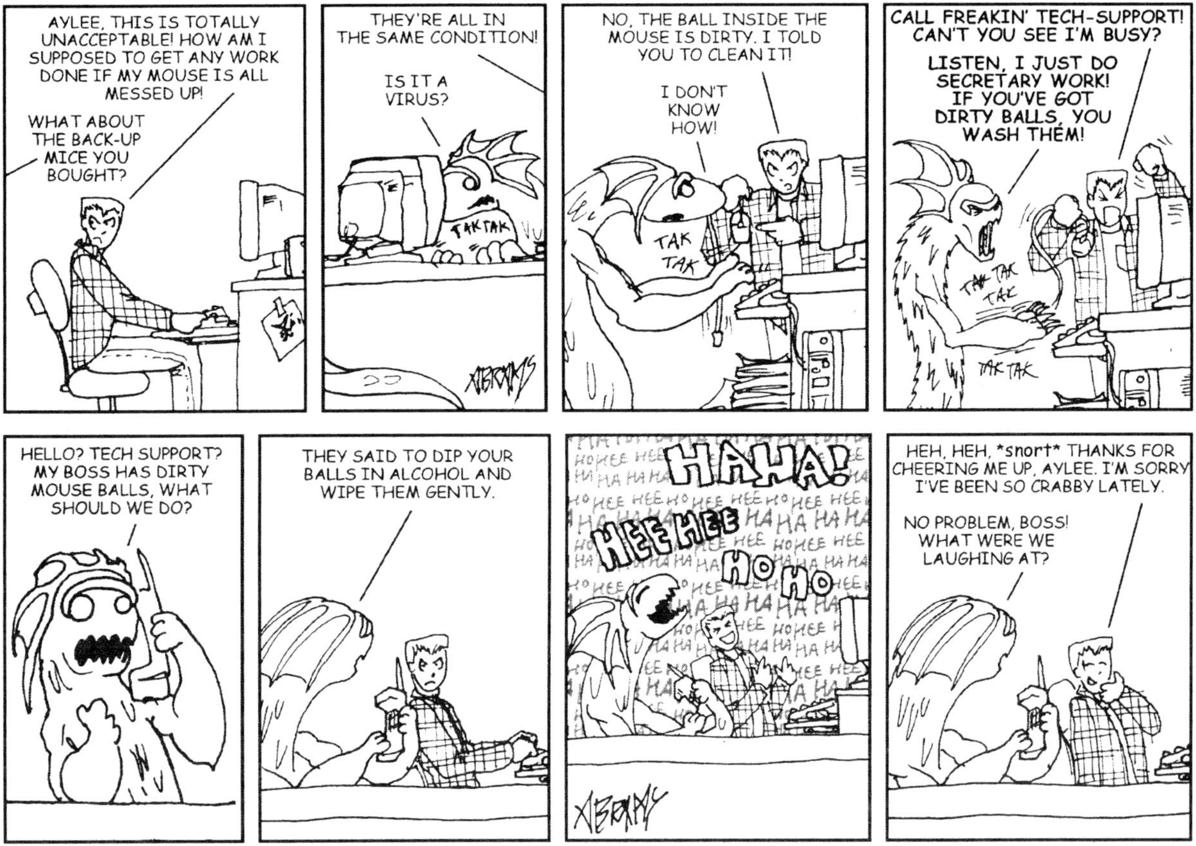
AYLEE, THIS IS TOTALLY UNACCEPTABLE! HOW AM I SUPPOSED TO GET ANY WORK DONE IF MY MOUSE IS ALL MESSED UP!
WHAT ABOUT THE BACK-UP MICE YOU BOUGHT?
THEY'RE ALL IN THE SAME CONDITION!
IS IT A VIRUS?
TAK TAK
NO, THE BALL INSIDE THE MOUSE IS DIRTY. I TOLD YOU TO CLEAN IT!
I DON'T KNOW HOW!
TAK TAK
CALL FREAKIN' TECH-SUPPORT! CAN'T YOU SEE I'M BUSY?
LISTEN, I JUST DO SECRETARY WORK! IF YOU'VE GOT DIRTY BALLS, YOU WASH THEM!
TAK TAK TAK
TAK TAK
HELLO? TECH SUPPORT? MY BOSS HAS DIRTY MOUSE BALLS, WHAT SHOULD WE DO?
THEY SAID TO DIP YOUR BALLS IN ALCOHOL AND WIPE THEM GENTLY.
HAHA!
HEE HEE
HO HO
HEH, HEH, *snort* THANKS FOR CHEERING ME UP, AYLEE. I'M SORRY I'VE BEEN SO CRABBY LATELY.
NO PROBLEM, BOSS! WHAT WERE WE LAUGHING AT?

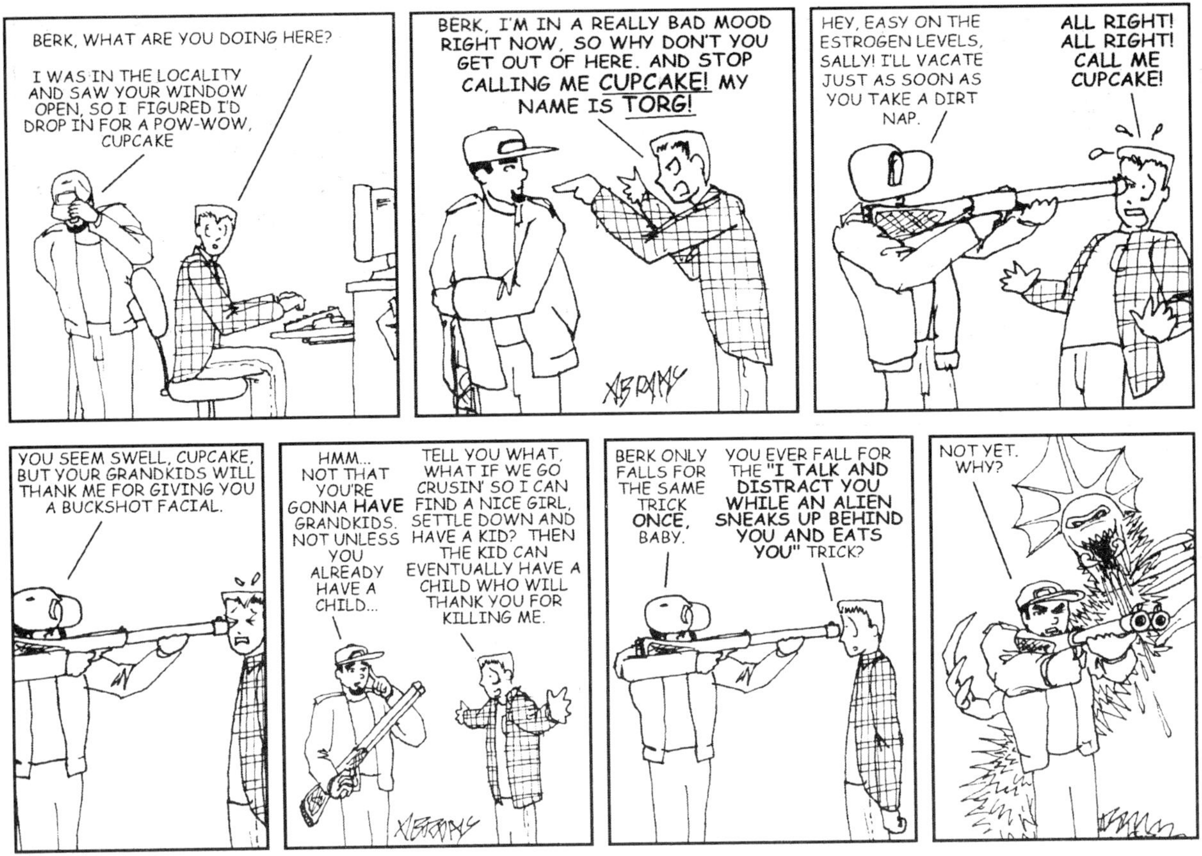
BERK, WHAT ARE YOU DOING HERE?
I WAS IN THE LOCALITY AND SAW YOUR WINDOW OPEN, SO I FIGURED I'D DROP IN FOR A POW-WOW, CUPCAKE
BERK, I'M IN A REALLY BAD MOOD RIGHT NOW, SO WHY DON'T YOU GET OUT OF HERE. AND STOP CALLING ME CUPCAKE! MY NAME IS TORG!
HEY, EASY ON THE ESTROGEN LEVELS, SALLY! I'LL VACATE JUST AS SOON AS YOU TAKE A DIRT NAP.
ALL RIGHT! ALL RIGHT! CALL ME CUPCAKE!
YOU SEEM SWELL, CUPCAKE, BUT YOUR GRANDKIDS WILL THANK ME FOR GIVING YOU A BUCKSHOT FACIAL.
HMM... NOT THAT YOU'RE GONNA HAVE GRANDKIDS. NOT UNLESS YOU ALREADY HAVE A CHILD...
TELL YOU WHAT. WHAT IF WE GO CRUSIN' SO I CAN FIND A NICE GIRL, SETTLE DOWN AND HAVE A KID? THEN THE KID CAN EVENTUALLY HAVE A CHILD WHO WILL THANK YOU FOR KILLING ME.
BERK ONLY FALLS FOR THE SAME TRICK ONCE, BABY.
YOU EVER FALL FOR THE "I TALK AND DISTRACT YOU WHILE AN ALIEN SNEAKS UP BEHIND YOU AND EATS YOU" TRICK?
NOT YET. WHY?

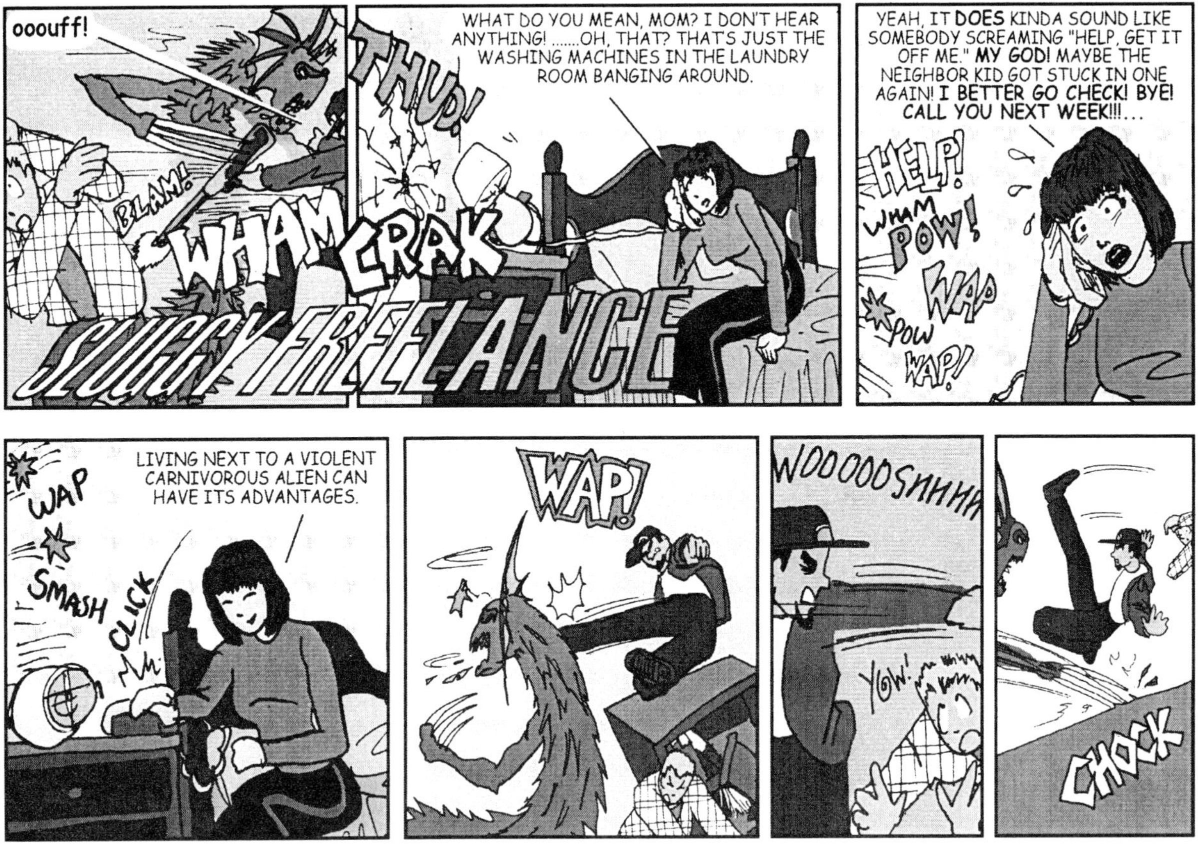
ooouff!
THUD!
BLAM!
WHAM
CRAK
SLUGGY FREELANCE
WHAT DO YOU MEAN, MOM? I DON'T HEAR ANYTHING! ....OH, THAT? THAT'S JUST THE WASHING MACHINES IN THE LAUNDRY ROOM BANGING AROUND.
YEAH, IT DOES KINDA SOUND LIKE SOMEBODY SCREAMING "HELP, GET IT OFF ME." MY GOD! MAYBE THE NEIGHBOR KID GOT STUCK IN ONE AGAIN! I BETTER GO CHECK! BYE! CALL YOU NEXT WEEK!!!...
HELP!
WHAM
POW!
WAP
POW
WAP!
WAP
SMASH
CLICK
LIVING NEXT TO A VIOLENT CARNIVOROUS ALIEN CAN HAVE ITS ADVANTAGES.
WAP!
WOOOOOOSHHHH
YOW!
CHOCK

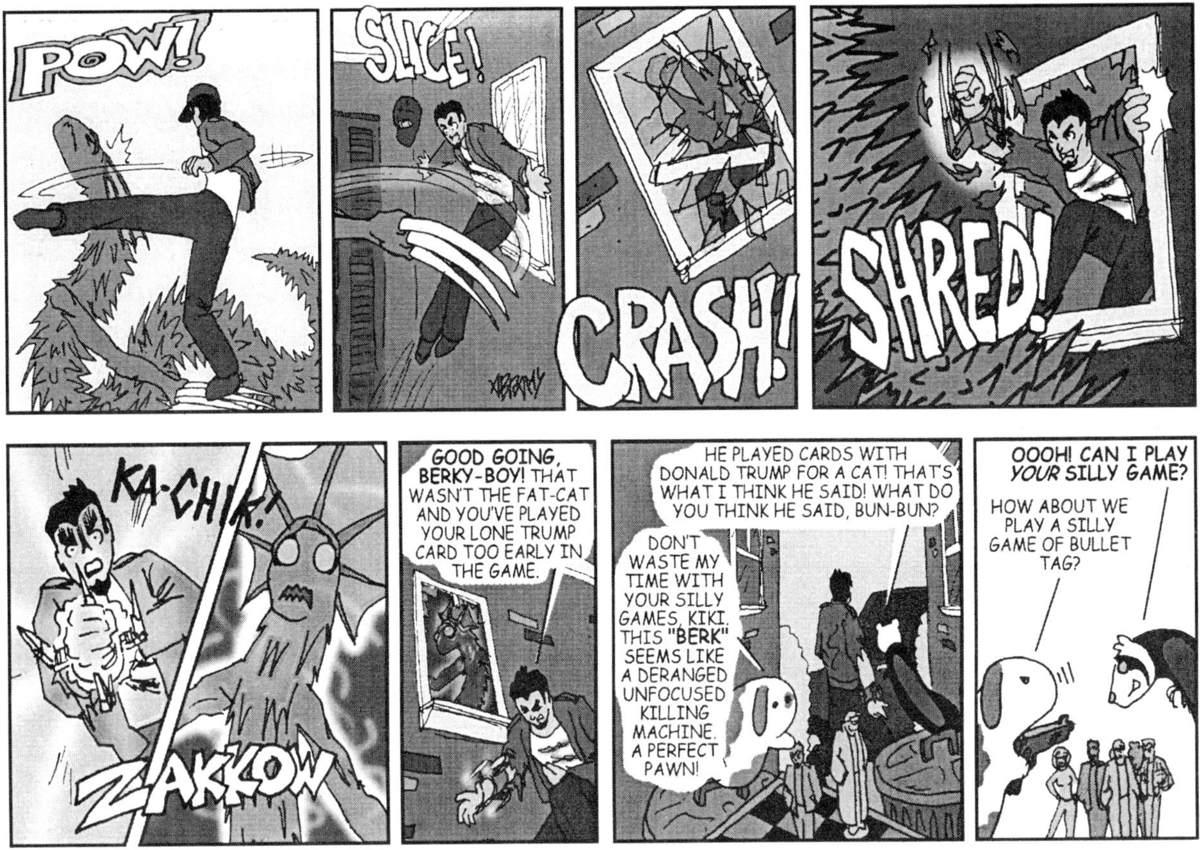

POW!
SLICE!
CRASH!
SHRED!
KA-CHIK!
ZAKKOW
GOOD GOING, BERKY-BOY! THAT WASN'T THE FAT-CAT AND YOU'VE PLAYED YOUR LONE TRUMP CARD TOO EARLY IN THE GAME.
HE PLAYED CARDS WITH DONALD TRUMP FOR A CAT! THAT'S WHAT I THINK HE SAID! WHAT DO YOU THINK HE SAID, BUN-BUN?
DON'T WASTE MY TIME WITH YOUR SILLY GAMES, KIKI. THIS "BERK" SEEMS LIKE A DERANGED UNFOCUSED KILLING MACHINE. A PERFECT PAWN!
OOOH! CAN I PLAY *YOUR* SILLY GAME?
HOW ABOUT WE PLAY A SILLY GAME OF BULLET TAG?

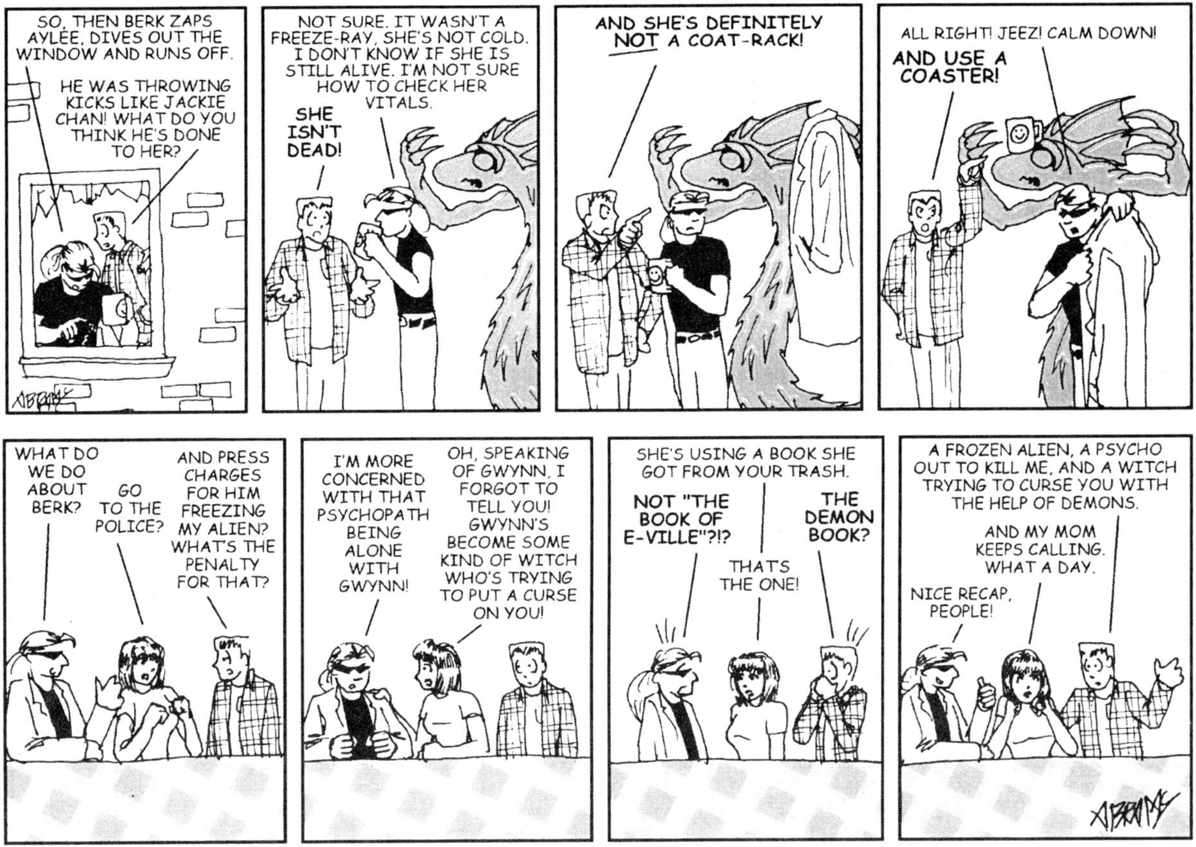
SO, THEN BERK ZAPS AYLÉE, DIVES OUT THE WINDOW AND RUNS OFF.
HE WAS THROWING KICKS LIKE JACKIE CHAN! WHAT DO YOU THINK HE'S DONE TO HER?
NOT SURE. IT WASN'T A FREEZE-RAY, SHE'S NOT COLD. I DON'T KNOW IF SHE IS STILL ALIVE. I'M NOT SURE HOW TO CHECK HER VITALS.
SHE ISN'T DEAD!
AND SHE'S DEFINITELY NOT A COAT-RACK!
ALL RIGHT! JEEZ! CALM DOWN!
AND USE A COASTER!
WHAT DO WE DO ABOUT BERK?
GO TO THE POLICE?
AND PRESS CHARGES FOR HIM FREEZING MY ALIEN? WHAT'S THE PENALTY FOR THAT?
I'M MORE CONCERNED WITH THAT PSYCHOPATH BEING ALONE WITH GWYNN!
OH, SPEAKING OF GWYNN, I FORGOT TO TELL YOU! GWYNN'S BECOME SOME KIND OF WITCH WHO'S TRYING TO PUT A CURSE ON YOU!
SHE'S USING A BOOK SHE GOT FROM YOUR TRASH.
NOT "THE BOOK OF E-VILLE"?!?
THE DEMON BOOK?
THAT'S THE ONE!
A FROZEN ALIEN, A PSYCHO OUT TO KILL ME, AND A WITCH TRYING TO CURSE YOU WITH THE HELP OF DEMONS.
AND MY MOM KEEPS CALLING. WHAT A DAY.
NICE RECAP, PEOPLE!

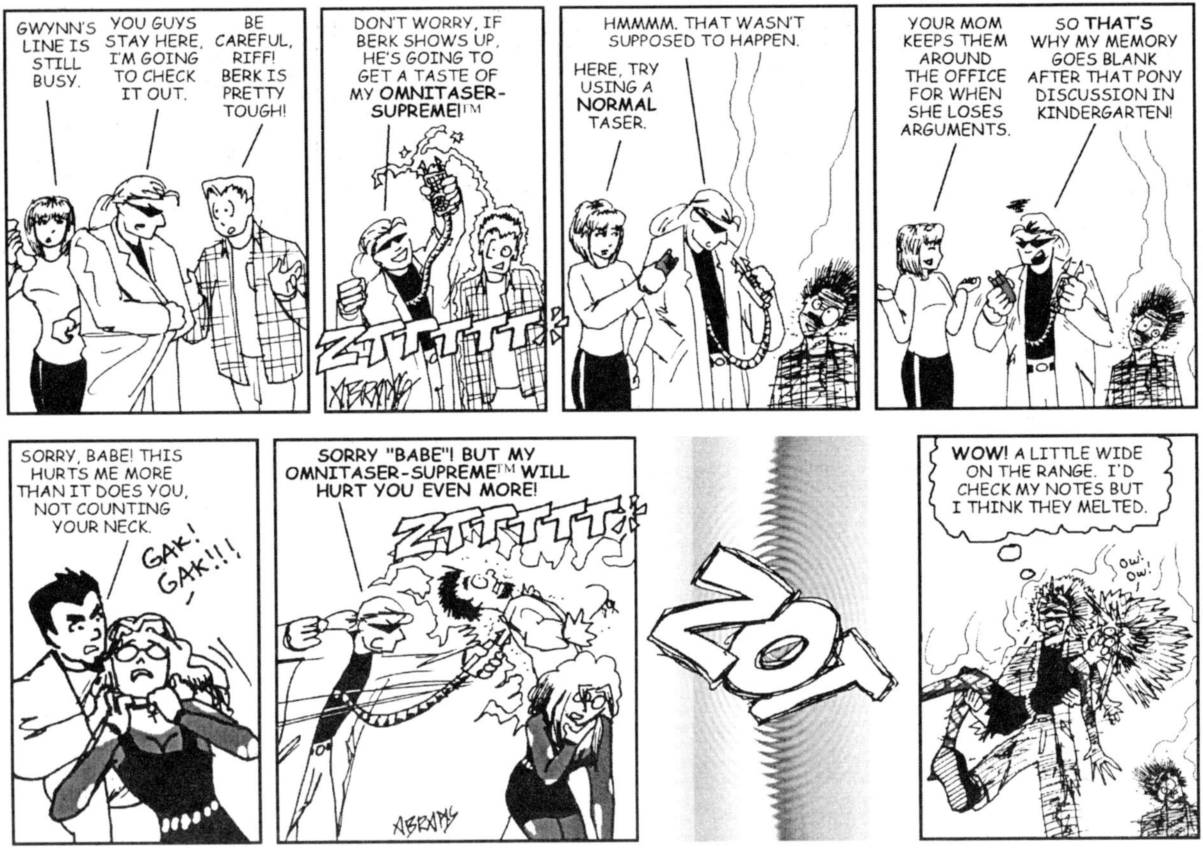
GWYNN'S LINE IS STILL BUSY.
YOU GUYS STAY HERE, I'M GOING TO CHECK IT OUT.
BE CAREFUL, RIFF! BERK IS PRETTY TOUGH!
DON'T WORRY, IF BERK SHOWS UP, HE'S GOING TO GET A TASTE OF MY OMNITASER-SUPREME!TM
ZTTTTTT!
ABRAMS
HMMMM. THAT WASN'T SUPPOSED TO HAPPEN.
HERE, TRY USING A NORMAL TASER.
YOUR MOM KEEPS THEM AROUND THE OFFICE FOR WHEN SHE LOSES ARGUMENTS.
SO THAT'S WHY MY MEMORY GOES BLANK AFTER THAT PONY DISCUSSION IN KINDERGARTEN!
SORRY, BABE! THIS HURTS ME MORE THAN IT DOES YOU, NOT COUNTING YOUR NECK.
GAK! GAK!!!
SORRY "BABE"! BUT MY OMNITASER-SUPREMETM WILL HURT YOU EVEN MORE!
ZTTTTTT!
ABRAMS
ZOT
WOW! A LITTLE WIDE ON THE RANGE. I'D CHECK MY NOTES BUT I THINK THEY MELTED.
OW! OW!

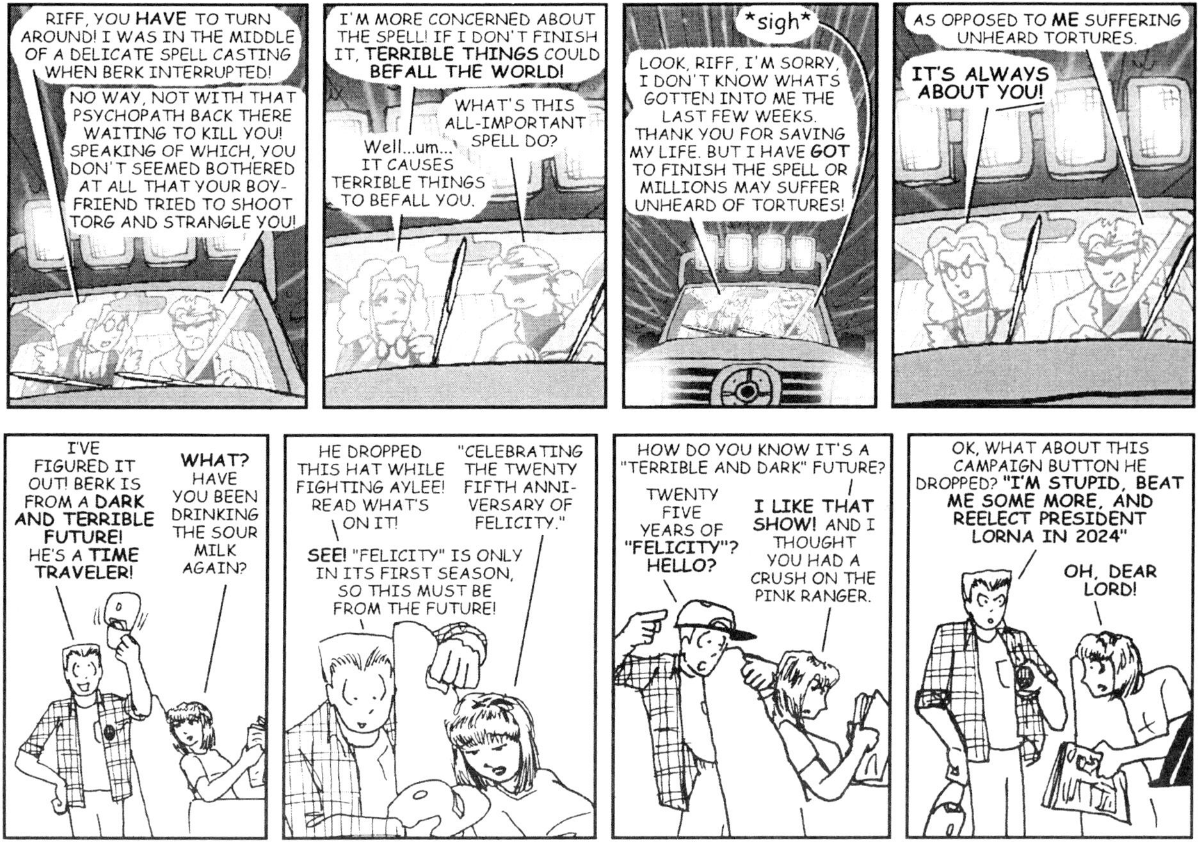

RIFF, YOU **HAVE** TO TURN AROUND! I WAS IN THE MIDDLE OF A DELICATE SPELL CASTING WHEN BERK INTERRUPTED!
NO WAY, NOT WITH THAT PSYCHOPATH BACK THERE WAITING TO KILL YOU! SPEAKING OF WHICH, YOU DON'T SEEMED BOTHERED AT ALL THAT YOUR BOY-FRIEND TRIED TO SHOOT TORG AND STRANGLE YOU!
I'M MORE CONCERNED ABOUT THE SPELL! IF I DON'T FINISH IT, **TERRIBLE THINGS** COULD **BEFALL THE WORLD!**
WHAT'S THIS ALL-IMPORTANT SPELL DO?
Well...um... IT CAUSES TERRIBLE THINGS TO BEFALL YOU.
sigh
LOOK, RIFF, I'M SORRY, I DON'T KNOW WHAT'S GOTTEN INTO ME THE LAST FEW WEEKS. THANK YOU FOR SAVING MY LIFE. BUT I HAVE **GOT** TO FINISH THE SPELL OR MILLIONS MAY SUFFER UNHEARD OF TORTURES!
AS OPPOSED TO **ME** SUFFERING UNHEARD TORTURES.
IT'S ALWAYS ABOUT YOU!
I'VE FIGURED IT OUT! BERK IS FROM A **DARK AND TERRIBLE FUTURE!** HE'S A **TIME TRAVELER!**
WHAT? HAVE YOU BEEN DRINKING THE SOUR MILK AGAIN?
HE DROPPED THIS HAT WHILE FIGHTING AYLEE! READ WHAT'S ON IT!
"CELEBRATING THE TWENTY FIFTH ANNI-VERSARY OF FELICITY."
SEE! "FELICITY" IS ONLY IN ITS FIRST SEASON, SO THIS MUST BE FROM THE FUTURE!
HOW DO YOU KNOW IT'S A "TERRIBLE AND DARK" FUTURE?
TWENTY FIVE YEARS OF **"FELICITY"? HELLO?**
I LIKE THAT SHOW! AND I THOUGHT YOU HAD A CRUSH ON THE PINK RANGER.
OK, WHAT ABOUT THIS CAMPAIGN BUTTON HE DROPPED? **"I'M STUPID, BEAT ME SOME MORE, AND REELECT PRESIDENT LORNA IN 2024"**
OH, DEAR LORD!

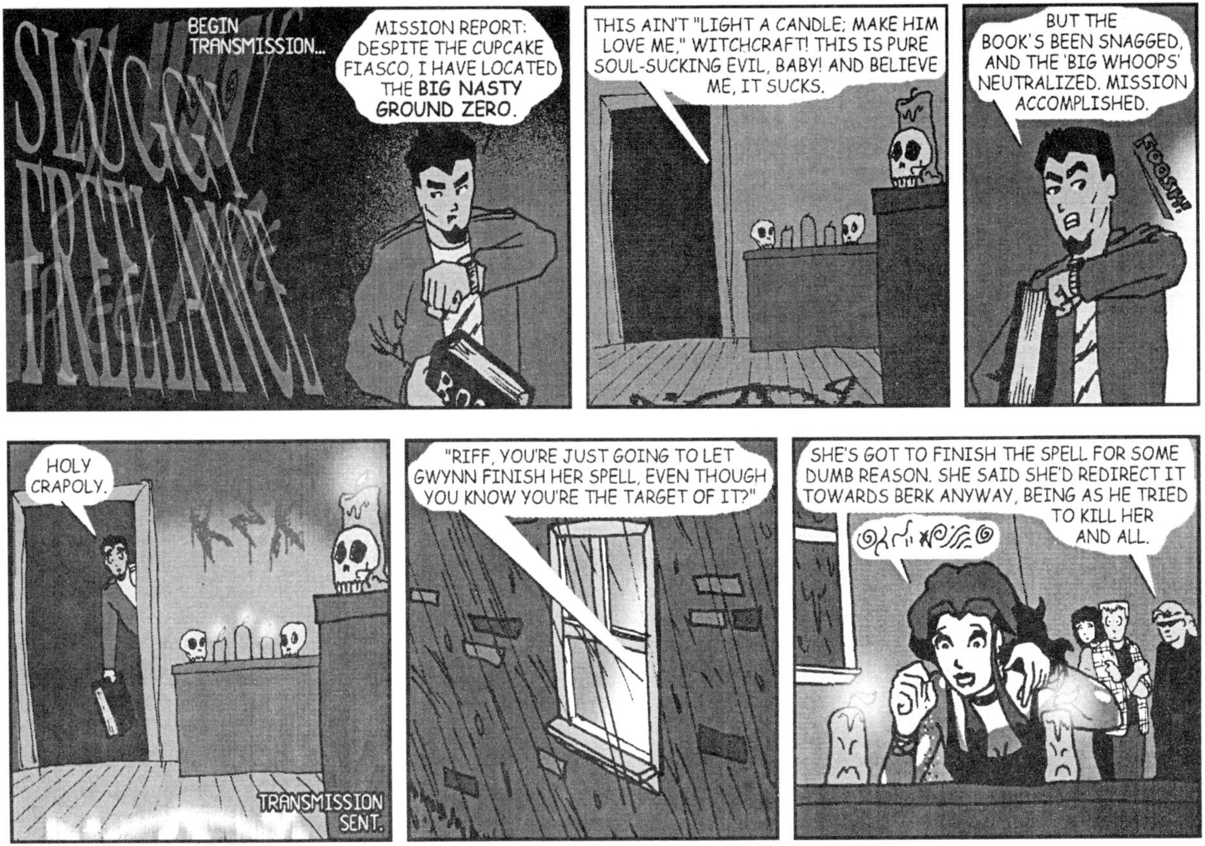
SLUGGY FREELANCE
BEGIN TRANSMISSION...
MISSION REPORT: DESPITE THE CUPCAKE FIASCO, I HAVE LOCATED THE BIG NASTY GROUND ZERO.
THIS AIN'T "LIGHT A CANDLE; MAKE HIM LOVE ME," WITCHCRAFT! THIS IS PURE SOUL-SUCKING EVIL, BABY! AND BELIEVE ME, IT SUCKS.
BUT THE BOOK'S BEEN SNAGGED, AND THE 'BIG WHOOPS' NEUTRALIZED. MISSION ACCOMPLISHED.
HOLY CRAPOLY.
TRANSMISSION SENT.
"RIFF, YOU'RE JUST GOING TO LET GWYNN FINISH HER SPELL, EVEN THOUGH YOU KNOW YOU'RE THE TARGET OF IT?"
SHE'S GOT TO FINISH THE SPELL FOR SOME DUMB REASON. SHE SAID SHE'D REDIRECT IT TOWARDS BERK ANYWAY, BEING AS HE TRIED TO KILL HER AND ALL.

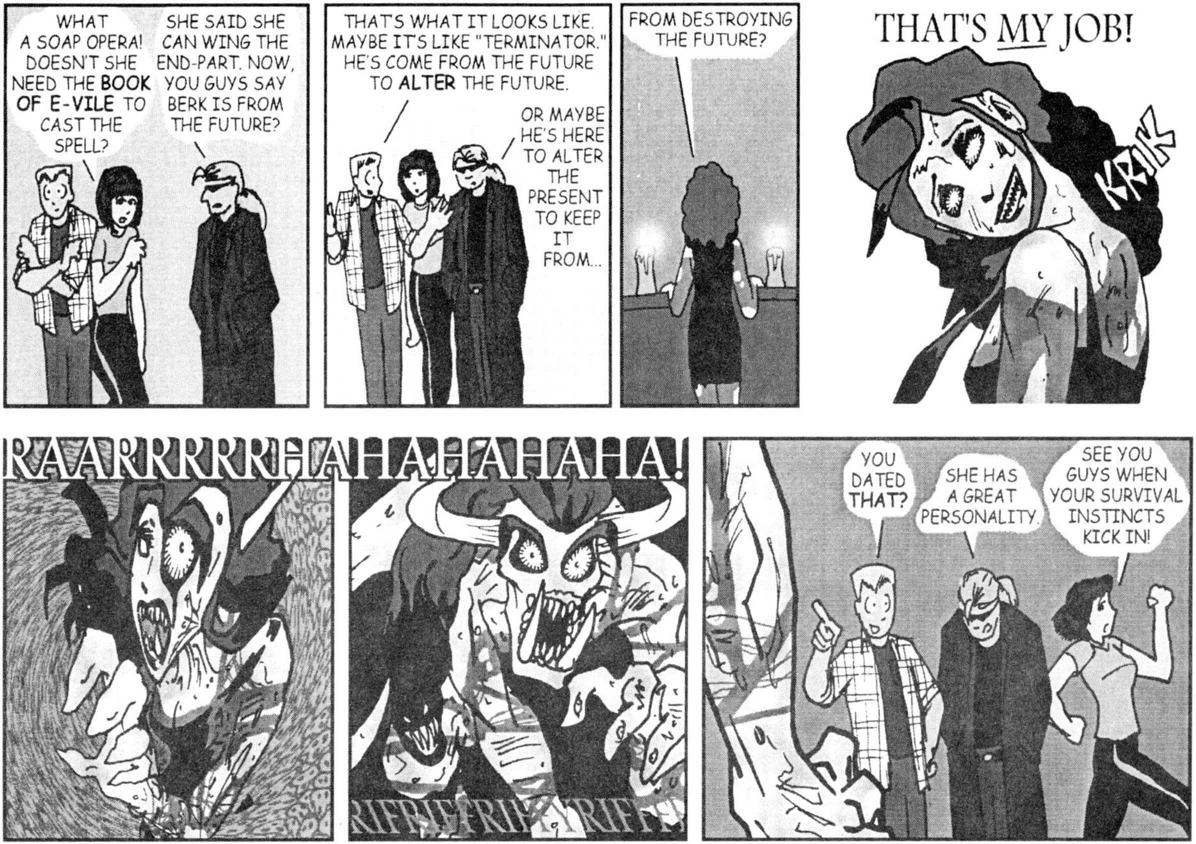
WHAT A SOAP OPERA! DOESN'T SHE NEED THE BOOK OF E-VILE TO CAST THE SPELL?
SHE SAID SHE CAN WING THE END-PART. NOW, YOU GUYS SAY BERK IS FROM THE FUTURE?
THAT'S WHAT IT LOOKS LIKE. MAYBE IT'S LIKE "TERMINATOR." HE'S COME FROM THE FUTURE TO ALTER THE FUTURE.
OR MAYBE HE'S HERE TO ALTER THE PRESENT TO KEEP IT FROM...
FROM DESTROYING THE FUTURE?
THAT'S MY JOB!
KRIK
RAARRRRRRHAHAHAHAHA!
RIFRIFRIFRIFRIF
YOU DATED THAT?
SHE HAS A GREAT PERSONALITY.
SEE YOU GUYS WHEN YOUR SURVIVAL INSTINCTS KICK IN!

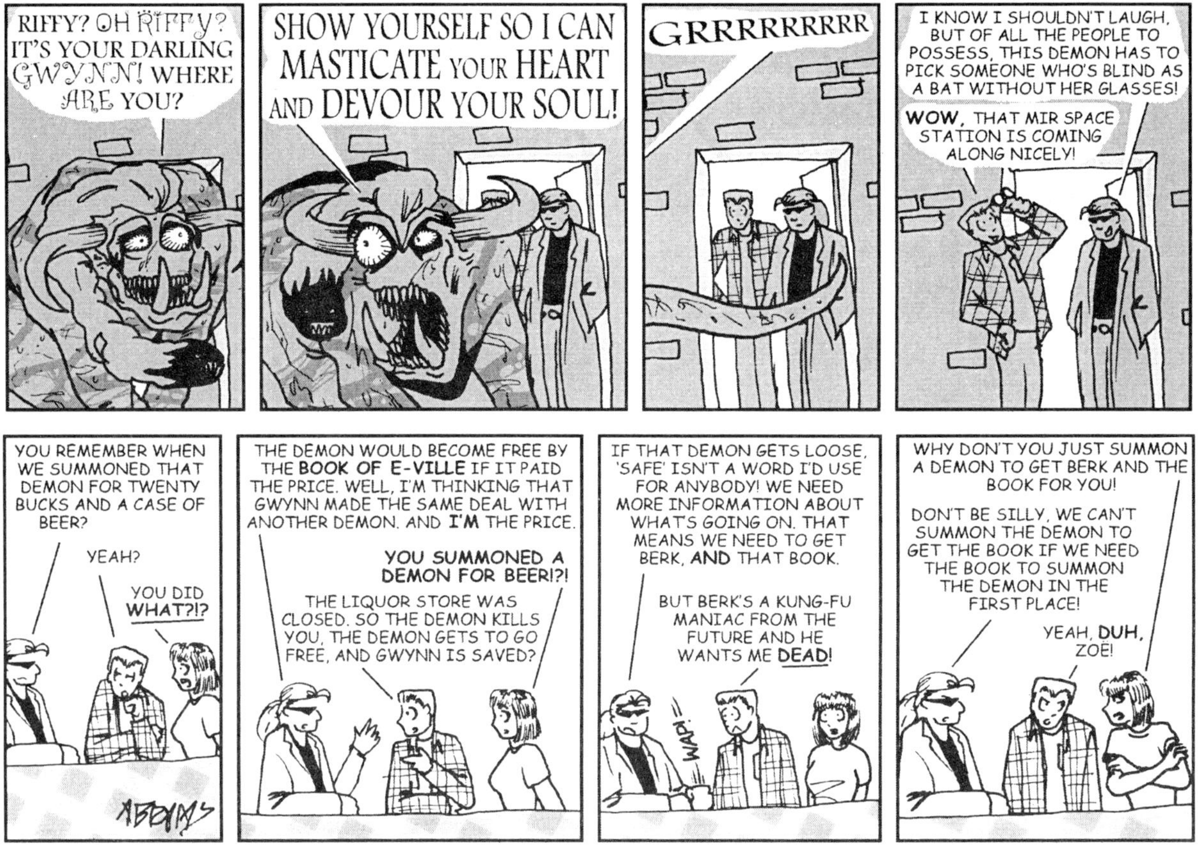
RIFFY? OH RIFFY? IT'S YOUR DARLING GWYNN! WHERE ARE YOU?
SHOW YOURSELF SO I CAN MASTICATE YOUR HEART AND DEVOUR YOUR SOUL!
GRRRRRRRRR
I KNOW I SHOULDN'T LAUGH, BUT OF ALL THE PEOPLE TO POSSESS, THIS DEMON HAS TO PICK SOMEONE WHO'S BLIND AS A BAT WITHOUT HER GLASSES!
WOW, THAT MIR SPACE STATION IS COMING ALONG NICELY!
YOU REMEMBER WHEN WE SUMMONED THAT DEMON FOR TWENTY BUCKS AND A CASE OF BEER?
YEAH?
YOU DID WHAT?!?
ABRAMS
THE DEMON WOULD BECOME FREE BY THE BOOK OF E-VILLE IF IT PAID THE PRICE. WELL, I'M THINKING THAT GWYNN MADE THE SAME DEAL WITH ANOTHER DEMON. AND I'M THE PRICE.
YOU SUMMONED A DEMON FOR BEER!?!
THE LIQUOR STORE WAS CLOSED. SO THE DEMON KILLS YOU, THE DEMON GETS TO GO FREE, AND GWYNN IS SAVED?
IF THAT DEMON GETS LOOSE, 'SAFE' ISN'T A WORD I'D USE FOR ANYBODY! WE NEED MORE INFORMATION ABOUT WHAT'S GOING ON. THAT MEANS WE NEED TO GET BERK, AND THAT BOOK.
BUT BERK'S A KUNG-FU MANIAC FROM THE FUTURE AND HE WANTS ME DEAD!
WAP!
WHY DON'T YOU JUST SUMMON A DEMON TO GET BERK AND THE BOOK FOR YOU!
DON'T BE SILLY, WE CAN'T SUMMON THE DEMON TO GET THE BOOK IF WE NEED THE BOOK TO SUMMON THE DEMON IN THE FIRST PLACE!
YEAH, DUH, ZOË!

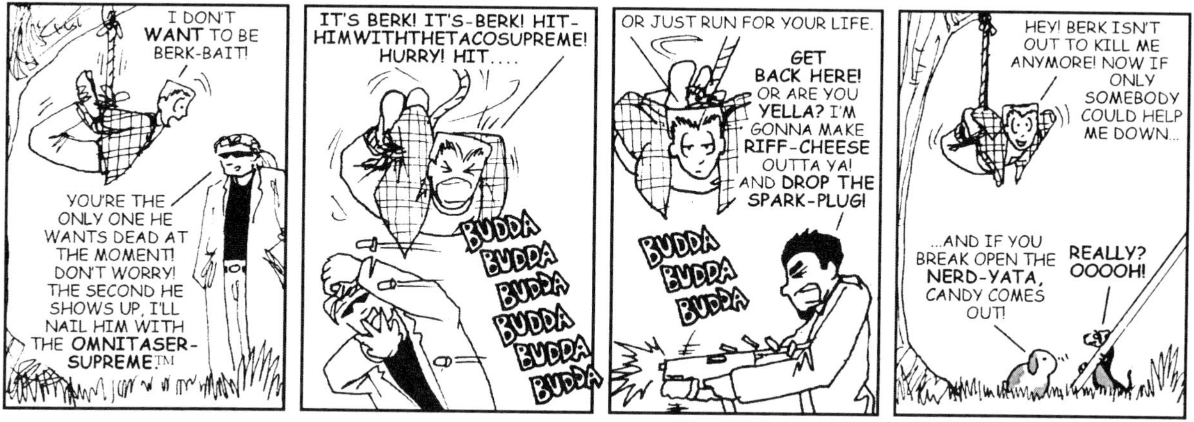
I DON'T WANT TO BE BERK-BAIT!
YOU'RE THE ONLY ONE HE WANTS DEAD AT THE MOMENT! DON'T WORRY! THE SECOND HE SHOWS UP, I'LL NAIL HIM WITH THE OMNITASER-SUPREME.™
IT'S BERK! IT'S-BERK! HIT-HIMWITHTHETACOSUPREME! HURRY! HIT....
BUDDA BUDDA BUDDA BUDDA BUDDA BUDDA
OR JUST RUN FOR YOUR LIFE.
GET BACK HERE! OR ARE YOU YELLA? I'M GONNA MAKE RIFF-CHEESE OUTTA YA! AND DROP THE SPARK-PLUG!
BUDDA BUDDA BUDDA
HEY! BERK ISN'T OUT TO KILL ME ANYMORE! NOW IF ONLY SOMEBODY COULD HELP ME DOWN...
...AND IF YOU BREAK OPEN THE NERD-YATA, CANDY COMES OUT!
REALLY? OOOOH!

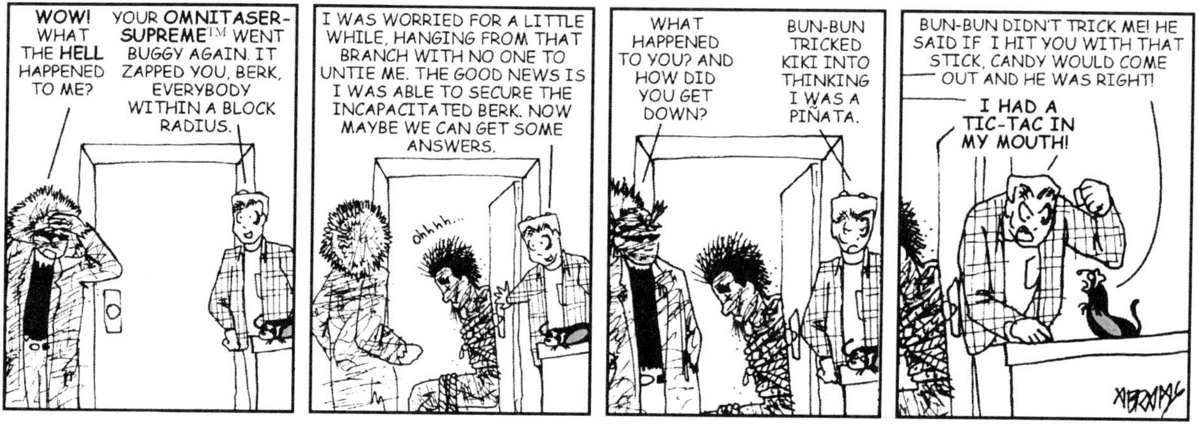
WOW! WHAT THE HELL HAPPENED TO ME?
YOUR OMNITASER-SUPREME™ WENT BUGGY AGAIN. IT ZAPPED YOU, BERK, EVERYBODY WITHIN A BLOCK RADIUS.
I WAS WORRIED FOR A LITTLE WHILE, HANGING FROM THAT BRANCH WITH NO ONE TO UNTIE ME. THE GOOD NEWS IS I WAS ABLE TO SECURE THE INCAPACITATED BERK. NOW MAYBE WE CAN GET SOME ANSWERS.
Ohhhh...
WHAT HAPPENED TO YOU? AND HOW DID YOU GET DOWN?
BUN-BUN TRICKED KIKI INTO THINKING I WAS A PIÑATA.
BUN-BUN DIDN'T TRICK ME! HE SAID IF I HIT YOU WITH THAT STICK, CANDY WOULD COME OUT AND HE WAS RIGHT!
I HAD A TIC-TAC IN MY MOUTH!

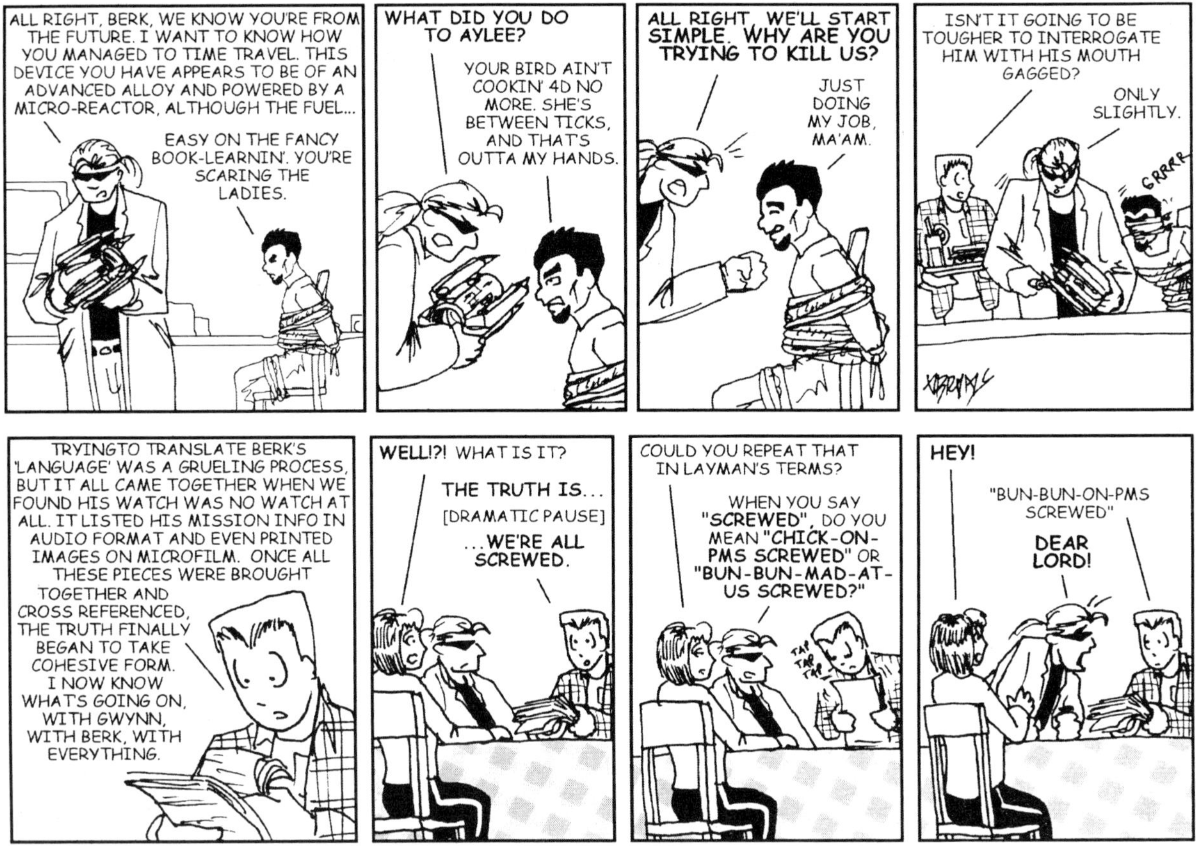
ALL RIGHT, BERK, WE KNOW YOU'RE FROM THE FUTURE. I WANT TO KNOW HOW YOU MANAGED TO TIME TRAVEL. THIS DEVICE YOU HAVE APPEARS TO BE OF AN ADVANCED ALLOY AND POWERED BY A MICRO-REACTOR, ALTHOUGH THE FUEL...
EASY ON THE FANCY BOOK-LEARNIN'. YOU'RE SCARING THE LADIES.
WHAT DID YOU DO TO AYLEE?
YOUR BIRD AIN'T COOKIN' 4D NO MORE. SHE'S BETWEEN TICKS, AND THAT'S OUTTA MY HANDS.
ALL RIGHT, WE'LL START SIMPLE. WHY ARE YOU TRYING TO KILL US?
JUST DOING MY JOB, MA'AM.
ISN'T IT GOING TO BE TOUGHER TO INTERROGATE HIM WITH HIS MOUTH GAGGED?
ONLY SLIGHTLY.
GRRRR
TRYINGTO TRANSLATE BERK'S 'LANGUAGE' WAS A GRUELING PROCESS, BUT IT ALL CAME TOGETHER WHEN WE FOUND HIS WATCH WAS NO WATCH AT ALL. IT LISTED HIS MISSION INFO IN AUDIO FORMAT AND EVEN PRINTED IMAGES ON MICROFILM. ONCE ALL THESE PIECES WERE BROUGHT TOGETHER AND CROSS REFERENCED, THE TRUTH FINALLY BEGAN TO TAKE COHESIVE FORM. I NOW KNOW WHAT'S GOING ON, WITH GWYNN, WITH BERK, WITH EVERYTHING.
WELL!?! WHAT IS IT?
THE TRUTH IS...
[DRAMATIC PAUSE]
...WE'RE ALL SCREWED.
COULD YOU REPEAT THAT IN LAYMAN'S TERMS?
WHEN YOU SAY "SCREWED", DO YOU MEAN "CHICK-ON-PMS SCREWED" OR "BUN-BUN-MAD-AT-US SCREWED?"
TAP TAP TAP
HEY!
"BUN-BUN-ON-PMS SCREWED"
DEAR LORD!

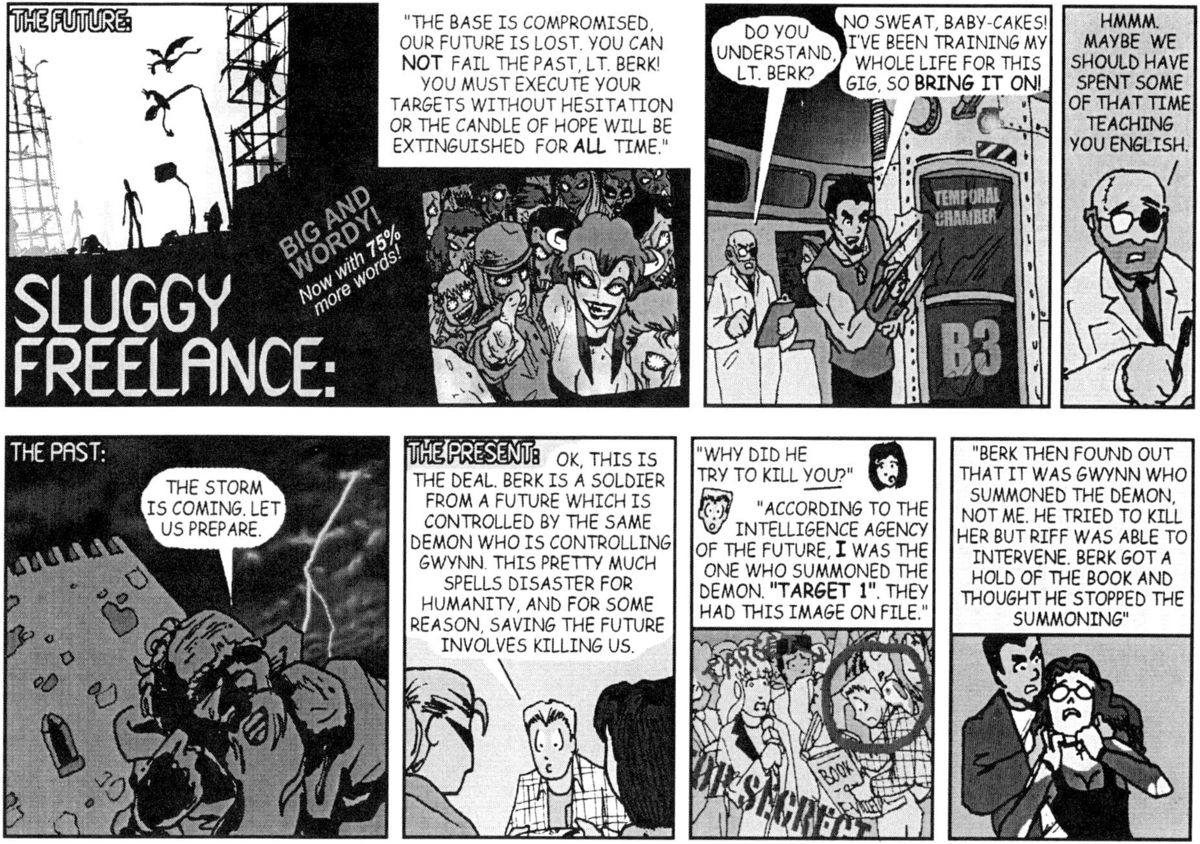

THE FUTURE:
SLUGGY FREELANCE:
BIG AND WORDY! Now with 75% more words!
"THE BASE IS COMPROMISED, OUR FUTURE IS LOST. YOU CAN NOT FAIL THE PAST, LT. BERK! YOU MUST EXECUTE YOUR TARGETS WITHOUT HESITATION OR THE CANDLE OF HOPE WILL BE EXTINGUISHED FOR ALL TIME."
DO YOU UNDERSTAND, LT. BERK?
NO SWEAT, BABY-CAKES! I'VE BEEN TRAINING MY WHOLE LIFE FOR THIS GIG, SO BRING IT ON!
TEMPORAL CHAMBER
B3
HMMM. MAYBE WE SHOULD HAVE SPENT SOME OF THAT TIME TEACHING YOU ENGLISH.
THE PAST:
THE STORM IS COMING. LET US PREPARE.
THE PRESENT: OK, THIS IS THE DEAL. BERK IS A SOLDIER FROM A FUTURE WHICH IS CONTROLLED BY THE SAME DEMON WHO IS CONTROLLING GWYNN. THIS PRETTY MUCH SPELLS DISASTER FOR HUMANITY, AND FOR SOME REASON, SAVING THE FUTURE INVOLVES KILLING US.
"WHY DID HE TRY TO KILL YOU?"
"ACCORDING TO THE INTELLIGENCE AGENCY OF THE FUTURE, I WAS THE ONE WHO SUMMONED THE DEMON. "TARGET 1". THEY HAD THIS IMAGE ON FILE."
BOOK
"BERK THEN FOUND OUT THAT IT WAS GWYNN WHO SUMMONED THE DEMON, NOT ME. HE TRIED TO KILL HER BUT RIFF WAS ABLE TO INTERVENE. BERK GOT A HOLD OF THE BOOK AND THOUGHT HE STOPPED THE SUMMONING"

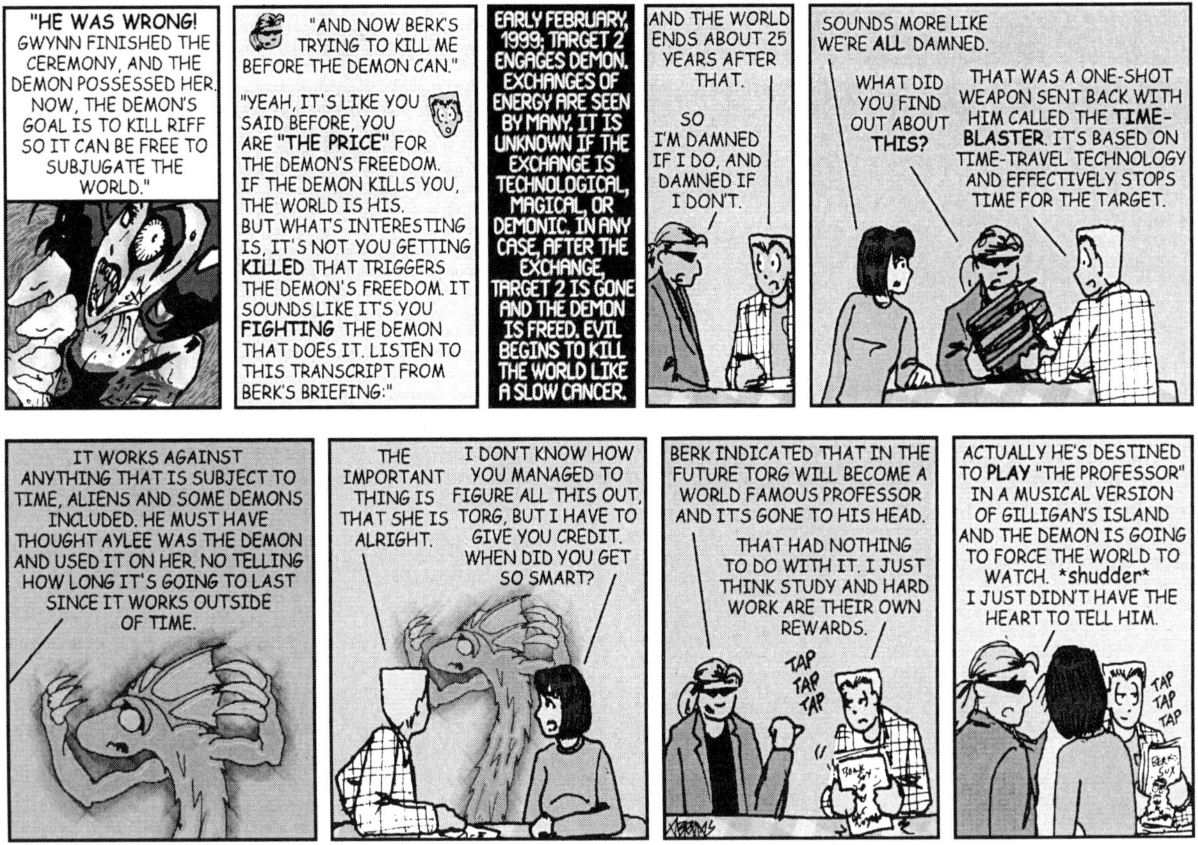
"HE WAS WRONG! GWYNN FINISHED THE CEREMONY, AND THE DEMON POSSESSED HER. NOW, THE DEMON'S GOAL IS TO KILL RIFF SO IT CAN BE FREE TO SUBJUGATE THE WORLD."
"AND NOW BERK'S TRYING TO KILL ME BEFORE THE DEMON CAN."
"YEAH, IT'S LIKE YOU SAID BEFORE, YOU ARE "THE PRICE" FOR THE DEMON'S FREEDOM. IF THE DEMON KILLS YOU, THE WORLD IS HIS. BUT WHAT'S INTERESTING IS, IT'S NOT YOU GETTING KILLED THAT TRIGGERS THE DEMON'S FREEDOM. IT SOUNDS LIKE IT'S YOU FIGHTING THE DEMON THAT DOES IT. LISTEN TO THIS TRANSCRIPT FROM BERK'S BRIEFING:"
EARLY FEBRUARY, 1999; TARGET 2 ENGAGES DEMON. EXCHANGES OF ENERGY ARE SEEN BY MANY. IT IS UNKNOWN IF THE EXCHANGE IS TECHNOLOGICAL, MAGICAL, OR DEMONIC. IN ANY CASE, AFTER THE EXCHANGE, TARGET 2 IS GONE AND THE DEMON IS FREED. EVIL BEGINS TO KILL THE WORLD LIKE A SLOW CANCER.
AND THE WORLD ENDS ABOUT 25 YEARS AFTER THAT.
SO I'M DAMNED IF I DO, AND DAMNED IF I DON'T.
SOUNDS MORE LIKE WE'RE ALL DAMNED.
WHAT DID YOU FIND OUT ABOUT THIS?
THAT WAS A ONE-SHOT WEAPON SENT BACK WITH HIM CALLED THE TIME-BLASTER. IT'S BASED ON TIME-TRAVEL TECHNOLOGY AND EFFECTIVELY STOPS TIME FOR THE TARGET.
IT WORKS AGAINST ANYTHING THAT IS SUBJECT TO TIME, ALIENS AND SOME DEMONS INCLUDED. HE MUST HAVE THOUGHT AYLEE WAS THE DEMON AND USED IT ON HER. NO TELLING HOW LONG IT'S GOING TO LAST SINCE IT WORKS OUTSIDE OF TIME.
THE IMPORTANT THING IS THAT SHE IS ALRIGHT.
I DON'T KNOW HOW YOU MANAGED TO FIGURE ALL THIS OUT, TORG, BUT I HAVE TO GIVE YOU CREDIT. WHEN DID YOU GET SO SMART?
BERK INDICATED THAT IN THE FUTURE TORG WILL BECOME A WORLD FAMOUS PROFESSOR AND IT'S GONE TO HIS HEAD.
THAT HAD NOTHING TO DO WITH IT. I JUST THINK STUDY AND HARD WORK ARE THEIR OWN REWARDS.
TAP TAP TAP
ACTUALLY HE'S DESTINED TO PLAY "THE PROFESSOR" IN A MUSICAL VERSION OF GILLIGAN'S ISLAND AND THE DEMON IS GOING TO FORCE THE WORLD TO WATCH. *shudder* I JUST DIDN'T HAVE THE HEART TO TELL HIM.
TAP TAP TAP
BERK SUX

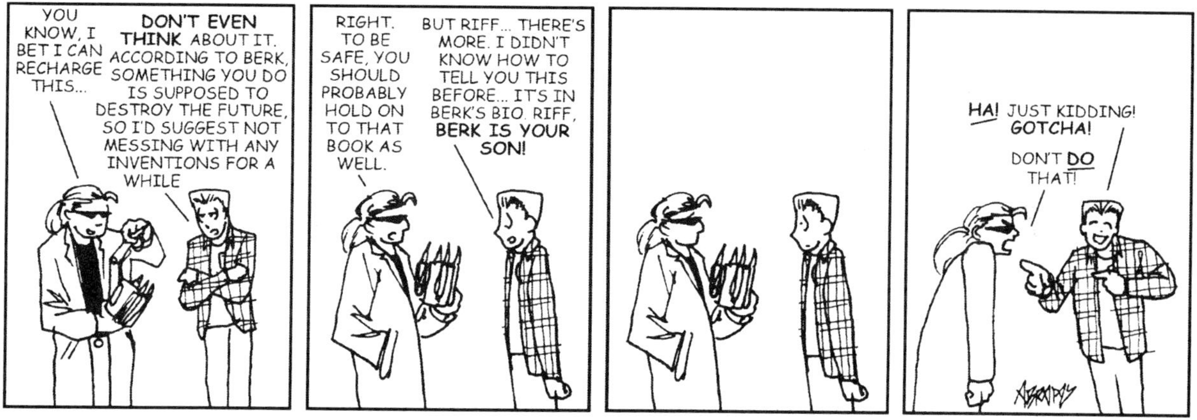
YOU KNOW, I BET I CAN RECHARGE THIS...
DON'T EVEN THINK ABOUT IT. ACCORDING TO BERK, SOMETHING YOU DO IS SUPPOSED TO DESTROY THE FUTURE, SO I'D SUGGEST NOT MESSING WITH ANY INVENTIONS FOR A WHILE
RIGHT. TO BE SAFE, YOU SHOULD PROBABLY HOLD ON TO THAT BOOK AS WELL.
BUT RIFF... THERE'S MORE. I DIDN'T KNOW HOW TO TELL YOU THIS BEFORE... IT'S IN BERK'S BIO. RIFF, BERK IS YOUR SON!
HA! JUST KIDDING! GOTCHA!
DON'T DO THAT!

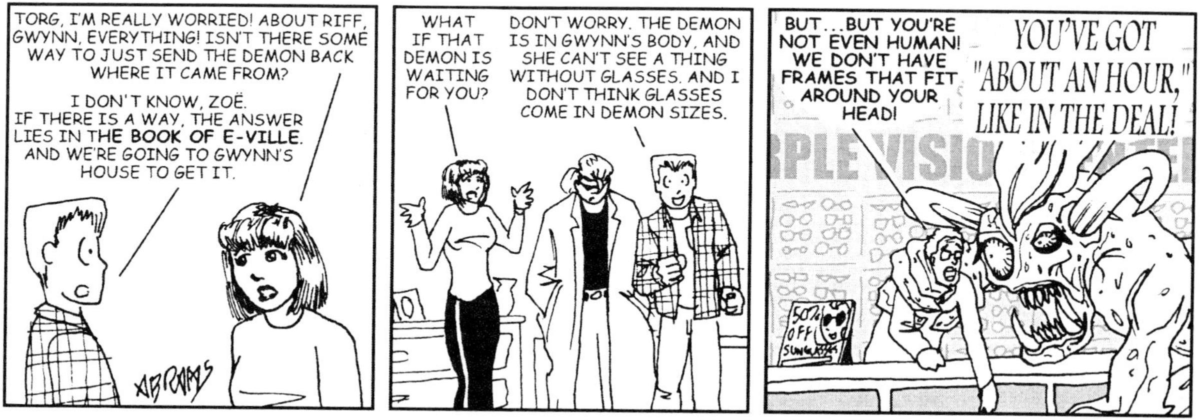
TORG, I'M REALLY WORRIED! ABOUT RIFF, GWYNN, EVERYTHING! ISN'T THERE SOME WAY TO JUST SEND THE DEMON BACK WHERE IT CAME FROM?
I DON'T KNOW, ZOË. IF THERE IS A WAY, THE ANSWER LIES IN THE BOOK OF E-VILLE. AND WE'RE GOING TO GWYNN'S HOUSE TO GET IT.
WHAT IF THAT DEMON IS WAITING FOR YOU?
DON'T WORRY. THE DEMON IS IN GWYNN'S BODY, AND SHE CAN'T SEE A THING WITHOUT GLASSES. AND I DON'T THINK GLASSES COME IN DEMON SIZES.
BUT...BUT YOU'RE NOT EVEN HUMAN! WE DON'T HAVE FRAMES THAT FIT AROUND YOUR HEAD!
YOU'VE GOT "ABOUT AN HOUR," LIKE IN THE DEAL!
50% OFF SUNGLASSES

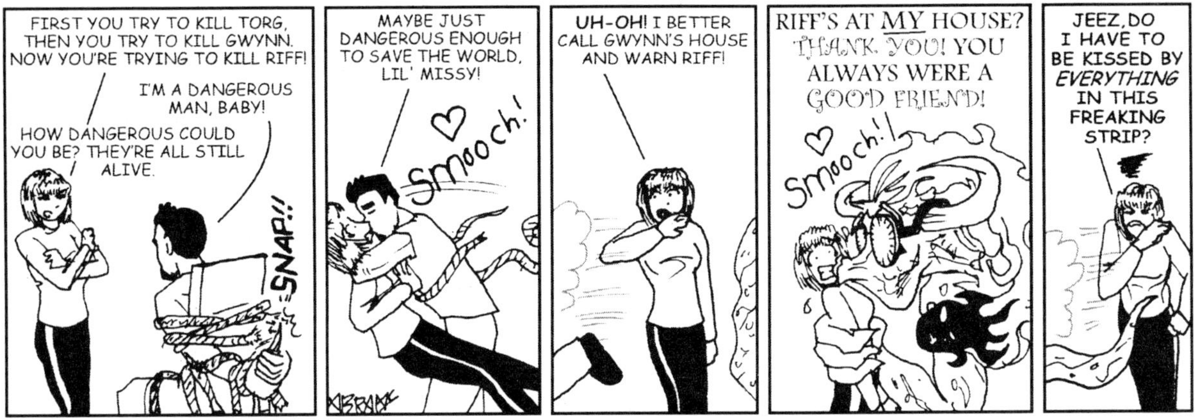
FIRST YOU TRY TO KILL TORG, THEN YOU TRY TO KILL GWYNN. NOW YOU'RE TRYING TO KILL RIFF!
I'M A DANGEROUS MAN, BABY!
HOW DANGEROUS COULD YOU BE? THEY'RE ALL STILL ALIVE.
SNAP!!
MAYBE JUST DANGEROUS ENOUGH TO SAVE THE WORLD, LIL' MISSY!
Smooch!
UH-OH! I BETTER CALL GWYNN'S HOUSE AND WARN RIFF!
RIFF'S AT MY HOUSE? THANK YOU! YOU ALWAYS WERE A GOOD FRIEND!
Smooch!
JEEZ, DO I HAVE TO BE KISSED BY EVERYTHING IN THIS FREAKING STRIP?

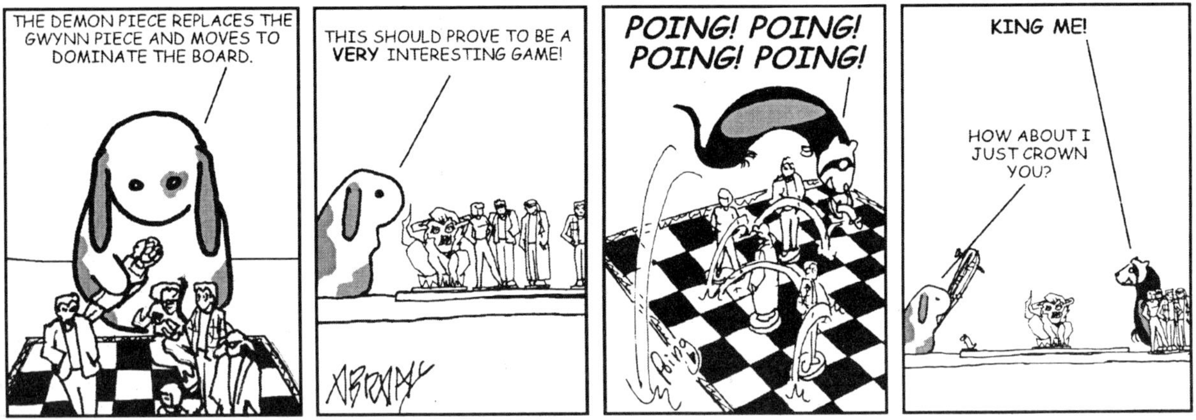
THE DEMON PIECE REPLACES THE GWYNN PIECE AND MOVES TO DOMINATE THE BOARD.
THIS SHOULD PROVE TO BE A VERY INTERESTING GAME!
POING! POING! POING! POING!
Poing
KING ME!
HOW ABOUT I JUST CROWN YOU?

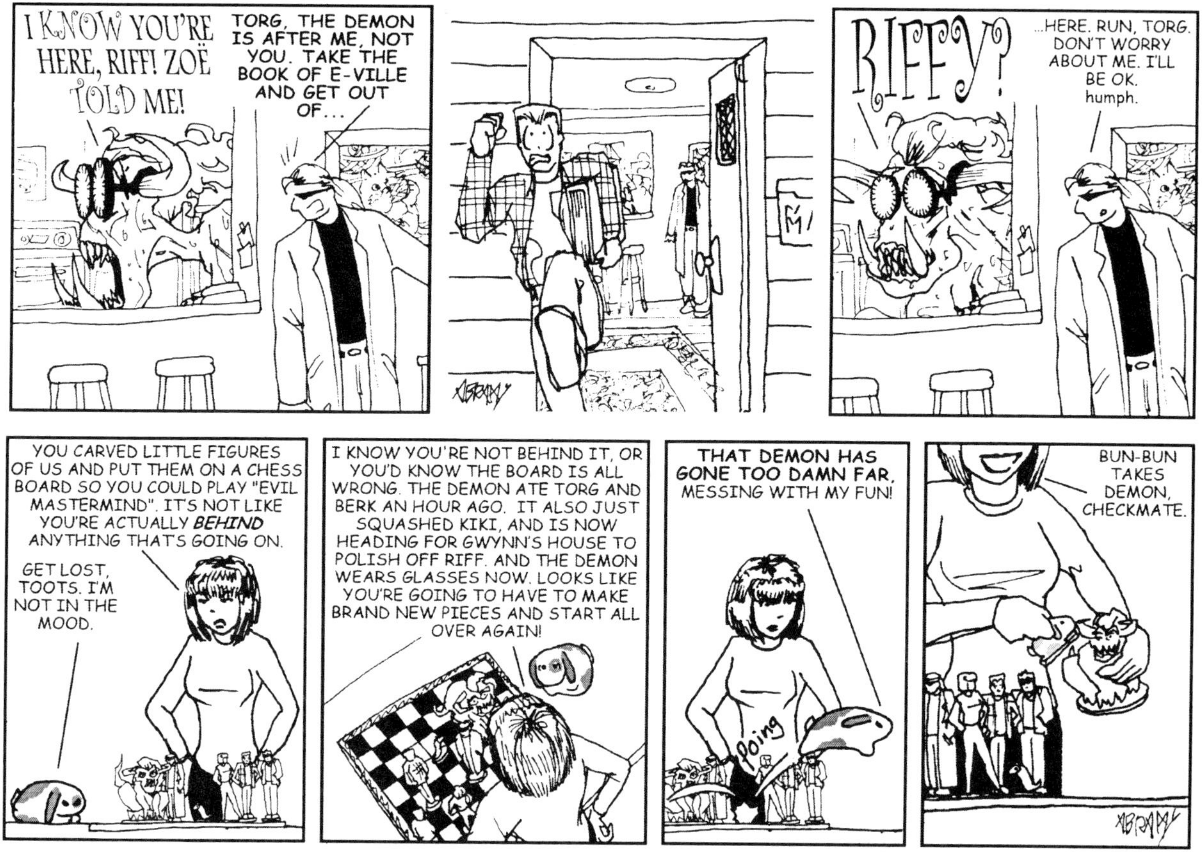
I KNOW YOU'RE HERE, RIFF! ZOË TOLD ME!
TORG, THE DEMON IS AFTER ME, NOT YOU. TAKE THE BOOK OF E-VILLE AND GET OUT OF...
RIFFY?
...HERE. RUN, TORG. DON'T WORRY ABOUT ME. I'LL BE OK. humph.
YOU CARVED LITTLE FIGURES OF US AND PUT THEM ON A CHESS BOARD SO YOU COULD PLAY "EVIL MASTERMIND". IT'S NOT LIKE YOU'RE ACTUALLY BEHIND ANYTHING THAT'S GOING ON.
GET LOST, TOOTS. I'M NOT IN THE MOOD.
I KNOW YOU'RE NOT BEHIND IT, OR YOU'D KNOW THE BOARD IS ALL WRONG. THE DEMON ATE TORG AND BERK AN HOUR AGO. IT ALSO JUST SQUASHED KIKI, AND IS NOW HEADING FOR GWYNN'S HOUSE TO POLISH OFF RIFF. AND THE DEMON WEARS GLASSES NOW. LOOKS LIKE YOU'RE GOING TO HAVE TO MAKE BRAND NEW PIECES AND START ALL OVER AGAIN!
THAT DEMON HAS GONE TOO DAMN FAR, MESSING WITH MY FUN!
poing
BUN-BUN TAKES DEMON, CHECKMATE.

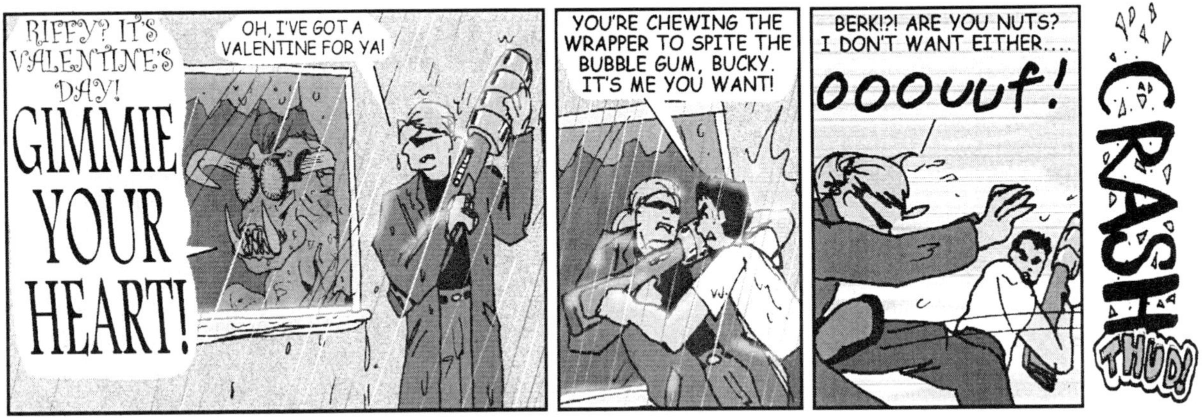
RIFFY? IT'S VALENTINE'S DAY!
GIMMIE YOUR HEART!
OH, I'VE GOT A VALENTINE FOR YA!
YOU'RE CHEWING THE WRAPPER TO SPITE THE BUBBLE GUM, BUCKY. IT'S ME YOU WANT!
BERK!?! ARE YOU NUTS? I DON'T WANT EITHER....
OOOUUF!
CRASH
THUD!

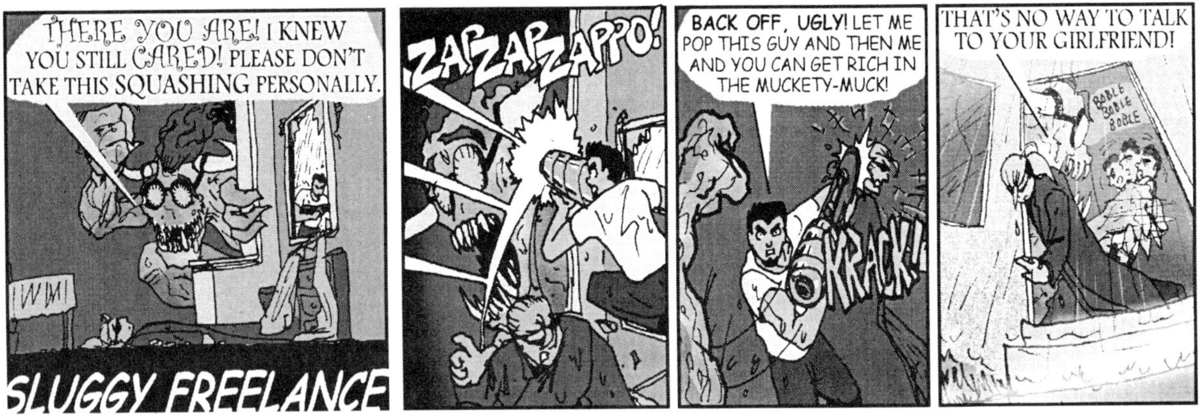
THERE YOU ARE! I KNEW YOU STILL CARED! PLEASE DON'T TAKE THIS SQUASHING PERSONALLY.
SLUGGY FREELANCE
ZAPZAPZAPPO!
BACK OFF, UGLY! LET ME POP THIS GUY AND THEN ME AND YOU CAN GET RICH IN THE MUCKETY-MUCK!
KRACK!
THAT'S NO WAY TO TALK TO YOUR GIRLFRIEND!
BOBLE BOBLE BOBLE

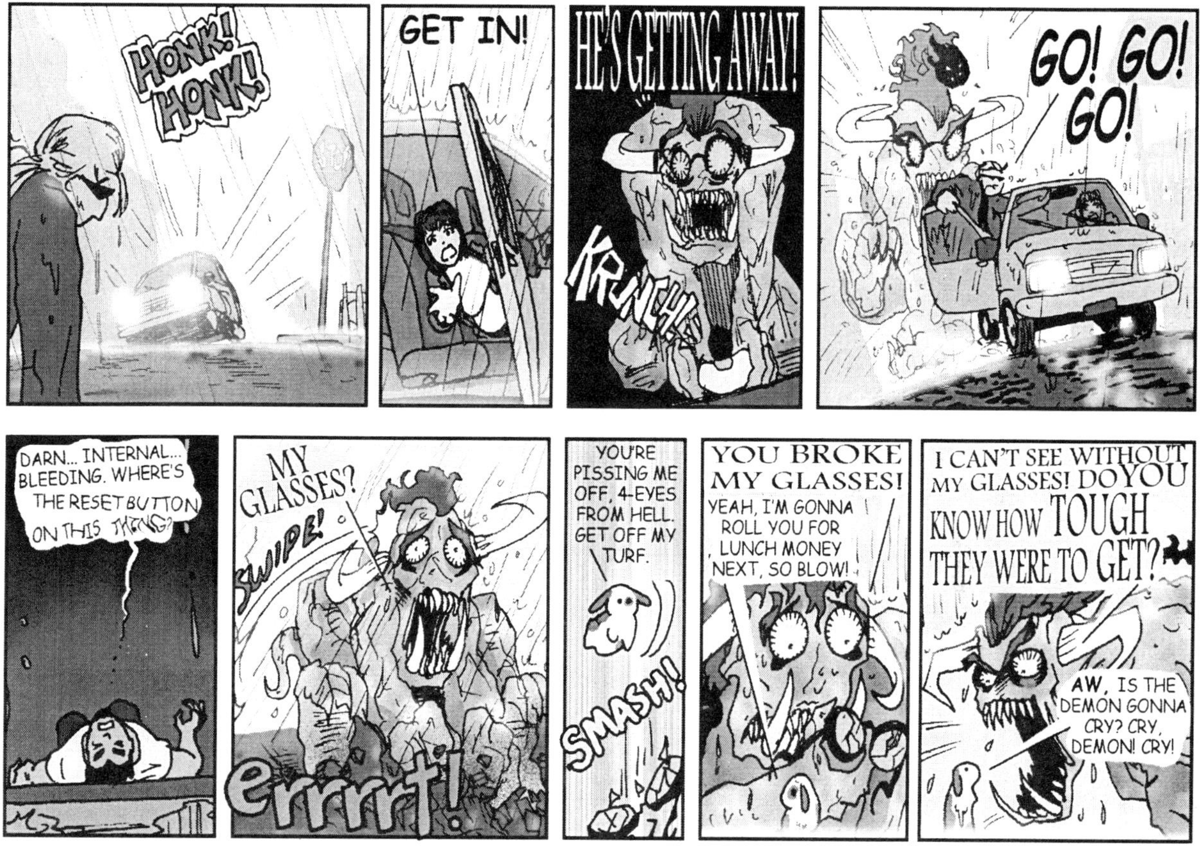

HONK! HONK!
GET IN!
HE'S GETTING AWAY!
KRUNCH!
GO! GO! GO!
DARN... INTERNAL... BLEEDING. WHERE'S THE RESET BUTTON ON THIS THING?
MY GLASSES?
SWIPE!
errrrt!
YOU'RE PISSING ME OFF, 4-EYES FROM HELL. GET OFF MY TURF.
SMASH!
YOU BROKE MY GLASSES!
YEAH, I'M GONNA ROLL YOU FOR LUNCH MONEY NEXT, SO BLOW!
I CAN'T SEE WITHOUT MY GLASSES! DO YOU KNOW HOW TOUGH THEY WERE TO GET?
AW, IS THE DEMON GONNA CRY? CRY, DEMON! CRY!

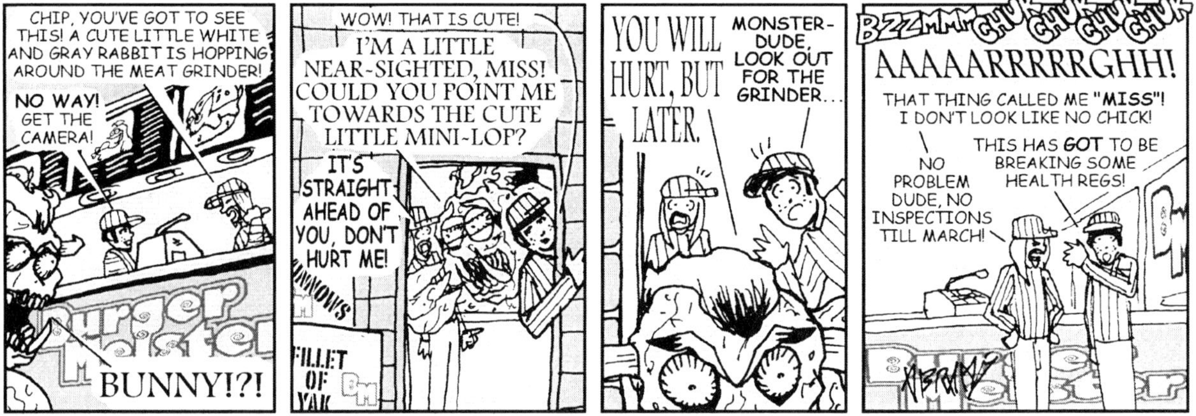

CHIP, YOU'VE GOT TO SEE THIS! A CUTE LITTLE WHITE AND GRAY RABBIT IS HOPPING AROUND THE MEAT GRINDER!
NO WAY! GET THE CAMERA!
BUNNY!?!
WOW! THAT IS CUTE!
I'M A LITTLE NEAR-SIGHTED, MISS! COULD YOU POINT ME TOWARDS THE CUTE LITTLE MINI-LOP?
IT'S STRAIGHT AHEAD OF YOU, DON'T HURT ME!
FILLET OF YAK
YOU WILL HURT, BUT LATER.
MONSTER-DUDE, LOOK OUT FOR THE GRINDER...
BZZMMM CHUK CHUK CHUK CHUK
AAAAAARRRRRGHH!
THAT THING CALLED ME **"MISS"**! I DON'T LOOK LIKE NO CHICK!
THIS HAS **GOT** TO BE BREAKING SOME HEALTH REGS!
NO PROBLEM DUDE, NO INSPECTIONS TILL MARCH!

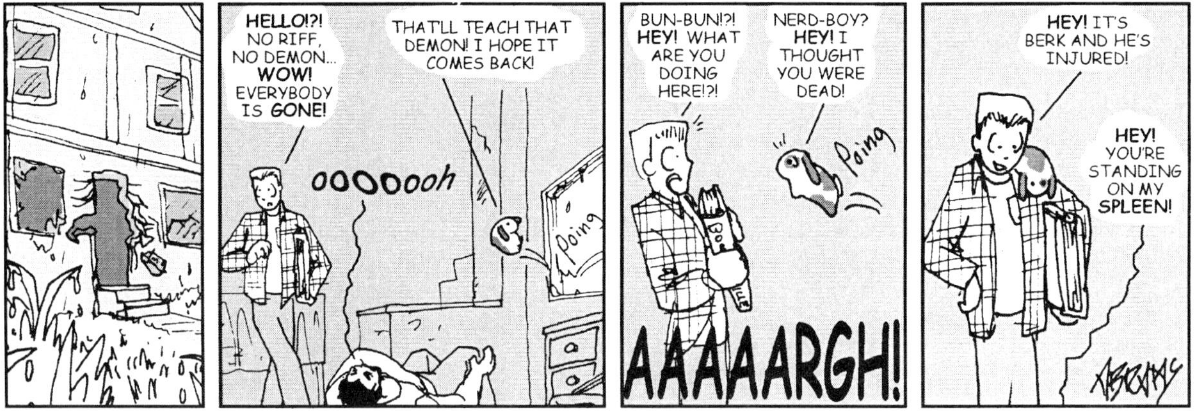

HELLO!?! NO RIFF, NO DEMON... **WOW!** EVERYBODY IS **GONE!**
OOOOOooh
THAT'LL TEACH THAT DEMON! I HOPE IT COMES BACK!
Poing
BUN-BUN!?! **HEY!** WHAT ARE YOU DOING HERE!?!
NERD-BOY? **HEY!** I THOUGHT YOU WERE DEAD!
Poing
AAAAARGH!
HEY! IT'S BERK AND HE'S INJURED!
HEY! YOU'RE STANDING ON MY **SPLEEN!**

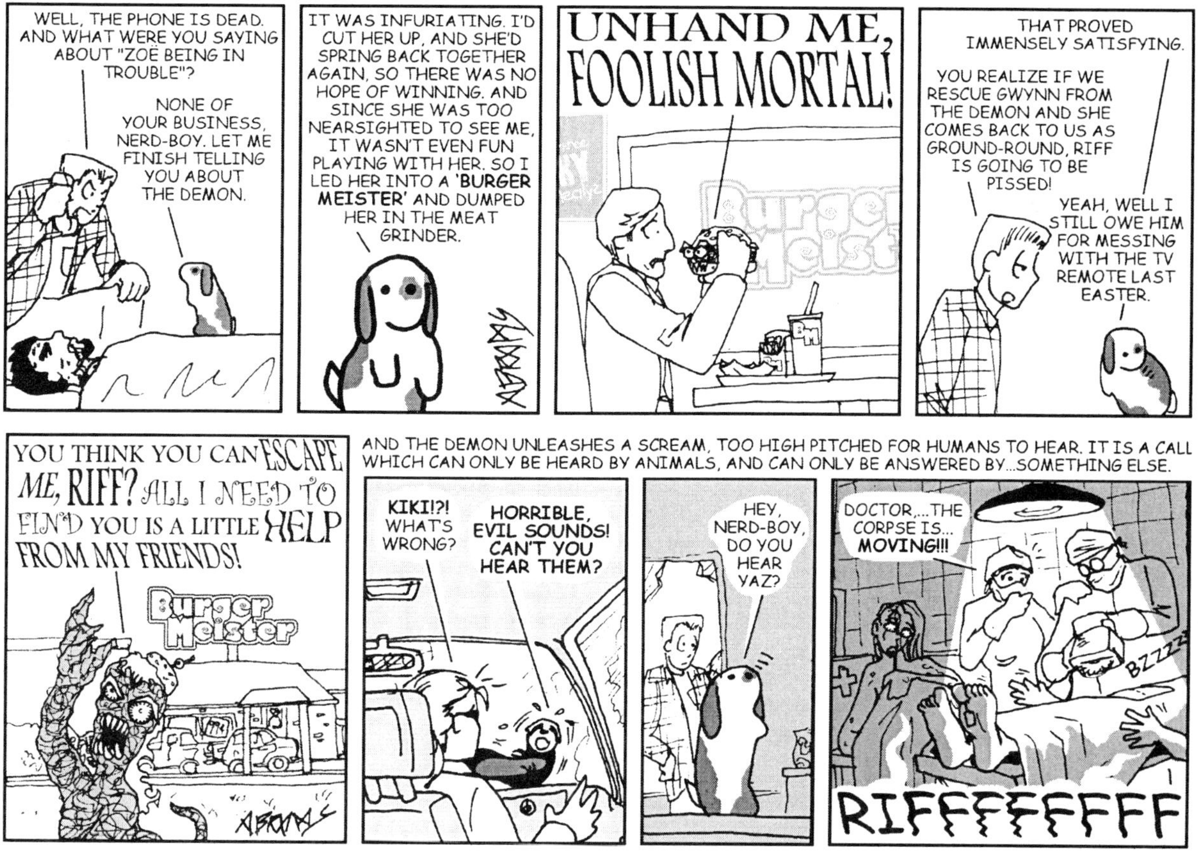
WELL, THE PHONE IS DEAD. AND WHAT WERE YOU SAYING ABOUT "ZOË BEING IN TROUBLE"?
NONE OF YOUR BUSINESS, NERD-BOY. LET ME FINISH TELLING YOU ABOUT THE DEMON.
IT WAS INFURIATING. I'D CUT HER UP, AND SHE'D SPRING BACK TOGETHER AGAIN, SO THERE WAS NO HOPE OF WINNING. AND SINCE SHE WAS TOO NEARSIGHTED TO SEE ME, IT WASN'T EVEN FUN PLAYING WITH HER. SO I LED HER INTO A 'BURGER MEISTER' AND DUMPED HER IN THE MEAT GRINDER.
UNHAND ME, FOOLISH MORTAL!
THAT PROVED IMMENSELY SATISFYING.
YOU REALIZE IF WE RESCUE GWYNN FROM THE DEMON AND SHE COMES BACK TO US AS GROUND-ROUND, RIFF IS GOING TO BE PISSED!
YEAH, WELL I STILL OWE HIM FOR MESSING WITH THE TV REMOTE LAST EASTER.
YOU THINK YOU CAN ESCAPE ME, RIFF? ALL I NEED TO FIND YOU IS A LITTLE HELP FROM MY FRIENDS!
Burger Meister
AND THE DEMON UNLEASHES A SCREAM, TOO HIGH PITCHED FOR HUMANS TO HEAR. IT IS A CALL WHICH CAN ONLY BE HEARD BY ANIMALS, AND CAN ONLY BE ANSWERED BY...SOMETHING ELSE.
KIKI!?! WHAT'S WRONG?
HORRIBLE, EVIL SOUNDS! CAN'T YOU HEAR THEM?
HEY, NERD-BOY, DO YOU HEAR YAZ?
DOCTOR,...THE CORPSE IS... MOVING!!!
BZZZZ
RIFFFFFFFF

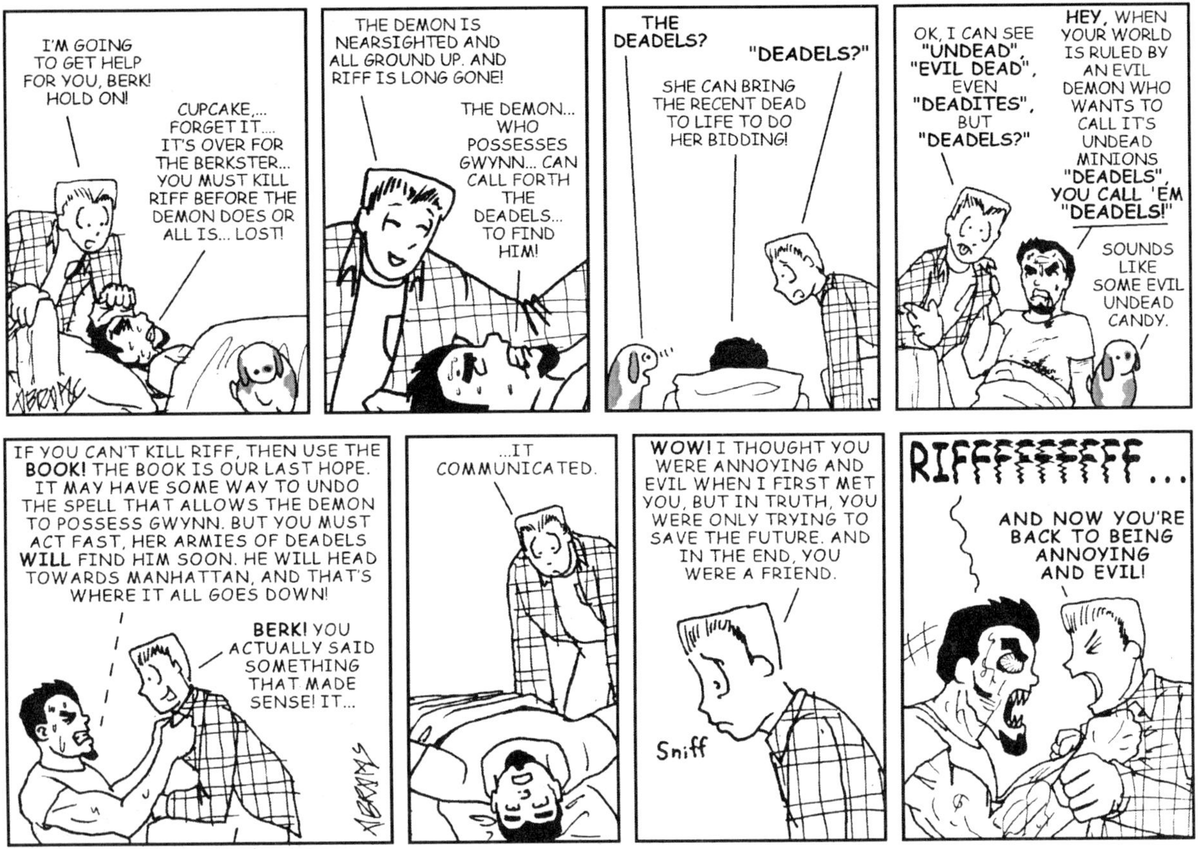
I'M GOING TO GET HELP FOR YOU, BERK! HOLD ON!
CUPCAKE,... FORGET IT.... IT'S OVER FOR THE BERKSTER... YOU MUST KILL RIFF BEFORE THE DEMON DOES OR ALL IS... LOST!
THE DEMON IS NEARSIGHTED AND ALL GROUND UP. AND RIFF IS LONG GONE!
THE DEMON... WHO POSSESSES GWYNN... CAN CALL FORTH THE DEADELS... TO FIND HIM!
THE DEADELS?
"DEADELS?"
SHE CAN BRING THE RECENT DEAD TO LIFE TO DO HER BIDDING!
OK, I CAN SEE "UNDEAD", "EVIL DEAD", EVEN "DEADITES", BUT "DEADELS?"
HEY, WHEN YOUR WORLD IS RULED BY AN EVIL DEMON WHO WANTS TO CALL IT'S UNDEAD MINIONS "DEADELS", YOU CALL 'EM "DEADELS!"
SOUNDS LIKE SOME EVIL UNDEAD CANDY.
IF YOU CAN'T KILL RIFF, THEN USE THE BOOK! THE BOOK IS OUR LAST HOPE. IT MAY HAVE SOME WAY TO UNDO THE SPELL THAT ALLOWS THE DEMON TO POSSESS GWYNN. BUT YOU MUST ACT FAST, HER ARMIES OF DEADELS WILL FIND HIM SOON. HE WILL HEAD TOWARDS MANHATTAN, AND THAT'S WHERE IT ALL GOES DOWN!
BERK! YOU ACTUALLY SAID SOMETHING THAT MADE SENSE! IT...
...IT COMMUNICATED.
WOW! I THOUGHT YOU WERE ANNOYING AND EVIL WHEN I FIRST MET YOU, BUT IN TRUTH, YOU WERE ONLY TRYING TO SAVE THE FUTURE. AND IN THE END, YOU WERE A FRIEND.
Sniff
RIFFFFFFFFF...
AND NOW YOU'RE BACK TO BEING ANNOYING AND EVIL!

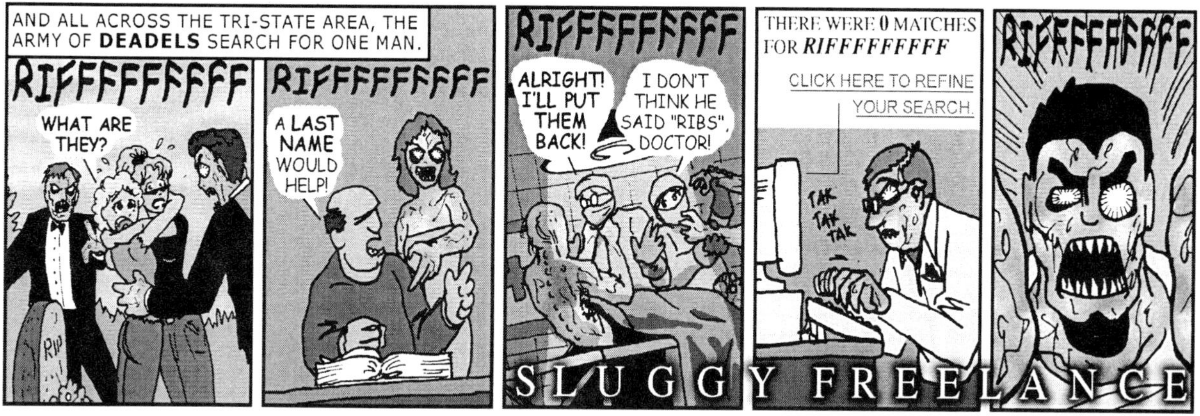
AND ALL ACROSS THE TRI-STATE AREA, THE ARMY OF DEADELS SEARCH FOR ONE MAN.
RIFFFFFFFFF
WHAT ARE THEY?
RIP
RIFFFFFFFFF
A LAST NAME WOULD HELP!
RIFFFFFFFFF
ALRIGHT! I'LL PUT THEM BACK!
I DON'T THINK HE SAID "RIBS", DOCTOR!
THERE WERE 0 MATCHES FOR RIFFFFFFFFF
CLICK HERE TO REFINE YOUR SEARCH.
TAK TAK TAK
RIFFFFFFFFF
SLUGGY FREELANCE

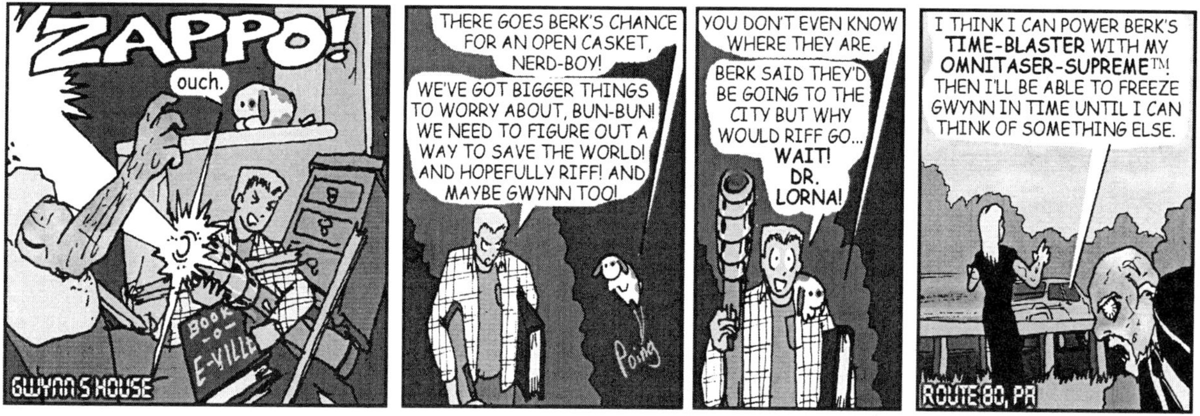
ZAPPO!
ouch.
BOOK-O-E-VILLE
GWYNN'S HOUSE
THERE GOES BERK'S CHANCE FOR AN OPEN CASKET, NERD-BOY!
WE'VE GOT BIGGER THINGS TO WORRY ABOUT, BUN-BUN! WE NEED TO FIGURE OUT A WAY TO SAVE THE WORLD! AND HOPEFULLY RIFF! AND MAYBE GWYNN TOO!
Poing
YOU DON'T EVEN KNOW WHERE THEY ARE.
BERK SAID THEY'D BE GOING TO THE CITY BUT WHY WOULD RIFF GO... WAIT! DR. LORNA!
I THINK I CAN POWER BERK'S TIME-BLASTER WITH MY OMNITASER-SUPREME™! THEN I'LL BE ABLE TO FREEZE GWYNN IN TIME UNTIL I CAN THINK OF SOMETHING ELSE.
ROUTE 80, PA

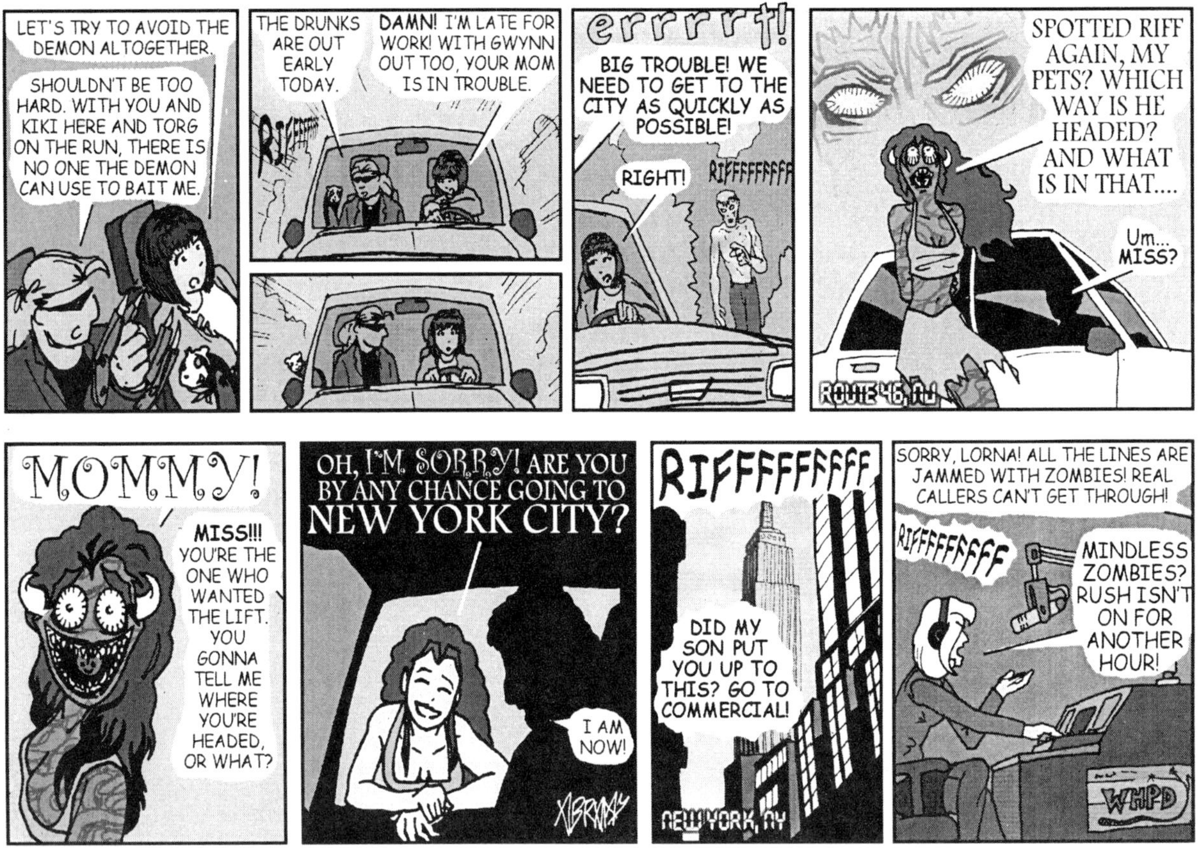
LET'S TRY TO AVOID THE DEMON ALTOGETHER.
SHOULDN'T BE TOO HARD. WITH YOU AND KIKI HERE AND TORG ON THE RUN, THERE IS NO ONE THE DEMON CAN USE TO BAIT ME.
THE DRUNKS ARE OUT EARLY TODAY.
DAMN! I'M LATE FOR WORK! WITH GWYNN OUT TOO, YOUR MOM IS IN TROUBLE.
errrrrt!
BIG TROUBLE! WE NEED TO GET TO THE CITY AS QUICKLY AS POSSIBLE!
RIGHT!
RIFFFFFFFFF
SPOTTED RIFF AGAIN, MY PETS? WHICH WAY IS HE HEADED? AND WHAT IS IN THAT....
Um... MISS?
ROUTE 46, NJ
MOMMY!
MISS!!! YOU'RE THE ONE WHO WANTED THE LIFT. YOU GONNA TELL ME WHERE YOU'RE HEADED, OR WHAT?
OH, I'M SORRY! ARE YOU BY ANY CHANCE GOING TO NEW YORK CITY?
I AM NOW!
RIFFFFFFFFF
DID MY SON PUT YOU UP TO THIS? GO TO COMMERCIAL!
NEW YORK, NY
SORRY, LORNA! ALL THE LINES ARE JAMMED WITH ZOMBIES! REAL CALLERS CAN'T GET THROUGH!
RIFFFFFFFFF
MINDLESS ZOMBIES? RUSH ISN'T ON FOR ANOTHER HOUR!
WHPD

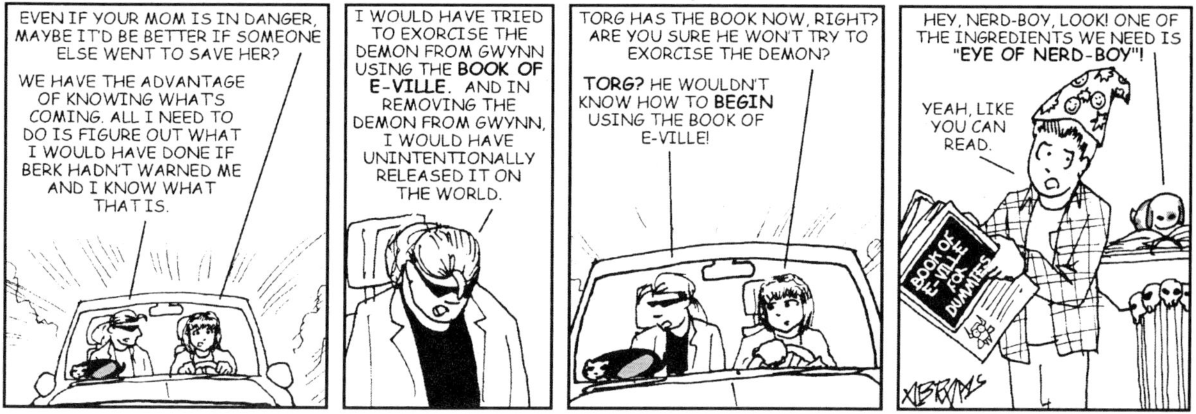
EVEN IF YOUR MOM IS IN DANGER, MAYBE IT'D BE BETTER IF SOMEONE ELSE WENT TO SAVE HER?
WE HAVE THE ADVANTAGE OF KNOWING WHAT'S COMING. ALL I NEED TO DO IS FIGURE OUT WHAT I WOULD HAVE DONE IF BERK HADN'T WARNED ME AND I KNOW WHAT THAT IS.
I WOULD HAVE TRIED TO EXORCISE THE DEMON FROM GWYNN USING THE BOOK OF E-VILLE. AND IN REMOVING THE DEMON FROM GWYNN, I WOULD HAVE UNINTENTIONALLY RELEASED IT ON THE WORLD.
TORG HAS THE BOOK NOW, RIGHT? ARE YOU SURE HE WON'T TRY TO EXORCISE THE DEMON?
TORG? HE WOULDN'T KNOW HOW TO BEGIN USING THE BOOK OF E-VILLE!
HEY, NERD-BOY, LOOK! ONE OF THE INGREDIENTS WE NEED IS "EYE OF NERD-BOY"!
YEAH, LIKE YOU CAN READ.
BOOK OF E-VILLE FOR DUMMIES

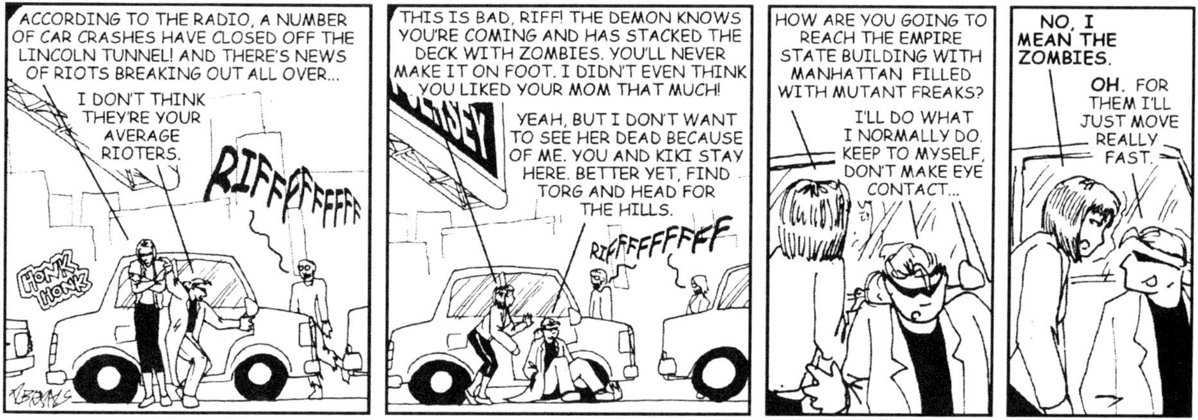
ACCORDING TO THE RADIO, A NUMBER OF CAR CRASHES HAVE CLOSED OFF THE LINCOLN TUNNEL! AND THERE'S NEWS OF RIOTS BREAKING OUT ALL OVER...
I DON'T THINK THEY'RE YOUR AVERAGE RIOTERS.
RIFFFFFFFF
HONK HONK
THIS IS BAD, RIFF! THE DEMON KNOWS YOU'RE COMING AND HAS STACKED THE DECK WITH ZOMBIES. YOU'LL NEVER MAKE IT ON FOOT. I DIDN'T EVEN THINK YOU LIKED YOUR MOM THAT MUCH!
YEAH, BUT I DON'T WANT TO SEE HER DEAD BECAUSE OF ME. YOU AND KIKI STAY HERE. BETTER YET, FIND TORG AND HEAD FOR THE HILLS.
RIFFFFFFFFF
HOW ARE YOU GOING TO REACH THE EMPIRE STATE BUILDING WITH MANHATTAN FILLED WITH MUTANT FREAKS?
I'LL DO WHAT I NORMALLY DO. KEEP TO MYSELF, DON'T MAKE EYE CONTACT...
NO, I MEAN THE ZOMBIES.
OH. FOR THEM I'LL JUST MOVE REALLY FAST.

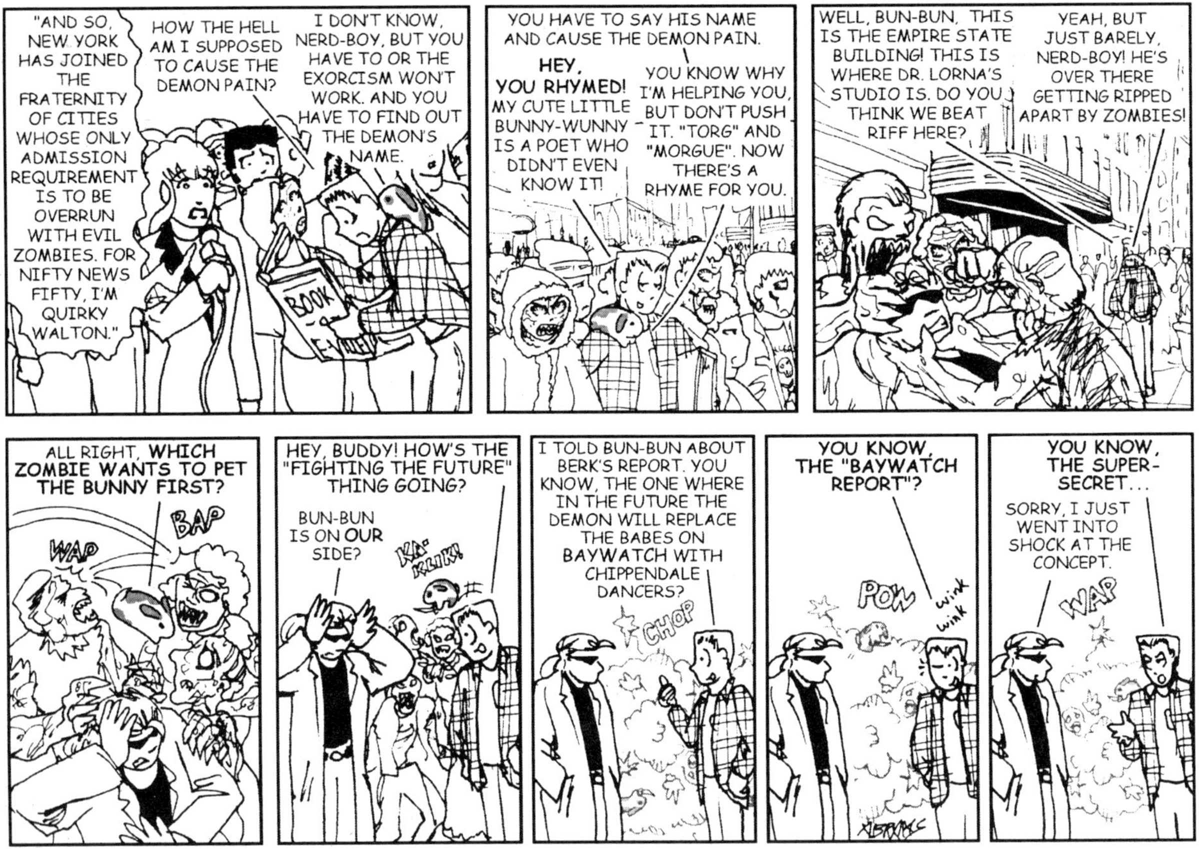
"AND SO, NEW YORK HAS JOINED THE FRATERNITY OF CITIES WHOSE ONLY ADMISSION REQUIREMENT IS TO BE OVERRUN WITH EVIL ZOMBIES. FOR NIFTY NEWS FIFTY, I'M QUIRKY WALTON."
HOW THE HELL AM I SUPPOSED TO CAUSE THE DEMON PAIN?
I DON'T KNOW, NERD-BOY, BUT YOU HAVE TO OR THE EXORCISM WON'T WORK. AND YOU HAVE TO FIND OUT THE DEMON'S NAME.
BOOK OF EVIL
YOU HAVE TO SAY HIS NAME AND CAUSE THE DEMON PAIN.
HEY, YOU RHYMED! MY CUTE LITTLE BUNNY-WUNNY IS A POET WHO DIDN'T EVEN KNOW IT!
YOU KNOW WHY I'M HELPING YOU, BUT DON'T PUSH IT. "TORG" AND "MORGUE". NOW THERE'S A RHYME FOR YOU.
WELL, BUN-BUN, THIS IS THE EMPIRE STATE BUILDING! THIS IS WHERE DR. LORNA'S STUDIO IS. DO YOU THINK WE BEAT RIFF HERE?
YEAH, BUT JUST BARELY, NERD-BOY! HE'S OVER THERE GETTING RIPPED APART BY ZOMBIES!
ALL RIGHT, WHICH ZOMBIE WANTS TO PET THE BUNNY FIRST?
WAP
BAP
HEY, BUDDY! HOW'S THE "FIGHTING THE FUTURE" THING GOING?
BUN-BUN IS ON OUR SIDE?
KA-KLIK!
I TOLD BUN-BUN ABOUT BERK'S REPORT. YOU KNOW, THE ONE WHERE IN THE FUTURE THE DEMON WILL REPLACE THE BABES ON BAYWATCH WITH CHIPPENDALE DANCERS?
CHOP
YOU KNOW, THE "BAYWATCH REPORT"?
POW
wink wink
YOU KNOW, THE SUPER-SECRET...
SORRY, I JUST WENT INTO SHOCK AT THE CONCEPT.
WAP

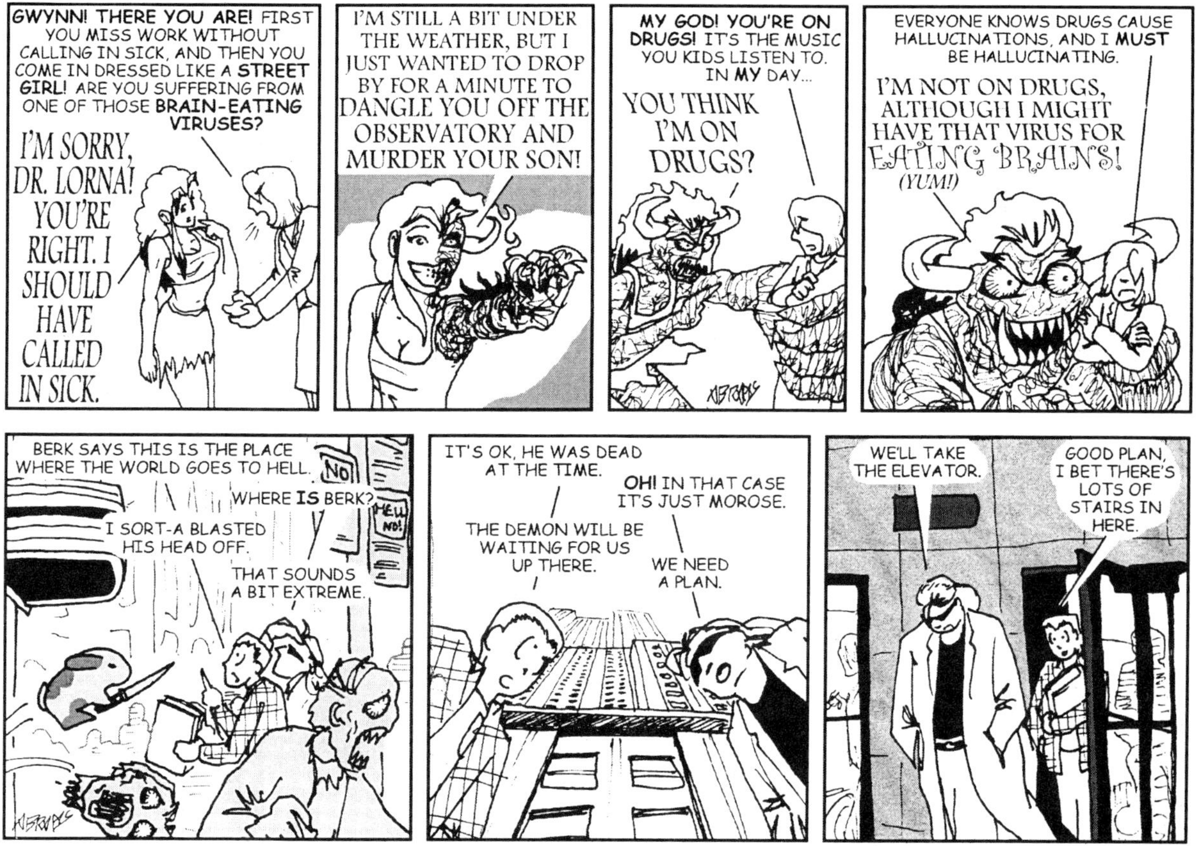
GWYNN! THERE YOU ARE! FIRST YOU MISS WORK WITHOUT CALLING IN SICK, AND THEN YOU COME IN DRESSED LIKE A STREET GIRL! ARE YOU SUFFERING FROM ONE OF THOSE BRAIN-EATING VIRUSES?
I'M SORRY, DR. LORNA! YOU'RE RIGHT. I SHOULD HAVE CALLED IN SICK.
I'M STILL A BIT UNDER THE WEATHER, BUT I JUST WANTED TO DROP BY FOR A MINUTE TO DANGLE YOU OFF THE OBSERVATORY AND MURDER YOUR SON!
YOU THINK I'M ON DRUGS?
MY GOD! YOU'RE ON DRUGS! IT'S THE MUSIC YOU KIDS LISTEN TO. IN MY DAY...
I'M NOT ON DRUGS, ALTHOUGH I MIGHT HAVE THAT VIRUS FOR EATING BRAINS!
(YUM!)
EVERYONE KNOWS DRUGS CAUSE HALLUCINATIONS, AND I MUST BE HALLUCINATING.
BERK SAYS THIS IS THE PLACE WHERE THE WORLD GOES TO HELL.
WHERE IS BERK?
I SORT-A BLASTED HIS HEAD OFF.
THAT SOUNDS A BIT EXTREME.
IT'S OK, HE WAS DEAD AT THE TIME.
OH! IN THAT CASE IT'S JUST MOROSE.
THE DEMON WILL BE WAITING FOR US UP THERE.
WE NEED A PLAN.
WE'LL TAKE THE ELEVATOR.
GOOD PLAN, I BET THERE'S LOTS OF STAIRS IN HERE.

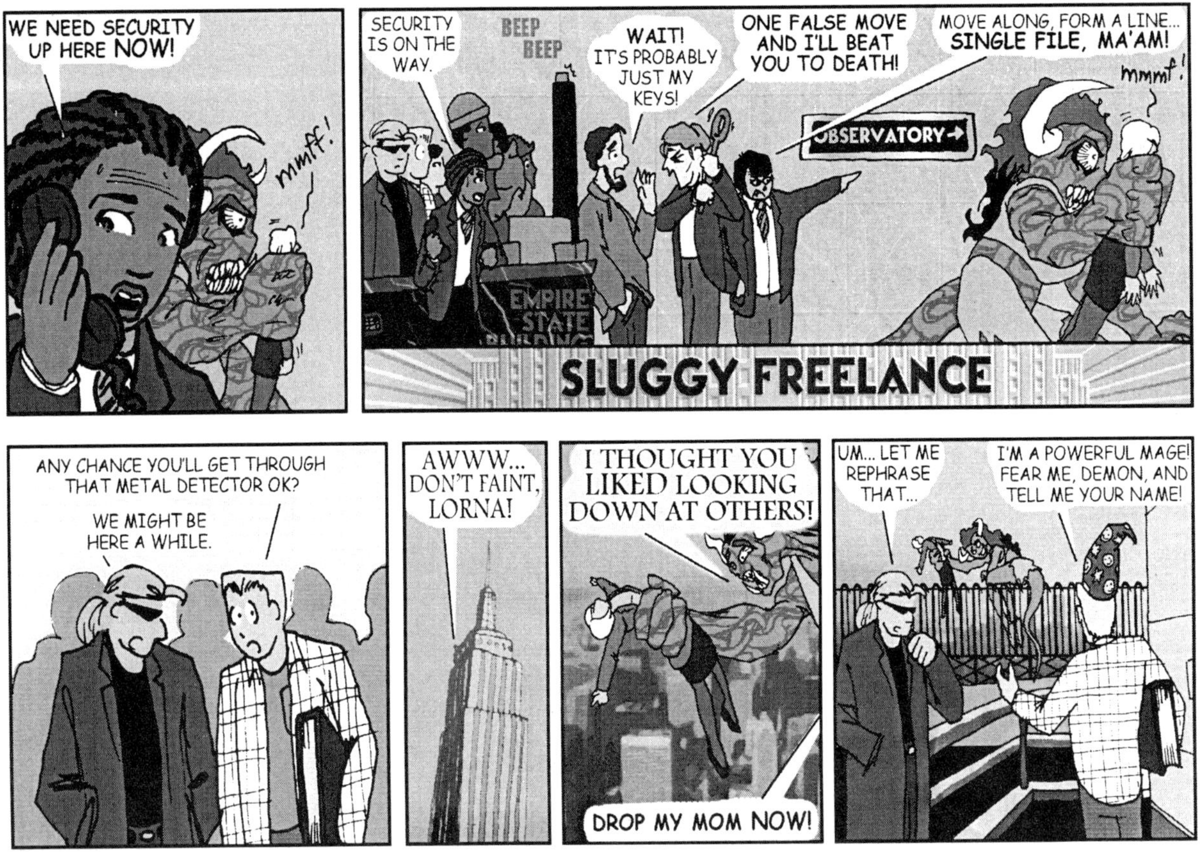

WE NEED SECURITY UP HERE NOW!
mmff!
SECURITY IS ON THE WAY.
BEEP BEEP
WAIT! IT'S PROBABLY JUST MY KEYS!
ONE FALSE MOVE AND I'LL BEAT YOU TO DEATH!
MOVE ALONG, FORM A LINE... SINGLE FILE, MA'AM!
mmmf!
OBSERVATORY
EMPIRE STATE BUILDING
SLUGGY FREELANCE
ANY CHANCE YOU'LL GET THROUGH THAT METAL DETECTOR OK?
WE MIGHT BE HERE A WHILE.
AWWW... DON'T FAINT, LORNA!
I THOUGHT YOU LIKED LOOKING DOWN AT OTHERS!
DROP MY MOM NOW!
UM... LET ME REPHRASE THAT...
I'M A POWERFUL MAGE! FEAR ME, DEMON, AND TELL ME YOUR NAME!

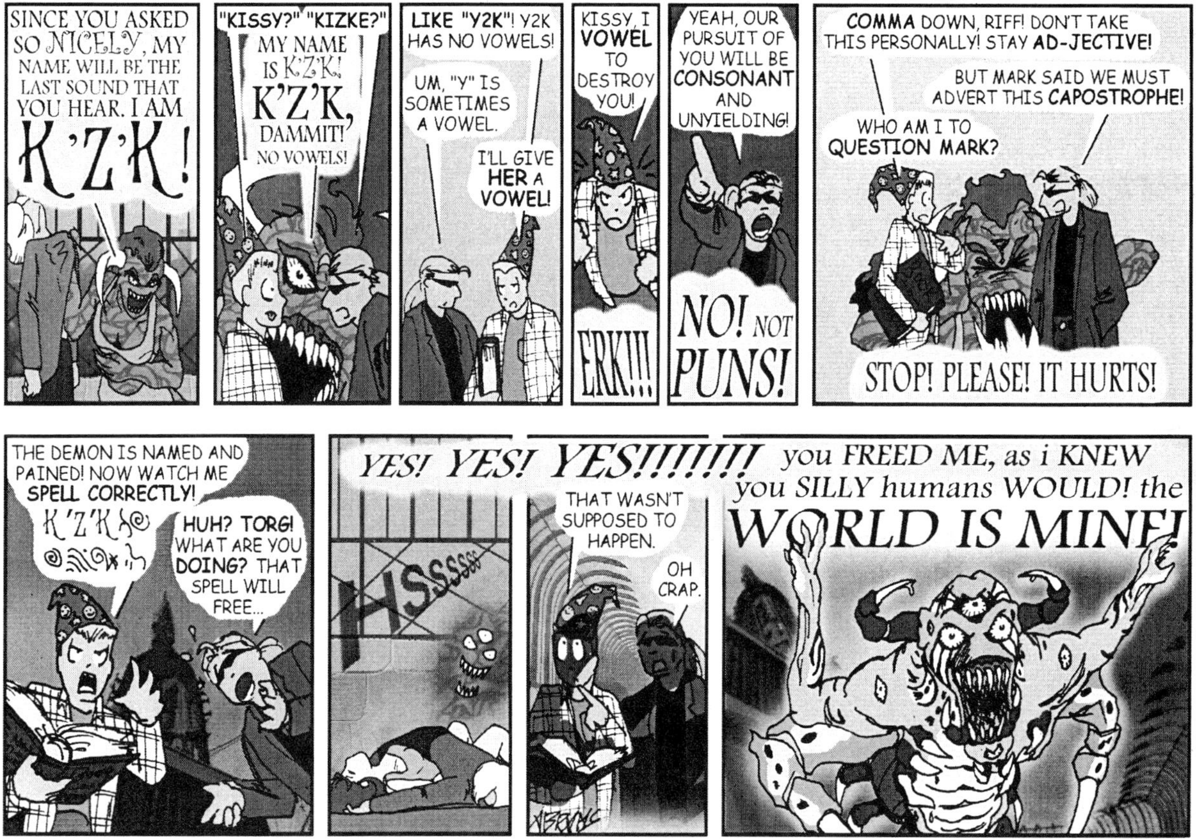
SINCE YOU ASKED SO NICELY, MY NAME WILL BE THE LAST SOUND THAT YOU HEAR. I AM K'Z'K!
"KISSY?" "KIZKE?"
MY NAME IS K'Z'K! K'Z'K, DAMMIT! NO VOWELS!
LIKE "Y2K"! Y2K HAS NO VOWELS!
UM, "Y" IS SOMETIMES A VOWEL.
I'LL GIVE HER A VOWEL!
KISSY, I VOWEL TO DESTROY YOU!
ERK!!!
YEAH, OUR PURSUIT OF YOU WILL BE CONSONANT AND UNYIELDING!
NO! NOT PUNS!
COMMA DOWN, RIFF! DON'T TAKE THIS PERSONALLY! STAY AD-JECTIVE!
BUT MARK SAID WE MUST ADVERT THIS CAPOSTROPHE!
WHO AM I TO QUESTION MARK?
STOP! PLEASE! IT HURTS!
THE DEMON IS NAMED AND PAINED! NOW WATCH ME SPELL CORRECTLY!
HUH? TORG! WHAT ARE YOU DOING? THAT SPELL WILL FREE...
HSSSSS
YES! YES! YES!!!!!!!!
THAT WASN'T SUPPOSED TO HAPPEN.
OH CRAP.
you FREED ME, as i KNEW you SILLY humans WOULD! the WORLD IS MINE!

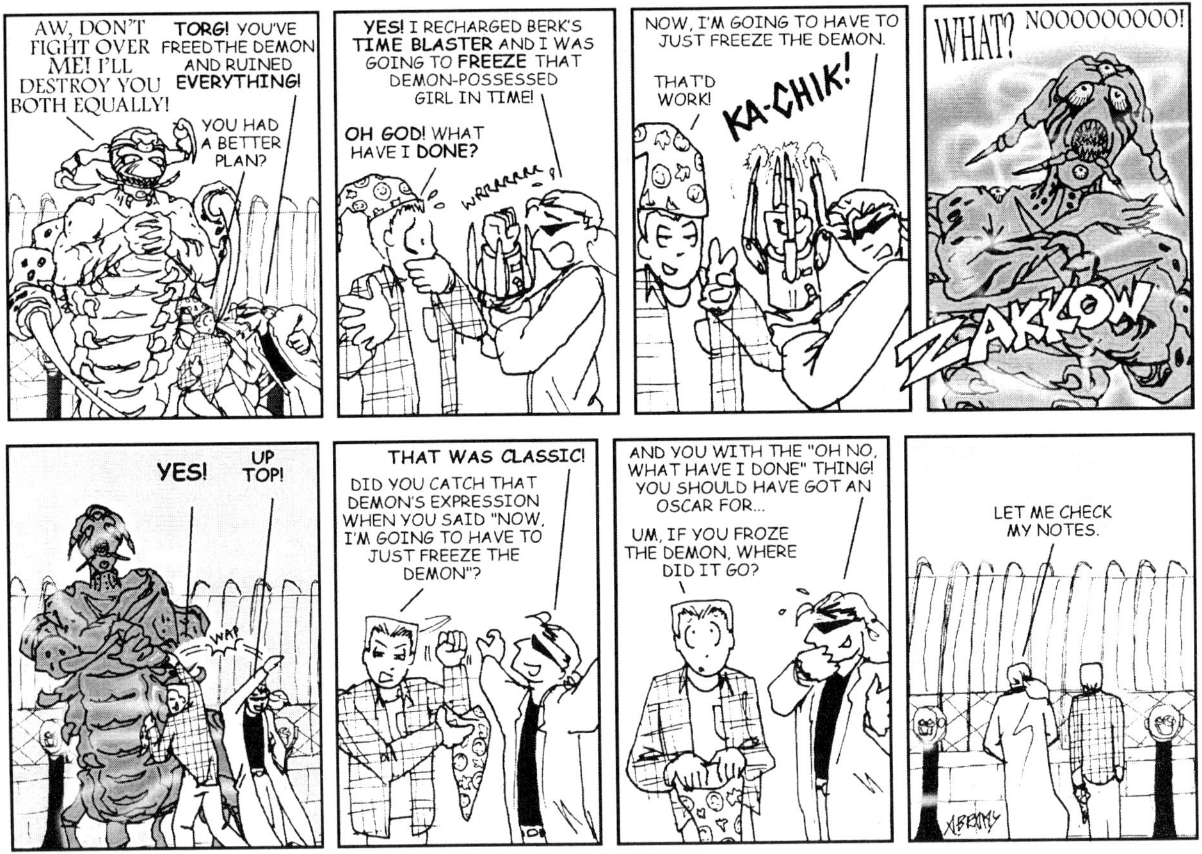
AW, DON'T FIGHT OVER ME! I'LL DESTROY YOU BOTH EQUALLY!
TORG! YOU'VE FREED THE DEMON AND RUINED EVERYTHING!
YOU HAD A BETTER PLAN?
YES! I RECHARGED BERK'S TIME BLASTER AND I WAS GOING TO FREEZE THAT DEMON-POSSESSED GIRL IN TIME!
OH GOD! WHAT HAVE I DONE?
WRRRRRRR
NOW, I'M GOING TO HAVE TO JUST FREEZE THE DEMON.
THAT'D WORK!
KA-CHIK!
WHAT? NOOOOOOOOO!
ZAKKOW
YES!
UP TOP!
WAP
THAT WAS CLASSIC!
DID YOU CATCH THAT DEMON'S EXPRESSION WHEN YOU SAID "NOW, I'M GOING TO HAVE TO JUST FREEZE THE DEMON"?
AND YOU WITH THE "OH NO, WHAT HAVE I DONE" THING! YOU SHOULD HAVE GOT AN OSCAR FOR...
UM, IF YOU FROZE THE DEMON, WHERE DID IT GO?
LET ME CHECK MY NOTES.

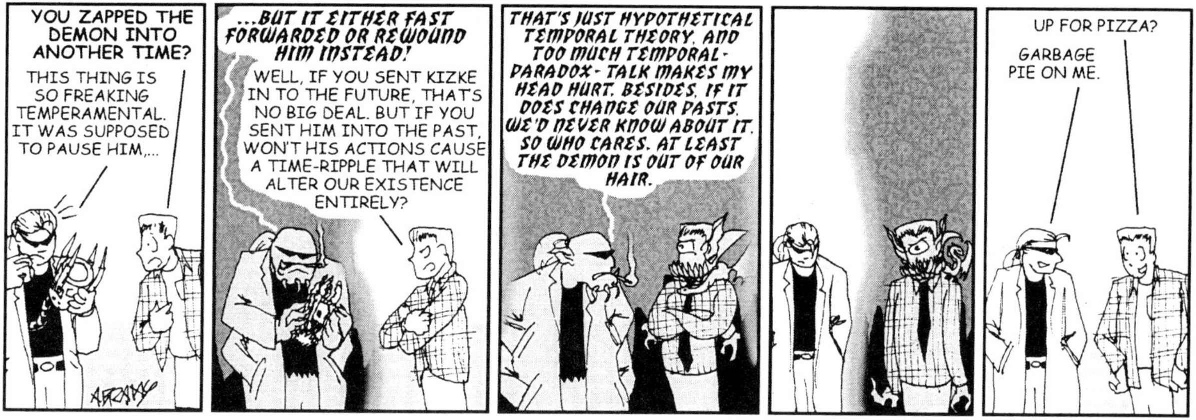

YOU ZAPPED THE DEMON INTO ANOTHER TIME?
THIS THING IS SO FREAKING TEMPERAMENTAL. IT WAS SUPPOSED TO PAUSE HIM,...
...BUT IT EITHER FAST FORWARDED OR REWOUND HIM INSTEAD!
WELL, IF YOU SENT KIZKE IN TO THE FUTURE, THAT'S NO BIG DEAL. BUT IF YOU SENT HIM INTO THE PAST, WON'T HIS ACTIONS CAUSE A TIME-RIPPLE THAT WILL ALTER OUR EXISTENCE ENTIRELY?
THAT'S JUST HYPOTHETICAL TEMPORAL THEORY, AND TOO MUCH TEMPORAL-PARADOX-TALK MAKES MY HEAD HURT. BESIDES, IF IT DOES CHANGE OUR PASTS, WE'D NEVER KNOW ABOUT IT. SO WHO CARES. AT LEAST THE DEMON IS OUT OF OUR HAIR.
UP FOR PIZZA?
GARBAGE PIE ON ME.

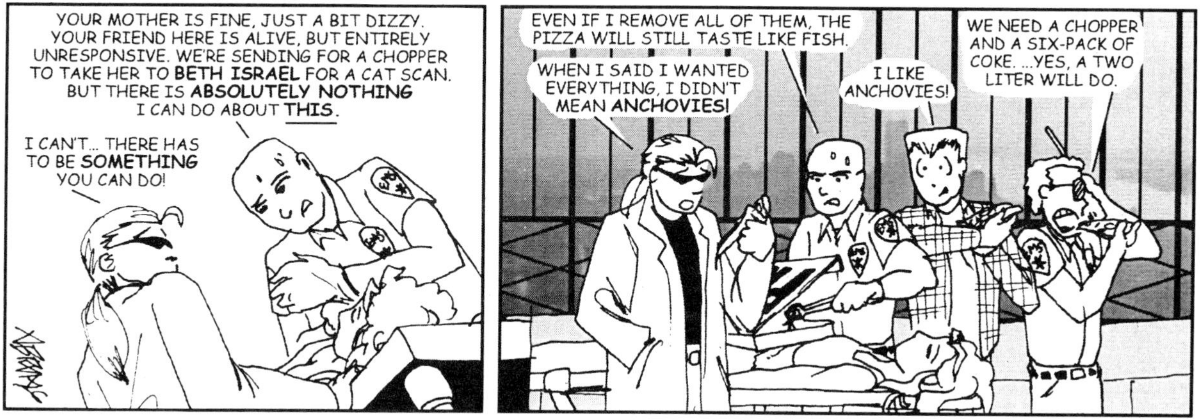

YOUR MOTHER IS FINE, JUST A BIT DIZZY. YOUR FRIEND HERE IS ALIVE, BUT ENTIRELY UNRESPONSIVE. WE'RE SENDING FOR A CHOPPER TO TAKE HER TO BETH ISRAEL FOR A CAT SCAN. BUT THERE IS ABSOLUTELY NOTHING I CAN DO ABOUT THIS.
I CAN'T... THERE HAS TO BE SOMETHING YOU CAN DO!
WHEN I SAID I WANTED EVERYTHING, I DIDN'T MEAN ANCHOVIES!
EVEN IF I REMOVE ALL OF THEM, THE PIZZA WILL STILL TASTE LIKE FISH.
I LIKE ANCHOVIES!
WE NEED A CHOPPER AND A SIX-PACK OF COKE. ...YES, A TWO LITER WILL DO.

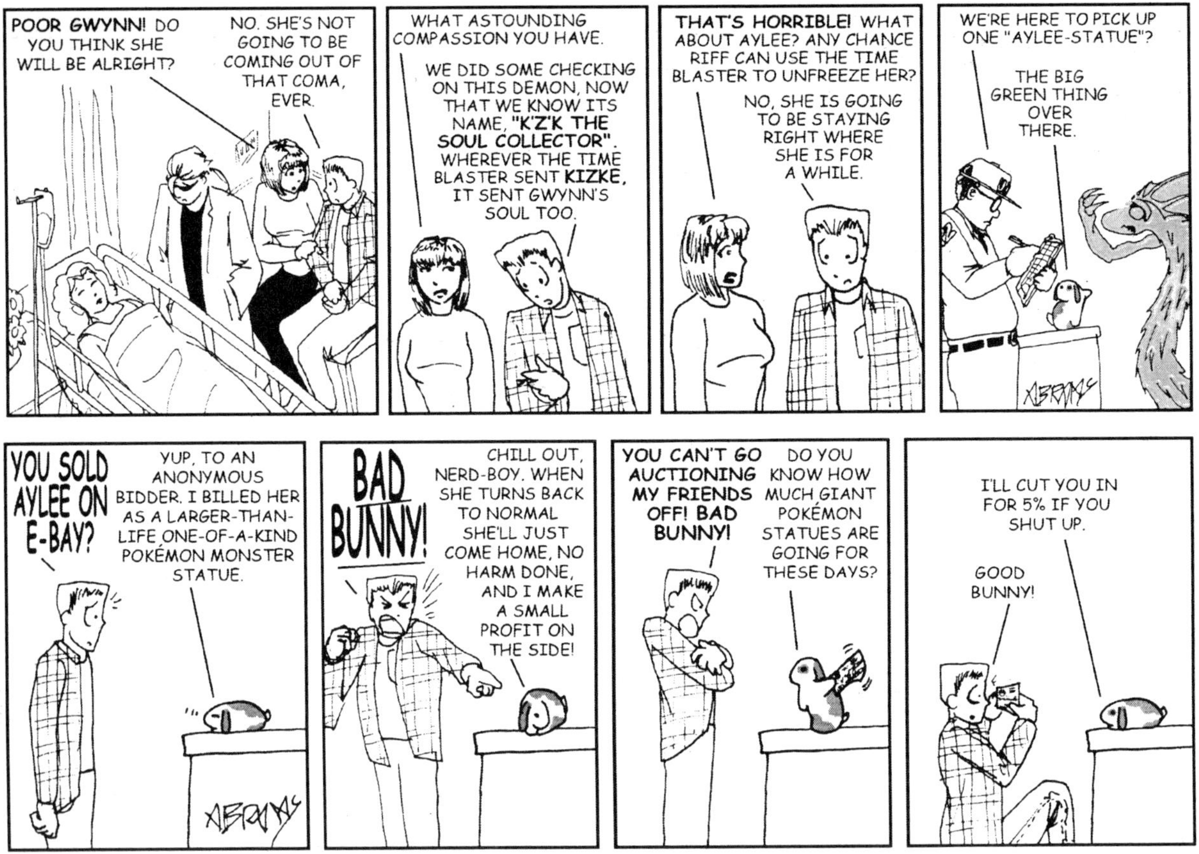

POOR GWYNN! DO YOU THINK SHE WILL BE ALRIGHT?
NO. SHE'S NOT GOING TO BE COMING OUT OF THAT COMA, EVER.
WHAT ASTOUNDING COMPASSION YOU HAVE.
WE DID SOME CHECKING ON THIS DEMON, NOW THAT WE KNOW ITS NAME, "K'Z'K THE SOUL COLLECTOR". WHEREVER THE TIME BLASTER SENT KIZKE, IT SENT GWYNN'S SOUL TOO.
THAT'S HORRIBLE! WHAT ABOUT AYLEE? ANY CHANCE RIFF CAN USE THE TIME BLASTER TO UNFREEZE HER?
NO, SHE IS GOING TO BE STAYING RIGHT WHERE SHE IS FOR A WHILE.
WE'RE HERE TO PICK UP ONE "AYLEE-STATUE"?
THE BIG GREEN THING OVER THERE.
YOU SOLD AYLEE ON E-BAY?
YUP, TO AN ANONYMOUS BIDDER. I BILLED HER AS A LARGER-THAN-LIFE ONE-OF-A-KIND POKÉMON MONSTER STATUE.
BAD BUNNY!
CHILL OUT, NERD-BOY. WHEN SHE TURNS BACK TO NORMAL SHE'LL JUST COME HOME, NO HARM DONE, AND I MAKE A SMALL PROFIT ON THE SIDE!
YOU CAN'T GO AUCTIONING MY FRIENDS OFF! BAD BUNNY!
DO YOU KNOW HOW MUCH GIANT POKÉMON STATUES ARE GOING FOR THESE DAYS?
I'LL CUT YOU IN FOR 5% IF YOU SHUT UP.
GOOD BUNNY!

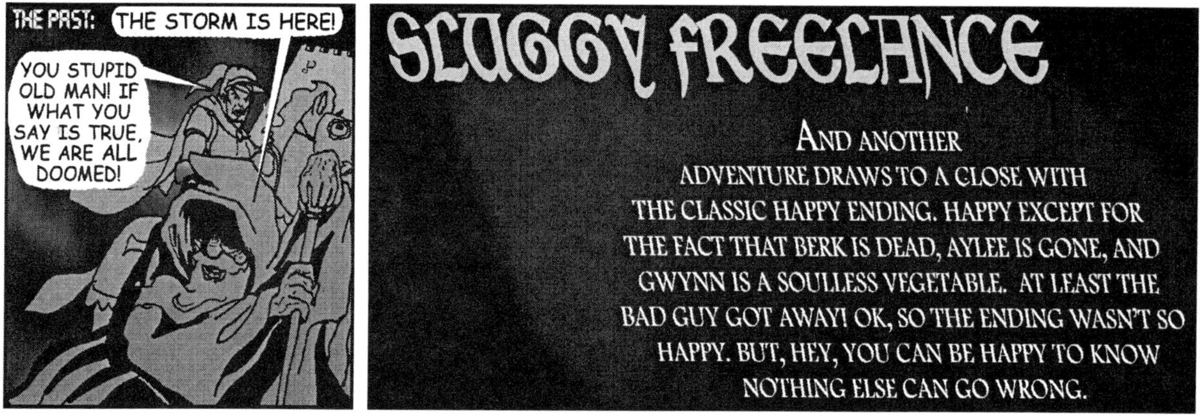
THE PAST:
THE STORM IS HERE!
YOU STUPID OLD MAN! IF WHAT YOU SAY IS TRUE, WE ARE ALL DOOMED!
SLUGGY FREELANCE
AND ANOTHER ADVENTURE DRAWS TO A CLOSE WITH THE CLASSIC HAPPY ENDING. HAPPY EXCEPT FOR THE FACT THAT BERK IS DEAD, AYLEE IS GONE, AND GWYNN IS A SOULLESS VEGETABLE. AT LEAST THE BAD GUY GOT AWAY! OK, SO THE ENDING WASN'T SO HAPPY. BUT, HEY, YOU CAN BE HAPPY TO KNOW NOTHING ELSE CAN GO WRONG.

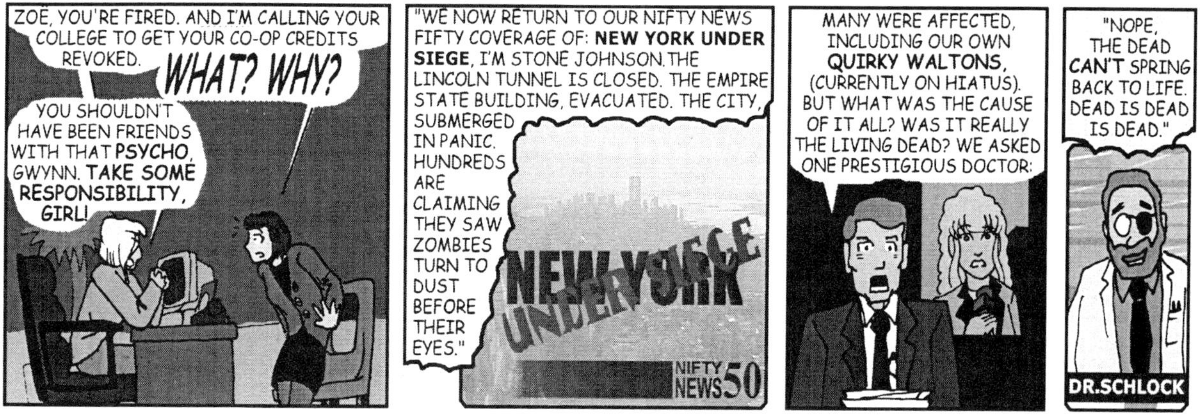
ZOË, YOU'RE FIRED. AND I'M CALLING YOUR COLLEGE TO GET YOUR CO-OP CREDITS REVOKED.
WHAT? WHY?
YOU SHOULDN'T HAVE BEEN FRIENDS WITH THAT PSYCHO, GWYNN. TAKE SOME RESPONSIBILITY, GIRL!
"WE NOW RETURN TO OUR NIFTY NEWS FIFTY COVERAGE OF: NEW YORK UNDER SIEGE, I'M STONE JOHNSON.THE LINCOLN TUNNEL IS CLOSED. THE EMPIRE STATE BUILDING, EVACUATED. THE CITY, SUBMERGED IN PANIC. HUNDREDS ARE CLAIMING THEY SAW ZOMBIES TURN TO DUST BEFORE THEIR EYES."
NEW YORK UNDER SIEGE
NIFTY NEWS 50
MANY WERE AFFECTED, INCLUDING OUR OWN QUIRKY WALTONS, (CURRENTLY ON HIATUS). BUT WHAT WAS THE CAUSE OF IT ALL? WAS IT REALLY THE LIVING DEAD? WE ASKED ONE PRESTIGIOUS DOCTOR:
"NOPE, THE DEAD CAN'T SPRING BACK TO LIFE. DEAD IS DEAD IS DEAD."
DR.SCHLOCK

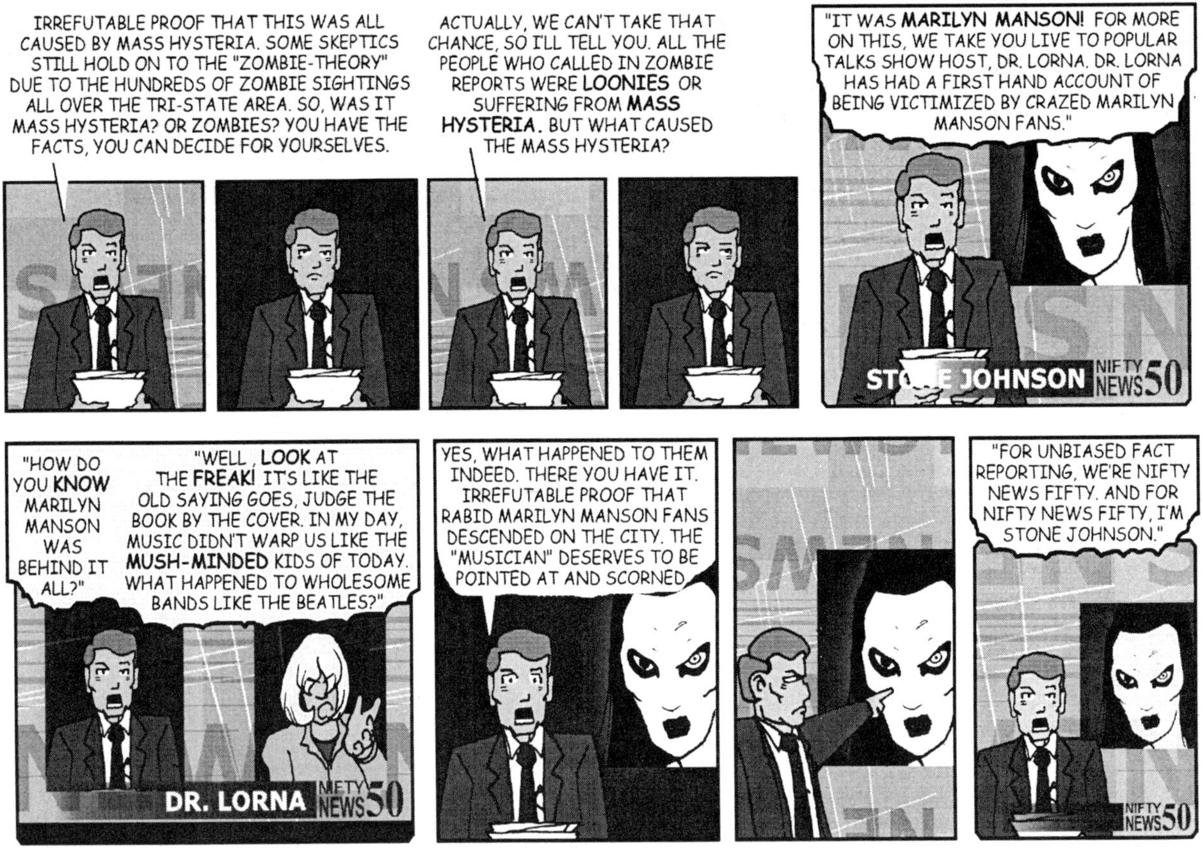
IRREFUTABLE PROOF THAT THIS WAS ALL CAUSED BY MASS HYSTERIA. SOME SKEPTICS STILL HOLD ON TO THE "ZOMBIE-THEORY" DUE TO THE HUNDREDS OF ZOMBIE SIGHTINGS ALL OVER THE TRI-STATE AREA. SO, WAS IT MASS HYSTERIA? OR ZOMBIES? YOU HAVE THE FACTS, YOU CAN DECIDE FOR YOURSELVES.
ACTUALLY, WE CAN'T TAKE THAT CHANCE, SO I'LL TELL YOU. ALL THE PEOPLE WHO CALLED IN ZOMBIE REPORTS WERE **LOONIES** OR SUFFERING FROM **MASS HYSTERIA**. BUT WHAT CAUSED THE MASS HYSTERIA?
"IT WAS **MARILYN MANSON!** FOR MORE ON THIS, WE TAKE YOU LIVE TO POPULAR TALKS SHOW HOST, DR. LORNA. DR. LORNA HAS HAD A FIRST HAND ACCOUNT OF BEING VICTIMIZED BY CRAZED MARILYN MANSON FANS."
STONE JOHNSON
NIFTY NEWS 50
"HOW DO YOU **KNOW** MARILYN MANSON WAS BEHIND IT ALL?"
"WELL, **LOOK** AT THE **FREAK!** IT'S LIKE THE OLD SAYING GOES, JUDGE THE BOOK BY THE COVER. IN MY DAY, MUSIC DIDN'T WARP US LIKE THE **MUSH-MINDED** KIDS OF TODAY. WHAT HAPPENED TO WHOLESOME BANDS LIKE THE BEATLES?"
DR. LORNA
NIFTY NEWS 50
YES, WHAT HAPPENED TO THEM INDEED. THERE YOU HAVE IT. IRREFUTABLE PROOF THAT RABID MARILYN MANSON FANS DESCENDED ON THE CITY. THE "MUSICIAN" DESERVES TO BE POINTED AT AND SCORNED.
"FOR UNBIASED FACT REPORTING, WE'RE NIFTY NEWS FIFTY. AND FOR NIFTY NEWS FIFTY, I'M STONE JOHNSON."
NIFTY NEWS 50

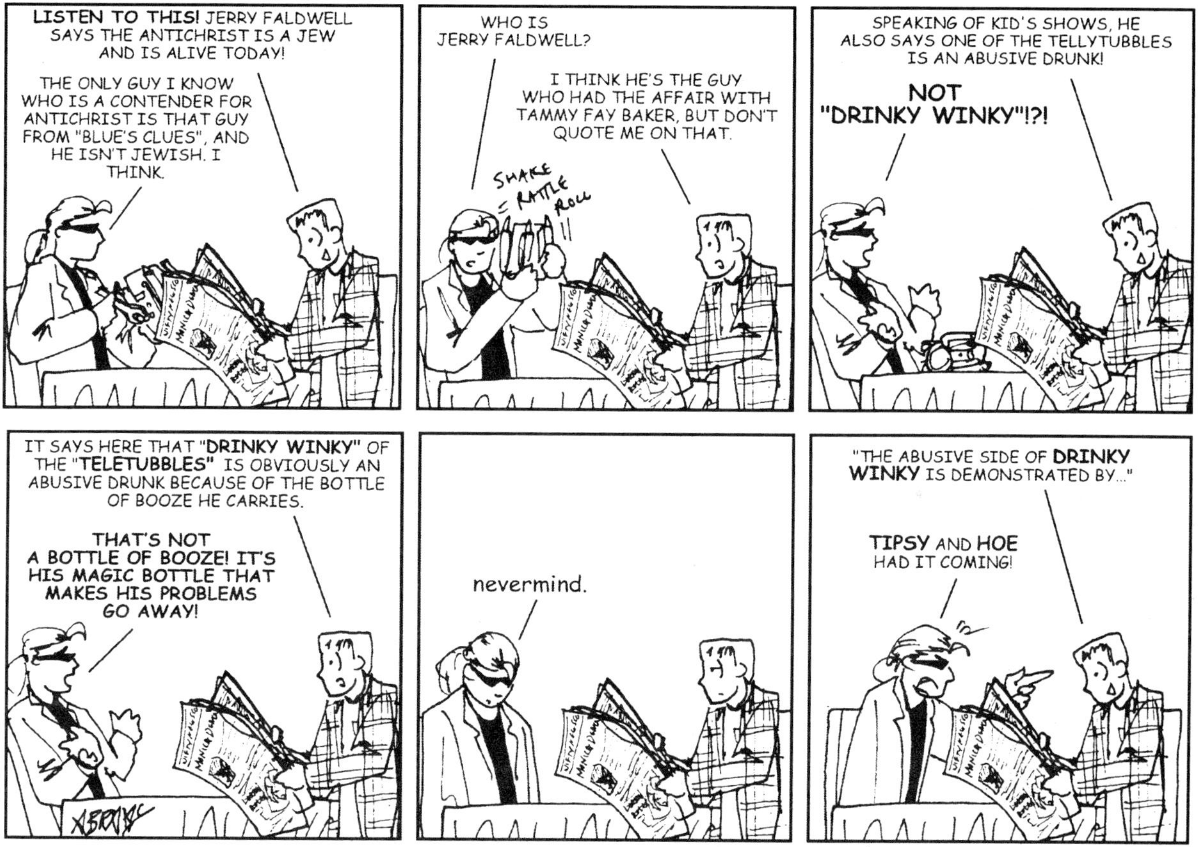
LISTEN TO THIS! JERRY FALDWELL SAYS THE ANTICHRIST IS A JEW AND IS ALIVE TODAY!
THE ONLY GUY I KNOW WHO IS A CONTENDER FOR ANTICHRIST IS THAT GUY FROM "BLUE'S CLUES", AND HE ISN'T JEWISH. I THINK.
WHO IS JERRY FALDWELL?
I THINK HE'S THE GUY WHO HAD THE AFFAIR WITH TAMMY FAY BAKER, BUT DON'T QUOTE ME ON THAT.
SHAKE
RATTLE
ROLL
SPEAKING OF KID'S SHOWS, HE ALSO SAYS ONE OF THE TELLYTUBBLES IS AN ABUSIVE DRUNK!
NOT "DRINKY WINKY"!?!
IT SAYS HERE THAT "DRINKY WINKY" OF THE "TELETUBBLES" IS OBVIOUSLY AN ABUSIVE DRUNK BECAUSE OF THE BOTTLE OF BOOZE HE CARRIES.
THAT'S NOT A BOTTLE OF BOOZE! IT'S HIS MAGIC BOTTLE THAT MAKES HIS PROBLEMS GO AWAY!
nevermind.
"THE ABUSIVE SIDE OF DRINKY WINKY IS DEMONSTRATED BY..."
TIPSY AND HOE HAD IT COMING!

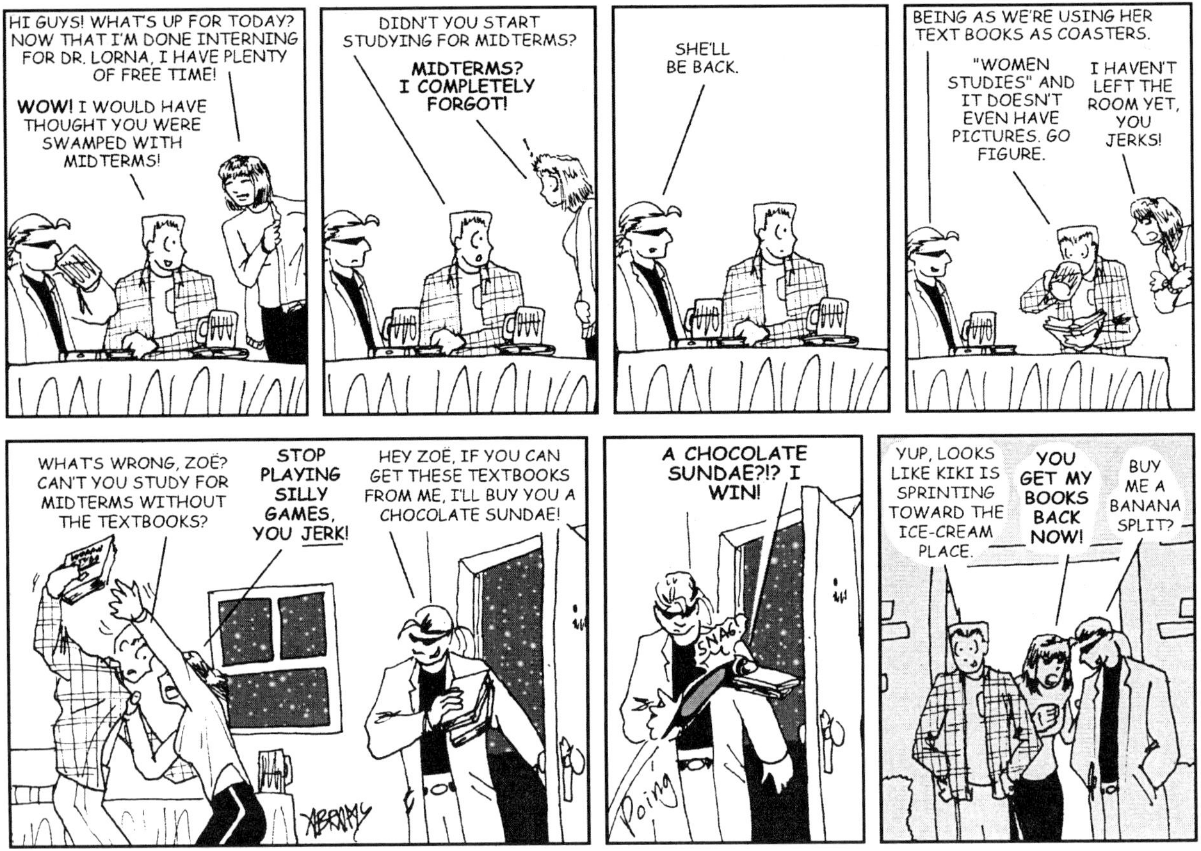
HI GUYS! WHAT'S UP FOR TODAY? NOW THAT I'M DONE INTERNING FOR DR. LORNA, I HAVE PLENTY OF FREE TIME!
WOW! I WOULD HAVE THOUGHT YOU WERE SWAMPED WITH MIDTERMS!
DIDN'T YOU START STUDYING FOR MIDTERMS?
MIDTERMS? I COMPLETELY FORGOT!
SHE'LL BE BACK.
BEING AS WE'RE USING HER TEXT BOOKS AS COASTERS.
"WOMEN STUDIES" AND IT DOESN'T EVEN HAVE PICTURES. GO FIGURE.
I HAVEN'T LEFT THE ROOM YET, YOU JERKS!
WHAT'S WRONG, ZOË? CAN'T YOU STUDY FOR MIDTERMS WITHOUT THE TEXTBOOKS?
STOP PLAYING SILLY GAMES, YOU JERK!
HEY ZOË, IF YOU CAN GET THESE TEXTBOOKS FROM ME, I'LL BUY YOU A CHOCOLATE SUNDAE!
A CHOCOLATE SUNDAE?!? I WIN!
SNAG!
Poing
YUP, LOOKS LIKE KIKI IS SPRINTING TOWARD THE ICE-CREAM PLACE.
YOU GET MY BOOKS BACK NOW!
BUY ME A BANANA SPLIT?

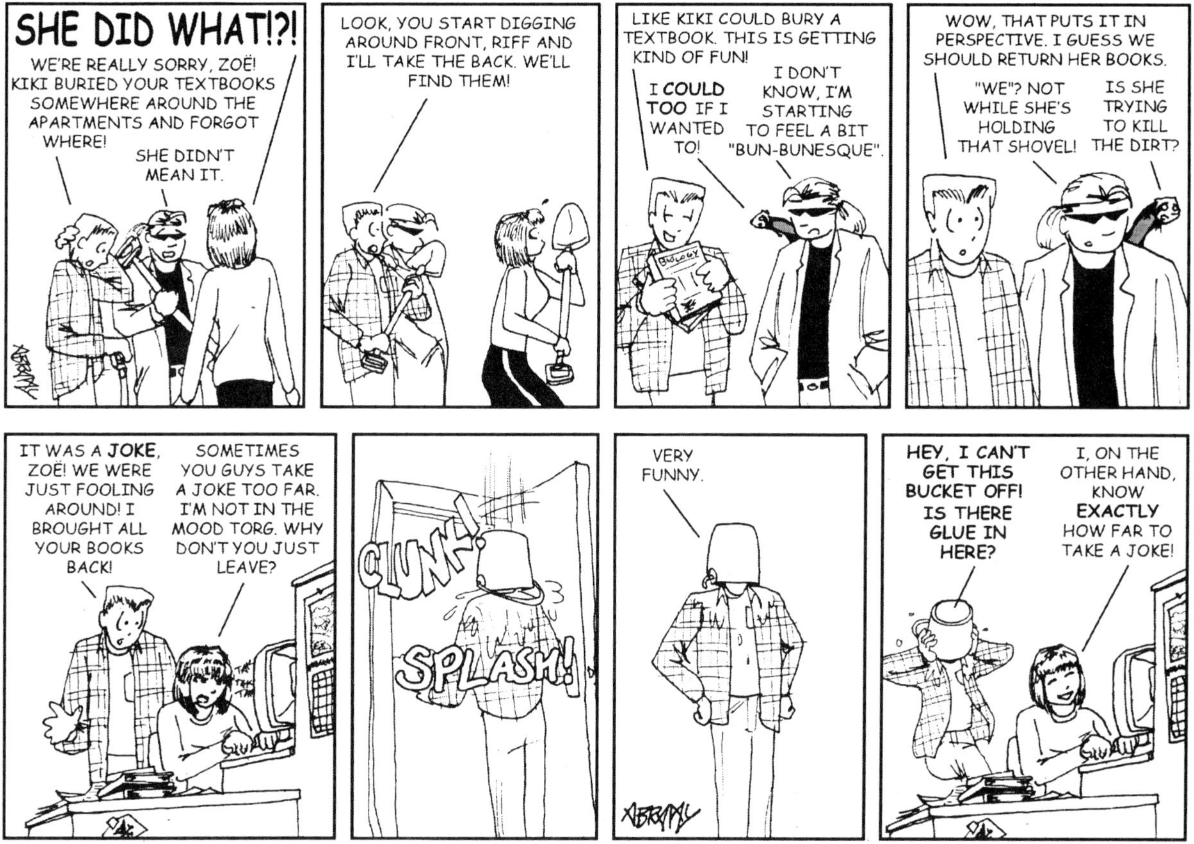
SHE DID WHAT!?!
WE'RE REALLY SORRY, ZOË! KIKI BURIED YOUR TEXTBOOKS SOMEWHERE AROUND THE APARTMENTS AND FORGOT WHERE!
SHE DIDN'T MEAN IT.
LOOK, YOU START DIGGING AROUND FRONT, RIFF AND I'LL TAKE THE BACK. WE'LL FIND THEM!
LIKE KIKI COULD BURY A TEXTBOOK. THIS IS GETTING KIND OF FUN!
I COULD TOO IF I WANTED TO!
I DON'T KNOW, I'M STARTING TO FEEL A BIT "BUN-BUNESQUE".
BIOLOGY
WOW, THAT PUTS IT IN PERSPECTIVE. I GUESS WE SHOULD RETURN HER BOOKS.
"WE"? NOT WHILE SHE'S HOLDING THAT SHOVEL!
IS SHE TRYING TO KILL THE DIRT?
IT WAS A JOKE, ZOË! WE WERE JUST FOOLING AROUND! I BROUGHT ALL YOUR BOOKS BACK!
SOMETIMES YOU GUYS TAKE A JOKE TOO FAR. I'M NOT IN THE MOOD TORG. WHY DON'T YOU JUST LEAVE?
CLUNK!
SPLASH!
VERY FUNNY.
HEY, I CAN'T GET THIS BUCKET OFF! IS THERE GLUE IN HERE?
I, ON THE OTHER HAND, KNOW EXACTLY HOW FAR TO TAKE A JOKE!

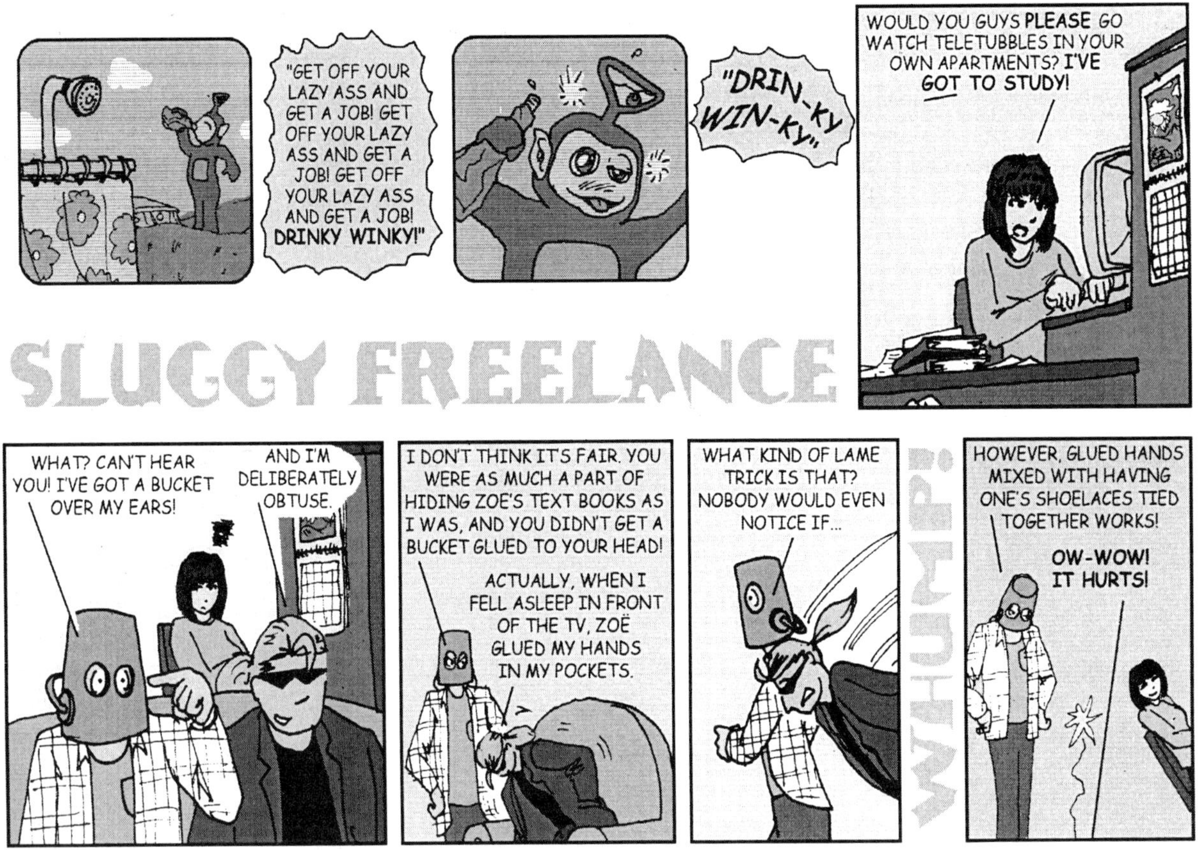
"GET OFF YOUR LAZY ASS AND GET A JOB! GET OFF YOUR LAZY ASS AND GET A JOB! GET OFF YOUR LAZY ASS AND GET A JOB! DRINKY WINKY!"
"DRIN-KY WIN-KY"
WOULD YOU GUYS PLEASE GO WATCH TELETUBBLES IN YOUR OWN APARTMENTS? I'VE GOT TO STUDY!
SLUGGY FREELANCE
WHAT? CAN'T HEAR YOU! I'VE GOT A BUCKET OVER MY EARS!
AND I'M DELIBERATELY OBTUSE.
I DON'T THINK IT'S FAIR. YOU WERE AS MUCH A PART OF HIDING ZOE'S TEXT BOOKS AS I WAS, AND YOU DIDN'T GET A BUCKET GLUED TO YOUR HEAD!
ACTUALLY, WHEN I FELL ASLEEP IN FRONT OF THE TV, ZOË GLUED MY HANDS IN MY POCKETS.
WHAT KIND OF LAME TRICK IS THAT? NOBODY WOULD EVEN NOTICE IF...
WHUMP!
HOWEVER, GLUED HANDS MIXED WITH HAVING ONE'S SHOELACES TIED TOGETHER WORKS!
OW-WOW! IT HURTS!

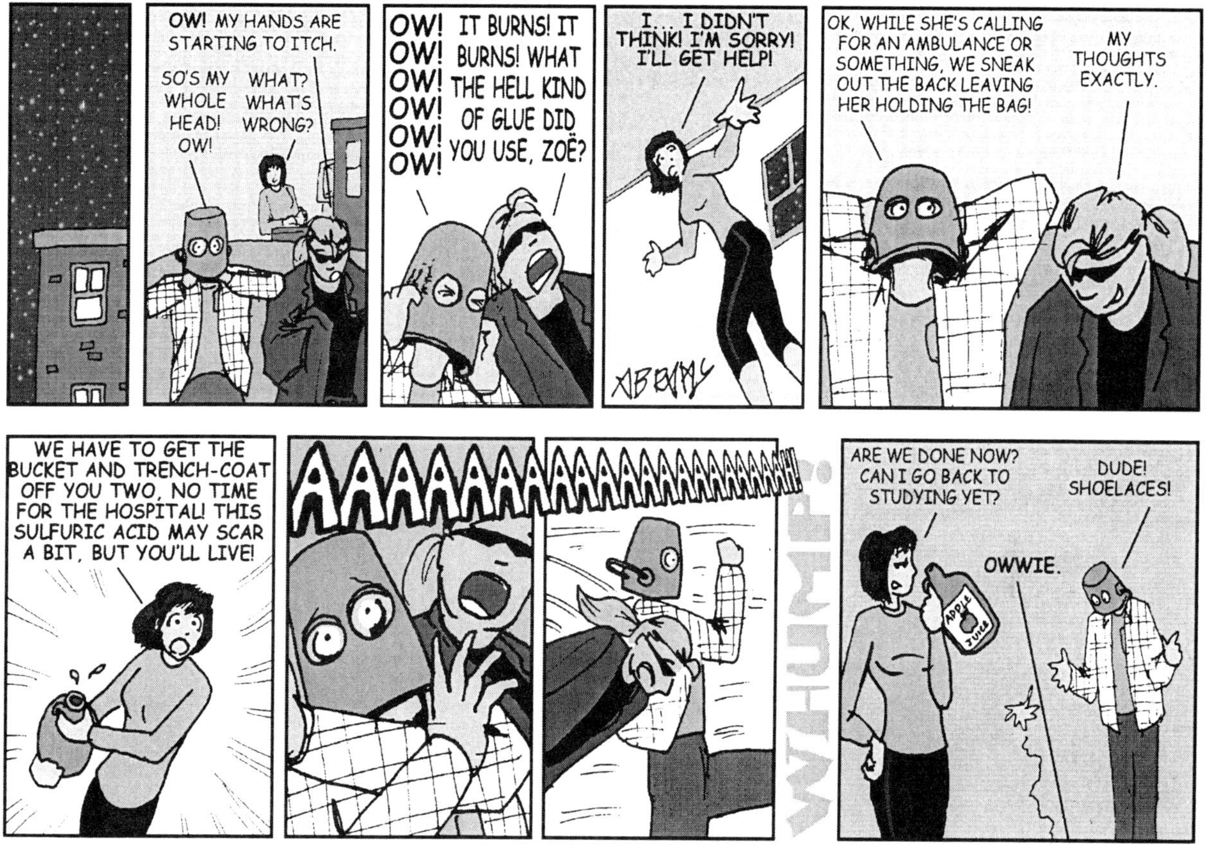
OW! MY HANDS ARE STARTING TO ITCH.
SO'S MY WHOLE HEAD! OW!
WHAT? WHAT'S WRONG?
OW! OW! OW! OW! OW! OW!
IT BURNS! IT BURNS! WHAT THE HELL KIND OF GLUE DID YOU USE, ZOË?
I... I DIDN'T THINK! I'M SORRY! I'LL GET HELP!
OK, WHILE SHE'S CALLING FOR AN AMBULANCE OR SOMETHING, WE SNEAK OUT THE BACK LEAVING HER HOLDING THE BAG!
MY THOUGHTS EXACTLY.
WE HAVE TO GET THE BUCKET AND TRENCH-COAT OFF YOU TWO, NO TIME FOR THE HOSPITAL! THIS SULFURIC ACID MAY SCAR A BIT, BUT YOU'LL LIVE!
AAAAAAAAAAAAAAAAAAAAAAAAAH!
WHUMP!
ARE WE DONE NOW? CAN I GO BACK TO STUDYING YET?
OWWIE.
DUDE! SHOELACES!
APPLE JUICE

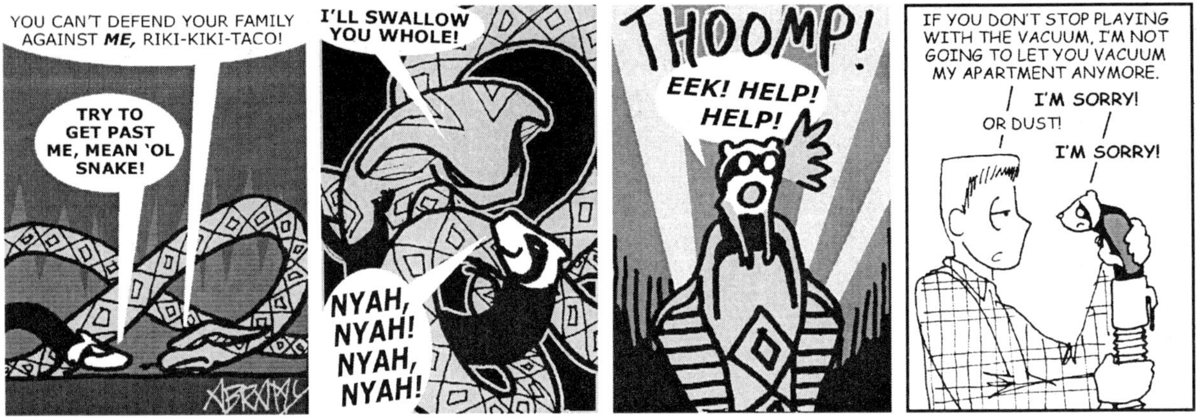
YOU CAN'T DEFEND YOUR FAMILY AGAINST *ME,* RIKI-KIKI-TACO!
TRY TO GET PAST ME, MEAN 'OL SNAKE!
I'LL SWALLOW YOU WHOLE!
NYAH, NYAH! NYAH, NYAH!
THOOMP!
EEK! HELP! HELP!
IF YOU DON'T STOP PLAYING WITH THE VACUUM, I'M NOT GOING TO LET YOU VACUUM MY APARTMENT ANYMORE.
OR DUST!
I'M SORRY!
I'M SORRY!

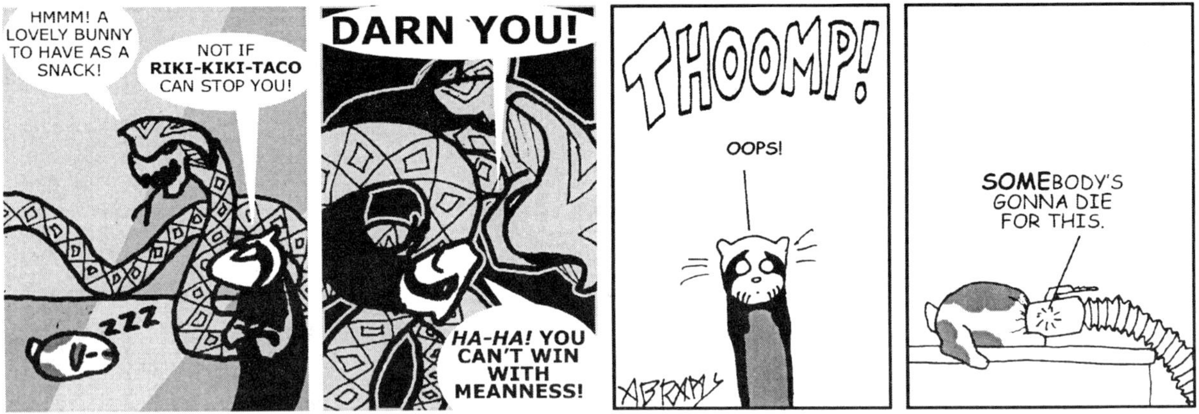
HMMM! A LOVELY BUNNY TO HAVE AS A SNACK!
NOT IF **RIKI-KIKI-TACO** CAN STOP YOU!
ZZZ
DARN YOU!
HA-HA! YOU CAN'T WIN WITH MEANNESS!
THOOMP!
OOPS!
SOMEBODY'S GONNA DIE FOR THIS.

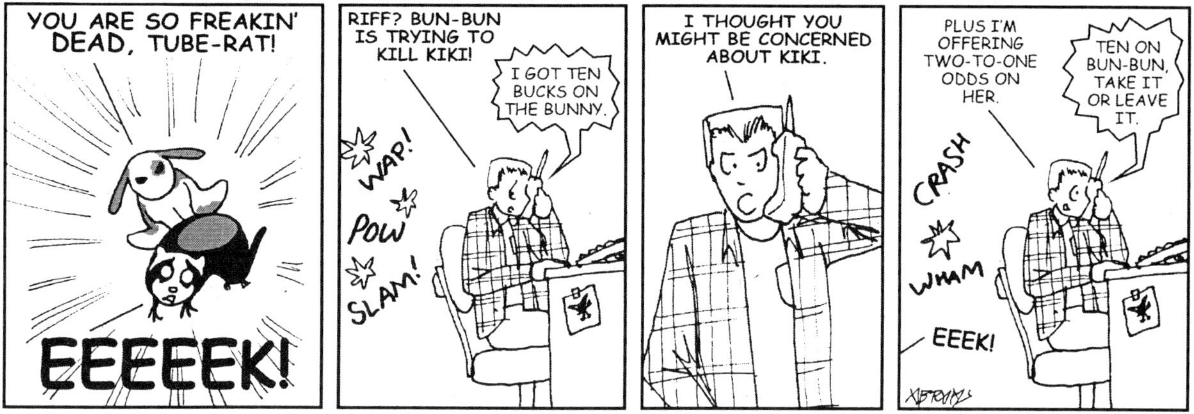
YOU ARE SO FREAKIN' DEAD, TUBE-RAT!
EEEEEK!
RIFF? BUN-BUN IS TRYING TO KILL KIKI!
I GOT TEN BUCKS ON THE BUNNY.
WAP!
POW
SLAM!
I THOUGHT YOU MIGHT BE CONCERNED ABOUT KIKI.
PLUS I'M OFFERING TWO-TO-ONE ODDS ON HER.
TEN ON BUN-BUN, TAKE IT OR LEAVE IT.
CRASH
WHAM
EEEK!

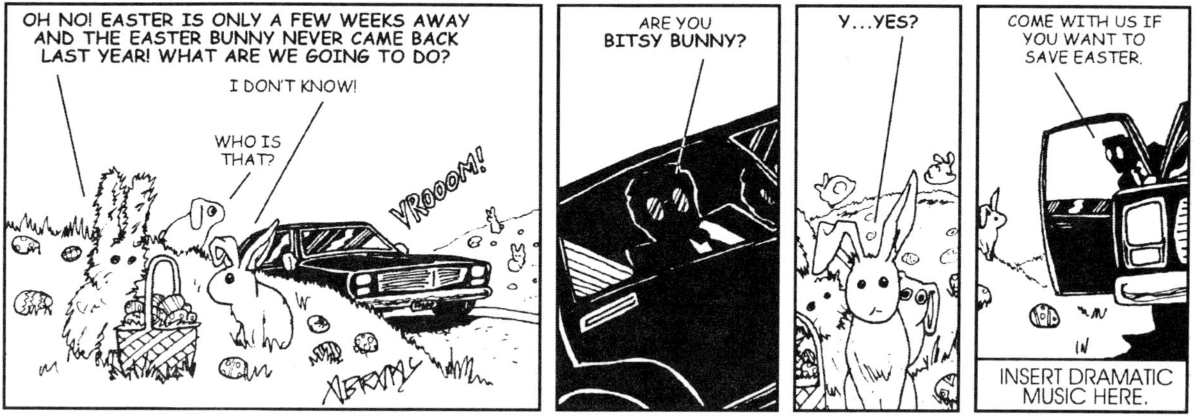
OH NO! EASTER IS ONLY A FEW WEEKS AWAY AND THE EASTER BUNNY NEVER CAME BACK LAST YEAR! WHAT ARE WE GOING TO DO?
I DON'T KNOW!
WHO IS THAT?
VROOOM!
ARE YOU BITSY BUNNY?
Y...YES?
COME WITH US IF YOU WANT TO SAVE EASTER.
INSERT DRAMATIC MUSIC HERE.

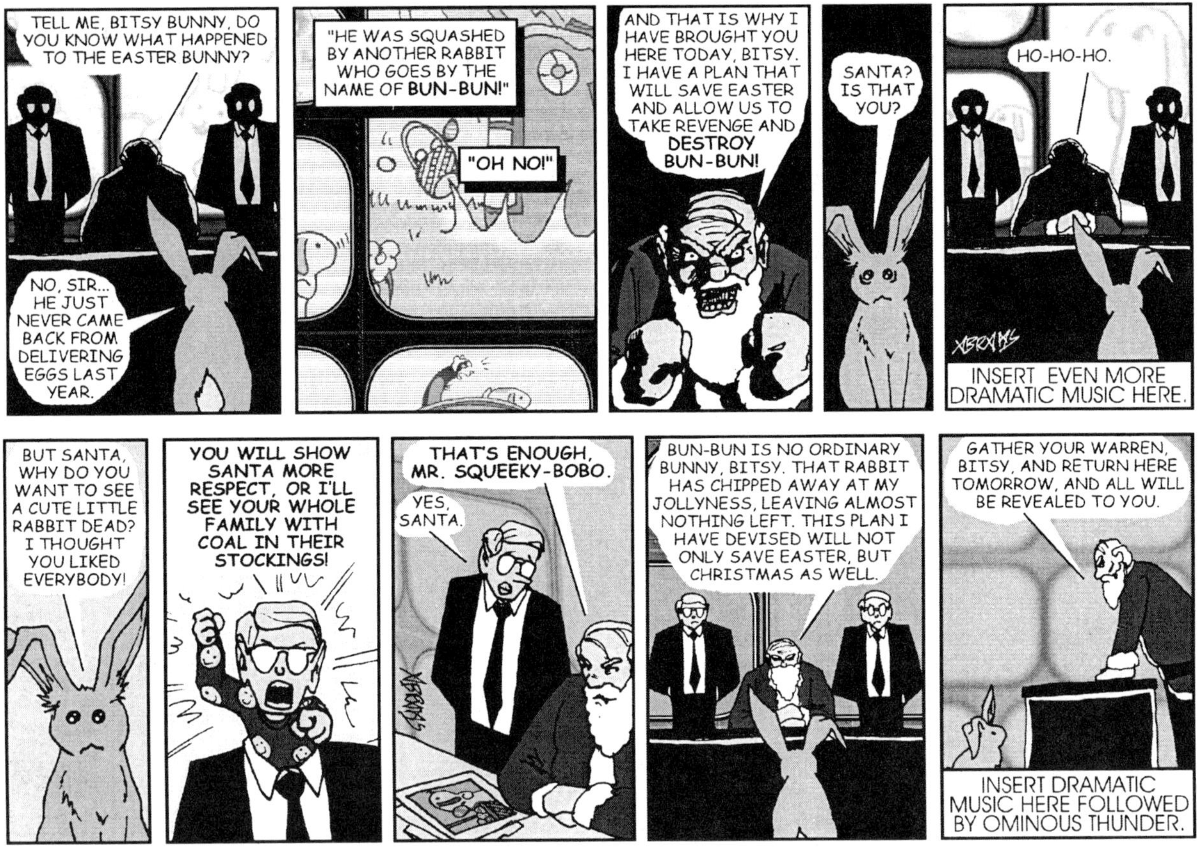

TELL ME, BITSY BUNNY, DO YOU KNOW WHAT HAPPENED TO THE EASTER BUNNY?
NO, SIR... HE JUST NEVER CAME BACK FROM DELIVERING EGGS LAST YEAR.
"HE WAS SQUASHED BY ANOTHER RABBIT WHO GOES BY THE NAME OF BUN-BUN!"
"OH NO!"
AND THAT IS WHY I HAVE BROUGHT YOU HERE TODAY, BITSY. I HAVE A PLAN THAT WILL SAVE EASTER AND ALLOW US TO TAKE REVENGE AND DESTROY BUN-BUN!
SANTA? IS THAT YOU?
HO-HO-HO.
INSERT EVEN MORE DRAMATIC MUSIC HERE.
BUT SANTA, WHY DO YOU WANT TO SEE A CUTE LITTLE RABBIT DEAD? I THOUGHT YOU LIKED EVERYBODY!
YOU WILL SHOW SANTA MORE RESPECT, OR I'LL SEE YOUR WHOLE FAMILY WITH COAL IN THEIR STOCKINGS!
THAT'S ENOUGH, MR. SQUEEKY-BOBO.
YES, SANTA.
BUN-BUN IS NO ORDINARY BUNNY, BITSY. THAT RABBIT HAS CHIPPED AWAY AT MY JOLLYNESS, LEAVING ALMOST NOTHING LEFT. THIS PLAN I HAVE DEVISED WILL NOT ONLY SAVE EASTER, BUT CHRISTMAS AS WELL.
GATHER YOUR WARREN, BITSY, AND RETURN HERE TOMORROW, AND ALL WILL BE REVEALED TO YOU.
INSERT DRAMATIC MUSIC HERE FOLLOWED BY OMINOUS THUNDER.

"THIS PROJECT BEGAN A YEAR AGO, WHEN WE SALVAGED SOME DNA FROM THE FIRST EASTER-BUNNY."
"MY ELF-GENETICISTS COMBINED RAPID GROWTH HORMONES WITH THE MOST ADVANCED CYBORG TECHNOLOGY."
"THE CYBORG WAS THEN PROTECTED BY AN EXOSKELETON BUILT FROM SPACE-METALS AND THE STUFF USED TO MAKE GOBSTOPPERS."
OVERALL RATING: IMPERVIOUS 90%
RAT TAT TAT TAT TAT TAT TAT TAT
ping ting tang tong ping
SLUGGY FREELANCE
"THEN, ADDING THE LATEST R&D WEAPONRY FROM THE PENTAGON (THE HEAD GUY THERE HAS A THING FOR TEDDY BEARS), WE DESIGNED THE MOST ADVANCED AND LETHAL CYBORG-CLONE RABBIT EVER CREATED!"
PROJECT: Happy Easter!
FLAME
MISSLE
LASER
BOMB
BLADE
AND ALL THAT TOPPED OFF WITH A COMPUTER-ENHANCED BRAIN COMPLETELY UNDER OUR CONTROL, I PRESENT TO YOU, MECHA-EASTER-BUNNY!
THIS UNSTOPPABLE FORCE HAS BUT ONE GOAL....TO DESTROY BUN-BUN!
Whisper Whisper Whisper

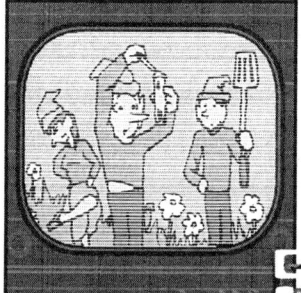

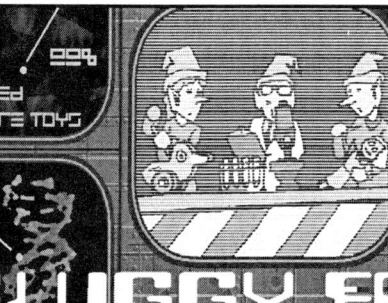

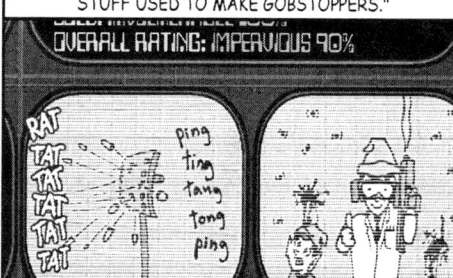

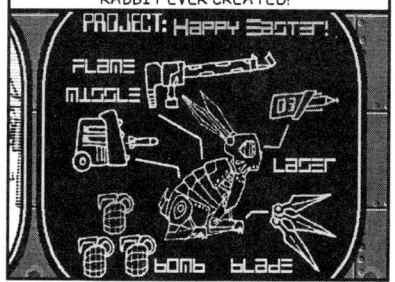

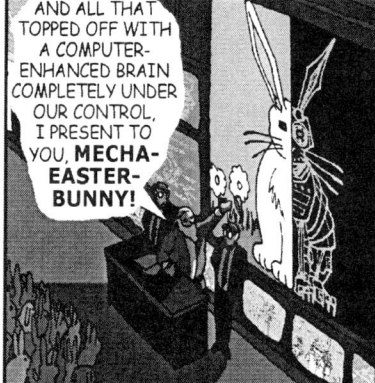

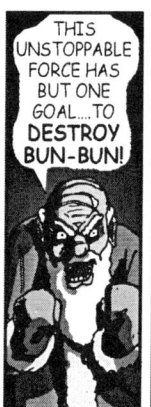

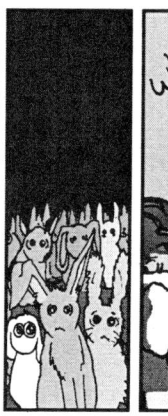

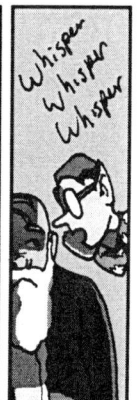

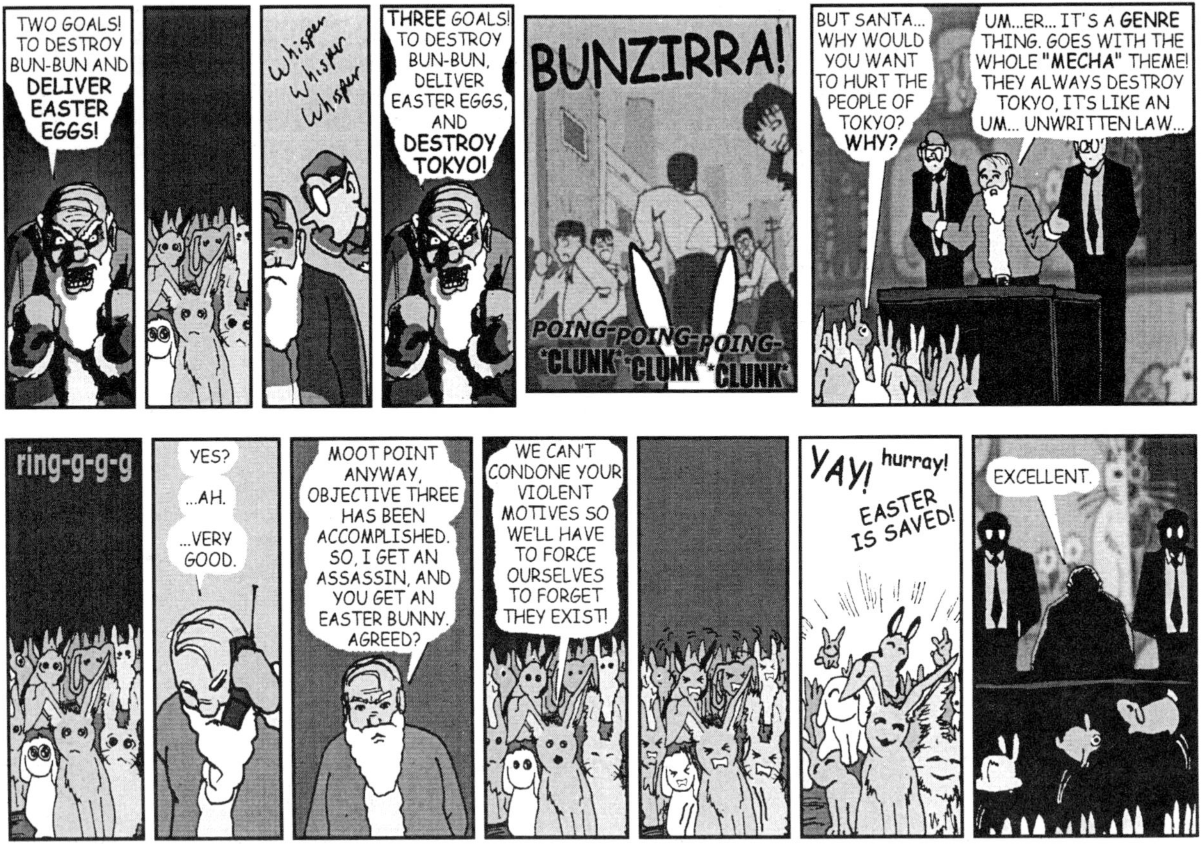
TWO GOALS! TO DESTROY BUN-BUN AND DELIVER EASTER EGGS!
Whisper Whisper Whisper
THREE GOALS! TO DESTROY BUN-BUN, DELIVER EASTER EGGS, AND DESTROY TOKYO!
BUNZIRRA!
POING-POING-POING-
CLUNK *CLUNK* *CLUNK*
BUT SANTA... WHY WOULD YOU WANT TO HURT THE PEOPLE OF TOKYO? WHY?
UM...ER... IT'S A GENRE THING. GOES WITH THE WHOLE "MECHA" THEME! THEY ALWAYS DESTROY TOKYO, IT'S LIKE AN UM... UNWRITTEN LAW...
ring-g-g-g
YES?
...AH.
...VERY GOOD.
MOOT POINT ANYWAY, OBJECTIVE THREE HAS BEEN ACCOMPLISHED. SO, I GET AN ASSASSIN, AND YOU GET AN EASTER BUNNY. AGREED?
WE CAN'T CONDONE YOUR VIOLENT MOTIVES SO WE'LL HAVE TO FORCE OURSELVES TO FORGET THEY EXIST!
YAY!
hurray!
EASTER IS SAVED!
EXCELLENT.

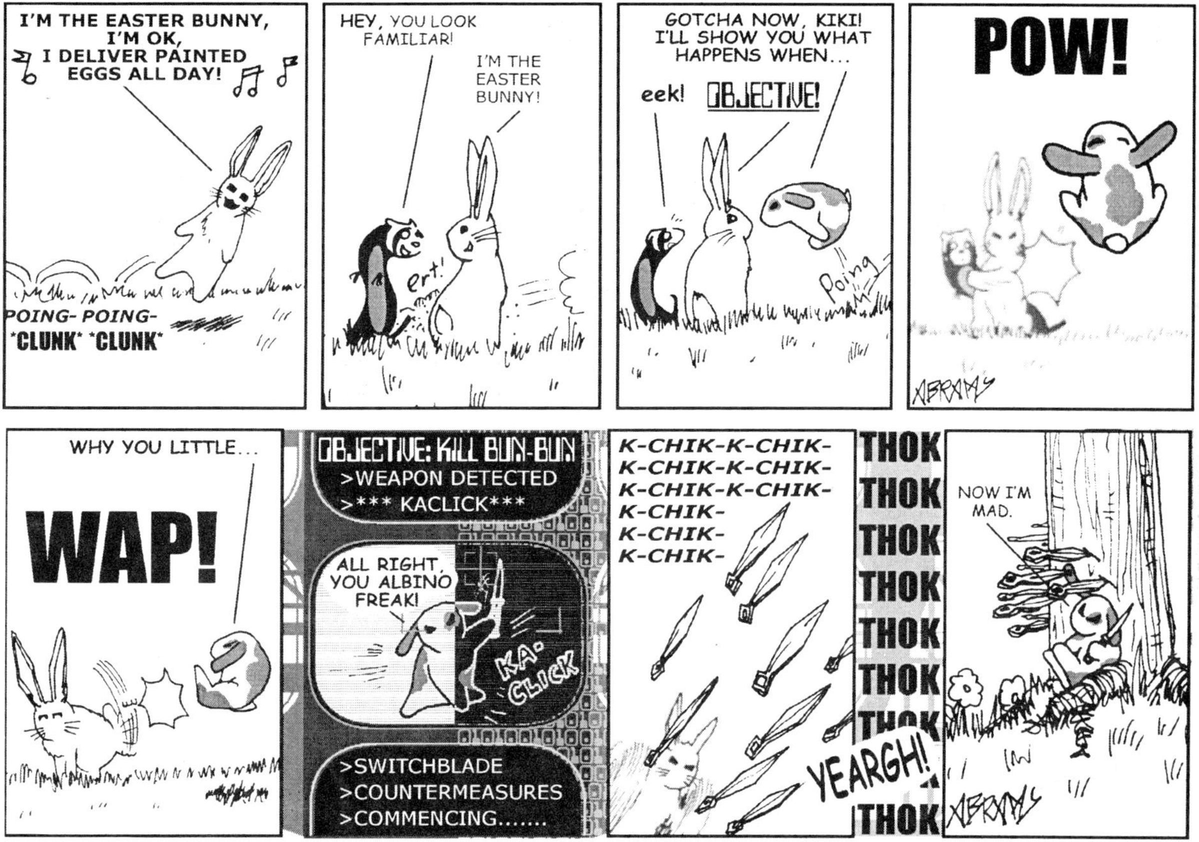
I'M THE EASTER BUNNY, I'M OK, I DELIVER PAINTED EGGS ALL DAY!
POING- POING-
CLUNK *CLUNK*
HEY, YOU LOOK FAMILIAR!
I'M THE EASTER BUNNY!
ert!
GOTCHA NOW, KIKI! I'LL SHOW YOU WHAT HAPPENS WHEN...
eek!
OBJECTIVE!
Poing
POW!
WHY YOU LITTLE...
WAP!
OBJECTIVE: KILL BUN-BUN
>WEAPON DETECTED
>*** KACLICK***
ALL RIGHT, YOU ALBINO FREAK!
KA-CLICK
>SWITCHBLADE
>COUNTERMEASURES
>COMMENCING.......
K-CHIK-K-CHIK-
K-CHIK-K-CHIK-
K-CHIK-K-CHIK-
K-CHIK-
K-CHIK-
K-CHIK-
THOK THOK THOK THOK THOK THOK THOK THOK
YEARGH!
NOW I'M MAD.

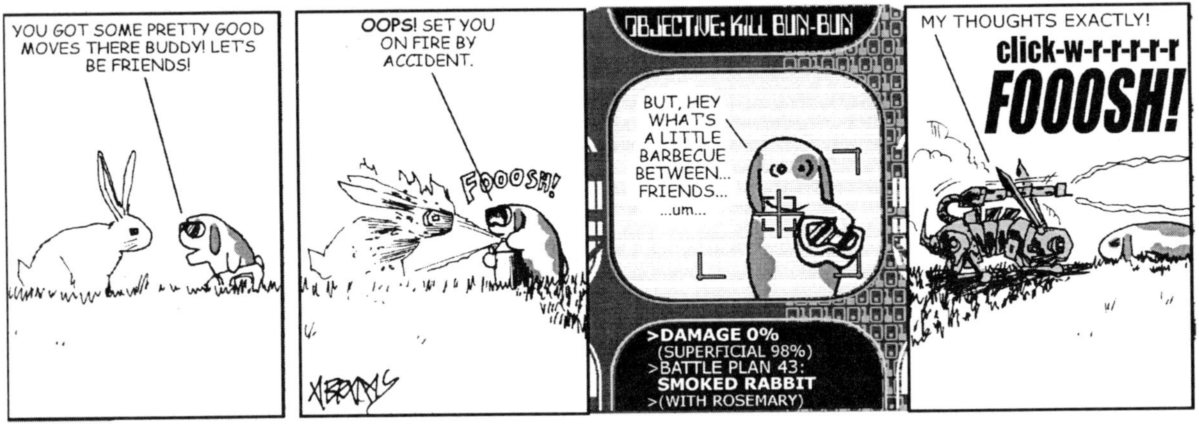
YOU GOT SOME PRETTY GOOD MOVES THERE BUDDY! LET'S BE FRIENDS!
OOPS! SET YOU ON FIRE BY ACCIDENT.
FOOOSH!
OBJECTIVE: KILL BUN-BUN
BUT, HEY WHAT'S A LITTLE BARBECUE BETWEEN... FRIENDS... ...um...
>DAMAGE 0%
(SUPERFICIAL 98%)
>BATTLE PLAN 43:
SMOKED RABBIT
>(WITH ROSEMARY)
MY THOUGHTS EXACTLY!
click-w-r-r-r-r-r
FOOOSH!

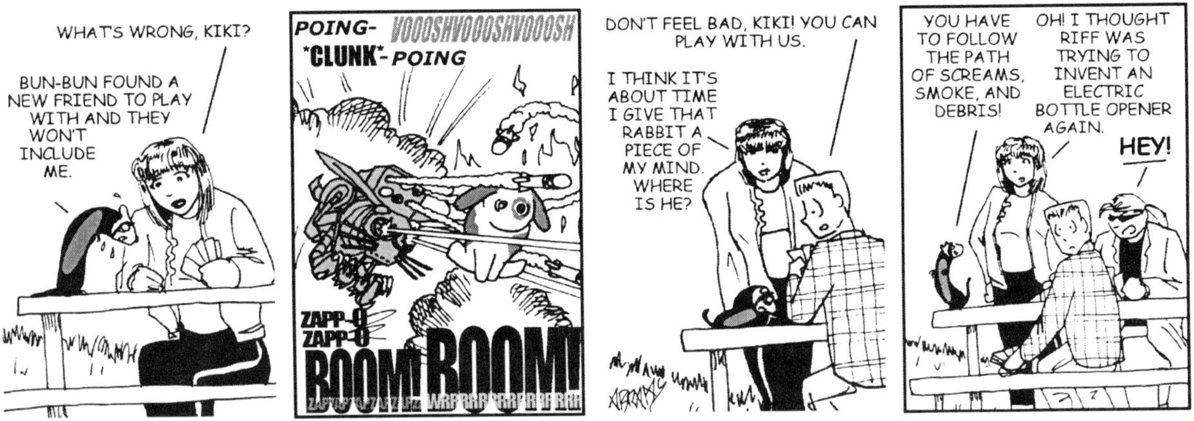
WHAT'S WRONG, KIKI?
BUN-BUN FOUND A NEW FRIEND TO PLAY WITH AND THEY WON'T INCLUDE ME.
POING-
VOOOSHVOOOSHVOOOSH
CLUNK-POING
ZAPP-
ZAPP-
BOOM! BOOM!
DON'T FEEL BAD, KIKI! YOU CAN PLAY WITH US.
I THINK IT'S ABOUT TIME I GIVE THAT RABBIT A PIECE OF MY MIND. WHERE IS HE?
YOU HAVE TO FOLLOW THE PATH OF SCREAMS, SMOKE, AND DEBRIS!
OH! I THOUGHT RIFF WAS TRYING TO INVENT AN ELECTRIC BOTTLE OPENER AGAIN.
HEY!

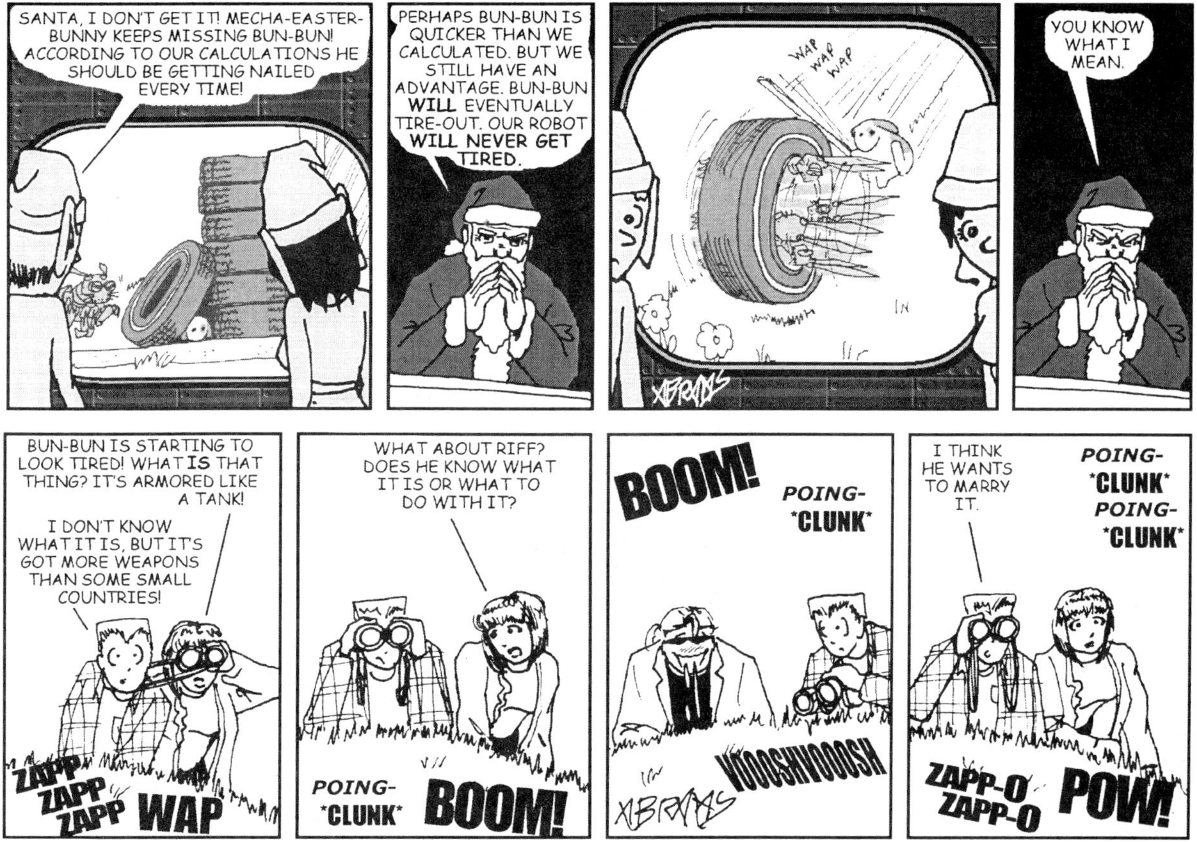
SANTA, I DON'T GET IT! MECHA-EASTER-BUNNY KEEPS MISSING BUN-BUN! ACCORDING TO OUR CALCULATIONS HE SHOULD BE GETTING NAILED EVERY TIME!
PERHAPS BUN-BUN IS QUICKER THAN WE CALCULATED. BUT WE STILL HAVE AN ADVANTAGE. BUN-BUN WILL EVENTUALLY TIRE-OUT. OUR ROBOT WILL NEVER GET TIRED.
WAP WAP WAP
YOU KNOW WHAT I MEAN.
BUN-BUN IS STARTING TO LOOK TIRED! WHAT IS THAT THING? IT'S ARMORED LIKE A TANK!
I DON'T KNOW WHAT IT IS, BUT IT'S GOT MORE WEAPONS THAN SOME SMALL COUNTRIES!
ZAPP ZAPP ZAPP WAP
WHAT ABOUT RIFF? DOES HE KNOW WHAT IT IS OR WHAT TO DO WITH IT?
POING- *CLUNK* BOOM!
BOOM!
POING- *CLUNK*
VOOOSHVOOOSH
I THINK HE WANTS TO MARRY IT.
POING- *CLUNK* POING- *CLUNK*
ZAPP-O ZAPP-O POW!

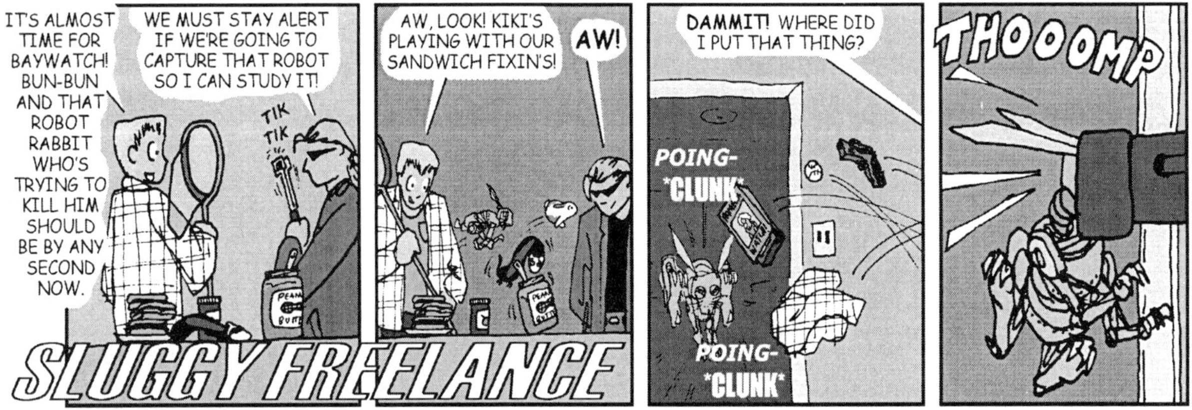
IT'S ALMOST TIME FOR BAYWATCH! BUN-BUN AND THAT ROBOT RABBIT WHO'S TRYING TO KILL HIM SHOULD BE BY ANY SECOND NOW.
WE MUST STAY ALERT IF WE'RE GOING TO CAPTURE THAT ROBOT SO I CAN STUDY IT!
TIK TIK
AW, LOOK! KIKI'S PLAYING WITH OUR SANDWICH FIXIN'S!
AW!
SLUGGY FREELANCE
DAMMIT! WHERE DID I PUT THAT THING?
POING- *CLUNK*
POING- *CLUNK*
THOOOMP

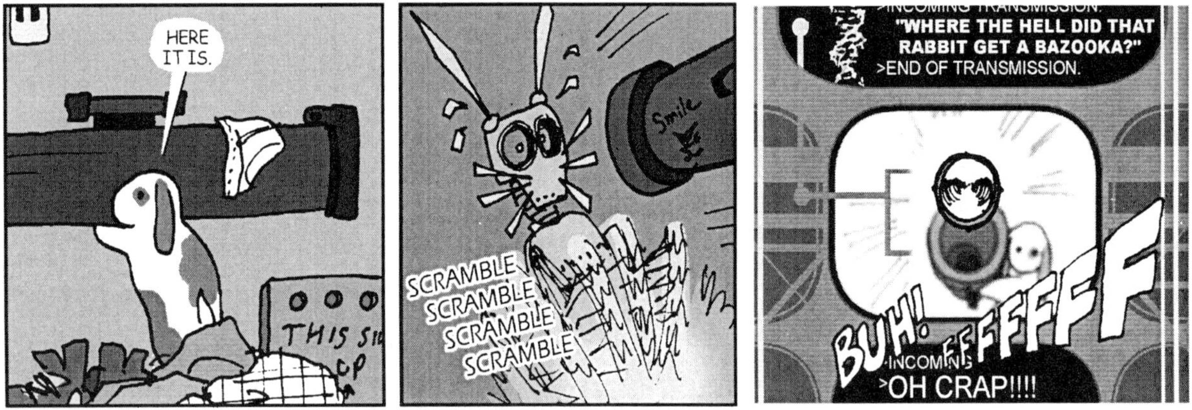
HERE IT IS.
SCRAMBLE SCRAMBLE SCRAMBLE SCRAMBLE
Smile
>INCOMING TRANSMISSION:
"WHERE THE HELL DID THAT RABBIT GET A BAZOOKA?"
>END OF TRANSMISSION.
BUH! FFFFFF
>INCOMING
>OH CRAP!!!!

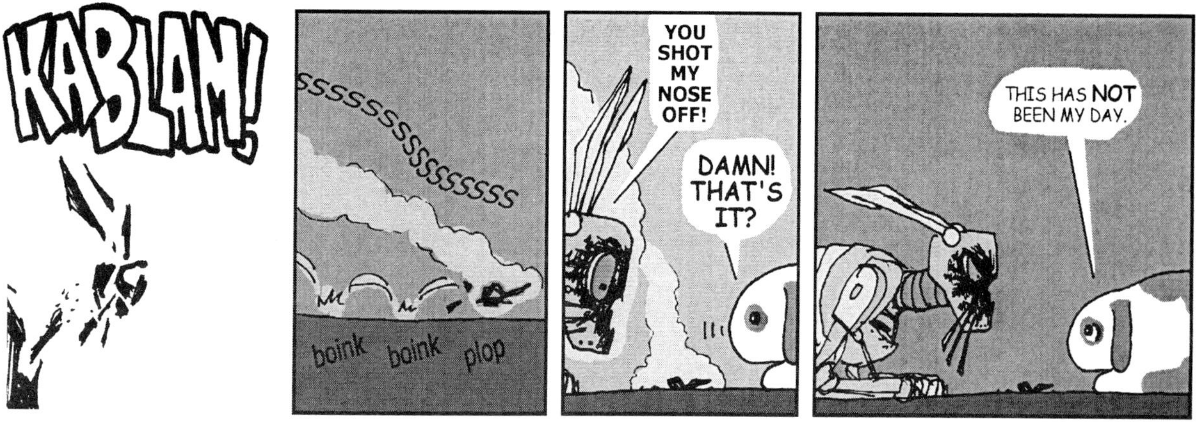
KABLAM!
SSSSSSSSSSSSSSSSSSSSSS
boink boink plop
YOU SHOT MY NOSE OFF!
DAMN! THAT'S IT?
THIS HAS NOT BEEN MY DAY.

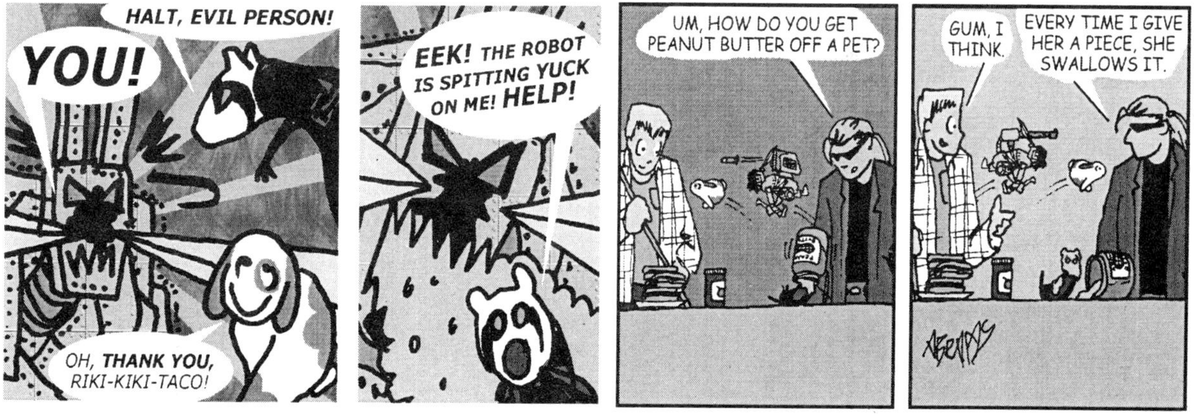
HALT, EVIL PERSON!
YOU!
OH, THANK YOU, RIKI-KIKI-TACO!
EEK! THE ROBOT IS SPITTING YUCK ON ME! HELP!
UM, HOW DO YOU GET PEANUT BUTTER OFF A PET?
GUM, I THINK.
EVERY TIME I GIVE HER A PIECE, SHE SWALLOWS IT.

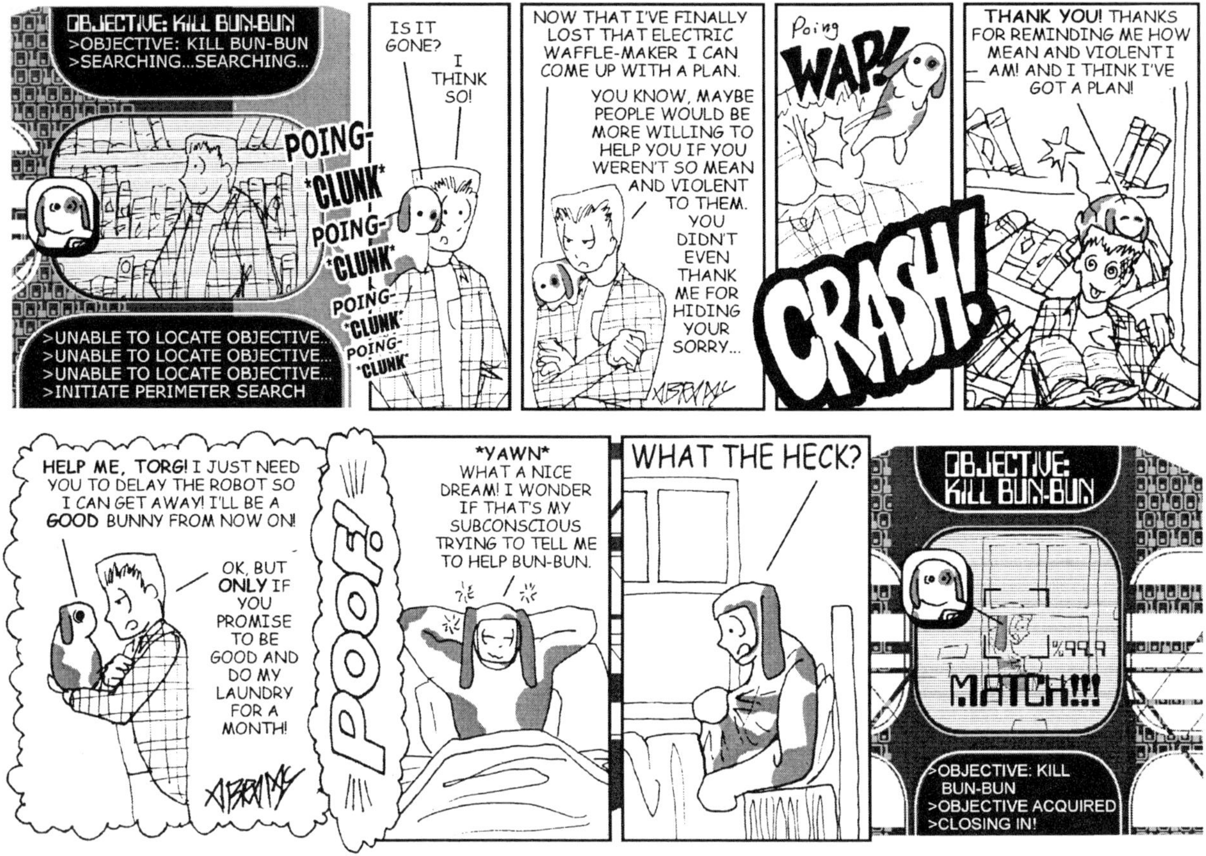
OBJECTIVE: KILL BUN-BUN
>OBJECTIVE: KILL BUN-BUN
>SEARCHING...SEARCHING...
>UNABLE TO LOCATE OBJECTIVE...
>UNABLE TO LOCATE OBJECTIVE...
>UNABLE TO LOCATE OBJECTIVE...
>INITIATE PERIMETER SEARCH
POING-
CLUNK
POING-
CLUNK
POING-
CLUNK
POING-
CLUNK
IS IT GONE?
I THINK SO!
NOW THAT I'VE FINALLY LOST THAT ELECTRIC WAFFLE-MAKER I CAN COME UP WITH A PLAN.
YOU KNOW, MAYBE PEOPLE WOULD BE MORE WILLING TO HELP YOU IF YOU WEREN'T SO MEAN AND VIOLENT TO THEM.
YOU DIDN'T EVEN THANK ME FOR HIDING YOUR SORRY...
Poing
WAP!
CRASH!
THANK YOU! THANKS FOR REMINDING ME HOW MEAN AND VIOLENT I AM! AND I THINK I'VE GOT A PLAN!
HELP ME, TORG! I JUST NEED YOU TO DELAY THE ROBOT SO I CAN GET AWAY! I'LL BE A GOOD BUNNY FROM NOW ON!
OK, BUT ONLY IF YOU PROMISE TO BE GOOD AND DO MY LAUNDRY FOR A MONTH!
POOF!
YAWN WHAT A NICE DREAM! I WONDER IF THAT'S MY SUBCONSCIOUS TRYING TO TELL ME TO HELP BUN-BUN.
WHAT THE HECK?
OBJECTIVE: KILL BUN-BUN
%99.9
MATCH!!!
>OBJECTIVE: KILL BUN-BUN
>OBJECTIVE ACQUIRED
>CLOSING IN!

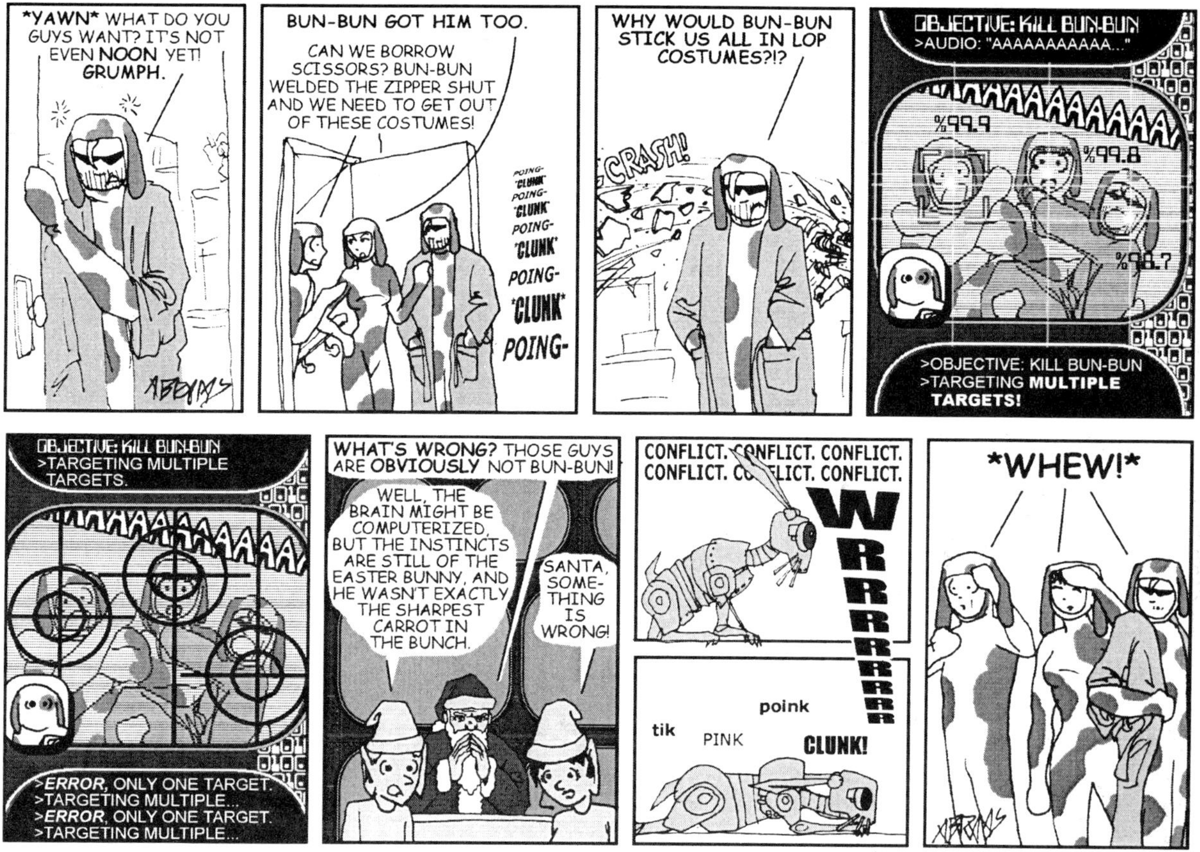
YAWN WHAT DO YOU GUYS WANT? IT'S NOT EVEN NOON YET! GRUMPH.
BUN-BUN GOT HIM TOO.
CAN WE BORROW SCISSORS? BUN-BUN WELDED THE ZIPPER SHUT AND WE NEED TO GET OUT OF THESE COSTUMES!
POING- CLUNK POING- CLUNK POING- CLUNK POING- CLUNK POING-
WHY WOULD BUN-BUN STICK US ALL IN LOP COSTUMES?!?
CRASH!
OBJECTIVE: KILL BUN-BUN
>AUDIO: "AAAAAAAAAAA..."
AAAAAAAAAAA
%99.9
%99.8
%98.7
>OBJECTIVE: KILL BUN-BUN
>TARGETING MULTIPLE TARGETS!
OBJECTIVE: KILL BUN-BUN
>TARGETING MULTIPLE TARGETS.
AAAAAAAAAAA
>ERROR, ONLY ONE TARGET.
>TARGETING MULTIPLE...
>ERROR, ONLY ONE TARGET.
>TARGETING MULTIPLE...
WHAT'S WRONG? THOSE GUYS ARE OBVIOUSLY NOT BUN-BUN!
WELL, THE BRAIN MIGHT BE COMPUTERIZED, BUT THE INSTINCTS ARE STILL OF THE EASTER BUNNY, AND HE WASN'T EXACTLY THE SHARPEST CARROT IN THE BUNCH.
SANTA, SOMETHING IS WRONG!
CONFLICT. CONFLICT. CONFLICT.
CONFLICT. CONFLICT. CONFLICT.
WRRRRRRRRR
tik
PINK
poink
CLUNK!
WHEW!

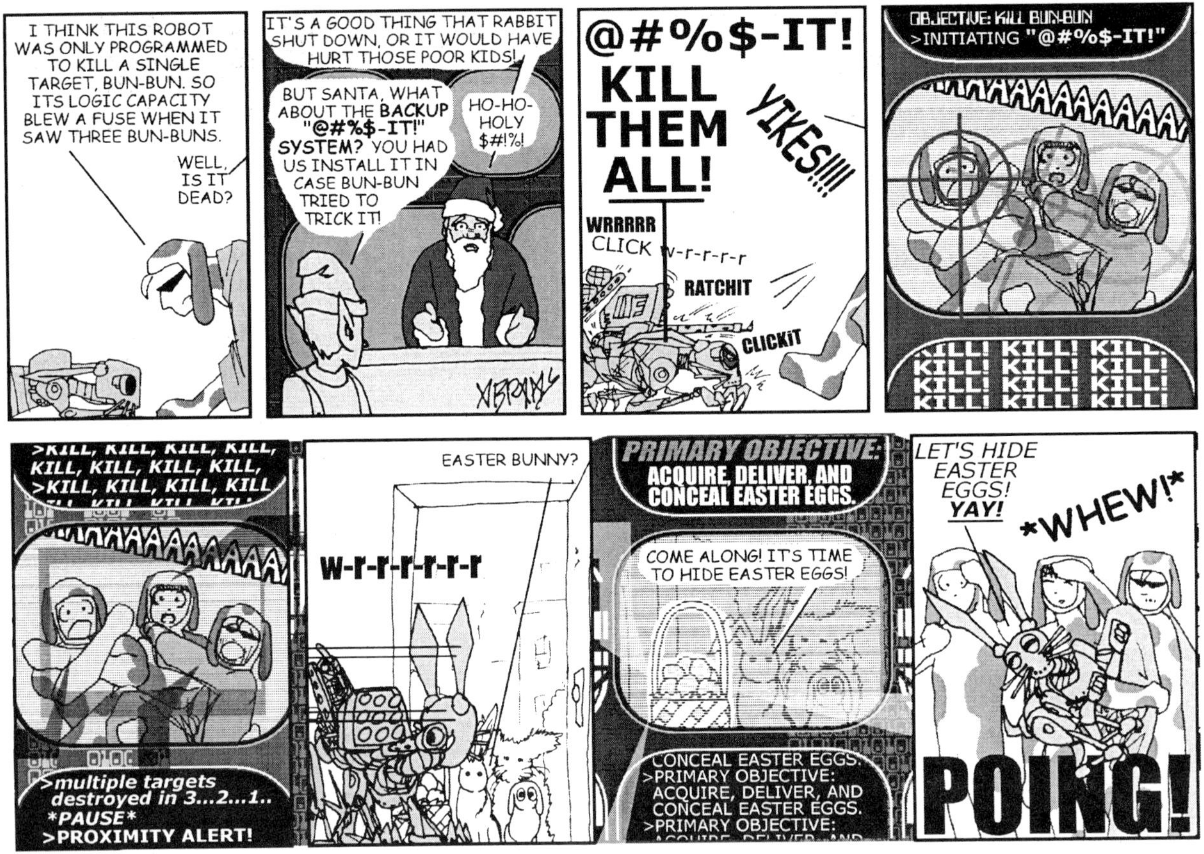

I THINK THIS ROBOT WAS ONLY PROGRAMMED TO KILL A SINGLE TARGET, BUN-BUN. SO ITS LOGIC CAPACITY BLEW A FUSE WHEN IT SAW THREE BUN-BUNS.
WELL, IS IT DEAD?
IT'S A GOOD THING THAT RABBIT SHUT DOWN, OR IT WOULD HAVE HURT THOSE POOR KIDS!
BUT SANTA, WHAT ABOUT THE BACKUP "@#%$-IT!" SYSTEM? YOU HAD US INSTALL IT IN CASE BUN-BUN TRIED TO TRICK IT!
HO-HO-HOLY $#!%!
@#%$-IT!
KILL THEM ALL!
YIKES!!!!!
WRRRRR
CLICK
w-r-r-r-r
RATCHIT
CLICKiT
OBJECTIVE: KILL BUN-BUN
>INITIATING "@#%$-IT!"
AAAAAAAAAAAA
KILL! KILL! KILL!
KILL! KILL! KILL!
KILL! KILL! KILL!
KILL! KILL! KILL!
>KILL, KILL, KILL, KILL,
KILL, KILL, KILL, KILL,
>KILL, KILL, KILL, KILL
AAAAAAAAAAAA
>multiple targets destroyed in 3...2...1..
PAUSE
>PROXIMITY ALERT!
EASTER BUNNY?
w-r-r-r-r-r-r
PRIMARY OBJECTIVE:
ACQUIRE, DELIVER, AND CONCEAL EASTER EGGS.
COME ALONG! IT'S TIME TO HIDE EASTER EGGS!
CONCEAL EASTER EGGS.
>PRIMARY OBJECTIVE:
ACQUIRE, DELIVER, AND
CONCEAL EASTER EGGS.
>PRIMARY OBJECTIVE:
LET'S HIDE EASTER EGGS! YAY!
WHEW!
POING!

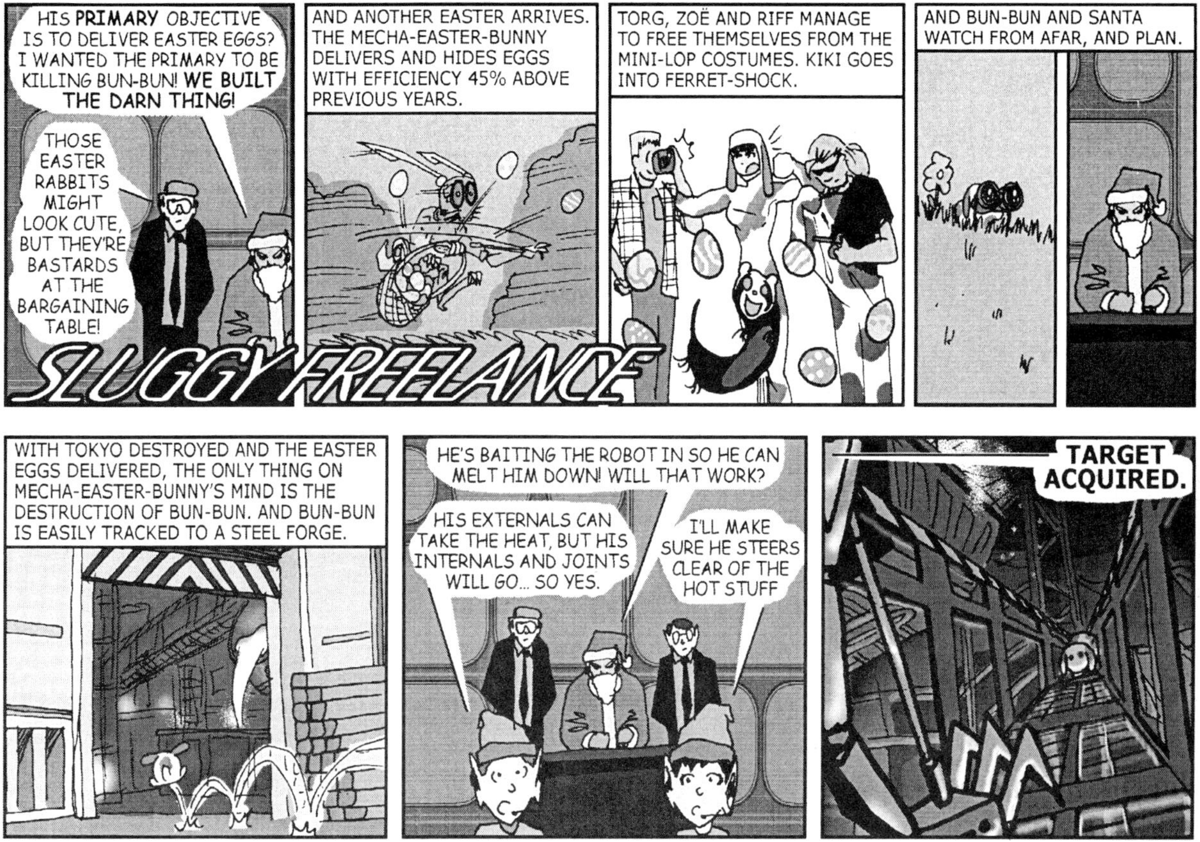
HIS PRIMARY OBJECTIVE IS TO DELIVER EASTER EGGS? I WANTED THE PRIMARY TO BE KILLING BUN-BUN! WE BUILT THE DARN THING!
THOSE EASTER RABBITS MIGHT LOOK CUTE, BUT THEY'RE BASTARDS AT THE BARGAINING TABLE!
SLUGGY FREELANCE
AND ANOTHER EASTER ARRIVES. THE MECHA-EASTER-BUNNY DELIVERS AND HIDES EGGS WITH EFFICIENCY 45% ABOVE PREVIOUS YEARS.
TORG, ZOË AND RIFF MANAGE TO FREE THEMSELVES FROM THE MINI-LOP COSTUMES. KIKI GOES INTO FERRET-SHOCK.
AND BUN-BUN AND SANTA WATCH FROM AFAR, AND PLAN.
WITH TOKYO DESTROYED AND THE EASTER EGGS DELIVERED, THE ONLY THING ON MECHA-EASTER-BUNNY'S MIND IS THE DESTRUCTION OF BUN-BUN. AND BUN-BUN IS EASILY TRACKED TO A STEEL FORGE.
HE'S BAITING THE ROBOT IN SO HE CAN MELT HIM DOWN! WILL THAT WORK?
HIS EXTERNALS CAN TAKE THE HEAT, BUT HIS INTERNALS AND JOINTS WILL GO... SO YES.
I'LL MAKE SURE HE STEERS CLEAR OF THE HOT STUFF
TARGET ACQUIRED.

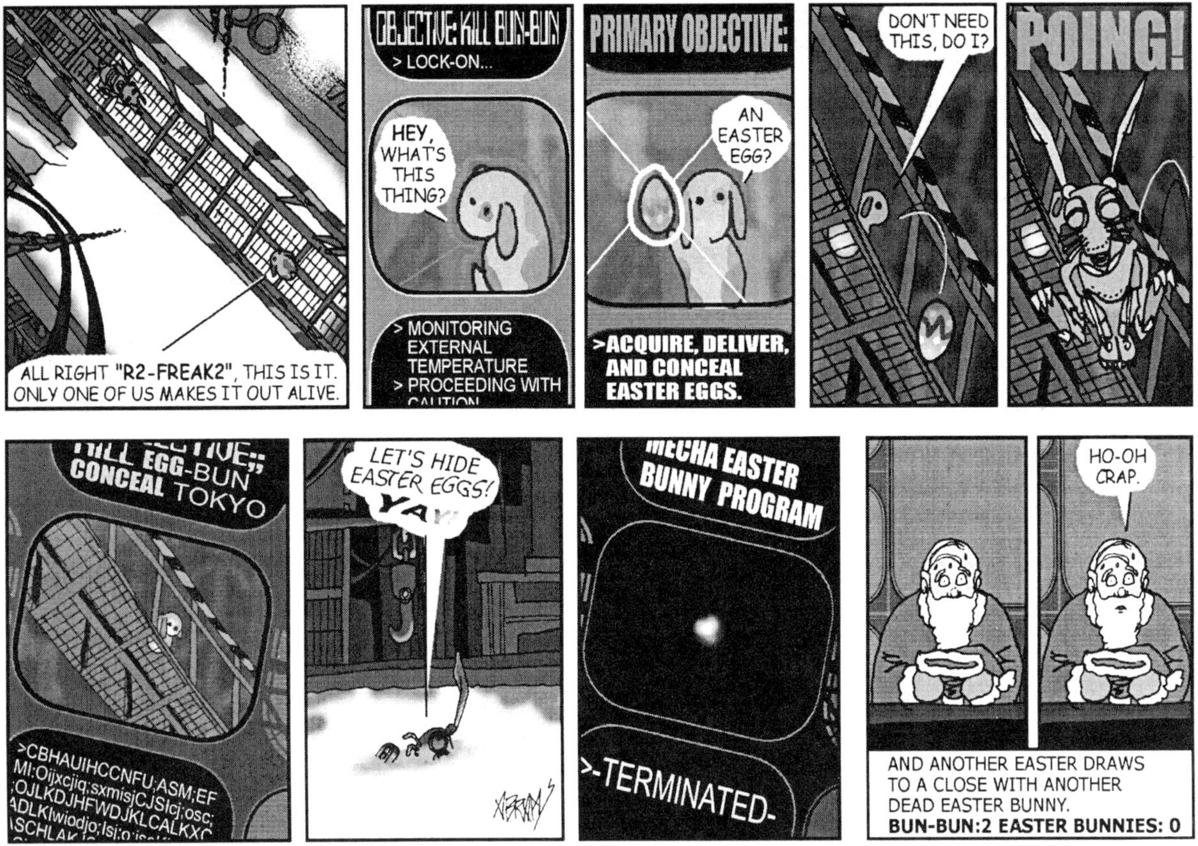
ALL RIGHT "R2-FREAK2", THIS IS IT. ONLY ONE OF US MAKES IT OUT ALIVE.
OBJECTIVE: KILL BUN-BUN
> LOCK-ON...
HEY, WHAT'S THIS THING?
> MONITORING EXTERNAL TEMPERATURE
> PROCEEDING WITH CAUTION
PRIMARY OBJECTIVE:
AN EASTER EGG?
>ACQUIRE, DELIVER, AND CONCEAL EASTER EGGS.
DON'T NEED THIS, DO I?
POING!
CONCEAL TOKYO
LET'S HIDE EASTER EGGS!
MECHA EASTER BUNNY PROGRAM
>-TERMINATED-
HO-OH CRAP.
AND ANOTHER EASTER DRAWS TO A CLOSE WITH ANOTHER DEAD EASTER BUNNY.
BUN-BUN:2 EASTER BUNNIES: 0

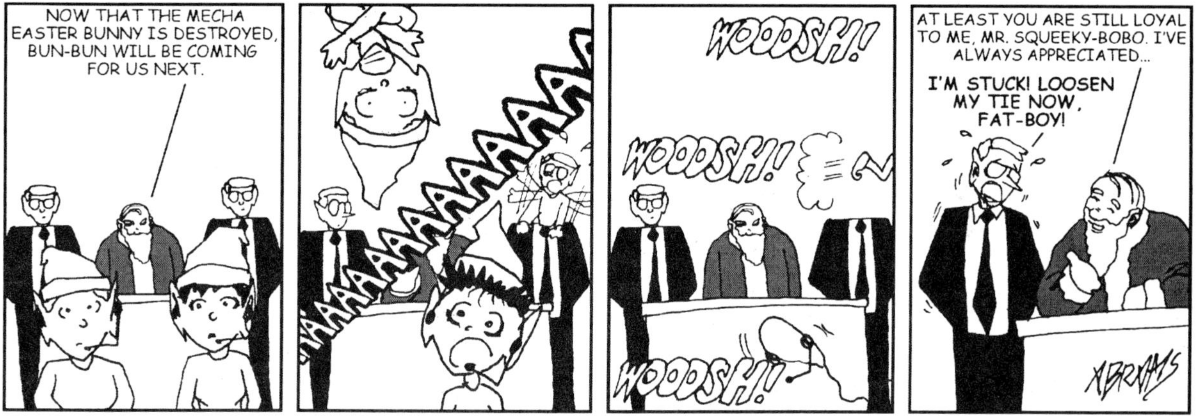
NOW THAT THE MECHA EASTER BUNNY IS DESTROYED, BUN-BUN WILL BE COMING FOR US NEXT.
WOOOSH!
WOOOSH!
WOOOSH!
AT LEAST YOU ARE STILL LOYAL TO ME, MR. SQUEEKY-BOBO. I'VE ALWAYS APPRECIATED...
I'M STUCK! LOOSEN MY TIE NOW, FAT-BOY!

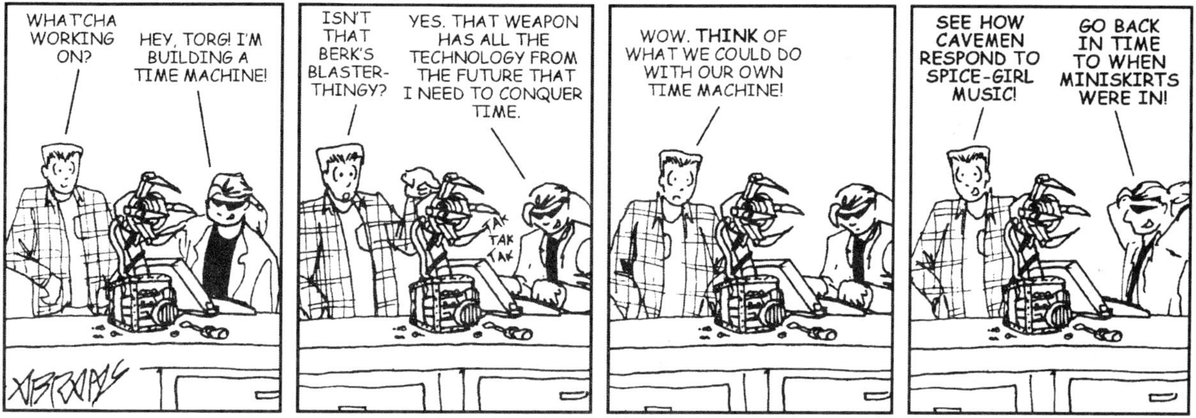
WHAT'CHA WORKING ON?
HEY, TORG! I'M BUILDING A TIME MACHINE!
ISN'T THAT BERK'S BLASTER-THINGY?
YES. THAT WEAPON HAS ALL THE TECHNOLOGY FROM THE FUTURE THAT I NEED TO CONQUER TIME.
TAK TAK TAK
WOW. THINK OF WHAT WE COULD DO WITH OUR OWN TIME MACHINE!
SEE HOW CAVEMEN RESPOND TO SPICE-GIRL MUSIC!
GO BACK IN TIME TO WHEN MINISKIRTS WERE IN!

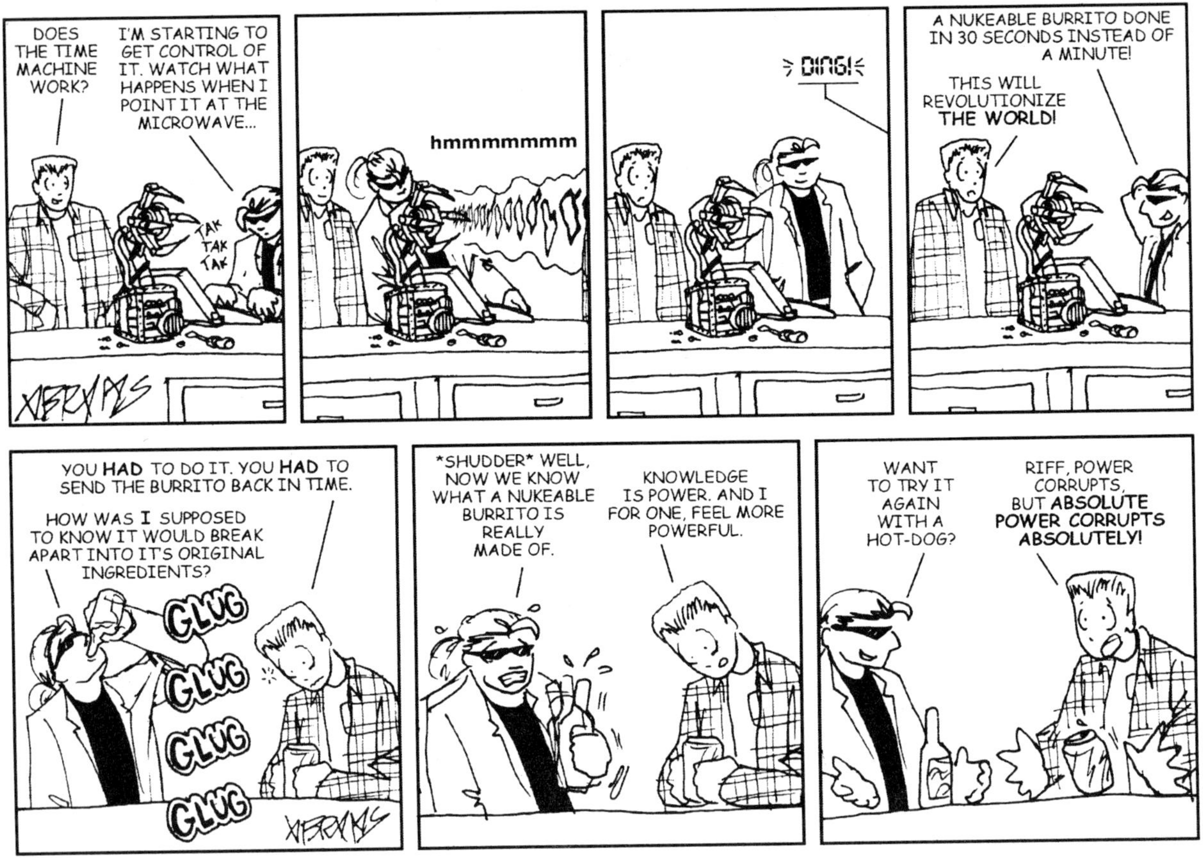

DOES THE TIME MACHINE WORK?
I'M STARTING TO GET CONTROL OF IT. WATCH WHAT HAPPENS WHEN I POINT IT AT THE MICROWAVE...
TAK TAK TAK
hmmmmmmm
DING!
A NUKEABLE BURRITO DONE IN 30 SECONDS INSTEAD OF A MINUTE!
THIS WILL REVOLUTIONIZE THE WORLD!
YOU HAD TO DO IT. YOU HAD TO SEND THE BURRITO BACK IN TIME.
HOW WAS I SUPPOSED TO KNOW IT WOULD BREAK APART INTO IT'S ORIGINAL INGREDIENTS?
GLUG GLUG GLUG GLUG
SHUDDER WELL, NOW WE KNOW WHAT A NUKEABLE BURRITO IS REALLY MADE OF.
KNOWLEDGE IS POWER. AND I FOR ONE, FEEL MORE POWERFUL.
WANT TO TRY IT AGAIN WITH A HOT-DOG?
RIFF, POWER CORRUPTS, BUT ABSOLUTE POWER CORRUPTS ABSOLUTELY!

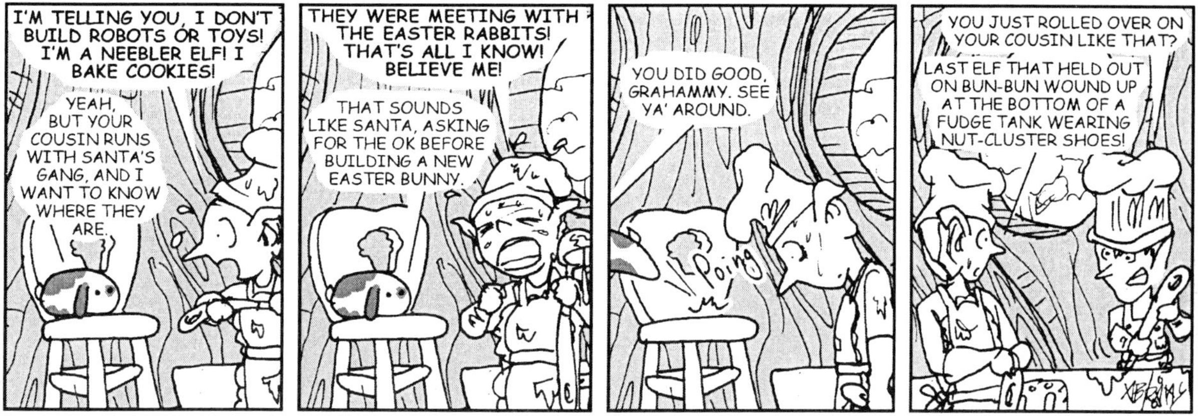
I'M TELLING YOU, I DON'T BUILD ROBOTS OR TOYS! I'M A NEEBLER ELF! I BAKE COOKIES!
YEAH, BUT YOUR COUSIN RUNS WITH SANTA'S GANG, AND I WANT TO KNOW WHERE THEY ARE.
THEY WERE MEETING WITH THE EASTER RABBITS! THAT'S ALL I KNOW! BELIEVE ME!
THAT SOUNDS LIKE SANTA, ASKING FOR THE OK BEFORE BUILDING A NEW EASTER BUNNY.
YOU DID GOOD, GRAHAMMY. SEE YA' AROUND.
Poing
YOU JUST ROLLED OVER ON YOUR COUSIN LIKE THAT?
LAST ELF THAT HELD OUT ON BUN-BUN WOUND UP AT THE BOTTOM OF A FUDGE TANK WEARING NUT-CLUSTER SHOES!

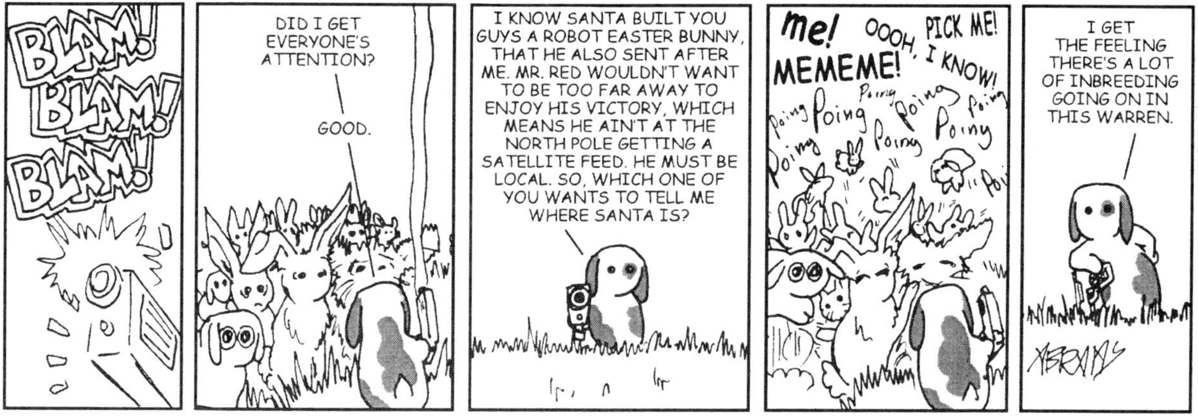
BLAM! BLAM! BLAM!
DID I GET EVERYONE'S ATTENTION?
GOOD.
I KNOW SANTA BUILT YOU GUYS A ROBOT EASTER BUNNY, THAT HE ALSO SENT AFTER ME. MR. RED WOULDN'T WANT TO BE TOO FAR AWAY TO ENJOY HIS VICTORY, WHICH MEANS HE AIN'T AT THE NORTH POLE GETTING A SATELLITE FEED. HE MUST BE LOCAL. SO, WHICH ONE OF YOU WANTS TO TELL ME WHERE SANTA IS?
me!
OOOH, I KNOW!
PICK ME!
MEMEME!
Poing Poing Poing Poing Poing Poing Poing
I GET THE FEELING THERE'S A LOT OF INBREEDING GOING ON IN THIS WARREN.

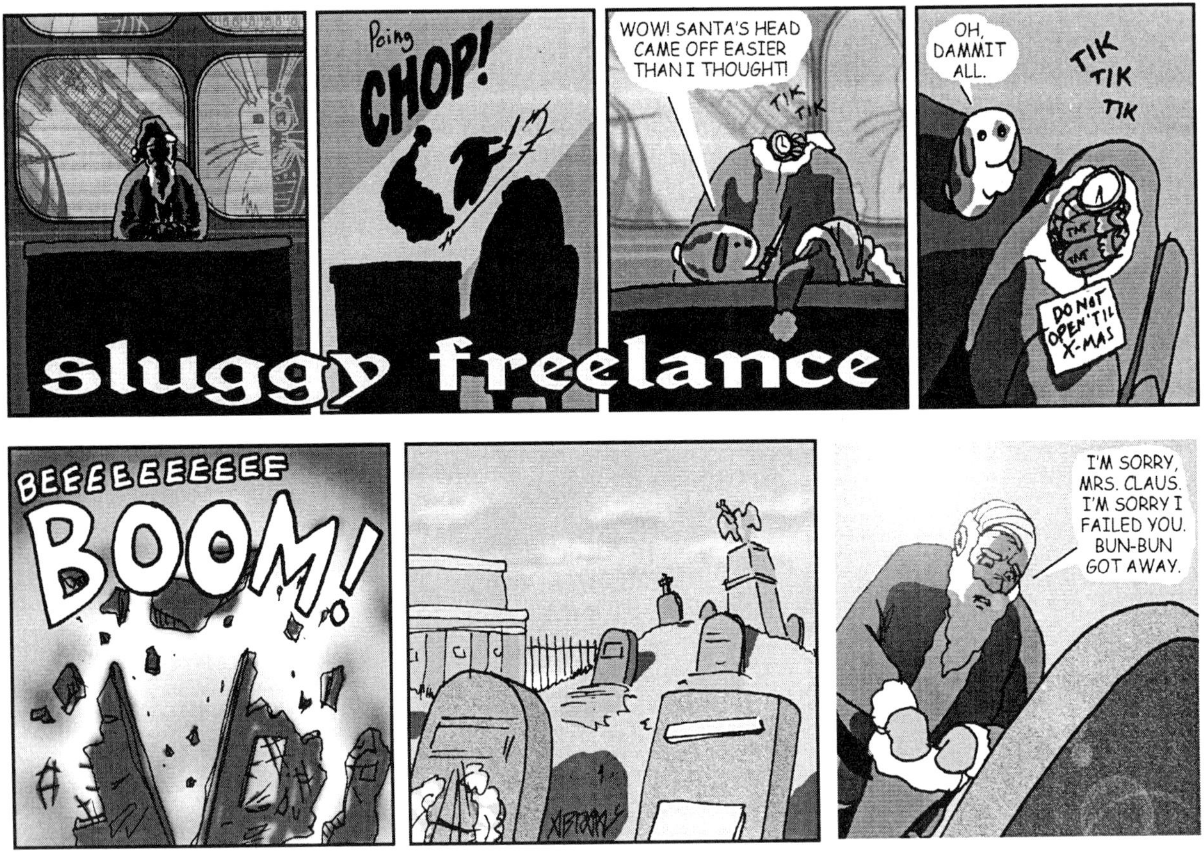
Poing
CHOP!
sluggy freelance
WOW! SANTA'S HEAD CAME OFF EASIER THAN I THOUGHT!
TIK TIK
OH, DAMMIT ALL.
TIK TIK TIK
DO NOT OPEN 'TIL X-MAS
BEEEEEEEEEE
BOOM!
I'M SORRY, MRS. CLAUS. I'M SORRY I FAILED YOU. BUN-BUN GOT AWAY.

I KNOW WHAT YOU'RE THINKING, I SWEAR I CAN ALMOST HEAR YOUR VOICE SAYING, "CHRISTMAS IS MORE IMPORTANT, JUST LET IT GO." YOU ALWAYS WERE MORE LEVEL HEADED THAN I.
BUT I VOWED I'D MAKE HIM PAY FOR WHAT HE HAD DONE. WITH THAT ONE BOMB, HE DESTROYED SO MUCH. MY WORKSHOP, SOME OF MY ELVES, AND WHAT HE DID TO US...
WHAT? YOU GOT THE WIND KNOCKED OUT OF YOU AND I WASN'T EVEN HOME WHEN THE WORKSHOP BLEW UP!
THAT'S NOT THE POINT, MRS. CLAUS! THAT BUNNY HAS GONE TOO FAR!
WELL, IT'S TIME TO GO HOME, DEAR.
BUT BUN-BUN ISN'T DEAD YET! I SET UP THIS GRAVE FOR HIM AND EVERYTHING!
STOP BEING SO MORBID. BESIDES, MAYBE THE EXPLOSIVES I LEFT FOR BUN-BUN BLEW HIM UP!
HERE LIES BUN-BUN
MAY HE REST IN PEACE
"IT WOULD TAKE MORE THAN EXPLOSIVES TO TAKE CARE OF HIM, MRS. CLAUS."
MAY HE REST IN PEACE

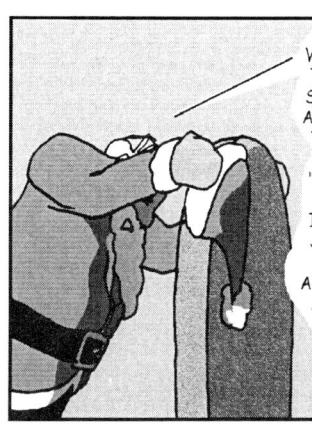

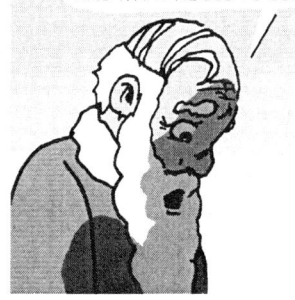

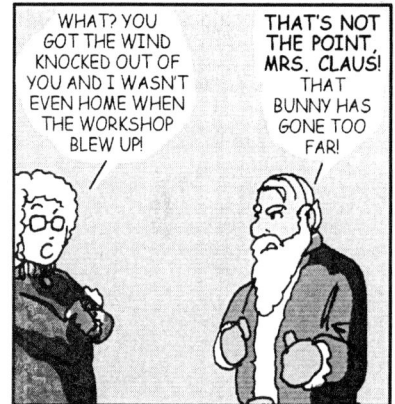

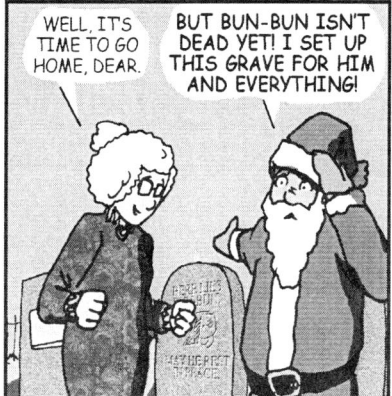

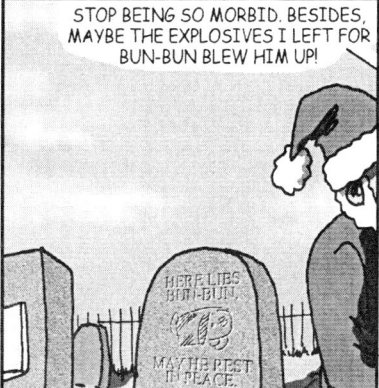

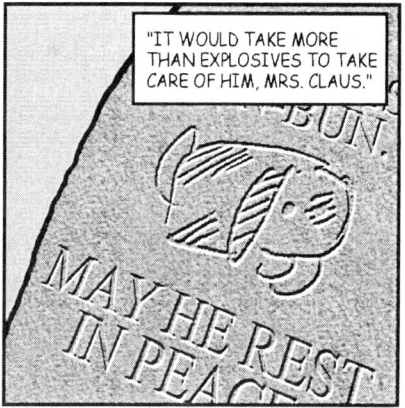

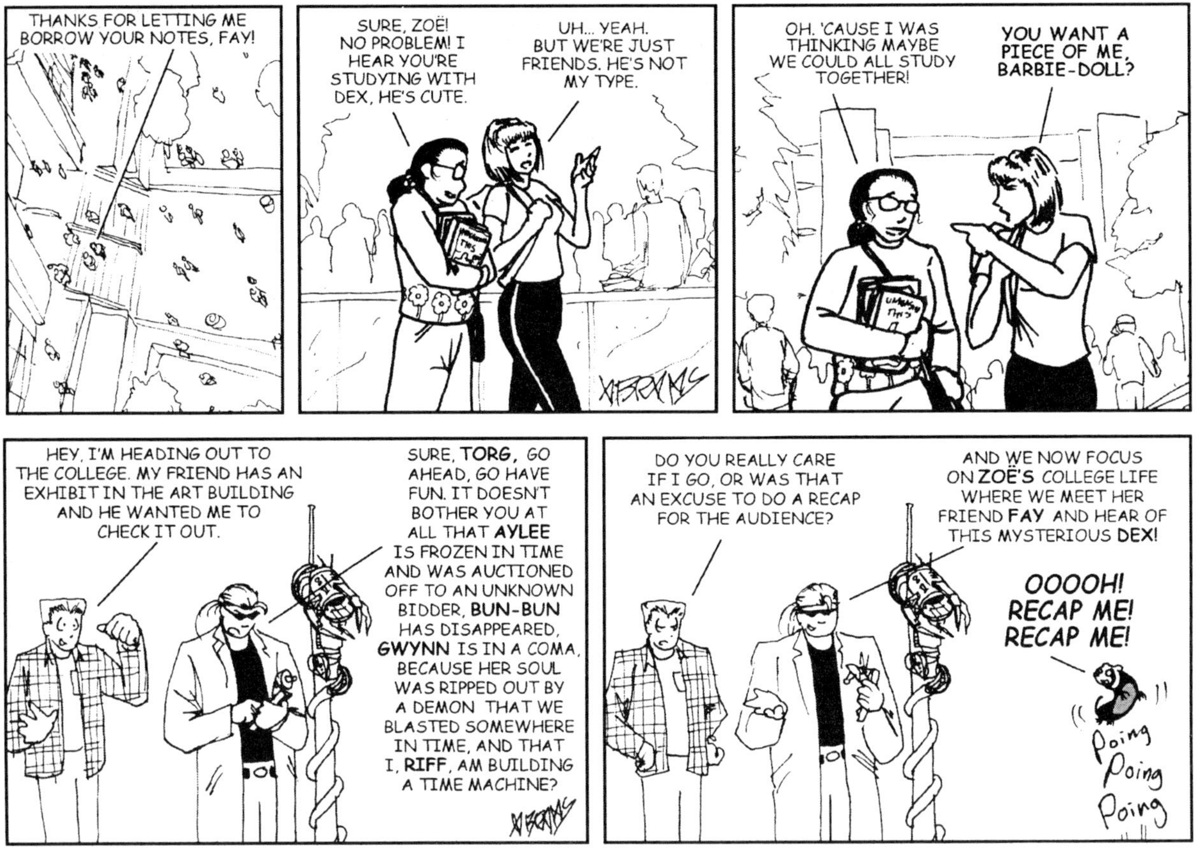

THANKS FOR LETTING ME BORROW YOUR NOTES, FAY!
SURE, ZOË! NO PROBLEM! I HEAR YOU'RE STUDYING WITH DEX, HE'S CUTE.
UH... YEAH. BUT WE'RE JUST FRIENDS. HE'S NOT MY TYPE.
OH. 'CAUSE I WAS THINKING MAYBE WE COULD ALL STUDY TOGETHER!
YOU WANT A PIECE OF ME, BARBIE-DOLL?
HEY, I'M HEADING OUT TO THE COLLEGE. MY FRIEND HAS AN EXHIBIT IN THE ART BUILDING AND HE WANTED ME TO CHECK IT OUT.
SURE, TORG, GO AHEAD, GO HAVE FUN. IT DOESN'T BOTHER YOU AT ALL THAT AYLEE IS FROZEN IN TIME AND WAS AUCTIONED OFF TO AN UNKNOWN BIDDER, BUN-BUN HAS DISAPPEARED, GWYNN IS IN A COMA, BECAUSE HER SOUL WAS RIPPED OUT BY A DEMON THAT WE BLASTED SOMEWHERE IN TIME, AND THAT I, RIFF, AM BUILDING A TIME MACHINE?
DO YOU REALLY CARE IF I GO, OR WAS THAT AN EXCUSE TO DO A RECAP FOR THE AUDIENCE?
AND WE NOW FOCUS ON ZOË'S COLLEGE LIFE WHERE WE MEET HER FRIEND FAY AND HEAR OF THIS MYSTERIOUS DEX!
OOOOH! RECAP ME! RECAP ME!
Poing Poing Poing

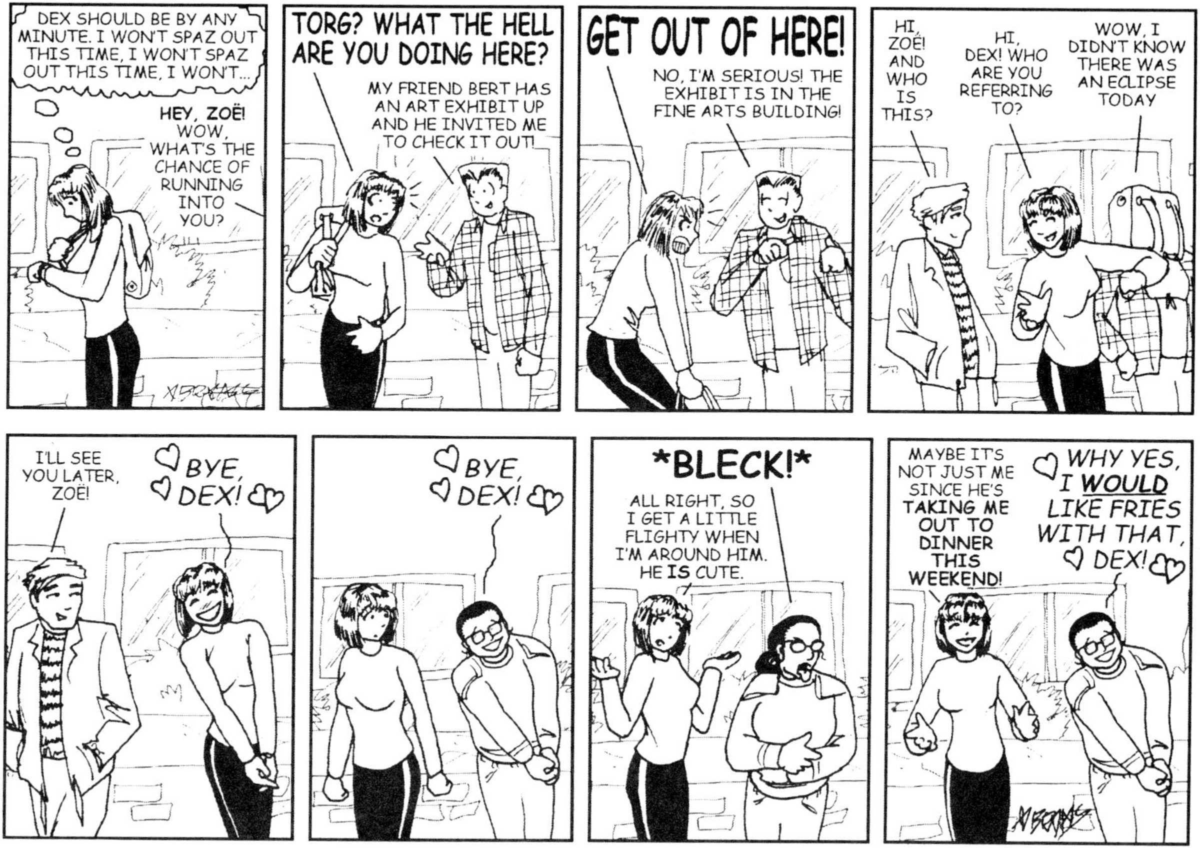
DEX SHOULD BE BY ANY MINUTE. I WON'T SPAZ OUT THIS TIME, I WON'T SPAZ OUT THIS TIME, I WON'T...
HEY, ZOË! WOW, WHAT'S THE CHANCE OF RUNNING INTO YOU?
TORG? WHAT THE HELL ARE YOU DOING HERE?
MY FRIEND BERT HAS AN ART EXHIBIT UP AND HE INVITED ME TO CHECK IT OUT!
GET OUT OF HERE!
NO, I'M SERIOUS! THE EXHIBIT IS IN THE FINE ARTS BUILDING!
HI, ZOË! AND WHO IS THIS?
HI, DEX! WHO ARE YOU REFERRING TO?
WOW, I DIDN'T KNOW THERE WAS AN ECLIPSE TODAY
I'LL SEE YOU LATER, ZOË!
BYE, DEX!
BYE, DEX!
BLECK!
ALL RIGHT, SO I GET A LITTLE FLIGHTY WHEN I'M AROUND HIM. HE IS CUTE.
MAYBE IT'S NOT JUST ME SINCE HE'S TAKING ME OUT TO DINNER THIS WEEKEND!
WHY YES, I WOULD LIKE FRIES WITH THAT, DEX!

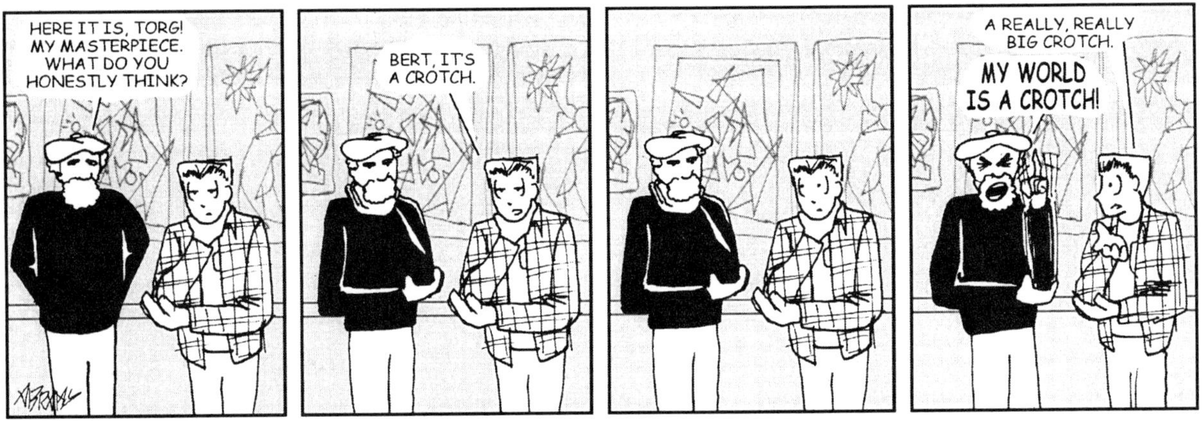
HERE IT IS, TORG! MY MASTERPIECE. WHAT DO YOU HONESTLY THINK?
BERT, IT'S A CROTCH.
A REALLY, REALLY BIG CROTCH.
MY WORLD IS A CROTCH!

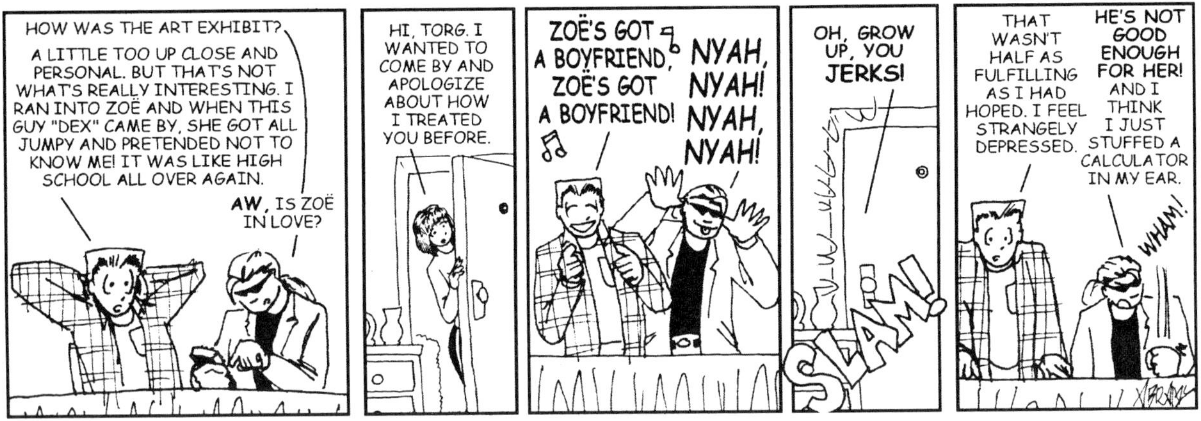
HOW WAS THE ART EXHIBIT?
A LITTLE TOO UP CLOSE AND PERSONAL. BUT THAT'S NOT WHAT'S REALLY INTERESTING. I RAN INTO ZOË AND WHEN THIS GUY "DEX" CAME BY, SHE GOT ALL JUMPY AND PRETENDED NOT TO KNOW ME! IT WAS LIKE HIGH SCHOOL ALL OVER AGAIN.
AW, IS ZOË IN LOVE?
HI, TORG. I WANTED TO COME BY AND APOLOGIZE ABOUT HOW I TREATED YOU BEFORE.
ZOË'S GOT A BOYFRIEND, ZOË'S GOT A BOYFRIEND!
NYAH, NYAH! NYAH, NYAH!
OH, GROW UP, YOU JERKS!
SLAM!
THAT WASN'T HALF AS FULFILLING AS I HAD HOPED. I FEEL STRANGELY DEPRESSED.
HE'S NOT GOOD ENOUGH FOR HER! AND I THINK I JUST STUFFED A CALCULATOR IN MY EAR.
WHAM!

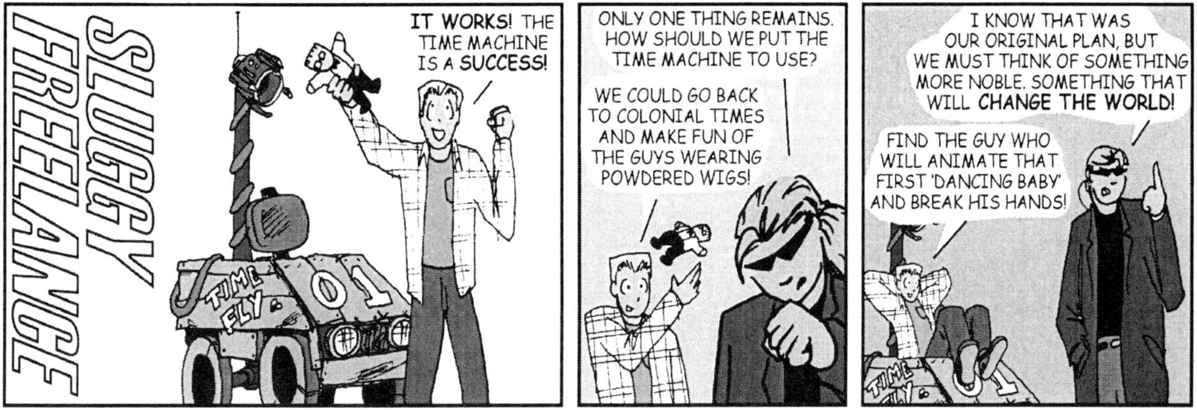
SLUGGY FREELANCE
IT WORKS! THE TIME MACHINE IS A SUCCESS!
TIME FLY 01
ONLY ONE THING REMAINS. HOW SHOULD WE PUT THE TIME MACHINE TO USE?
WE COULD GO BACK TO COLONIAL TIMES AND MAKE FUN OF THE GUYS WEARING POWDERED WIGS!
I KNOW THAT WAS OUR ORIGINAL PLAN, BUT WE MUST THINK OF SOMETHING MORE NOBLE. SOMETHING THAT WILL CHANGE THE WORLD!
FIND THE GUY WHO WILL ANIMATE THAT FIRST 'DANCING BABY' AND BREAK HIS HANDS!

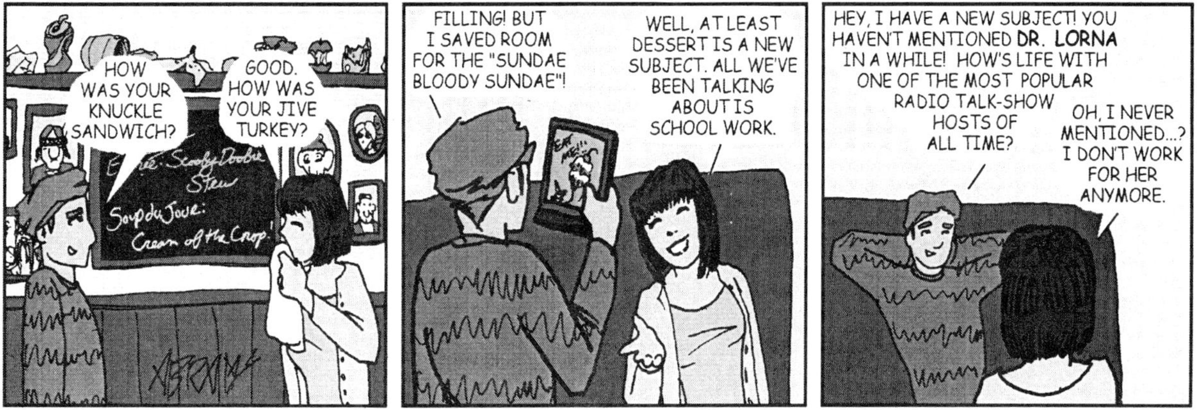
HOW WAS YOUR KNUCKLE SANDWICH?
GOOD. HOW WAS YOUR JIVE TURKEY?
Soup du Joue: Cream of the Crop!
FILLING! BUT I SAVED ROOM FOR THE "SUNDAE BLOODY SUNDAE"!
WELL, AT LEAST DESSERT IS A NEW SUBJECT. ALL WE'VE BEEN TALKING ABOUT IS SCHOOL WORK.
HEY, I HAVE A NEW SUBJECT! YOU HAVEN'T MENTIONED DR. LORNA IN A WHILE! HOW'S LIFE WITH ONE OF THE MOST POPULAR RADIO TALK-SHOW HOSTS OF ALL TIME?
OH, I NEVER MENTIONED...? I DON'T WORK FOR HER ANYMORE.

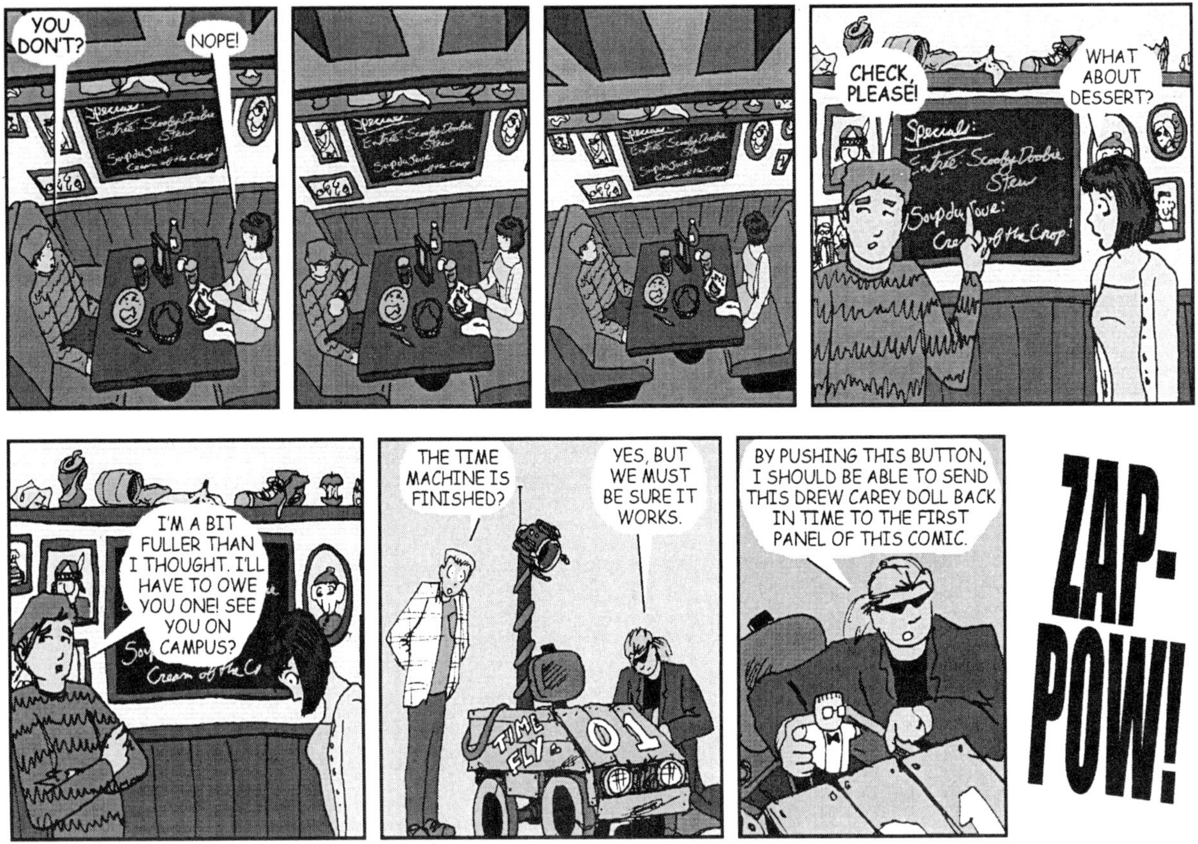
YOU DON'T?
NOPE!
Specials:
Entrée: Scooby Doobie Stew
Soup du Jour: Cream of the Crop!
CHECK, PLEASE!
WHAT ABOUT DESSERT?
I'M A BIT FULLER THAN I THOUGHT. I'LL HAVE TO OWE YOU ONE! SEE YOU ON CAMPUS?
THE TIME MACHINE IS FINISHED?
YES, BUT WE MUST BE SURE IT WORKS.
TIME FLY
01
BY PUSHING THIS BUTTON, I SHOULD BE ABLE TO SEND THIS DREW CAREY DOLL BACK IN TIME TO THE FIRST PANEL OF THIS COMIC.
ZAP-POW!!

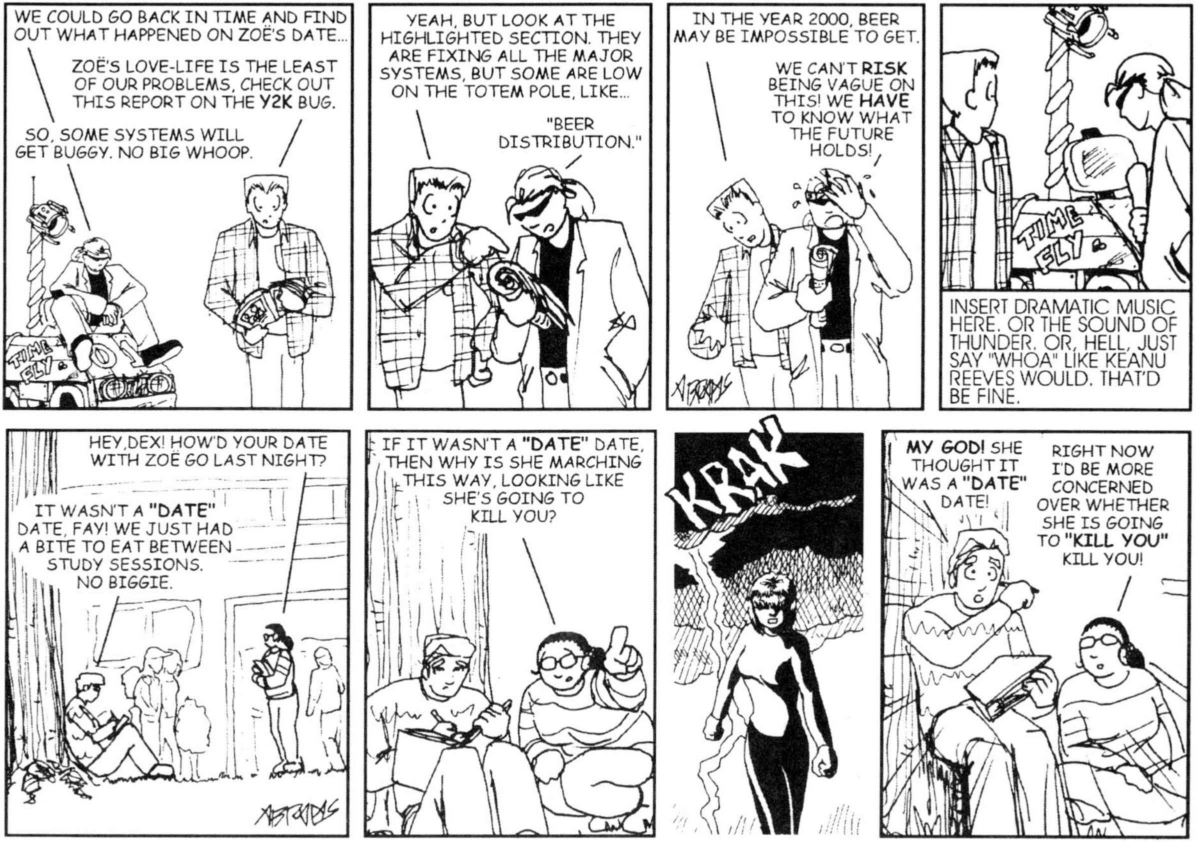
WE COULD GO BACK IN TIME AND FIND OUT WHAT HAPPENED ON ZOË'S DATE...
ZOË'S LOVE-LIFE IS THE LEAST OF OUR PROBLEMS, CHECK OUT THIS REPORT ON THE **Y2K** BUG.
SO, SOME SYSTEMS WILL GET BUGGY. NO BIG WHOOP.
TIME FLY
YEAH, BUT LOOK AT THE HIGHLIGHTED SECTION. THEY ARE FIXING ALL THE MAJOR SYSTEMS, BUT SOME ARE LOW ON THE TOTEM POLE, LIKE...
"BEER DISTRIBUTION."
IN THE YEAR 2000, BEER MAY BE IMPOSSIBLE TO GET.
WE CAN'T **RISK** BEING VAGUE ON THIS! WE **HAVE** TO KNOW WHAT THE FUTURE HOLDS!
TIME FLY
INSERT DRAMATIC MUSIC HERE. OR THE SOUND OF THUNDER. OR, HELL, JUST SAY "WHOA" LIKE KEANU REEVES WOULD. THAT'D BE FINE.
HEY, DEX! HOW'D YOUR DATE WITH ZOË GO LAST NIGHT?
IT WASN'T A **"DATE"** DATE, FAY! WE JUST HAD A BITE TO EAT BETWEEN STUDY SESSIONS. NO BIGGIE.
IF IT WASN'T A **"DATE"** DATE, THEN WHY IS SHE MARCHING THIS WAY, LOOKING LIKE SHE'S GOING TO KILL YOU?
KRAK
MY GOD! SHE THOUGHT IT WAS A **"DATE"** DATE!
RIGHT NOW I'D BE MORE CONCERNED OVER WHETHER SHE IS GOING TO **"KILL YOU"** KILL YOU!

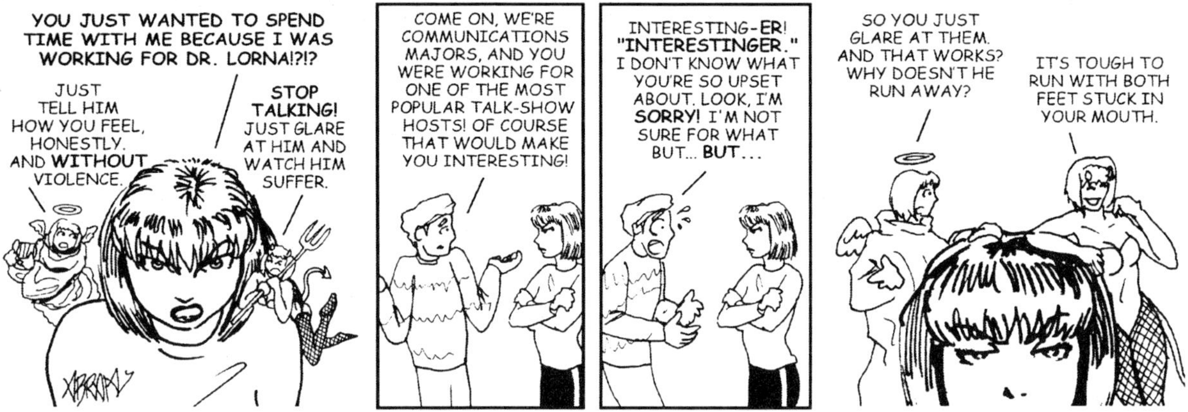
YOU JUST WANTED TO SPEND TIME WITH ME BECAUSE I WAS WORKING FOR DR. LORNA!?!?
JUST TELL HIM HOW YOU FEEL, HONESTLY. AND WITHOUT VIOLENCE.
STOP TALKING! JUST GLARE AT HIM AND WATCH HIM SUFFER.
COME ON, WE'RE COMMUNICATIONS MAJORS, AND YOU WERE WORKING FOR ONE OF THE MOST POPULAR TALK-SHOW HOSTS! OF COURSE THAT WOULD MAKE YOU INTERESTING!
INTERESTING-ER! "INTERESTINGER." I DON'T KNOW WHAT YOU'RE SO UPSET ABOUT. LOOK, I'M SORRY! I'M NOT SURE FOR WHAT BUT... BUT...
SO YOU JUST GLARE AT THEM. AND THAT WORKS? WHY DOESN'T HE RUN AWAY?
IT'S TOUGH TO RUN WITH BOTH FEET STUCK IN YOUR MOUTH.

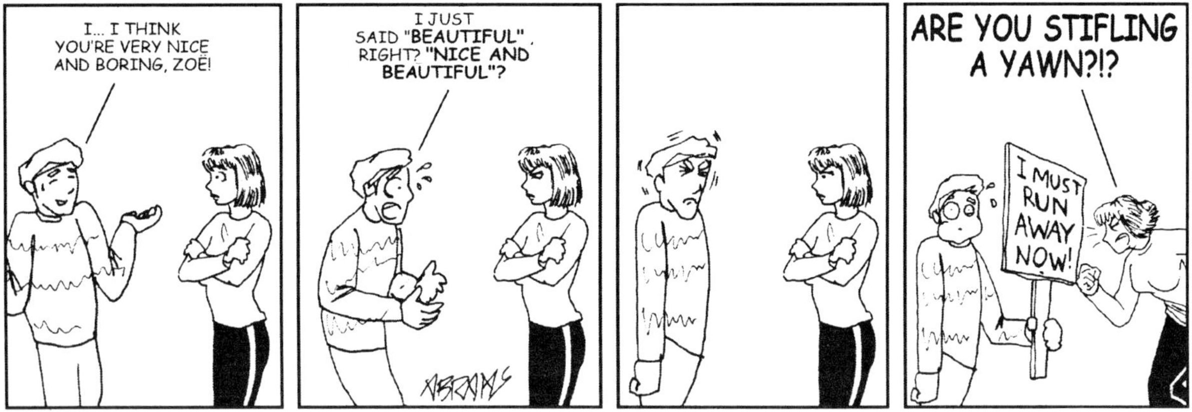
I... I THINK YOU'RE VERY NICE AND BORING, ZOË!
I JUST SAID "BEAUTIFUL", RIGHT? "NICE AND BEAUTIFUL"?
ARE YOU STIFLING A YAWN?!?
I MUST RUN AWAY NOW!

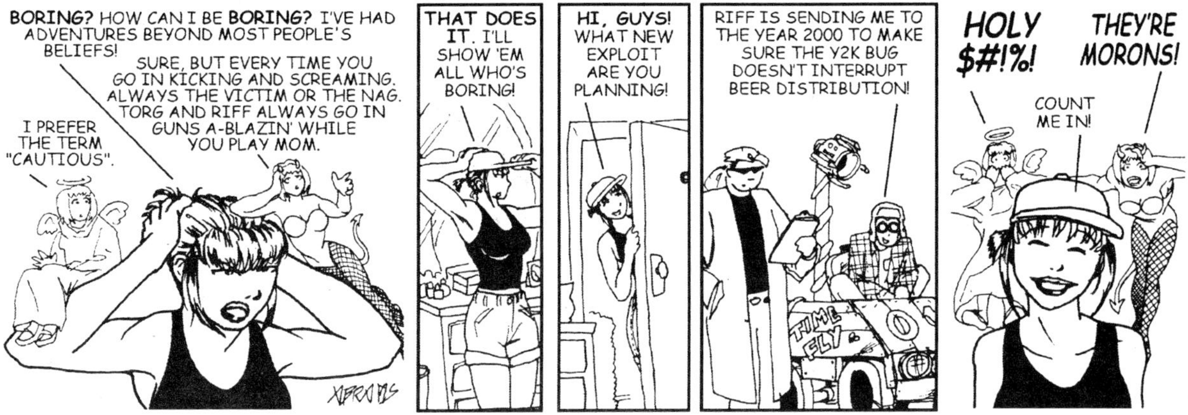
BORING? HOW CAN I BE BORING? I'VE HAD ADVENTURES BEYOND MOST PEOPLE'S BELIEFS!
SURE, BUT EVERY TIME YOU GO IN KICKING AND SCREAMING. ALWAYS THE VICTIM OR THE NAG. TORG AND RIFF ALWAYS GO IN GUNS A-BLAZIN' WHILE YOU PLAY MOM.
I PREFER THE TERM "CAUTIOUS".
THAT DOES IT. I'LL SHOW 'EM ALL WHO'S BORING!
HI, GUYS! WHAT NEW EXPLOIT ARE YOU PLANNING!
RIFF IS SENDING ME TO THE YEAR 2000 TO MAKE SURE THE Y2K BUG DOESN'T INTERRUPT BEER DISTRIBUTION!
HOLY $#!%!
THEY'RE MORONS!
COUNT ME IN!

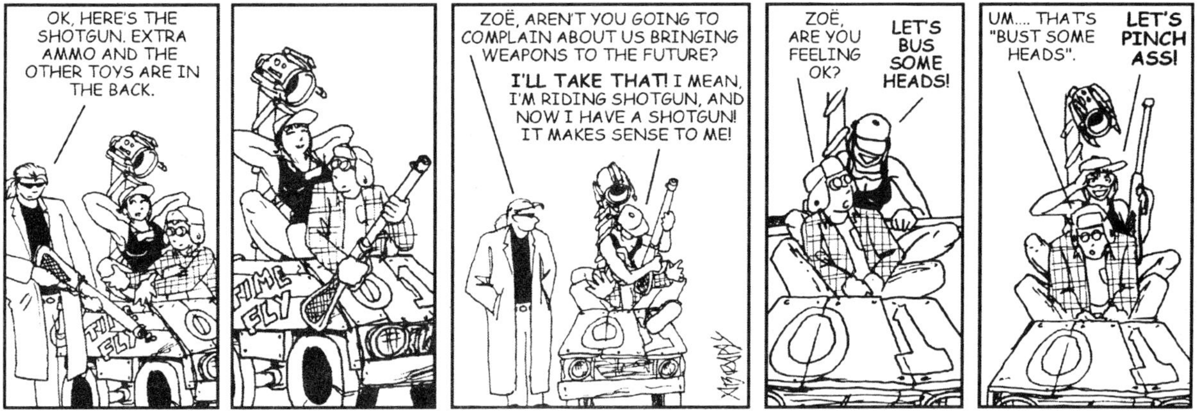
OK, HERE'S THE SHOTGUN. EXTRA AMMO AND THE OTHER TOYS ARE IN THE BACK.
ZOË, AREN'T YOU GOING TO COMPLAIN ABOUT US BRINGING WEAPONS TO THE FUTURE?
I'LL TAKE THAT! I MEAN, I'M RIDING SHOTGUN, AND NOW I HAVE A SHOTGUN! IT MAKES SENSE TO ME!
ZOË, ARE YOU FEELING OK?
LET'S BUS SOME HEADS!
UM.... THAT'S "BUST SOME HEADS".
LET'S PINCH ASS!

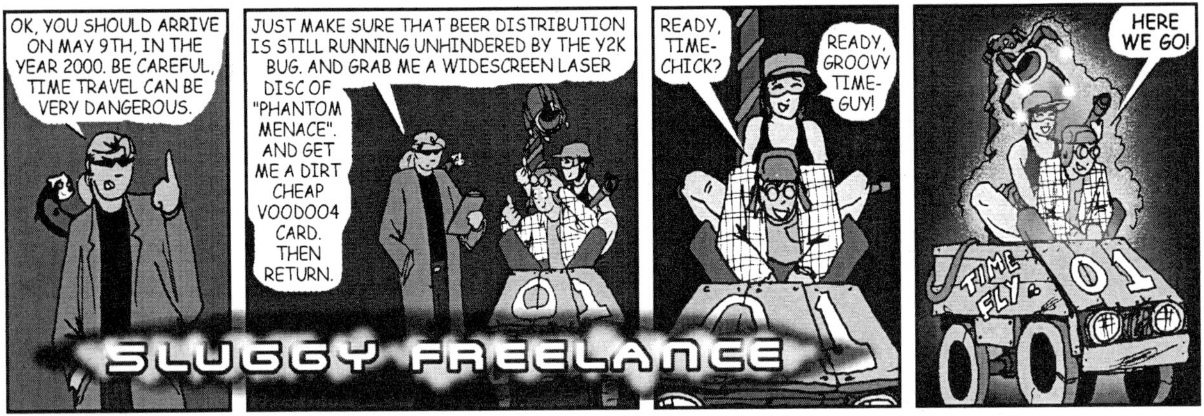
OK, YOU SHOULD ARRIVE ON MAY 9TH, IN THE YEAR 2000. BE CAREFUL, TIME TRAVEL CAN BE VERY DANGEROUS.
JUST MAKE SURE THAT BEER DISTRIBUTION IS STILL RUNNING UNHINDERED BY THE Y2K BUG. AND GRAB ME A WIDESCREEN LASER DISC OF "PHANTOM MENACE". AND GET ME A DIRT CHEAP VOODOO4 CARD. THEN RETURN.
SLUGGY FREELANCE
READY, TIME-CHICK?
READY, GROOVY TIME-GUY!
01
HERE WE GO!
TIME FLY
01

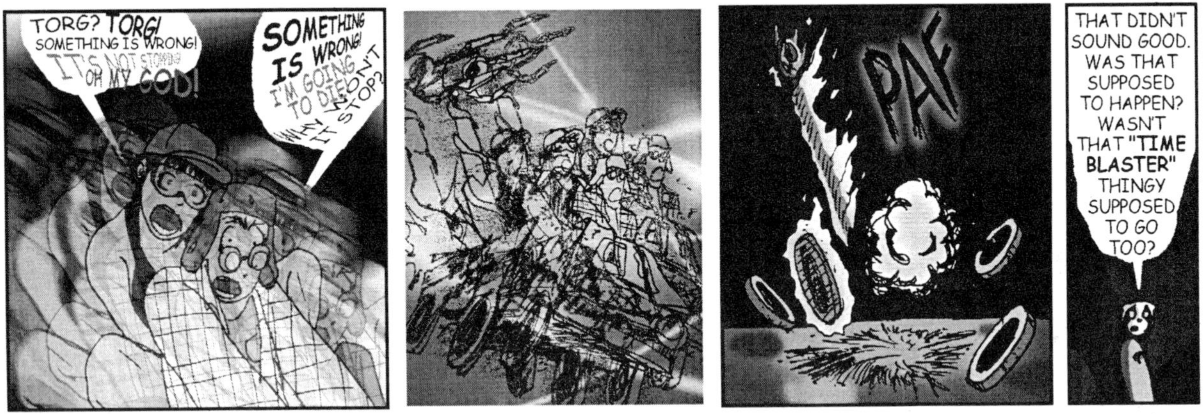
TORG? TORG! SOMETHING IS WRONG!
IT'S NOT STOPPING! OH MY GOD!
SOMETHING IS WRONG!
I'M GOING TO DIE!
WHY WON'T IT STOP?
PAF
THAT DIDN'T SOUND GOOD. WAS THAT SUPPOSED TO HAPPEN? WASN'T THAT "TIME BLASTER" THINGY SUPPOSED TO GO TOO?

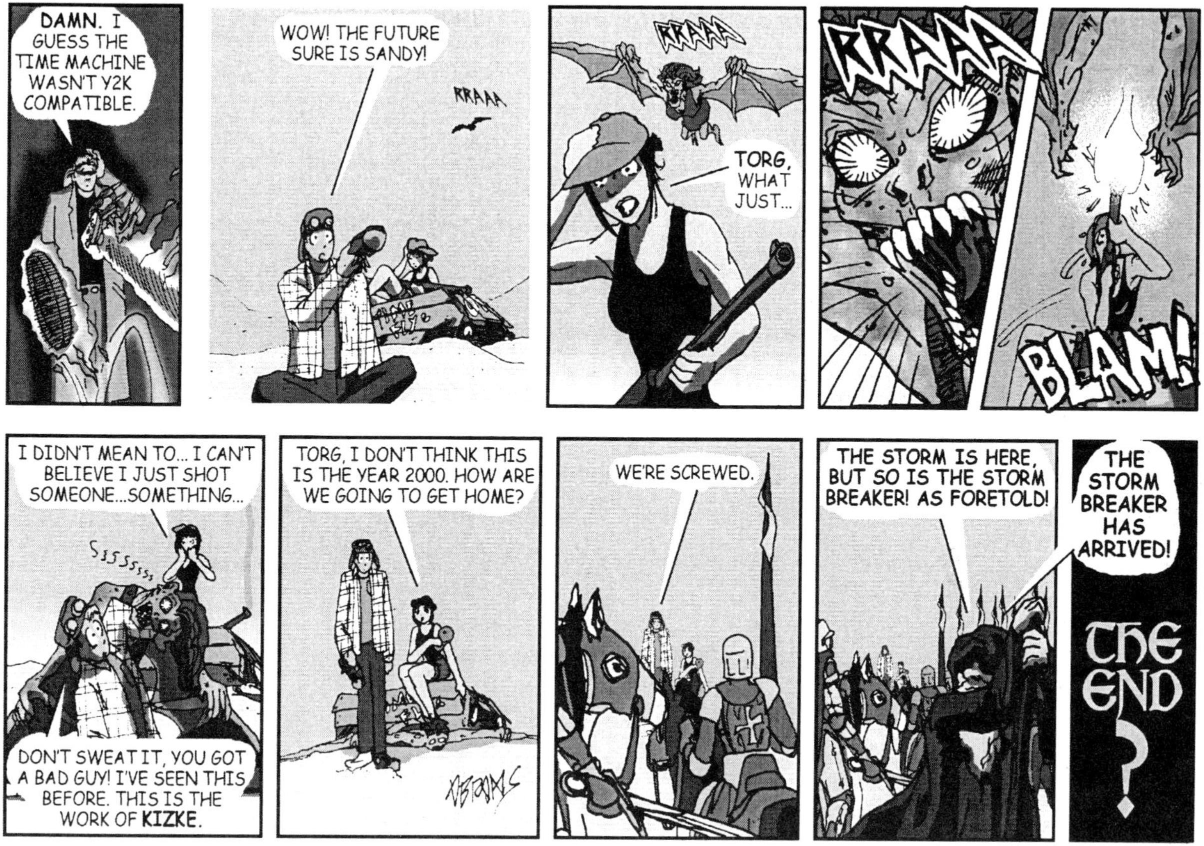
DAMN. I GUESS THE TIME MACHINE WASN'T Y2K COMPATIBLE.
WOW! THE FUTURE SURE IS SANDY!
RRAAA
RRAAA
TORG, WHAT JUST...
RRAAA
BLAM!
I DIDN'T MEAN TO... I CAN'T BELIEVE I JUST SHOT SOMEONE...SOMETHING...
SSSSSSSS
DON'T SWEAT IT, YOU GOT A BAD GUY! I'VE SEEN THIS BEFORE. THIS IS THE WORK OF KIZKE.
TORG, I DON'T THINK THIS IS THE YEAR 2000. HOW ARE WE GOING TO GET HOME?
WE'RE SCREWED.
THE STORM IS HERE, BUT SO IS THE STORM BREAKER! AS FORETOLD!
THE STORM BREAKER HAS ARRIVED!
THE END ?

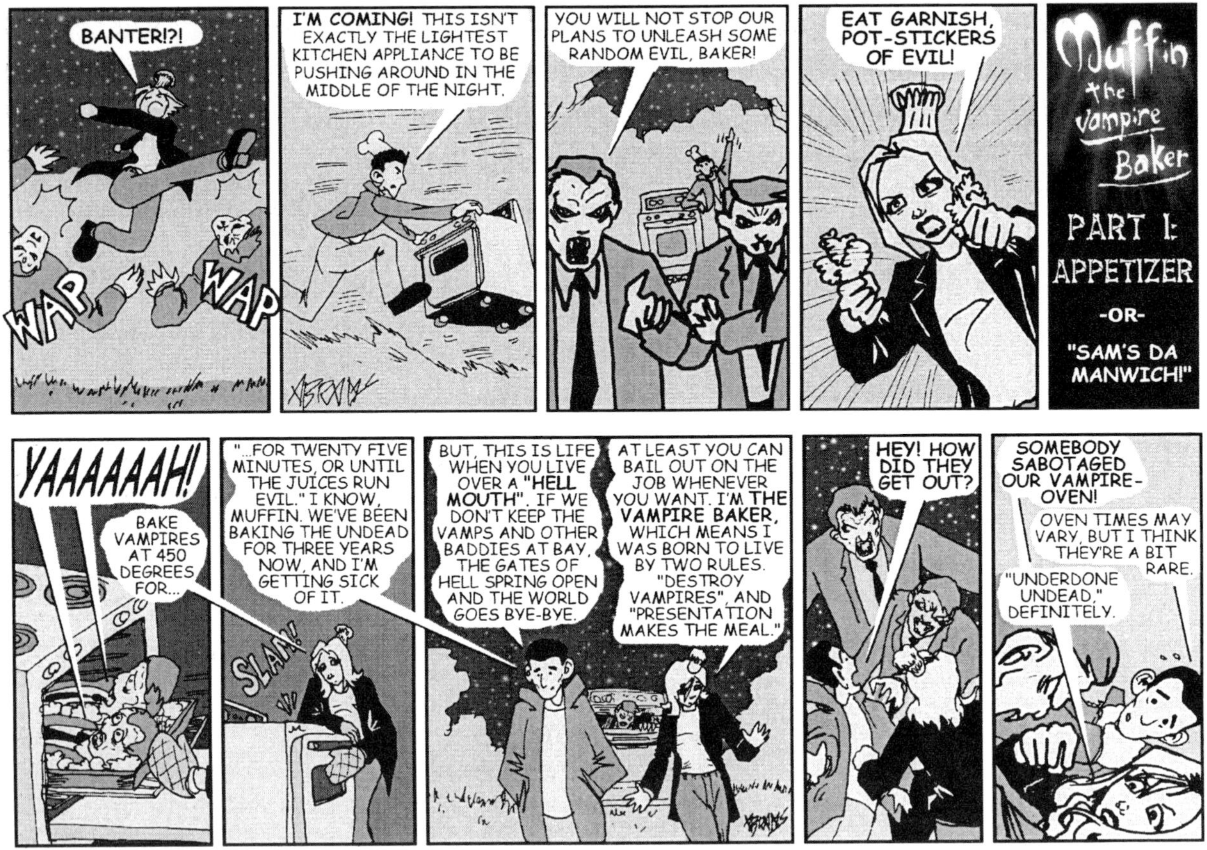

BANTER!?!
WAP
WAP
I'M COMING! THIS ISN'T EXACTLY THE LIGHTEST KITCHEN APPLIANCE TO BE PUSHING AROUND IN THE MIDDLE OF THE NIGHT.
YOU WILL NOT STOP OUR PLANS TO UNLEASH SOME RANDOM EVIL, BAKER!
EAT GARNISH, POT-STICKERS OF EVIL!
Muffin the Vampire Baker
PART 1: APPETIZER
-OR-
"SAM'S DA MANWICH!"
YAAAAAAH!
BAKE VAMPIRES AT 450 DEGREES FOR...
"...FOR TWENTY FIVE MINUTES, OR UNTIL THE JUICES RUN EVIL." I KNOW, MUFFIN. WE'VE BEEN BAKING THE UNDEAD FOR THREE YEARS NOW, AND I'M GETTING SICK OF IT.
SLAM!
BUT, THIS IS LIFE WHEN YOU LIVE OVER A "HELL MOUTH". IF WE DON'T KEEP THE VAMPS AND OTHER BADDIES AT BAY, THE GATES OF HELL SPRING OPEN AND THE WORLD GOES BYE-BYE.
AT LEAST YOU CAN BAIL OUT ON THE JOB WHENEVER YOU WANT. I'M THE VAMPIRE BAKER, WHICH MEANS I WAS BORN TO LIVE BY TWO RULES. "DESTROY VAMPIRES", AND "PRESENTATION MAKES THE MEAL."
HEY! HOW DID THEY GET OUT?
SOMEBODY SABOTAGED OUR VAMPIRE-OVEN!
OVEN TIMES MAY VARY, BUT I THINK THEY'RE A BIT RARE.
"UNDERDONE UNDEAD," DEFINITELY.

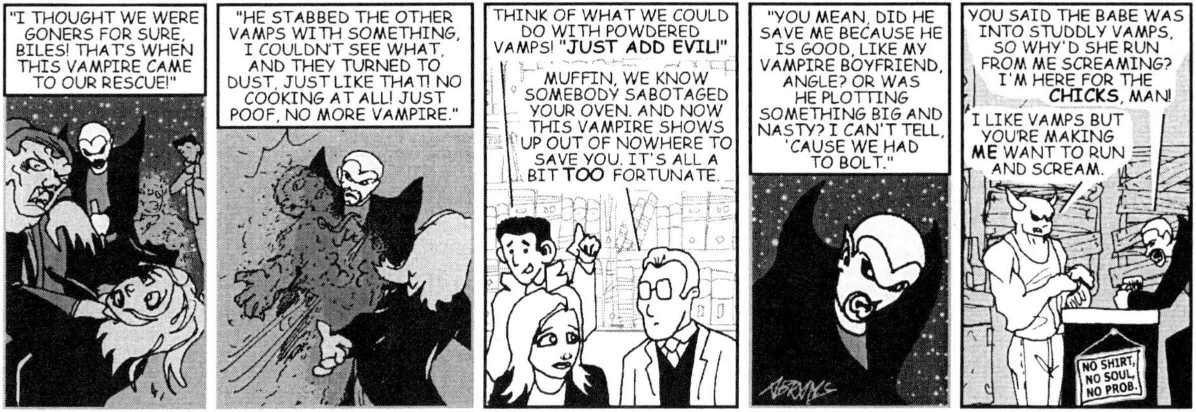
"I THOUGHT WE WERE GONERS FOR SURE, BILES! THAT'S WHEN THIS VAMPIRE CAME TO OUR RESCUE!"
"HE STABBED THE OTHER VAMPS WITH SOMETHING, I COULDN'T SEE WHAT, AND THEY TURNED TO DUST, JUST LIKE THAT! NO COOKING AT ALL! JUST POOF, NO MORE VAMPIRE."
THINK OF WHAT WE COULD DO WITH POWDERED VAMPS! **"JUST ADD EVIL!"**
MUFFIN, WE KNOW SOMEBODY SABOTAGED YOUR OVEN. AND NOW THIS VAMPIRE SHOWS UP OUT OF NOWHERE TO SAVE YOU. IT'S ALL A BIT **TOO** FORTUNATE.
"YOU MEAN, DID HE SAVE ME BECAUSE HE IS GOOD, LIKE MY VAMPIRE BOYFRIEND, ANGLE? OR WAS HE PLOTTING SOMETHING BIG AND NASTY? I CAN'T TELL, 'CAUSE WE HAD TO BOLT."
YOU SAID THE BABE WAS INTO STUDDLY VAMPS, SO WHY'D SHE RUN FROM ME SCREAMING? I'M HERE FOR THE **CHICKS**, MAN!
I LIKE VAMPS BUT YOU'RE MAKING **ME** WANT TO RUN AND SCREAM.
NO SHIRT, NO SOUL, NO PROB.

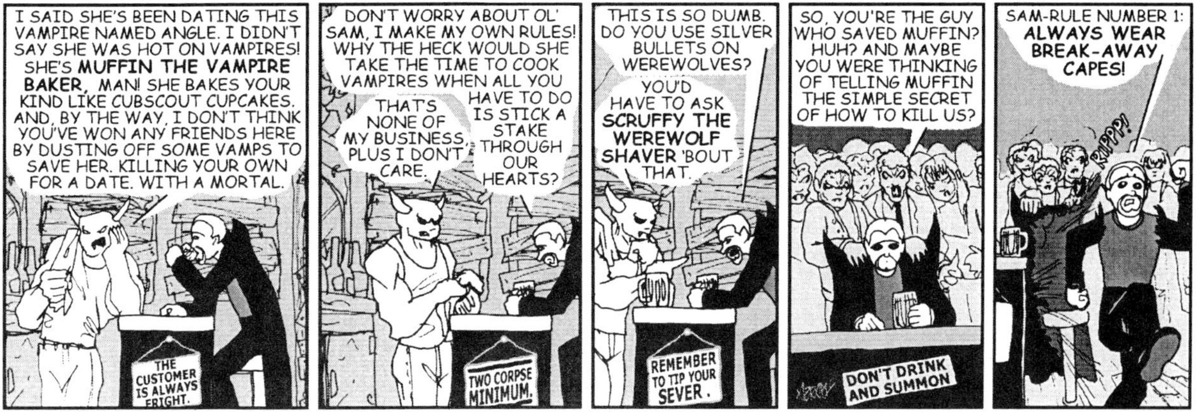
I SAID SHE'S BEEN DATING THIS VAMPIRE NAMED ANGLE. I DIDN'T SAY SHE WAS HOT ON VAMPIRES! SHE'S **MUFFIN THE VAMPIRE BAKER,** MAN! SHE BAKES YOUR KIND LIKE CUBSCOUT CUPCAKES. AND, BY THE WAY, I DON'T THINK YOU'VE WON ANY FRIENDS HERE BY DUSTING OFF SOME VAMPS TO SAVE HER. KILLING YOUR OWN FOR A DATE. WITH A MORTAL.
THE CUSTOMER IS ALWAYS FRIGHT.
DON'T WORRY ABOUT OL' SAM, I MAKE MY OWN RULES! WHY THE HECK WOULD SHE TAKE THE TIME TO COOK VAMPIRES WHEN ALL YOU HAVE TO DO IS STICK A STAKE THROUGH OUR HEARTS?
THAT'S NONE OF MY BUSINESS, PLUS I DON'T CARE.
TWO CORPSE MINIMUM.
THIS IS SO DUMB. DO YOU USE SILVER BULLETS ON WEREWOLVES?
YOU'D HAVE TO ASK **SCRUFFY THE WEREWOLF SHAVER** 'BOUT THAT.
REMEMBER TO TIP YOUR SEVER.
SO, YOU'RE THE GUY WHO SAVED MUFFIN? HUH? AND MAYBE YOU WERE THINKING OF TELLING MUFFIN THE SIMPLE SECRET OF HOW TO KILL US?
DON'T DRINK AND SUMMON
SAM-RULE NUMBER 1: **ALWAYS WEAR BREAK-AWAY CAPES!**
RIPPP!

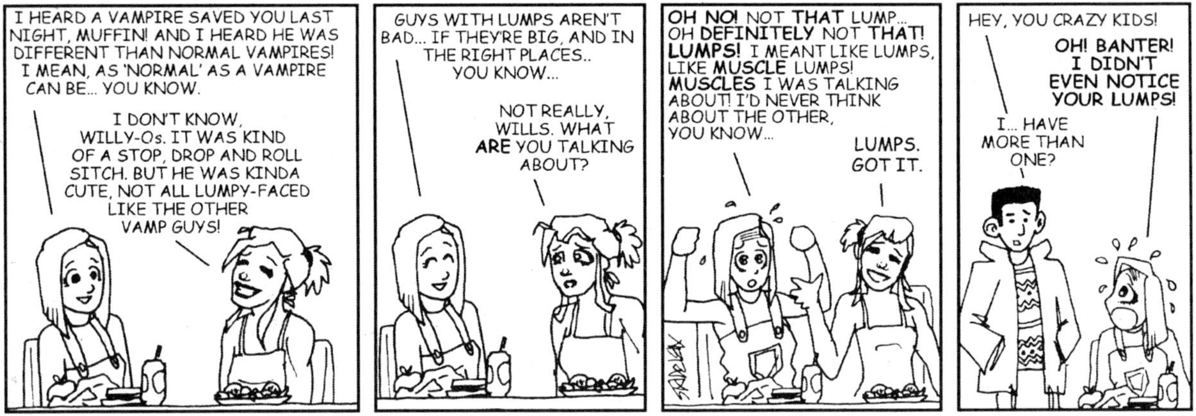
I HEARD A VAMPIRE SAVED YOU LAST NIGHT, MUFFIN! AND I HEARD HE WAS DIFFERENT THAN NORMAL VAMPIRES! I MEAN, AS 'NORMAL' AS A VAMPIRE CAN BE... YOU KNOW.
I DON'T KNOW, WILLY-Os. IT WAS KIND OF A STOP, DROP AND ROLL SITCH. BUT HE WAS KINDA CUTE, NOT ALL LUMPY-FACED LIKE THE OTHER VAMP GUYS!
GUYS WITH LUMPS AREN'T BAD... IF THEY'RE BIG, AND IN THE RIGHT PLACES.. YOU KNOW...
NOT REALLY, WILLS. WHAT **ARE** YOU TALKING ABOUT?
OH NO! NOT **THAT** LUMP... OH **DEFINITELY** NOT **THAT! LUMPS!** I MEANT LIKE LUMPS, LIKE **MUSCLE** LUMPS! **MUSCLES** I WAS TALKING ABOUT! I'D NEVER THINK ABOUT THE OTHER, YOU KNOW...
LUMPS. GOT IT.
HEY, YOU CRAZY KIDS!
OH! BANTER! I DIDN'T EVEN NOTICE YOUR LUMPS!
I... HAVE MORE THAN ONE?

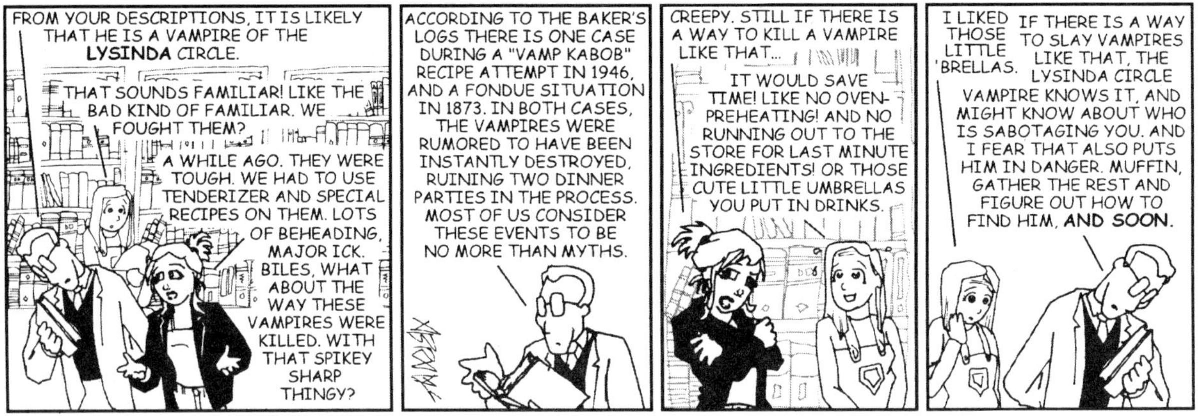
FROM YOUR DESCRIPTIONS, IT IS LIKELY THAT HE IS A VAMPIRE OF THE **LYSINDA** CIRCLE.
THAT SOUNDS FAMILIAR! LIKE THE BAD KIND OF FAMILIAR. WE FOUGHT THEM?
A WHILE AGO. THEY WERE TOUGH. WE HAD TO USE TENDERIZER AND SPECIAL RECIPES ON THEM. LOTS OF BEHEADING, MAJOR ICK. BILES, WHAT ABOUT THE WAY THESE VAMPIRES WERE KILLED. WITH THAT SPIKEY SHARP THINGY?
ACCORDING TO THE BAKER'S LOGS THERE IS ONE CASE DURING A "VAMP KABOB" RECIPE ATTEMPT IN 1946, AND A FONDUE SITUATION IN 1873. IN BOTH CASES, THE VAMPIRES WERE RUMORED TO HAVE BEEN INSTANTLY DESTROYED, RUINING TWO DINNER PARTIES IN THE PROCESS. MOST OF US CONSIDER THESE EVENTS TO BE NO MORE THAN MYTHS.
CREEPY. STILL IF THERE IS A WAY TO KILL A VAMPIRE LIKE THAT...
IT WOULD SAVE TIME! LIKE NO OVEN-PREHEATING! AND NO RUNNING OUT TO THE STORE FOR LAST MINUTE INGREDIENTS! OR THOSE CUTE LITTLE UMBRELLAS YOU PUT IN DRINKS.
I LIKED THOSE LITTLE 'BRELLAS.
IF THERE IS A WAY TO SLAY VAMPIRES LIKE THAT, THE LYSINDA CIRCLE VAMPIRE KNOWS IT, AND MIGHT KNOW ABOUT WHO IS SABOTAGING YOU. AND I FEAR THAT ALSO PUTS HIM IN DANGER. MUFFIN, GATHER THE REST AND FIGURE OUT HOW TO FIND HIM, **AND SOON.**

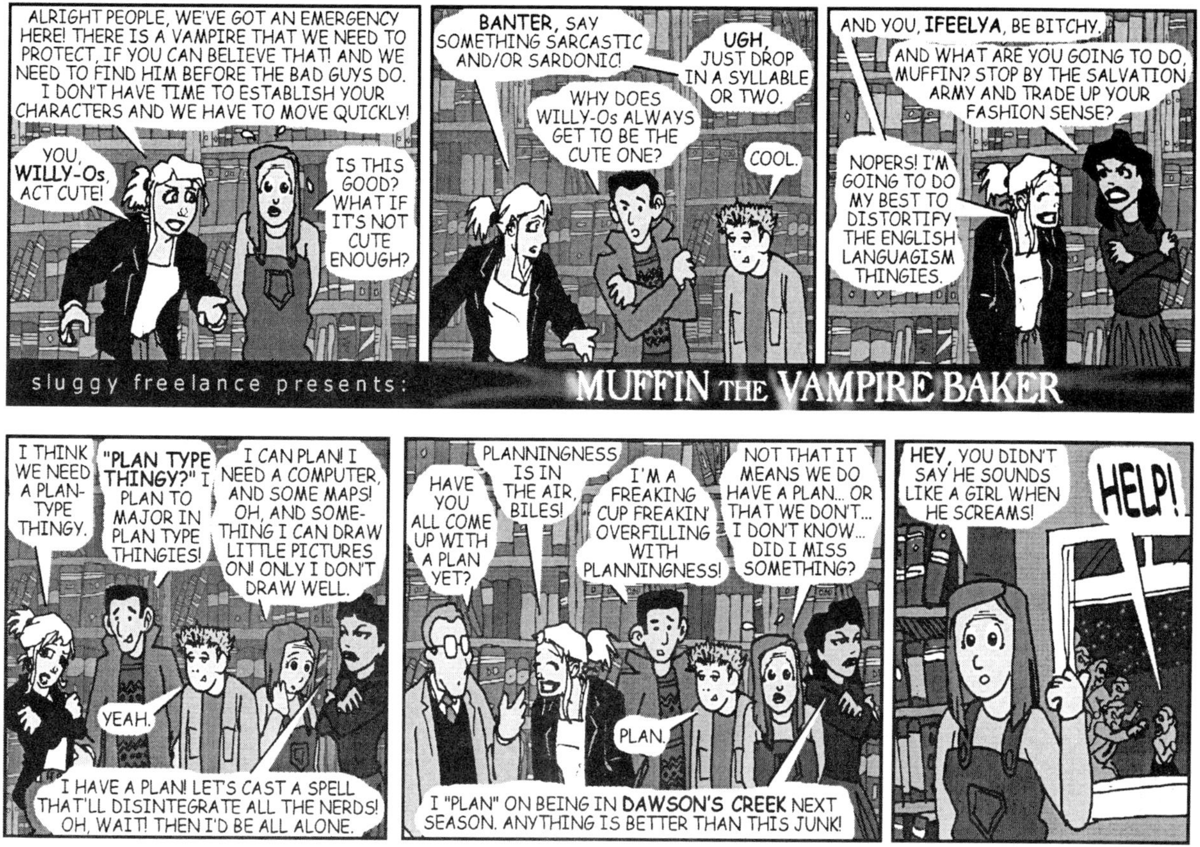
ALRIGHT PEOPLE, WE'VE GOT AN EMERGENCY HERE! THERE IS A VAMPIRE THAT WE NEED TO PROTECT, IF YOU CAN BELIEVE THAT! AND WE NEED TO FIND HIM BEFORE THE BAD GUYS DO. I DON'T HAVE TIME TO ESTABLISH YOUR CHARACTERS AND WE HAVE TO MOVE QUICKLY!
YOU, WILLY-Os, ACT CUTE!
IS THIS GOOD? WHAT IF IT'S NOT CUTE ENOUGH?
BANTER, SAY SOMETHING SARCASTIC AND/OR SARDONIC!
UGH, JUST DROP IN A SYLLABLE OR TWO.
WHY DOES WILLY-Os ALWAYS GET TO BE THE CUTE ONE?
COOL.
AND YOU, IFEELYA, BE BITCHY.
AND WHAT ARE YOU GOING TO DO, MUFFIN? STOP BY THE SALVATION ARMY AND TRADE UP YOUR FASHION SENSE?
NOPERS! I'M GOING TO DO MY BEST TO DISTORTIFY THE ENGLISH LANGUAGISM THINGIES.
sluggy freelance presents:
MUFFIN THE VAMPIRE BAKER
I THINK WE NEED A PLAN-TYPE THINGY.
"PLAN TYPE THINGY?" I PLAN TO MAJOR IN PLAN TYPE THINGIES!
I CAN PLAN! I NEED A COMPUTER, AND SOME MAPS! OH, AND SOME-THING I CAN DRAW LITTLE PICTURES ON! ONLY I DON'T DRAW WELL.
YEAH.
I HAVE A PLAN! LET'S CAST A SPELL THAT'LL DISINTEGRATE ALL THE NERDS! OH, WAIT! THEN I'D BE ALL ALONE.
HAVE YOU ALL COME UP WITH A PLAN YET?
PLANNINGNESS IS IN THE AIR, BILES!
I'M A FREAKING CUP FREAKIN' OVERFILLING WITH PLANNINGNESS!
NOT THAT IT MEANS WE DO HAVE A PLAN... OR THAT WE DON'T... I DON'T KNOW... DID I MISS SOMETHING?
PLAN.
I "PLAN" ON BEING IN DAWSON'S CREEK NEXT SEASON. ANYTHING IS BETTER THAN THIS JUNK!
HEY, YOU DIDN'T SAY HE SOUNDS LIKE A GIRL WHEN HE SCREAMS!
HELP!

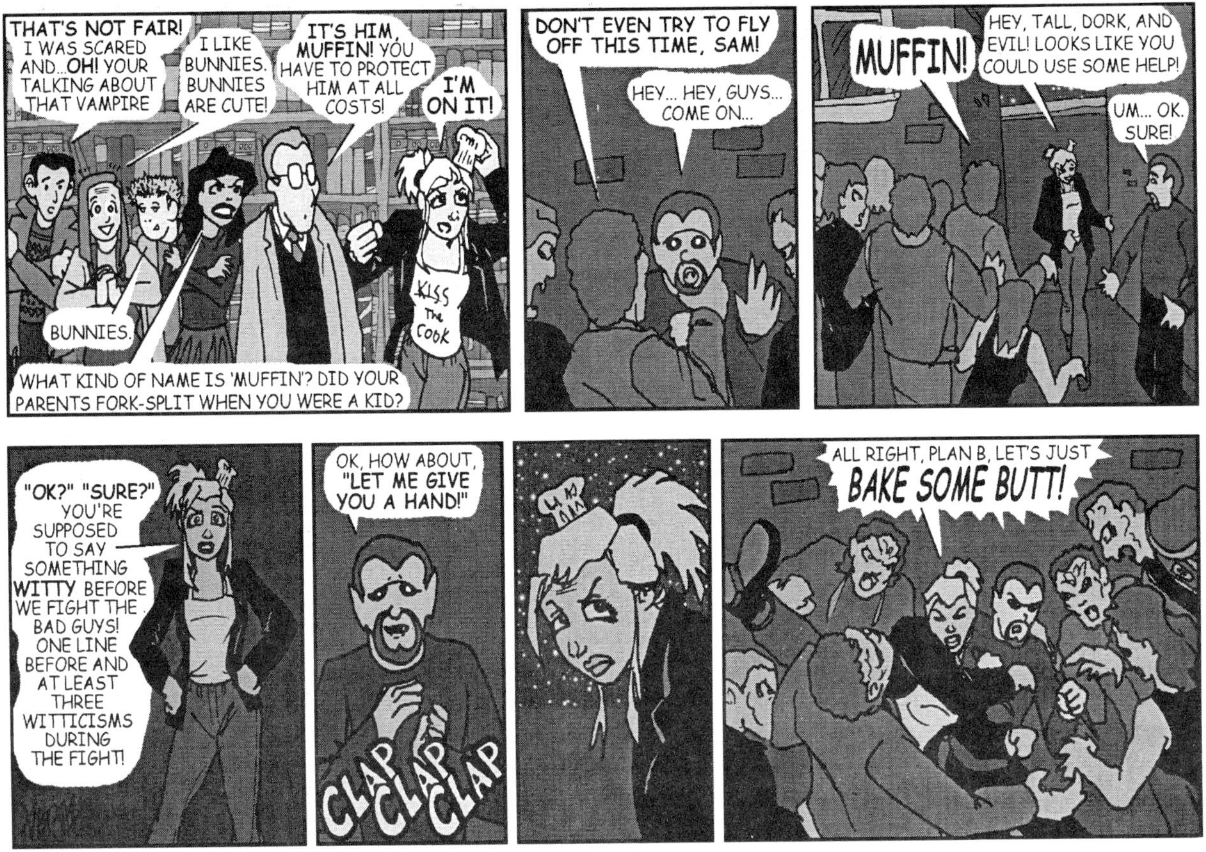
THAT'S NOT FAIR! I WAS SCARED AND...OH! YOUR TALKING ABOUT THAT VAMPIRE
I LIKE BUNNIES. BUNNIES ARE CUTE!
IT'S HIM, MUFFIN! YOU HAVE TO PROTECT HIM AT ALL COSTS!
I'M ON IT!
BUNNIES.
WHAT KIND OF NAME IS 'MUFFIN'? DID YOUR PARENTS FORK-SPLIT WHEN YOU WERE A KID?
KISS The COOK
DON'T EVEN TRY TO FLY OFF THIS TIME, SAM!
HEY... HEY, GUYS... COME ON...
MUFFIN!
HEY, TALL, DORK, AND EVIL! LOOKS LIKE YOU COULD USE SOME HELP!
UM... OK. SURE!
"OK?" "SURE?" YOU'RE SUPPOSED TO SAY SOMETHING WITTY BEFORE WE FIGHT THE BAD GUYS! ONE LINE BEFORE AND AT LEAST THREE WITTICISMS DURING THE FIGHT!
OK, HOW ABOUT, "LET ME GIVE YOU A HAND!"
CLAP CLAP CLAP
ALL RIGHT, PLAN B, LET'S JUST BAKE SOME BUTT!

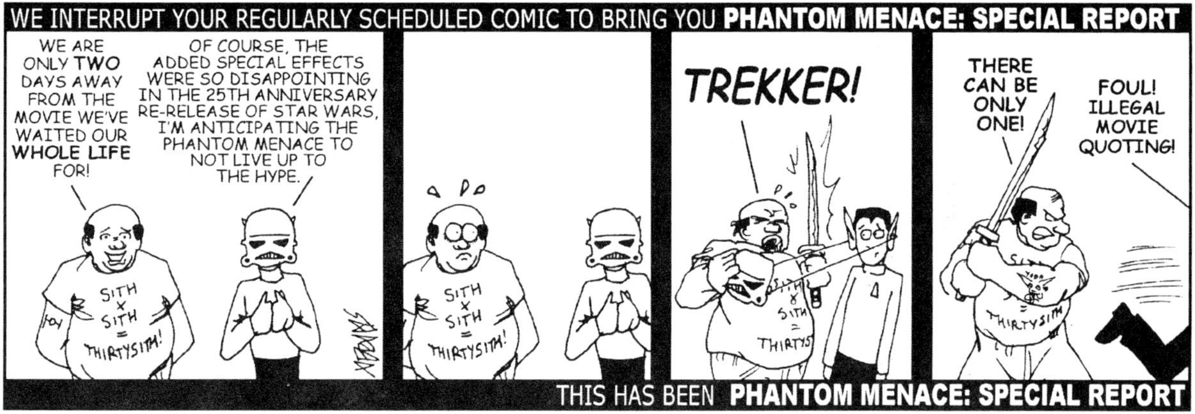
WE INTERRUPT YOUR REGULARLY SCHEDULED COMIC TO BRING YOU PHANTOM MENACE: SPECIAL REPORT
WE ARE ONLY TWO DAYS AWAY FROM THE MOVIE WE'VE WAITED OUR WHOLE LIFE FOR!
OF COURSE, THE ADDED SPECIAL EFFECTS WERE SO DISAPPOINTING IN THE 25TH ANNIVERSARY RE-RELEASE OF STAR WARS, I'M ANTICIPATING THE PHANTOM MENACE TO NOT LIVE UP TO THE HYPE.
SITH x SITH = THIRTYSITH!
TREKKER!
THERE CAN BE ONLY ONE!
FOUL! ILLEGAL MOVIE QUOTING!
THIS HAS BEEN PHANTOM MENACE: SPECIAL REPORT

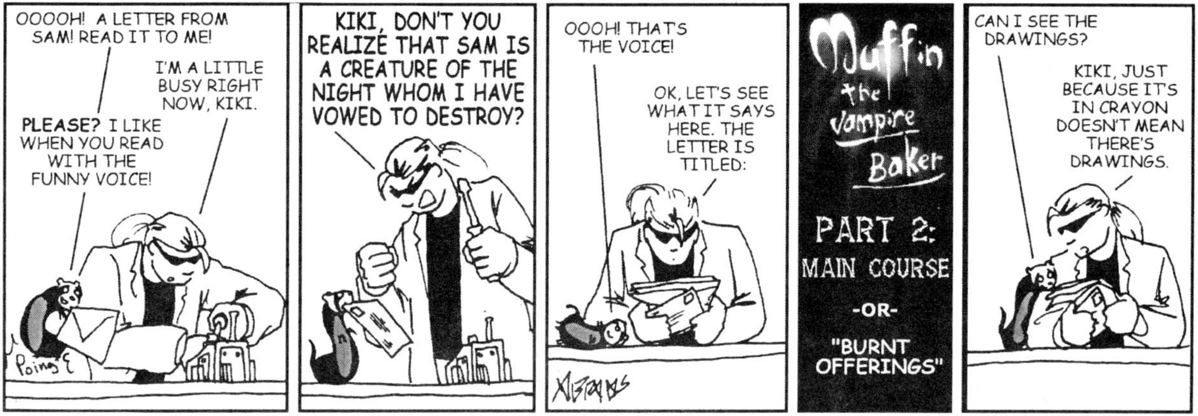
OOOOH! A LETTER FROM SAM! READ IT TO ME!
I'M A LITTLE BUSY RIGHT NOW, KIKI.
PLEASE? I LIKE WHEN YOU READ WITH THE FUNNY VOICE!
KIKI, DON'T YOU REALIZE THAT SAM IS A CREATURE OF THE NIGHT WHOM I HAVE VOWED TO DESTROY?
OOOH! THAT'S THE VOICE!
OK, LET'S SEE WHAT IT SAYS HERE. THE LETTER IS TITLED:
Muffin the Vampire Baker
PART 2: MAIN COURSE
-OR-
"BURNT OFFERINGS"
CAN I SEE THE DRAWINGS?
KIKI, JUST BECAUSE IT'S IN CRAYON DOESN'T MEAN THERE'S DRAWINGS.

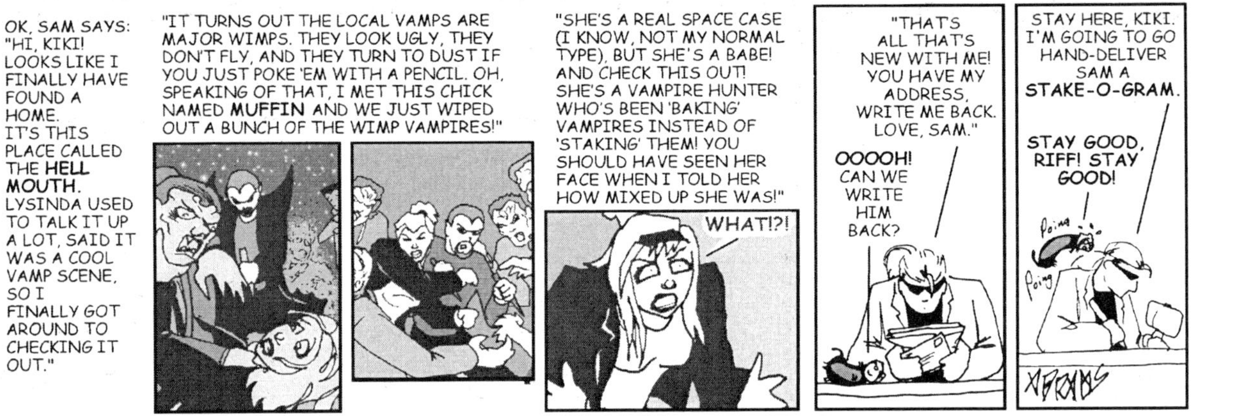
OK, SAM SAYS: "HI, KIKI! LOOKS LIKE I FINALLY HAVE FOUND A HOME. IT'S THIS PLACE CALLED THE **HELL MOUTH**. LYSINDA USED TO TALK IT UP A LOT, SAID IT WAS A COOL VAMP SCENE, SO I FINALLY GOT AROUND TO CHECKING IT OUT."
"IT TURNS OUT THE LOCAL VAMPS ARE MAJOR WIMPS. THEY LOOK UGLY, THEY DON'T FLY, AND THEY TURN TO DUST IF YOU JUST POKE 'EM WITH A PENCIL. OH, SPEAKING OF THAT, I MET THIS CHICK NAMED **MUFFIN** AND WE JUST WIPED OUT A BUNCH OF THE WIMP VAMPIRES!"
"SHE'S A REAL SPACE CASE (I KNOW, NOT MY NORMAL TYPE), BUT SHE'S A BABE! AND CHECK THIS OUT! SHE'S A VAMPIRE HUNTER WHO'S BEEN 'BAKING' VAMPIRES INSTEAD OF 'STAKING' THEM! YOU SHOULD HAVE SEEN HER FACE WHEN I TOLD HER HOW MIXED UP SHE WAS!"
WHAT!?!
"THAT'S ALL THAT'S NEW WITH ME! YOU HAVE MY ADDRESS, WRITE ME BACK. LOVE, SAM."
OOOOH! CAN WE WRITE HIM BACK?
STAY HERE, KIKI. I'M GOING TO GO HAND-DELIVER SAM A **STAKE-O-GRAM**.
STAY GOOD, RIFF! STAY GOOD!

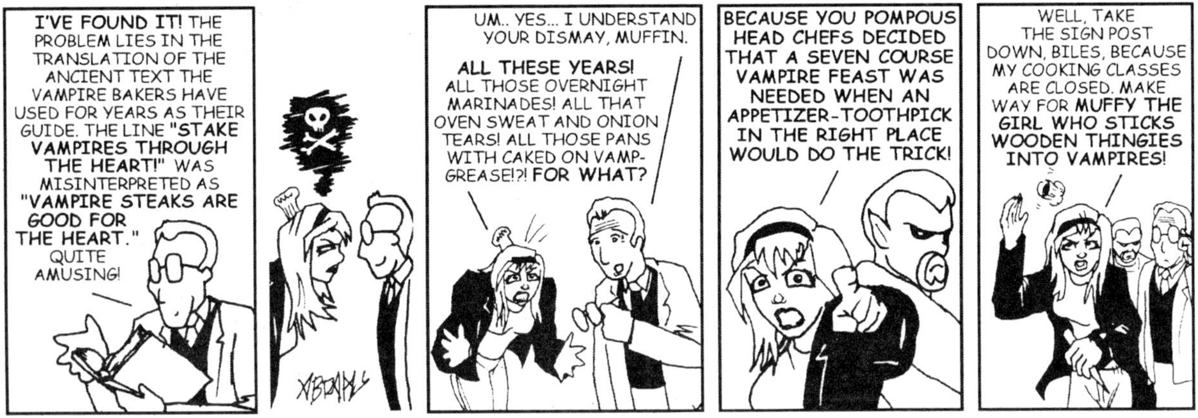
I'VE FOUND IT! THE PROBLEM LIES IN THE TRANSLATION OF THE ANCIENT TEXT THE VAMPIRE BAKERS HAVE USED FOR YEARS AS THEIR GUIDE. THE LINE **"STAKE VAMPIRES THROUGH THE HEART!"** WAS MISINTERPRETED AS **"VAMPIRE STEAKS ARE GOOD FOR THE HEART."** QUITE AMUSING!
UM.. YES... I UNDERSTAND YOUR DISMAY, MUFFIN.
ALL THESE YEARS! ALL THOSE OVERNIGHT MARINADES! ALL THAT OVEN SWEAT AND ONION TEARS! ALL THOSE PANS WITH CAKED ON VAMP-GREASE!?! **FOR WHAT?**
BECAUSE YOU POMPOUS HEAD CHEFS DECIDED THAT A SEVEN COURSE VAMPIRE FEAST WAS NEEDED WHEN AN APPETIZER-TOOTHPICK IN THE RIGHT PLACE WOULD DO THE TRICK!
WELL, TAKE THE SIGN POST DOWN, BILES, BECAUSE MY COOKING CLASSES ARE CLOSED. MAKE WAY FOR **MUFFY THE GIRL WHO STICKS WOODEN THINGIES INTO VAMPIRES!**

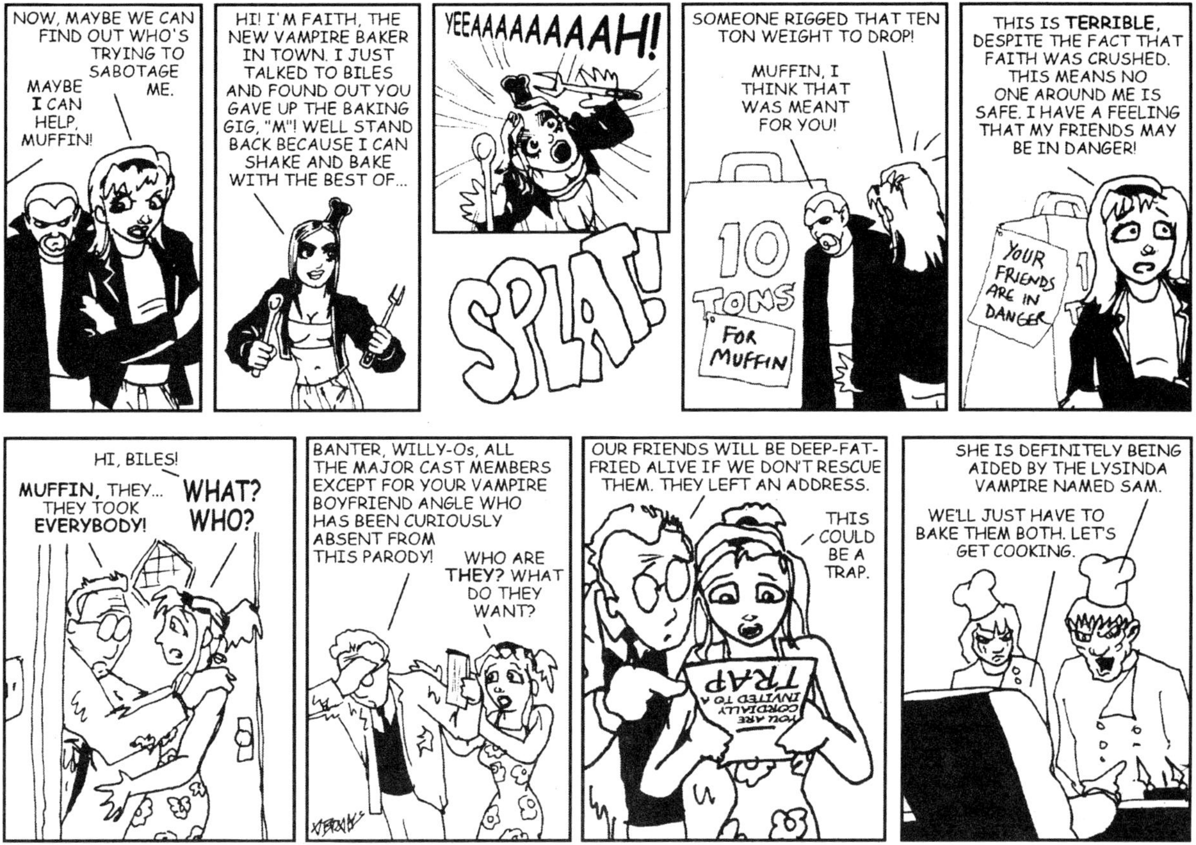
NOW, MAYBE WE CAN FIND OUT WHO'S TRYING TO SABOTAGE ME.
MAYBE I CAN HELP, MUFFIN!
HI! I'M FAITH, THE NEW VAMPIRE BAKER IN TOWN. I JUST TALKED TO BILES AND FOUND OUT YOU GAVE UP THE BAKING GIG, "M"! WELL STAND BACK BECAUSE I CAN SHAKE AND BAKE WITH THE BEST OF...
YEEAAAAAAAAAH!
SPLAT!
SOMEONE RIGGED THAT TEN TON WEIGHT TO DROP!
MUFFIN, I THINK THAT WAS MEANT FOR YOU!
10 TONS
FOR MUFFIN
THIS IS TERRIBLE, DESPITE THE FACT THAT FAITH WAS CRUSHED. THIS MEANS NO ONE AROUND ME IS SAFE. I HAVE A FEELING THAT MY FRIENDS MAY BE IN DANGER!
YOUR FRIENDS ARE IN DANGER
HI, BILES!
MUFFIN, THEY... THEY TOOK EVERYBODY!
WHAT? WHO?
BANTER, WILLY-Os, ALL THE MAJOR CAST MEMBERS EXCEPT FOR YOUR VAMPIRE BOYFRIEND ANGLE WHO HAS BEEN CURIOUSLY ABSENT FROM THIS PARODY!
WHO ARE THEY? WHAT DO THEY WANT?
OUR FRIENDS WILL BE DEEP-FAT-FRIED ALIVE IF WE DON'T RESCUE THEM. THEY LEFT AN ADDRESS.
THIS COULD BE A TRAP.
YOU ARE CORDIALLY INVITED TO A TRAP
SHE IS DEFINITELY BEING AIDED BY THE LYSINDA VAMPIRE NAMED SAM.
WE'LL JUST HAVE TO BAKE THEM BOTH. LET'S GET COOKING.

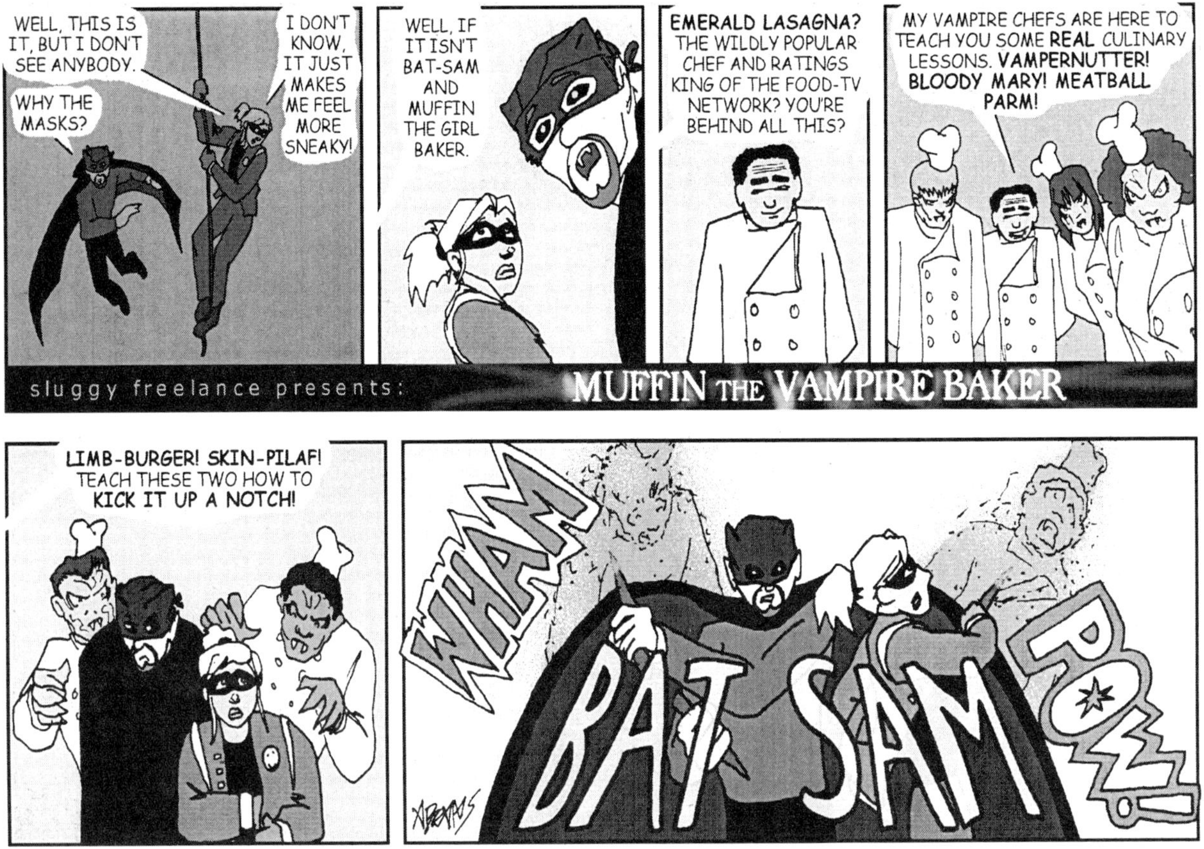
WELL, THIS IS IT, BUT I DON'T SEE ANYBODY.
WHY THE MASKS?
I DON'T KNOW, IT JUST MAKES ME FEEL MORE SNEAKY!
WELL, IF IT ISN'T BAT-SAM AND MUFFIN THE GIRL BAKER.
EMERALD LASAGNA? THE WILDLY POPULAR CHEF AND RATINGS KING OF THE FOOD-TV NETWORK? YOU'RE BEHIND ALL THIS?
MY VAMPIRE CHEFS ARE HERE TO TEACH YOU SOME REAL CULINARY LESSONS. VAMPERNUTTER! BLOODY MARY! MEATBALL PARM!
sluggy freelance presents:
MUFFIN THE VAMPIRE BAKER
LIMB-BURGER! SKIN-PILAF! TEACH THESE TWO HOW TO KICK IT UP A NOTCH!
WHAM
BAT SAM
POW!

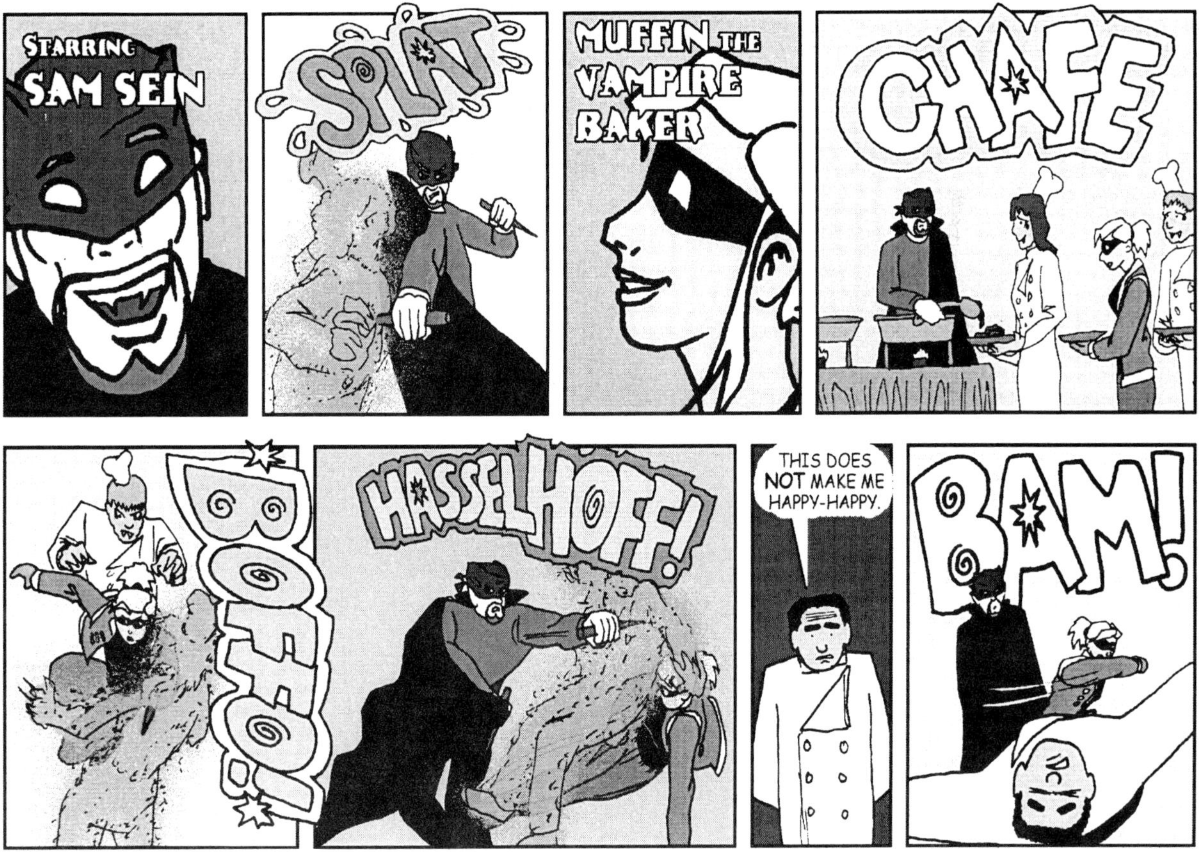

STARRING
SAM SEIN
SPLAT
MUFFIN THE VAMPIRE BAKER
CHAFE
BOFFO!
HASSELHOFF!
THIS DOES NOT MAKE ME HAPPY-HAPPY.
BAM!

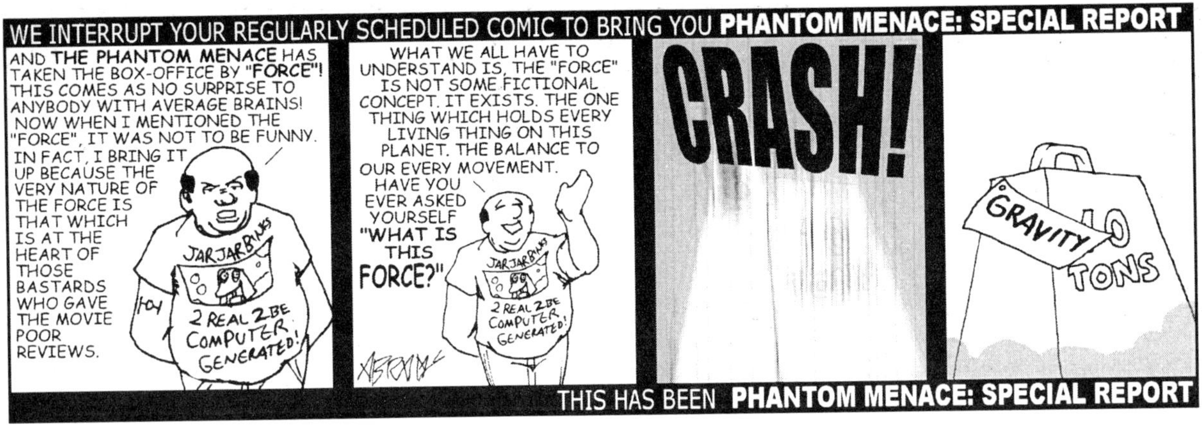
WE INTERRUPT YOUR REGULARLY SCHEDULED COMIC TO BRING YOU PHANTOM MENACE: SPECIAL REPORT
AND THE PHANTOM MENACE HAS TAKEN THE BOX-OFFICE BY "FORCE"! THIS COMES AS NO SURPRISE TO ANYBODY WITH AVERAGE BRAINS! NOW WHEN I MENTIONED THE "FORCE", IT WAS NOT TO BE FUNNY.
IN FACT, I BRING IT UP BECAUSE THE VERY NATURE OF THE FORCE IS THAT WHICH IS AT THE HEART OF THOSE BASTARDS WHO GAVE THE MOVIE POOR REVIEWS.
JAR JAR BINKS
2 REAL 2 BE COMPUTER GENERATED!
WHAT WE ALL HAVE TO UNDERSTAND IS, THE "FORCE" IS NOT SOME FICTIONAL CONCEPT. IT EXISTS. THE ONE THING WHICH HOLDS EVERY LIVING THING ON THIS PLANET. THE BALANCE TO OUR EVERY MOVEMENT.
HAVE YOU EVER ASKED YOURSELF "WHAT IS THIS FORCE?"
JAR JAR BINKS
2 REAL 2 BE COMPUTER GENERATED!
CRASH!
GRAVITY
10 TONS
THIS HAS BEEN PHANTOM MENACE: SPECIAL REPORT
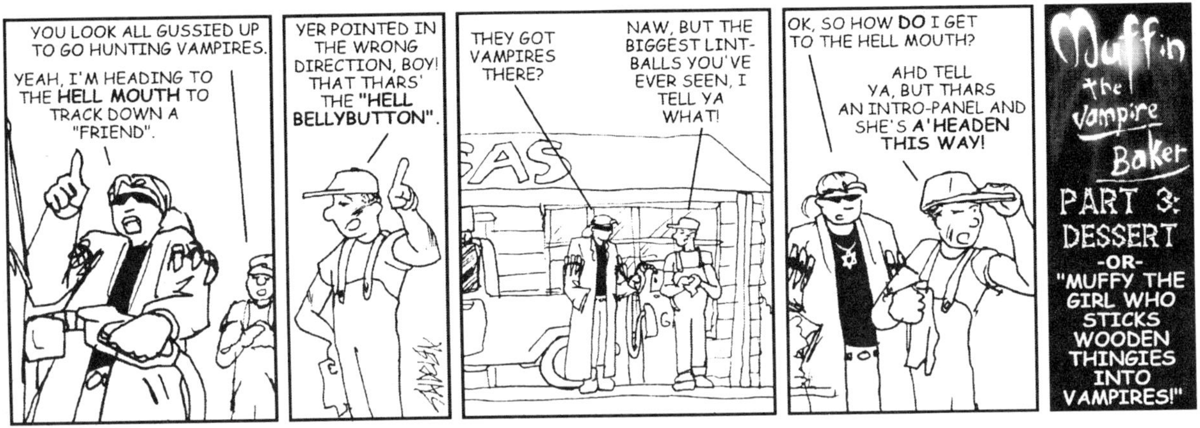
YOU LOOK ALL GUSSIED UP TO GO HUNTING VAMPIRES.
YEAH, I'M HEADING TO THE HELL MOUTH TO TRACK DOWN A "FRIEND".
YER POINTED IN THE WRONG DIRECTION, BOY! THAT THARS' THE "HELL BELLYBUTTON".
THEY GOT VAMPIRES THERE?
NAW, BUT THE BIGGEST LINT-BALLS YOU'VE EVER SEEN, I TELL YA WHAT!
OK, SO HOW DO I GET TO THE HELL MOUTH?
AHD TELL YA, BUT THARS AN INTRO-PANEL AND SHE'S A'HEADEN THIS WAY!
Muffin the Vampire Baker
PART 3: DESSERT
-OR-
"MUFFY THE GIRL WHO STICKS WOODEN THINGIES INTO VAMPIRES!"

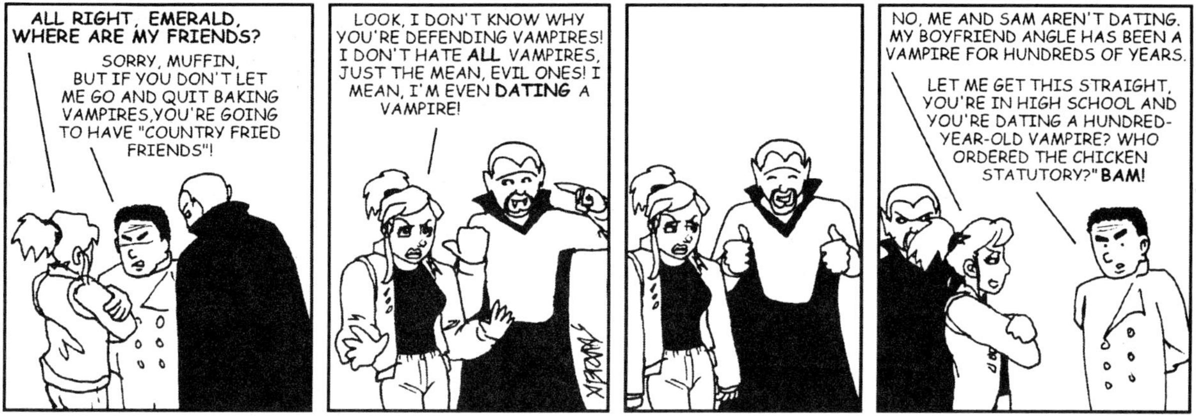
ALL RIGHT, EMERALD, WHERE ARE MY FRIENDS?
SORRY, MUFFIN, BUT IF YOU DON'T LET ME GO AND QUIT BAKING VAMPIRES,YOU'RE GOING TO HAVE "COUNTRY FRIED FRIENDS"!
LOOK, I DON'T KNOW WHY YOU'RE DEFENDING VAMPIRES! I DON'T HATE ALL VAMPIRES, JUST THE MEAN, EVIL ONES! I MEAN, I'M EVEN DATING A VAMPIRE!
NO, ME AND SAM AREN'T DATING. MY BOYFRIEND ANGLE HAS BEEN A VAMPIRE FOR HUNDREDS OF YEARS.
LET ME GET THIS STRAIGHT, YOU'RE IN HIGH SCHOOL AND YOU'RE DATING A HUNDRED-YEAR-OLD VAMPIRE? WHO ORDERED THE CHICKEN STATUTORY?" BAM!

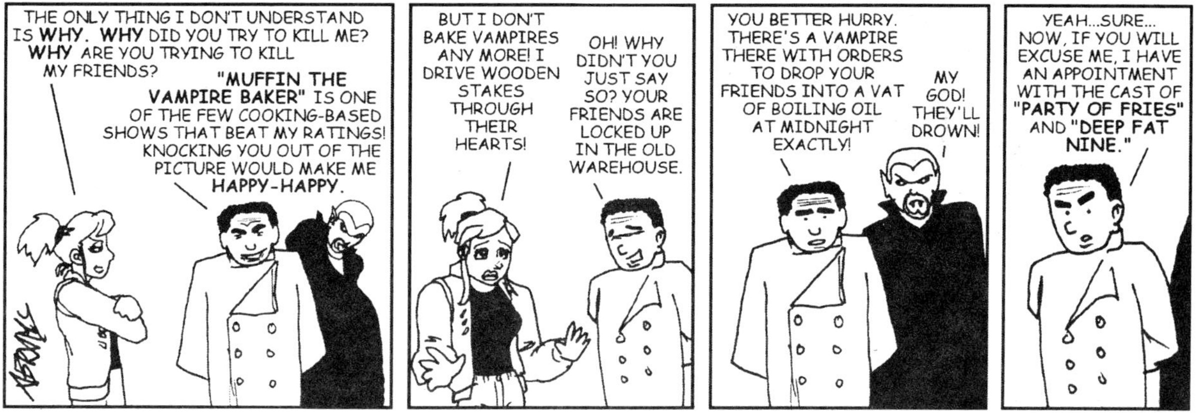
THE ONLY THING I DON'T UNDERSTAND IS WHY. WHY DID YOU TRY TO KILL ME? WHY ARE YOU TRYING TO KILL MY FRIENDS?
"MUFFIN THE VAMPIRE BAKER" IS ONE OF THE FEW COOKING-BASED SHOWS THAT BEAT MY RATINGS! KNOCKING YOU OUT OF THE PICTURE WOULD MAKE ME HAPPY-HAPPY.
BUT I DON'T BAKE VAMPIRES ANY MORE! I DRIVE WOODEN STAKES THROUGH THEIR HEARTS!
OH! WHY DIDN'T YOU JUST SAY SO? YOUR FRIENDS ARE LOCKED UP IN THE OLD WAREHOUSE.
YOU BETTER HURRY. THERE'S A VAMPIRE THERE WITH ORDERS TO DROP YOUR FRIENDS INTO A VAT OF BOILING OIL AT MIDNIGHT EXACTLY!
MY GOD! THEY'LL DROWN!
YEAH...SURE... NOW, IF YOU WILL EXCUSE ME, I HAVE AN APPOINTMENT WITH THE CAST OF "PARTY OF FRIES" AND "DEEP FAT NINE."

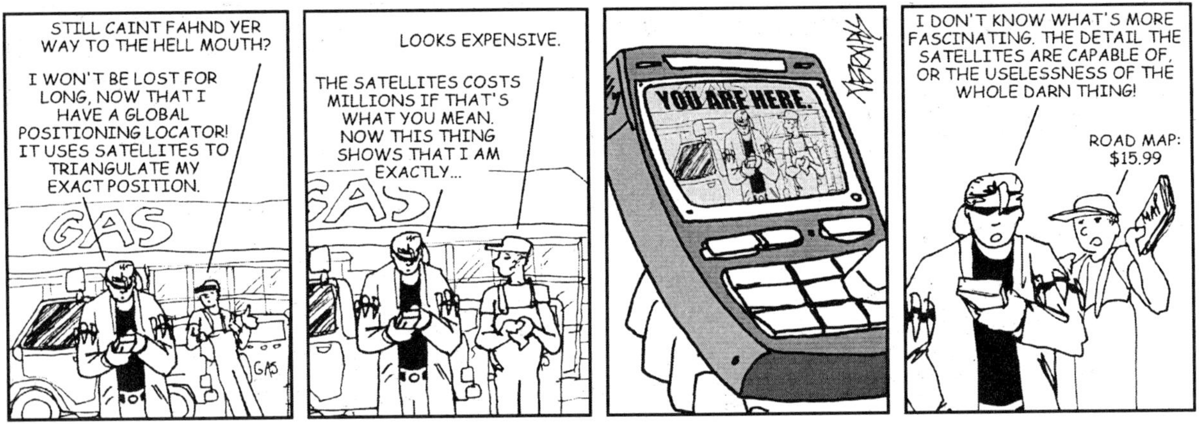
STILL CAINT FAHND YER WAY TO THE HELL MOUTH?
I WON'T BE LOST FOR LONG, NOW THAT I HAVE A GLOBAL POSITIONING LOCATOR! IT USES SATELLITES TO TRIANGULATE MY EXACT POSITION.
GAS
LOOKS EXPENSIVE.
THE SATELLITES COSTS MILLIONS IF THAT'S WHAT YOU MEAN. NOW THIS THING SHOWS THAT I AM EXACTLY...
GAS
YOU ARE HERE.
I DON'T KNOW WHAT'S MORE FASCINATING. THE DETAIL THE SATELLITES ARE CAPABLE OF, OR THE USELESSNESS OF THE WHOLE DARN THING!
ROAD MAP: $15.99
MAP

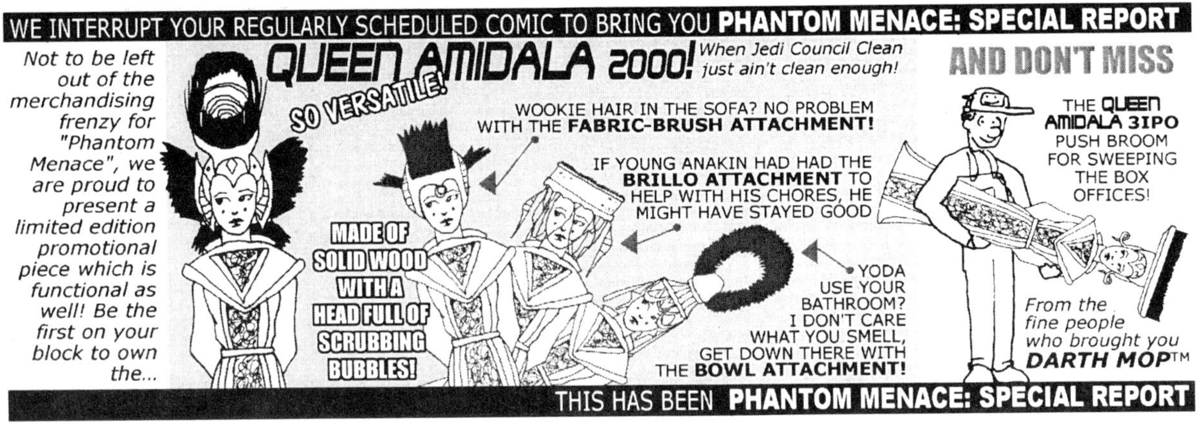
WE INTERRUPT YOUR REGULARLY SCHEDULED COMIC TO BRING YOU PHANTOM MENACE: SPECIAL REPORT
Not to be left out of the merchandising frenzy for "Phantom Menace", we are proud to present a limited edition promotional piece which is functional as well! Be the first on your block to own the...
QUEEN AMIDALA 2000!
When Jedi Council Clean just ain't clean enough!
SO VERSATILE!
WOOKIE HAIR IN THE SOFA? NO PROBLEM WITH THE FABRIC-BRUSH ATTACHMENT!
IF YOUNG ANAKIN HAD HAD THE BRILLO ATTACHMENT TO HELP WITH HIS CHORES, HE MIGHT HAVE STAYED GOOD
MADE OF SOLID WOOD WITH A HEAD FULL OF SCRUBBING BUBBLES!
YODA USE YOUR BATHROOM? I DON'T CARE WHAT YOU SMELL, GET DOWN THERE WITH THE BOWL ATTACHMENT!
AND DON'T MISS
THE QUEEN AMIDALA 3IPO PUSH BROOM FOR SWEEPING THE BOX OFFICES!
From the fine people who brought you DARTH MOP™
THIS HAS BEEN PHANTOM MENACE: SPECIAL REPORT

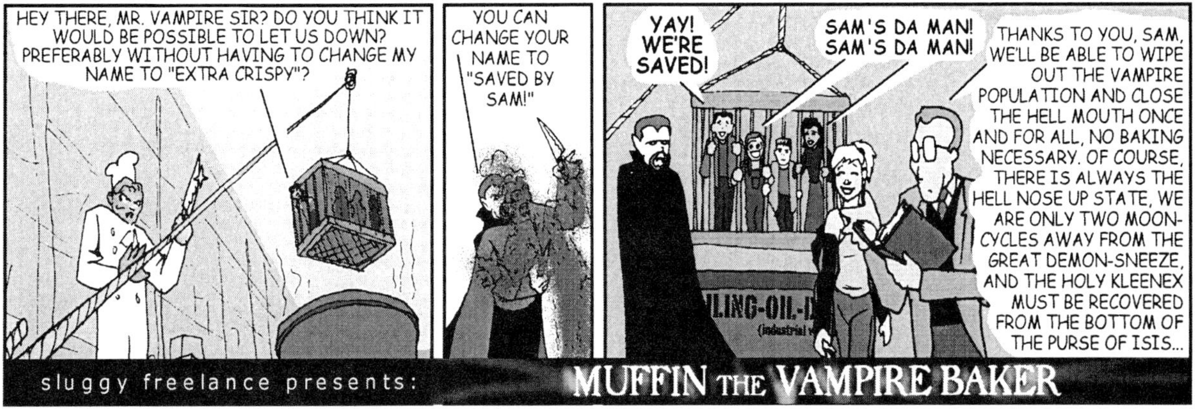
HEY THERE, MR. VAMPIRE SIR? DO YOU THINK IT WOULD BE POSSIBLE TO LET US DOWN? PREFERABLY WITHOUT HAVING TO CHANGE MY NAME TO "EXTRA CRISPY"?
YOU CAN CHANGE YOUR NAME TO "SAVED BY SAM!"
YAY! WE'RE SAVED!
SAM'S DA MAN! SAM'S DA MAN!
THANKS TO YOU, SAM, WE'LL BE ABLE TO WIPE OUT THE VAMPIRE POPULATION AND CLOSE THE HELL MOUTH ONCE AND FOR ALL, NO BAKING NECESSARY. OF COURSE, THERE IS ALWAYS THE HELL NOSE UP STATE, WE ARE ONLY TWO MOON-CYCLES AWAY FROM THE GREAT DEMON-SNEEZE, AND THE HOLY KLEENEX MUST BE RECOVERED FROM THE BOTTOM OF THE PURSE OF ISIS...
sluggy freelance presents:
MUFFIN THE VAMPIRE BAKER

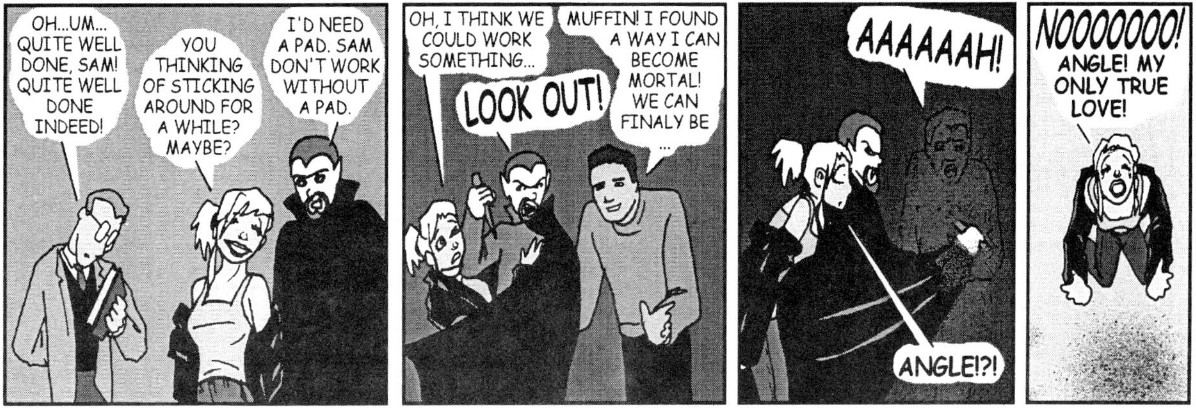
OH...UM... QUITE WELL DONE, SAM! QUITE WELL DONE INDEED!
YOU THINKING OF STICKING AROUND FOR A WHILE? MAYBE?
I'D NEED A PAD. SAM DON'T WORK WITHOUT A PAD.
OH, I THINK WE COULD WORK SOMETHING...
MUFFIN! I FOUND A WAY I CAN BECOME MORTAL! WE CAN FINALY BE ...
LOOK OUT!
AAAAAAH!
ANGLE!?!
NOOOOOOO! ANGLE! MY ONLY TRUE LOVE!

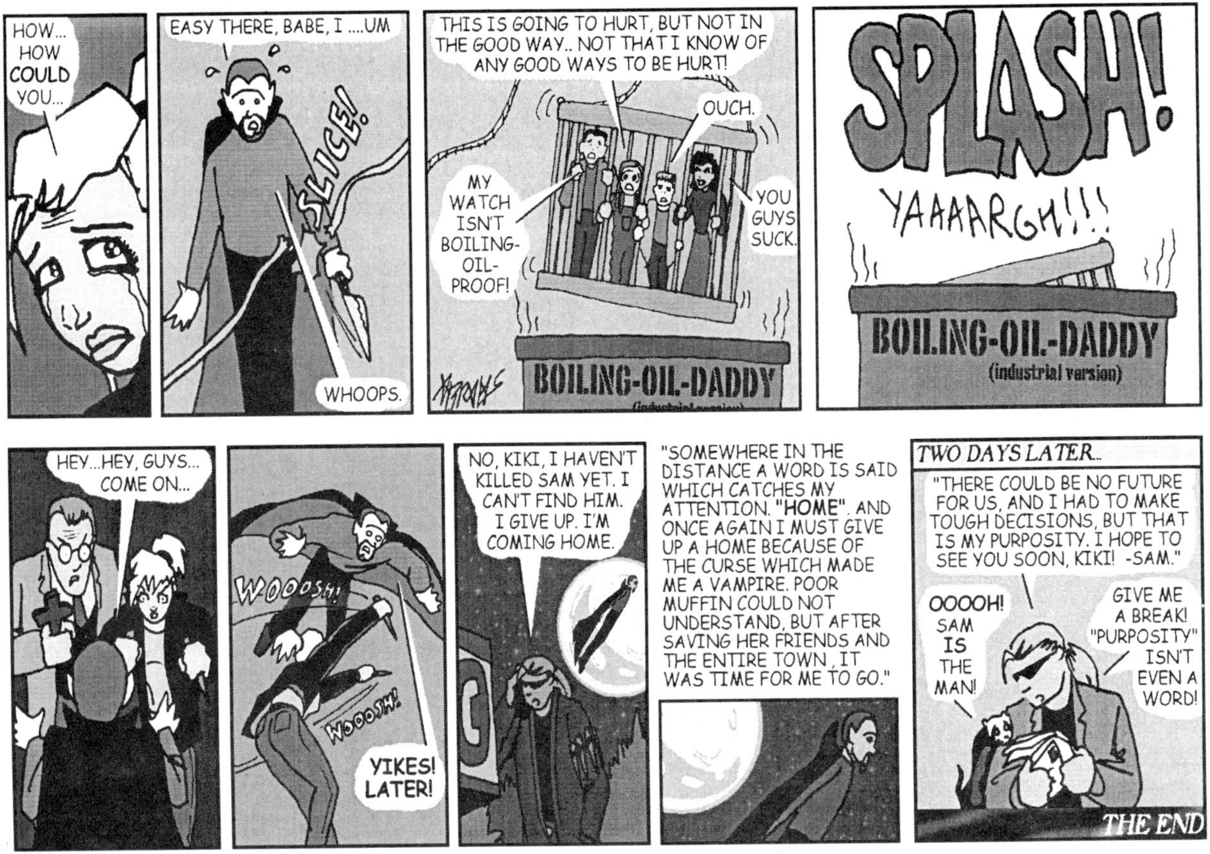
HOW... HOW COULD YOU...
EASY THERE, BABE, I ....UM
SLICE!
WHOOPS.
THIS IS GOING TO HURT, BUT NOT IN THE GOOD WAY.. NOT THAT I KNOW OF ANY GOOD WAYS TO BE HURT!
OUCH.
MY WATCH ISN'T BOILING-OIL-PROOF!
YOU GUYS SUCK.
BOILING-OIL-DADDY
SPLASH!
YAAAARGH!!!
BOILING-OIL.-DADDY
(industrial version)
HEY...HEY, GUYS... COME ON...
WOOOSH!
WOOOSH!
YIKES! LATER!
NO, KIKI, I HAVEN'T KILLED SAM YET. I CAN'T FIND HIM. I GIVE UP. I'M COMING HOME.
"SOMEWHERE IN THE DISTANCE A WORD IS SAID WHICH CATCHES MY ATTENTION. "HOME". AND ONCE AGAIN I MUST GIVE UP A HOME BECAUSE OF THE CURSE WHICH MADE ME A VAMPIRE. POOR MUFFIN COULD NOT UNDERSTAND, BUT AFTER SAVING HER FRIENDS AND THE ENTIRE TOWN , IT WAS TIME FOR ME TO GO."
TWO DAYS LATER...
"THERE COULD BE NO FUTURE FOR US, AND I HAD TO MAKE TOUGH DECISIONS, BUT THAT IS MY PURPOSITY. I HOPE TO SEE YOU SOON, KIKI! -SAM."
OOOOH! SAM IS THE MAN!
GIVE ME A BREAK! "PURPOSITY" ISN'T EVEN A WORD!
THE END

LUCK

A Sluggy Freelance Presentation.

A Zoë Story.

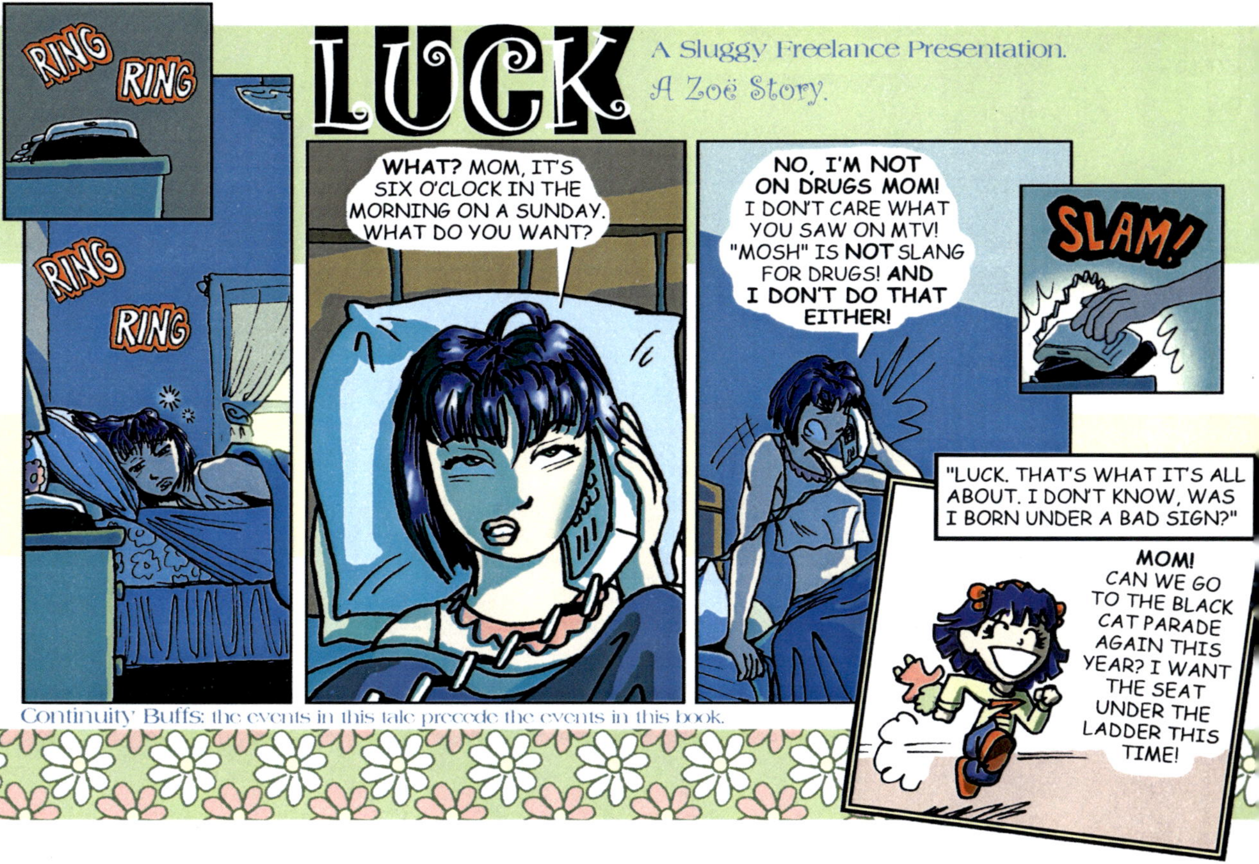
RING RING
RING
RING
WHAT? MOM, IT'S SIX O'CLOCK IN THE MORNING ON A SUNDAY. WHAT DO YOU WANT?
NO, I'M NOT ON DRUGS MOM! I DON'T CARE WHAT YOU SAW ON MTV! "MOSH" IS NOT SLANG FOR DRUGS! AND I DON'T DO THAT EITHER!
SLAM!
"LUCK. THAT'S WHAT IT'S ALL ABOUT. I DON'T KNOW, WAS I BORN UNDER A BAD SIGN?"
MOM! CAN WE GO TO THE BLACK CAT PARADE AGAIN THIS YEAR? I WANT THE SEAT UNDER THE LADDER THIS TIME!

Continuity Buffs: the events in this tale precede the events in this book.

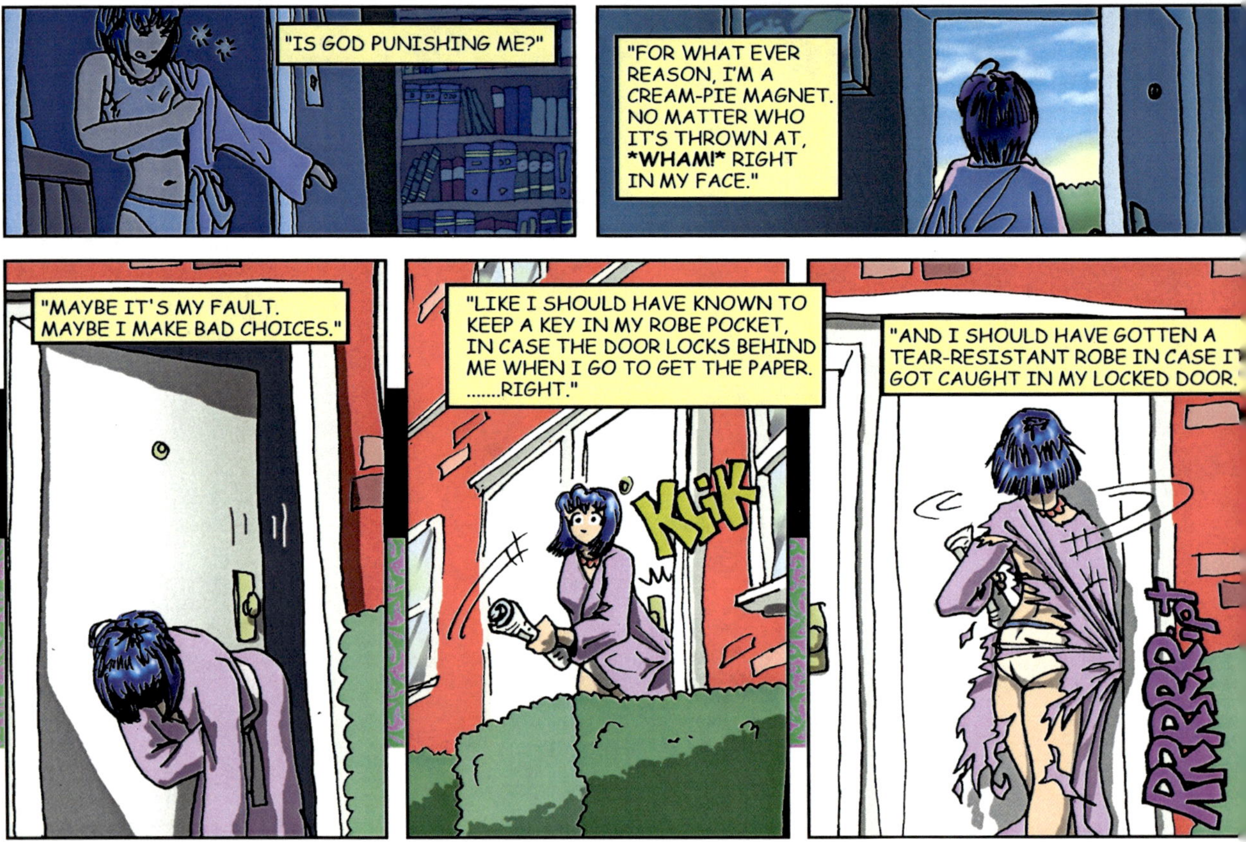
"IS GOD PUNISHING ME?"
"FOR WHAT EVER REASON, I'M A CREAM-PIE MAGNET. NO MATTER WHO IT'S THROWN AT, *WHAM!* RIGHT IN MY FACE."
"MAYBE IT'S MY FAULT. MAYBE I MAKE BAD CHOICES."
"LIKE I SHOULD HAVE KNOWN TO KEEP A KEY IN MY ROBE POCKET, IN CASE THE DOOR LOCKS BEHIND ME WHEN I GO TO GET THE PAPER. ....RIGHT."
KLIK
"AND I SHOULD HAVE GOTTEN A TEAR-RESISTANT ROBE IN CASE IT GOT CAUGHT IN MY LOCKED DOOR."
RRRRR...ript

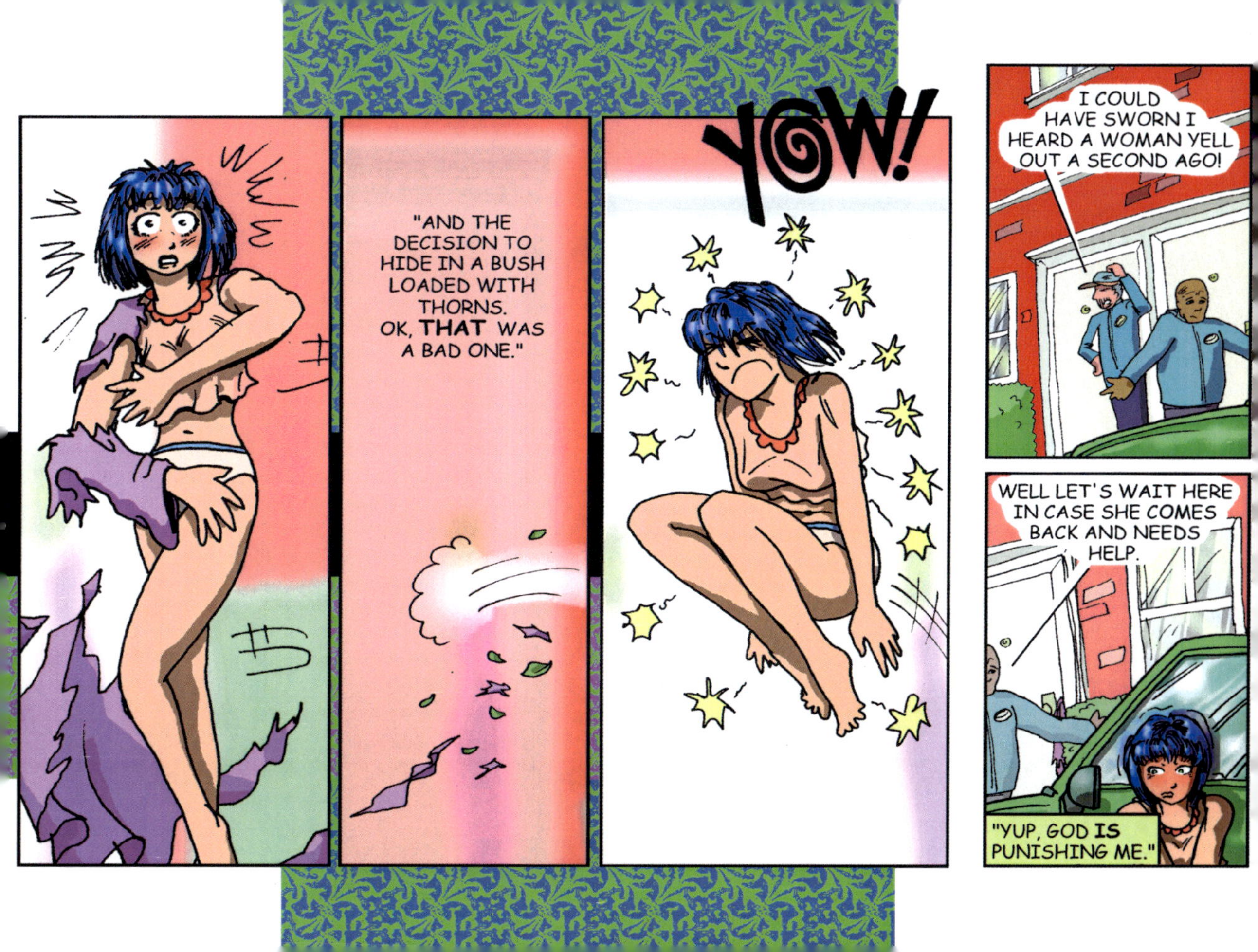
"AND THE DECISION TO HIDE IN A BUSH LOADED WITH THORNS. OK, THAT WAS A BAD ONE."
YOW!
I COULD HAVE SWORN I HEARD A WOMAN YELL OUT A SECOND AGO!
WELL LET'S WAIT HERE IN CASE SHE COMES BACK AND NEEDS HELP.
"YUP, GOD IS PUNISHING ME."

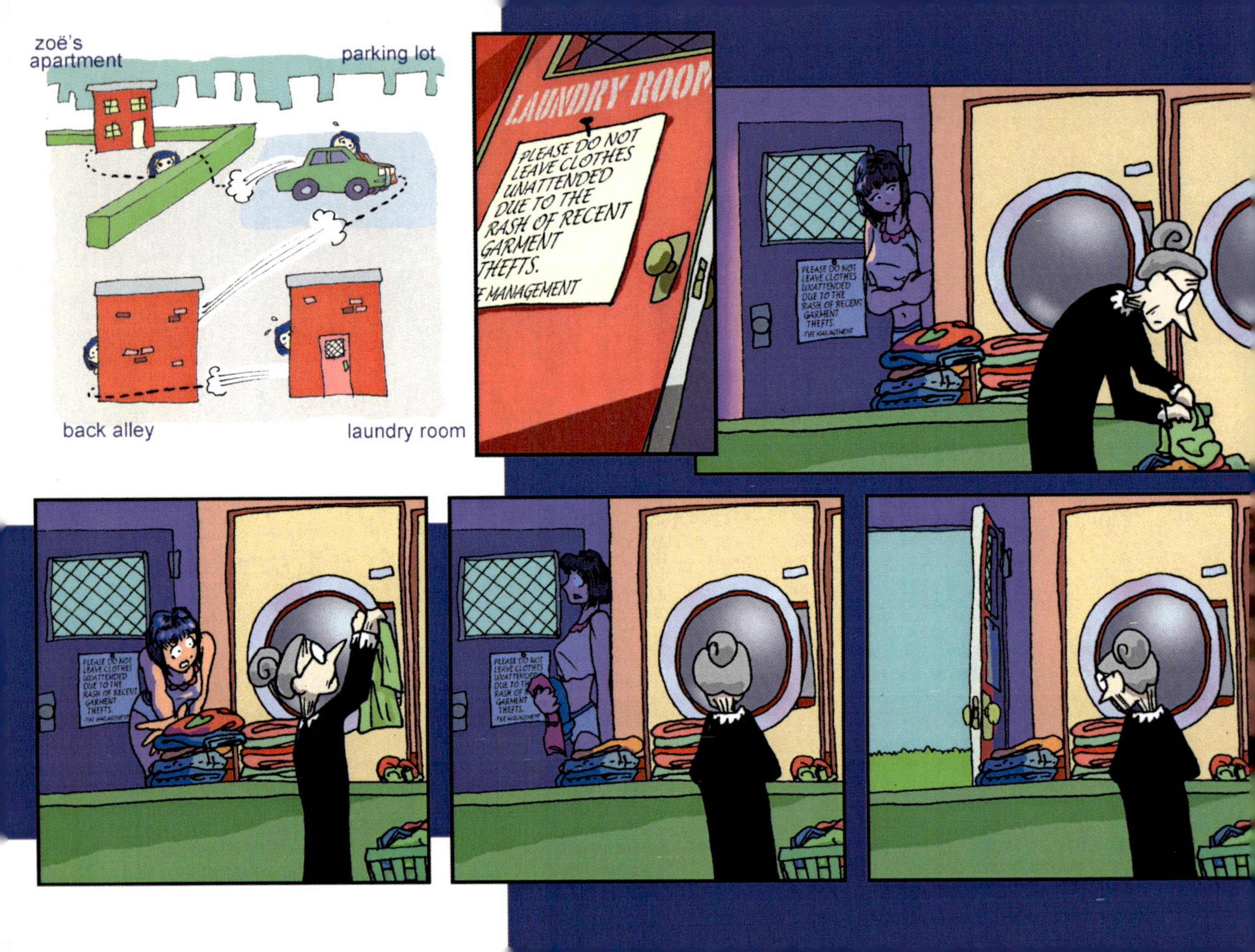
zoë's apartment
parking lot
back alley
laundry room
LAUNDRY ROOM
PLEASE DO NOT LEAVE CLOTHES UNATTENDED DUE TO THE RASH OF RECENT GARMENT THEFTS.
E MANAGEMENT

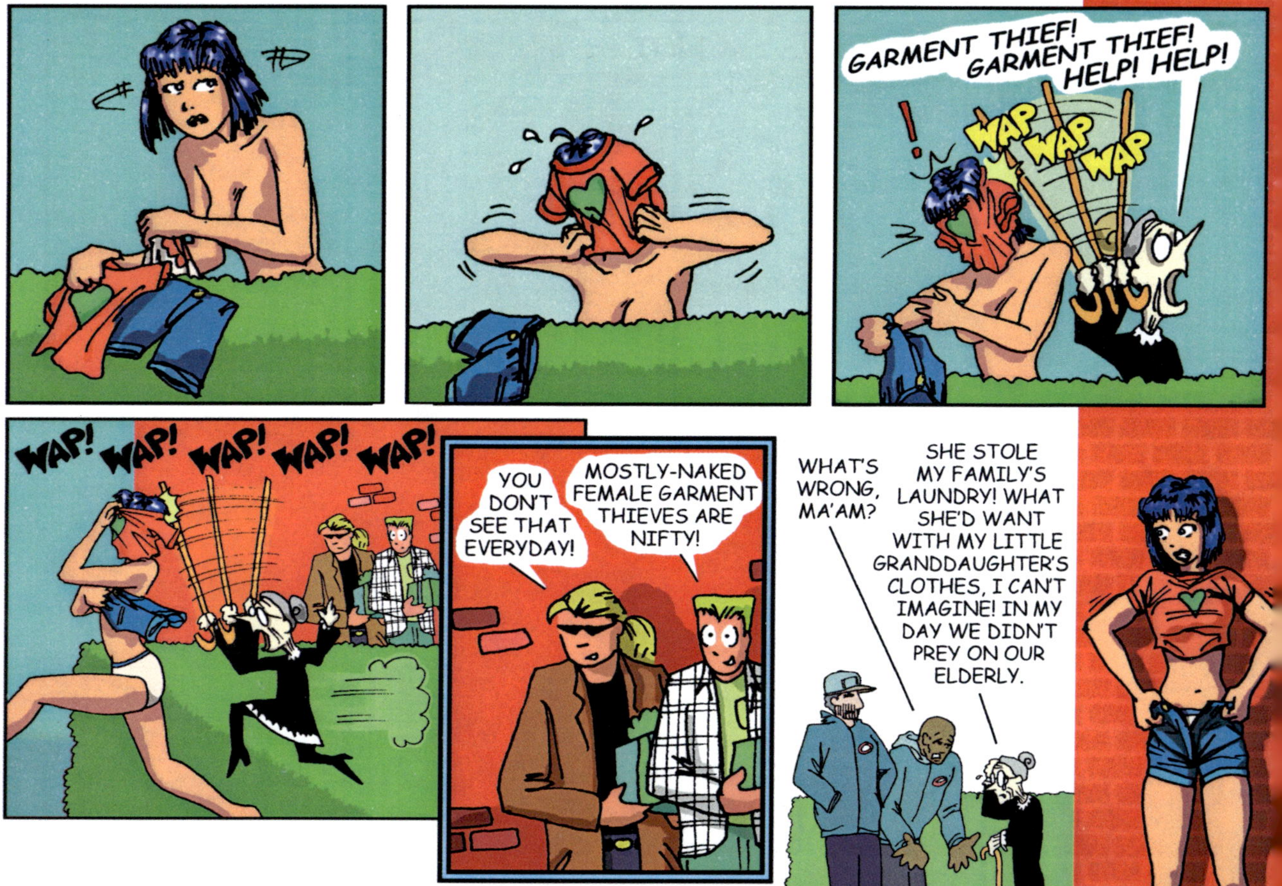
GARMENT THIEF! GARMENT THIEF! HELP! HELP!
!
WAP WAP WAP
WAP! WAP! WAP! WAP! WAP!
YOU DON'T SEE THAT EVERYDAY!
MOSTLY-NAKED FEMALE GARMENT THIEVES ARE NIFTY!
WHAT'S WRONG, MA'AM?
SHE STOLE MY FAMILY'S LAUNDRY! WHAT SHE'D WANT WITH MY LITTLE GRANDDAUGHTER'S CLOTHES, I CAN'T IMAGINE! IN MY DAY WE DIDN'T PREY ON OUR ELDERLY.

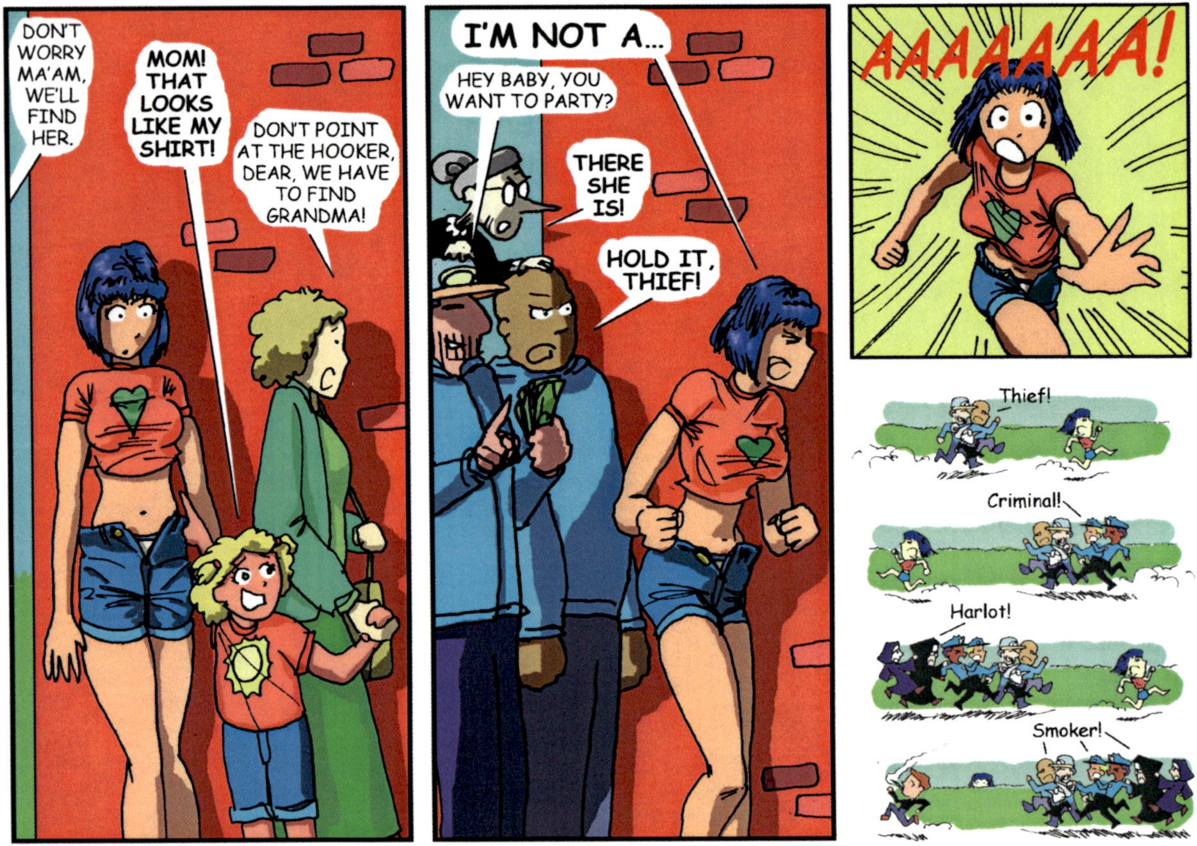
DON'T WORRY MA'AM, WE'LL FIND HER.
MOM! THAT LOOKS LIKE MY SHIRT!
DON'T POINT AT THE HOOKER, DEAR, WE HAVE TO FIND GRANDMA!
I'M NOT A...
HEY BABY, YOU WANT TO PARTY?
THERE SHE IS!
HOLD IT, THIEF!
AAAAAAA!
Thief!
Criminal!
Harlot!
Smoker!

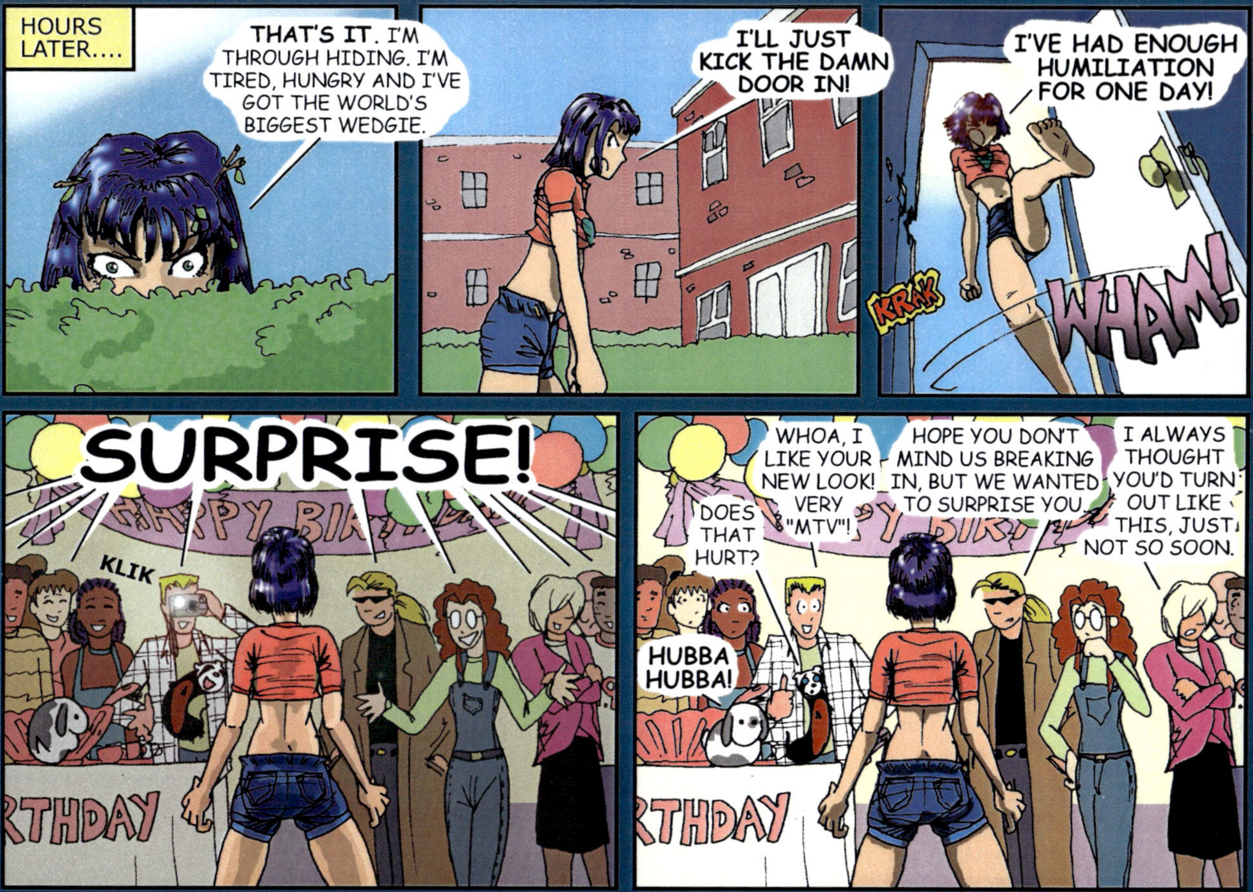
HOURS LATER....
THAT'S IT. I'M THROUGH HIDING. I'M TIRED, HUNGRY AND I'VE GOT THE WORLD'S BIGGEST WEDGIE.
I'LL JUST KICK THE DAMN DOOR IN!
I'VE HAD ENOUGH HUMILIATION FOR ONE DAY!
KRAK
WHAM!
SURPRISE!
KLIK
DOES THAT HURT?
WHOA, I LIKE YOUR NEW LOOK! VERY "MTV"!
HOPE YOU DON'T MIND US BREAKING IN, BUT WE WANTED TO SURPRISE YOU.
I ALWAYS THOUGHT YOU'D TURN OUT LIKE THIS, JUST NOT SO SOON.
HUBBA HUBBA!

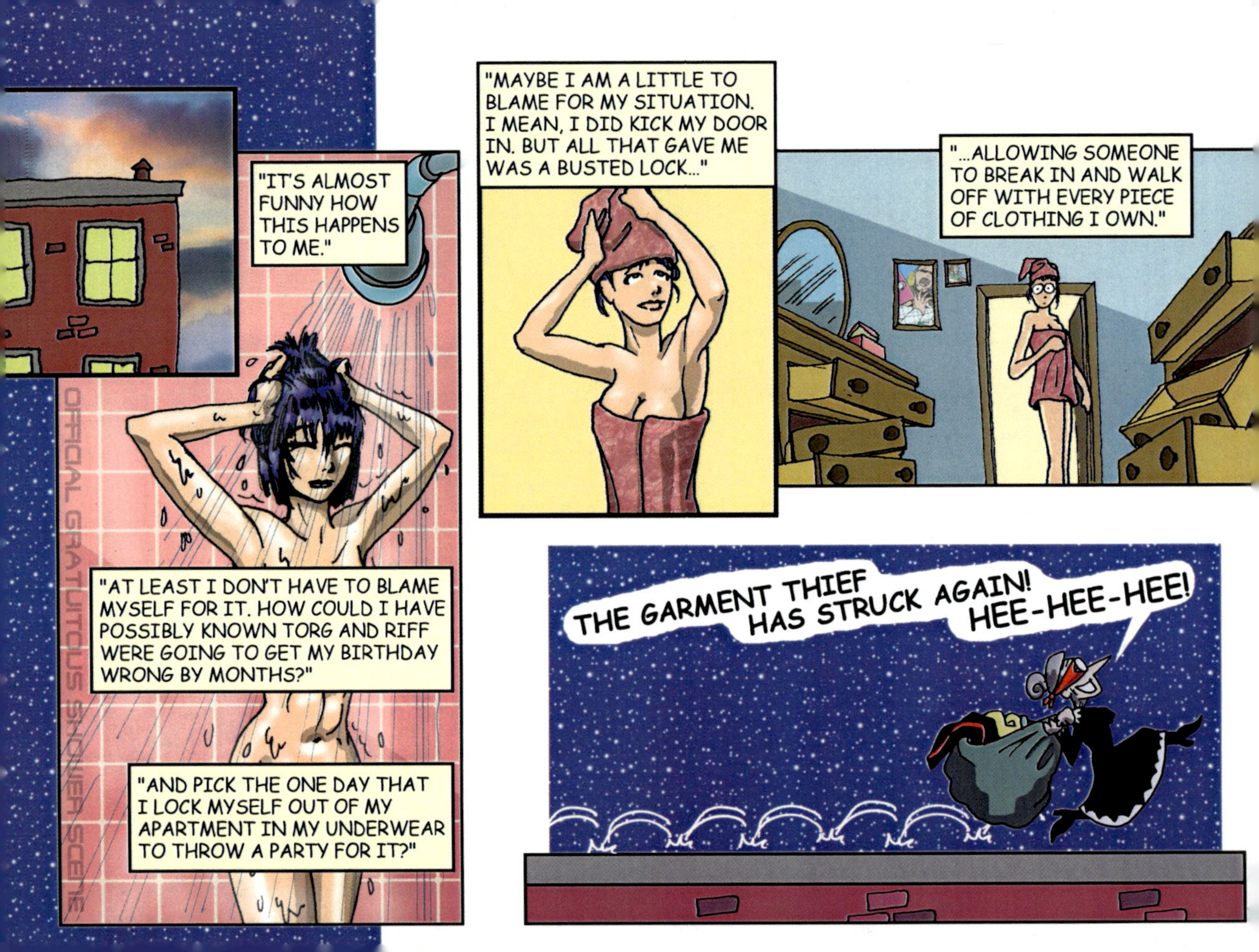
"IT'S ALMOST FUNNY HOW THIS HAPPENS TO ME."
OFFICIAL GRATUITOUS SHOWER SCENE
"AT LEAST I DON'T HAVE TO BLAME MYSELF FOR IT. HOW COULD I HAVE POSSIBLY KNOWN TORG AND RIFF WERE GOING TO GET MY BIRTHDAY WRONG BY MONTHS?"
"AND PICK THE ONE DAY THAT I LOCK MYSELF OUT OF MY APARTMENT IN MY UNDERWEAR TO THROW A PARTY FOR IT?"
"MAYBE I AM A LITTLE TO BLAME FOR MY SITUATION. I MEAN, I DID KICK MY DOOR IN. BUT ALL THAT GAVE ME WAS A BUSTED LOCK..."
"...ALLOWING SOMEONE TO BREAK IN AND WALK OFF WITH EVERY PIECE OF CLOTHING I OWN."
THE GARMENT THIEF HAS STRUCK AGAIN! HEE-HEE-HEE!

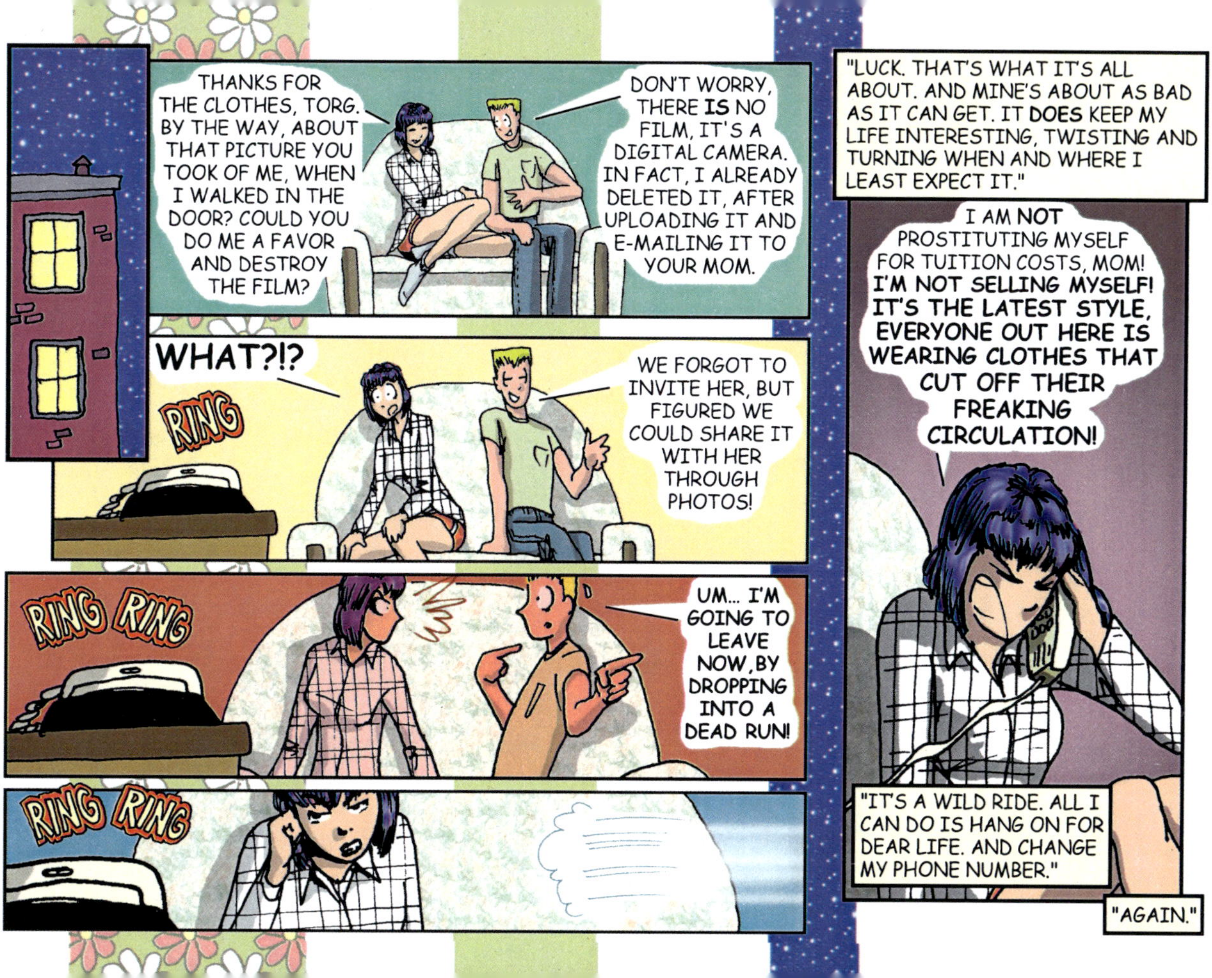

THANKS FOR THE CLOTHES, TORG. BY THE WAY, ABOUT THAT PICTURE YOU TOOK OF ME, WHEN I WALKED IN THE DOOR? COULD YOU DO ME A FAVOR AND DESTROY THE FILM?
DON'T WORRY, THERE IS NO FILM, IT'S A DIGITAL CAMERA. IN FACT, I ALREADY DELETED IT, AFTER UPLOADING IT AND E-MAILING IT TO YOUR MOM.
WHAT?!?
RING
WE FORGOT TO INVITE HER, BUT FIGURED WE COULD SHARE IT WITH HER THROUGH PHOTOS!
RING RING
UM... I'M GOING TO LEAVE NOW, BY DROPPING INTO A DEAD RUN!
RING RING
"LUCK. THAT'S WHAT IT'S ALL ABOUT. AND MINE'S ABOUT AS BAD AS IT CAN GET. IT DOES KEEP MY LIFE INTERESTING, TWISTING AND TURNING WHEN AND WHERE I LEAST EXPECT IT."
I AM NOT PROSTITUTING MYSELF FOR TUITION COSTS, MOM! I'M NOT SELLING MYSELF! IT'S THE LATEST STYLE, EVERYONE OUT HERE IS WEARING CLOTHES THAT CUT OFF THEIR FREAKING CIRCULATION!
"IT'S A WILD RIDE. ALL I CAN DO IS HANG ON FOR DEAR LIFE. AND CHANGE MY PHONE NUMBER."
"AGAIN."